Advertising Works 17

Proving the payback on
marketing investment

Case studies from the
IPA Effectiveness Awards 2008
Open to all agencies, media owners and
clients worldwide

Edited and introduced by
Neil Dawson

Convenor of Judges

WARC

First published 2009 by World Advertising Research Center
Farm Road, Henley-on-Thames, Oxfordshire RG9 1EJ, United Kingdom
Telephone: 01491 411000
Fax: 01491 418600
Email: enquiries@warc.com

A CIP catalogue record for this book is available from the British Library

ISBN: 978-1-84116-212-6

DVD of the 2008 IPA Effectiveness Awards winners produced by Xtreme Information Ltd,
London
Book produced by Sophie Petrou, World Advertising Research Center
Typeset by Godiva Publishing Services Ltd, Coventry
Printed by the MPG Books Group in the UK

Contents

Foreword

Apparently everyone's looking for value in this downturn and I think this book represents it: the wisdom and insight from 23 brands and their agencies on delivering maximum profit from advertising investments. But I don't need to persuade you of that; you're already reading it.

We can never have enough proof that advertising delivers incremental profit; we need it right now indisputably, but frankly, when won't we need it? So you'll be coming back to this book over the years. Long-term as well as short-term payback from your book purchase. That's the trick that advertising has to pull off too. They are not mutually exclusive ambitions.

There are many valuable lessons in this book, but one of my favourites is about the supermarket Morrisons. Its brand was already perceived as having low prices. What the case study proves is that by boosting perceptions of their quality, while hanging on to its price positioning, it was able to increase its share of the market. Consumers are seeking value, but value doesn't just mean price. Value is an intricate hybrid of quality and price. There are some potentially suicidal strategies being pursued at the moment; price-cutting and promotions, while cutting adspend, sacrifice the long-term health of the brand for the short term. They need to learn from Morrisons.

Thinkbox is dedicated to effectiveness and is a very proud sponsor of these important awards. Without rigorous analysis, TV wouldn't get the credit it deserves. One current frustration is the assumption that accountability equals effectiveness. 'Countability' is dangerously seductive but the enemy of proper econometric understanding.

Congratulations to all the winners and thank you for your immense efforts; we all benefit from them.

Tess Alps
Chief Executive

Sponsors

The success of the 2008 IPA Effectiveness Awards is in no small part down to its sponsors, and the IPA would like to thank the companies listed here for their continuing support. We are particularly grateful to Thinkbox, our overall sponsor, for their commitment to this competition until 2010.

IN ASSOCIATION WITH

AND

campaign

Acknowledgements

Many people worked hard to make the Awards a success, especially the following: Ian Priest, Chairman of the IPA Value of Advertising Group (VAG); Neil Dawson, Convenor of Judges; and David Golding, Deputy Convenor of Judges.

At the IPA, the core team were: Danielle Davies, Tessa Gooding, Julie London, Sylvia Ogden, Kathryn Patten and Sophie Walker.

We also owe a debt of gratitude to the following:

The IPA Awards Board:

IPA President, Moray MacLennan	M&C Saatchi
IPA Chairman of VAG, Ian Priest	VCCP
2006 Convenor of Judges, Laurence Green	Fallon
2007 Convenor of Judges, Richard Storey	M&C Saatchi
2008 Convenor of Judges, Neil Dawson	HMDG
2009 Convenor of Judges, Andy Nairn	MCBD
2010 Convenor of Judges, David Golding	Adam & Eve
IPA Director General, Hamish Pringle	
IPA Director of Communications, Tessa Gooding	
IPA Events Manager, Kathryn Patten	

The IPA Value of Advertising Group:

Ian Priest (Chairman)	VCCP
Neil Simpson (2009 Chairman-elect)	Publicis
Les Binet	DDB Matrix
Lucas Brown	Total Media
Simon Calvert	Draft FCB
Will Collin	Naked
Neil Dawson	HMDG
Ken Dixon	Newhaven Communications
Simeon Duckworth	Mindshare
David Golding	Adam & Eve
Lorna Hawtin	TBWA Manchester
Andy Nairn	MCBD
Charlie Snow	DLKW
Richard Storey	M&C Saatchi

We are also grateful to the following former members of the VAG for their contribution during the year: Dave Cobham, Ed Ling, Matthew Palmer and Gurdeep Puri.

The Judges

Neil Dawson
Convenor of Judges
Partner
Hurrell Moseley Dawson & Grimmer

David Golding
Deputy Convenor of Judges
Founding Partner
Adam & Eve

STAGE 1: INDUSTRY SPECIALISTS

Morag Blazey
Former CEO
PHD Group

Peter Bowman
General Manager
JICIMS

John Deighton
Brierley Professor of Business
Administration
Harvard Business School

Sara Donoghugh
Econometrician
Data2Decisions

Bryan Finn
Founder
Business Economics

Richard Foan
Managing Director
ABCe

Thayne Forbes
Joint Managing Director
Intangible Business

Kirsty Fuller
Chairman
Flamingo

Richard Jolly
Adjunct Associate Professor of
Organisational Behaviour
London Business School

Judie Lannon
Editor
Market Leader

Nick Manning
Chief Operating Officer
Ebiquity

Paul Phillips
Managing Director
AAR

Toby Reeks
Analyst
Merrill Lynch

Mark Stockdale
Founder
Wheelbarrow

John Tylee
Associate Editor
Campaign

David Wethey
Founder and Chairman
Agency Assessments

STAGE 2: CLIENT JURY

Sir John Sunderland
Chairman of Judges
Former Chairman
Cadbury plc

Alan Bishop
Chief Executive
Central Office of Information (COI)

Dan Cobley
Marketing Director, UK, Ireland and
Benelux
Google

Hilary Cross
Director of External Affairs
Macmillan Cancer Support

Jeremy Davies
Brand and Communications Director
E.on

Roisin Donnelly
Corporate Marketing Director
Procter & Gamble

Andy Gilson
Marketing Director
General Motors

Jo Kenrick
Former Marketing & Customer
Proposition Director
B&Q

David Pemsel
Group Marketing Director
ITV

Richard Tolley
Former Group Marketing Development
Director
Dairy Crest

David Wheldon
Global Brand Director
Vodafone

Introduction

So this is *Advertising Works 17*. Another milestone in the life of this unique competition whose core purpose is to demonstrate the financial payback for investment in marketing communications. And a fresh crop of winners to add further weight to the invaluable body of learning already contained in the IPA dataBANK about how communications works in hard commercial terms. In the challenging economic climate of late 2008, these Awards and the lessons they teach us feel more important than ever.

Practitioners, interested observers and enthusiasts from agency and client communities have already whetted their appetites by downloading winning papers from 2008 at www.warc.com (8,880 downloads at time of writing). So this printed publication aims to be more than a straightforward compendium of the winners of the 2008 IPA Effectiveness Awards. The full-strength Gold and Silver Award winners are indeed gathered in one place for the first time, along with 200-word summaries of the Bronze winners. But beyond this the reader will find seven chapters exploring different facets of 'new learning' providing insight and perspective on both the content of the winners and, importantly, the context in which they were written.

Let's begin with a brief overview of the class of 2008. Entries dipped to 50 in total – down from 63 in 2006. While no single factor can explain this, history indicates that during periods of economic growth levels of entry to these Awards tend to decline. (NB All these papers were written in the period before 25 April 2008.) Perhaps the need to justify investment in marketing communications is less pronounced during more buoyant times. If this remains true, we can expect a healthy rise in entries during the aftermath of the current global economic crisis.

Quantity should not, however, be confused with quality and these entries were certainly up to scratch. And the judging standards at both stages of the competition remain unswervingly high – reflecting both the competition rules and the calibre of those who kindly agree to give up their time and energy to support the Awards and assess the cases. It is often asked if there is a target number for papers that the industry judges are asked to shortlist and a requisite number of Golds, Silvers and Bronzes for the client judges to award. The answer to both questions is no. Both decisions are up to the judges themselves. The 23 shortlisted from 50 entries this year reflects a high bar and some healthy debate around the key judging criteria – scale of effect and strength of proof.

For the first time this competition was open to clients and media owners, as well as agencies – rightly so given the increasingly blurred lines between all three. Accordingly, the Award previously known as Effectiveness Agency of the Year is now Effectiveness Company of the Year. And while the winners remain dominated by the established creative agencies, there was a welcome influx of debutant authors and contributors from outside this arena. A rise in joint authorship was also noteworthy in the long list of entries.

Even more striking is the growing presence of both multi-market and ex-UK international papers. Prior to this competition the dataBANK contained only ten international or multi-market cases. 2008 saw six additions to this list, from the Grand Prix winner Johnnie Walker through to the Bronze-winning Motorola case from China. This was the year the Awards finally stepped onto the global stage. The two Asian cases in particular represent the beginnings of a body of new learning in their own right about how brands are being built in today's emerging economies. On reading them, it is clear that these papers are there on merit alone – no dispensation was given in the judging process.

However, taking the 2008 winners as a whole, the most striking advance is the extent and fluency of the use of multiple channels in delivering success – based on skilful and scientific blending of the right channels for the task and audiences involved. What were previously referred to as 'old' and 'new' media seem curiously anachronistic terms. The modern communications armoury is healthily silo-free and open-minded. While progress in the consideration and deployment of channels is both rapid and impressive, there remains limited attention to the delivery of hard commercial proof of the effects of media generally and the interactive channels in particular. There are several explanatory factors at work:

- Authorship: most entrants are still from established creative agencies and write from this perspective; the missing evidence may be available but overlooked.
- Entry format: the 4,000 word limit is already a challenge to most cases; additional media effectiveness data across all channels would only add to this.
- Investment, both financial and 'energy': the cost of measurement across the increasingly wide range of channels can be prohibitive; and things that are easy to measure tend to get measured.

Whatever the reason, more proof of undoubted promise of the multi-channel planning described among the winners in this area is essential if the Awards are to maintain their unrivalled reputation.

Moving to the New Learning chapters, these are primarily intended to stimulate the reader. Whatever your response to the views expressed, it is hoped that they will fulfil this objective. Some use the winning cases of 2008 to provide perspective. Others are more general ruminations on the issues surrounding payback and accountability in the marketing arena.

I provide an overview of the cases and what they tell us about the evolution of commercially effective communications. Trends and success factors are in evidence, although the reader seeking a formulaic approach to communications payback will be disappointed.

Nick Manning provides a comprehensive assessment of progress in the New Media Communications Model. His report card highlights the exemplars of best practice among the 2008 winners from the perspective of the two key media principles: consumer touchpoints and engagement planning. He then turns to the opportunity for future Awards entrants to genuinely embrace media effectiveness in the round.

Greg Grimmer casts a critical eye over the world of online effectiveness and warns against confusing counting actions and responses with measuring contribution to revenue or profit. Ironically given its perceived accountability, it is the online industry that has furthest to go in embracing multi-channel research to demonstrate its commercial value. Thinkbox and the IAB have taken steps in the right direction in 2008, but there is more work to do here.

Two chapters will be particularly illuminating for prospective authors or indeed anyone who wants to understand more about the behind-the-scenes of the awards. Jeremy Davies tells us what it feels like to be a client judge and in so doing provides invaluable guidance on what makes an outstanding paper. David Golding contrasts the mindset of the author with that of the judge and provides insight into how to succeed in this competition. Making the judges your bull's-eye target audience sounds simple, but is easily overlooked.

Les Binet on payback calculations is a must-read for any advertising or marketing practitioner, let alone a prospective author of an IPA case. Drawing on *Measuring Marketing Payback* – a guide specifically created for the IPA and ISBA, this piece explains the calculation of payback and the pitfalls therein. In the wake of the 2006 Awards, this issue was highlighted by industry and client judges alike as an area of significant weakness across the submissions as a whole. Thus it became a key point to rectify and it is clear that many of the 2008 winners have benefited from Les and Peter Field's sterling work.

In 'Effectiveness and two-thirds of the human race', Tim Broadbent describes the growth of an effectiveness culture in the Asian market. The debut of papers from this region offers fascinating glimpses into what to many of us is unfamiliar territory. It is to be hoped that these are just the vanguard of a significant Asian challenge in these Awards.

Finally, I would like to acknowledge all those who have contributed to the success of the 2008 Awards:

- all the industry and client judges who gave up their time and ensured that the standards of the competition are maintained; their commitment was beyond impressive
- Sir John Sunderland who chaired the Client Judges with skill and diplomacy
- David Golding the Deputy Convenor for his passionate support of the Awards and what they represent
- the IPA team who organise and administrate every aspect of the Awards over a period of 14 months from launch through the event itself to publication of this book
- the clients who gave permission for their cases to be entered, and contributed to the quality of the input
- and, finally, of course, all the authors, whether shortlisted or not; producing 4,000 words, excluding charts and appendices, is a hard task by any standards; it has been reasonably estimated that it takes up to 100 hours to deliver a case – such extraordinary effort is what makes this competition unique in the world.

As you benefit from the product of their collective endeavours in this volume, I'm sure you will join me in offering wholehearted thanks for their blood, sweat and tears.

Neil Dawson
Convenor of Judges, 2008

SECTION 1

Prize winners

GRAND PRIX

BBH for Johnnie Walker (pp.41–82)

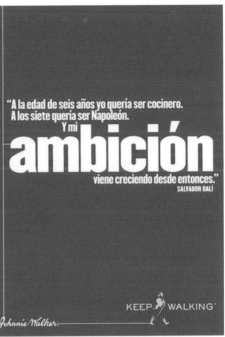

GOLD

RKCR/Y&R for Aquisition Crime (pp.83–111)

Red Bee Media & Uktv for Dave (pp.113–141)

BBH for KFC (pp.143–181)

AMV.BBDO for Sainsbury's (pp.183–205)

SILVER AWARDS

BBH for Audi (pp.209–251)

RKCR/Y&R for Danone Activia (pp.253–277)

JWT for De Beers (pp.279–314)

MCBD for Direct Payment (pp.315–333)

Ogilvy for Dove (pp.335–370)

MediaCom/M&C Saatchi for Lucozade Sport (pp.371–405)

Ogilvy Vietnam for Helmet Wearing (pp.407–418)

DDB London for Radley (pp.419–459)

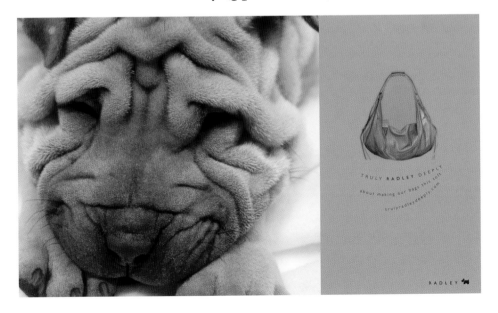

RKCR/Y&R for Virgin Atlantic (pp.461–492)

MCBD for Waitrose (pp.493–518)

BRONZE AWARDS

WCRS for CABWISE (pp.520–521)

BBH for Cadbury Biscuits (pp.522–523)

RKCR/Y&R for Learndirect (pp.524–525)

DDB London for Marmite (pp.526–527)

DLKW for Morrisons (pp.528–529)

Ogilvy & Mather Beijing for Motorola (pp.530–531)

LyleBailie International for Road Safety (pp.532–533)

MCBD for Trident (pp.534–535)

SPECIAL PRIZES

EFFECTIVENESS COMPANY OF THE YEAR
BBH

BEST DEDICATION TO EFFECTIVENESS
The Home Office for Aquisition Crime

BEST INTEGRATION
AMV.BBDO for Sainsbury's (Sainsbury's)

BEST INTERNATIONAL SINGLE MARKET
Ogilvy & Mather Vietnam for Public Awareness Campaign for Helmet Wearing (Asia Injury Prevention Foundation)

BEST INTERNATIONAL MULTI-MARKET
BBH for Johnnie Walker (Diageo)

BEST MEDIA
RKCR/Y&R and *The Home Office* for Acquisition Crime (The Home Office)

BEST NEW LEARNING
RKCR/Y&R and *The Home Office* for Acquisition Crime (The Home Office)

BEST SMALL BUDGET
DDB London for Radley (Radley & Co)

SECTION 2

New learning

Chapter 1

Effectiveness and two-thirds of the human race

By Tim Broadbent
Regional Planning and Effectiveness Director, Ogilvy & Mather Asia Pacific

Why Asia today is like Britain in the 1970s

British advertising had a problem. It was too creative. British agencies won more awards at Cannes than any other country for five straight years in a row in the 1970s. Why was that a problem? Because, to quote Jeremy Bullmore, they were 'doing work designed just to win awards', not to sell products.[1] They had lost their compass bearings. If the work was less effective, clients would turn to other ways of stimulating sales. Agencies were committing hara-kiri. The IPA Effectiveness Awards were launched in 1979, in response to this problem. They introduced a new competitive arena. Agencies could be compared not only on their creativity but also on their effectiveness.

There are parallels between the British agency scene then and the Asian scene now. Asian creativity is often world class. The most awarded commercial directors in the world are Thai, according to the Gunn Report. Ogilvy Singapore was one of the three most creative offices in the world in the 2007 Cannes Lions ranking, after Saatchi New York and DDB London. Steve Henry, founder of HHCL, came to Asia in 2007 to judge the Spikes, Asia's own creative awards, and commented, 'The quality of creativity here is stunning', but then added waspishly, 'though I'd like to see it done with clients that we're working on every day'. He was referring to work designed just to win awards.

To be fair, Asia has not had to worry about effectiveness as much as the West. Asia's economic miracle is well known. For instance, the Chinese economy has grown in real terms by 9% a year since reforms began in 1979. On current trends, it will overtake America to become the largest economy in the world early in the 2030s. Its advertising market has grown even faster. Chinese adspend grew by 1,200% in the 10 years from 1997 to 2006. China is likely to overtake Japan this year to become the second largest advertising market in the world, and will overtake the American advertising market in the 2020s – a seismic shift in the balance of global advertising power. In the circumstances, one can see why effectiveness has not been Asia's top priority. Sales and adspend have been growing anyway.

Growth of new effectiveness powers

However, things are changing fast. Effectiveness is becoming more important in Asia, and Asia is becoming more important in effectiveness. *Media* magazine, Asia's version of *Campaign*, carried out a survey of Asian marketers a couple of years ago. Asked for their 'priorities for improvement' next year, 'measuring the effectiveness of your campaigns' was top of the list. 'Coming up with creative marketing solutions' came second. Many Asian clients now think effectiveness is at least as important as creativity, if not more so.

Agencies and organisers have responded. Entries to the China Effies have more than tripled in the last three years. Ogilvy & Mather entered a dozen papers into the Asia Marketing Effectiveness Awards in 2006; this year we entered 110 papers. And new effectiveness competitions are being created, too. Last year saw the launch of the first Pan-Asian Effies. This year Malaysia joins Hong Kong, Singapore, India, China and New Zealand in running its own Effie competition; Sri Lanka plans to do so next year. A sign of Asia's growing importance in the effectiveness world is that the first World Effie Congress was held in Singapore this year, with British speakers of the quality of Nick Kendall (BBH), Lucy Jamieson (DDB) and Laurence Green (Fallon).

From slave to partner

However, there is still some way to go before Asian effectiveness cultures reach British levels. One barrier is the relationship between clients and agencies. Rather than partners, agencies are often seen merely as vendors of creative products. For instance, there are more than 60,000 agencies in China, and few local agencies have strategy or research functions. Most are not given sales data and wouldn't know what to do with them if they were. Effectiveness is of little or no interest to Asian agencies like these. They compete on low price, speed of response and, yes, creative awards. Other countries have different barriers. The Japanese advertising market is dominated by Dentsu, which works with multiple clients in the same category. A good sales result for its client Toyota, for example, might not be good news for its client Nissan. In Korea, many of the giant industrial conglomerates use in-house agencies, which do not compete for business in the same way as independent agencies. And in many markets there is less research available. The TGI, for example, an indispensable tool in the UK, is available in only seven Asian countries.

One thing Asia has going for it is a greater willingness to experiment and change. London and New York seem sclerotic in comparison. The pace of change is faster here. Asian marketing will catch up with the best of the West and then surpass it – it's only a matter of time. This year saw Asia's first entries in the IPA

Effectiveness Awards, and both papers won prizes; a silver, best international single market and a bronze. One is for Motorola from Ogilvy Beijing, and the other is about a safety campaign for wearing motorcycle helmets from Ogilvy Vietnam.

Learning about growing economies

This year international entries were also received from Brazil, Romania, South Africa, Ireland and America, with entries for global campaigns for Dove, Johnnie Walker and HP. Entries such as these help fill gaps in the IPA dataBANK, but they also do much more than this. There are relatively few published cases about how the economic growth in emerging countries is being built from the ground up, brand by brand and campaign by campaign. These cases have enormous value for agencies and clients whose growth now depends on these countries. They teach us about their consumers, markets and media; they set benchmarks for future campaigns; and, above all, they prove that evaluation *is* possible, despite the barriers.

Should the IPA Awards lower its standards for entries from emerging countries, to encourage more entries? I don't think so. I was the Convenor of Judges in 2000 and proposed the rule change that let agencies from all over the world enter the Awards. To my mind, it's like the Olympics. There is one standard of excellence and it applies to every entrant. Asian manufacturers don't ask for special treatment in Western consumer markets, so why should Asian planners and account teams be treated differently? And to lower the IPA's standards would be to misunderstand what it is that motivates authors to put in the extra hours that an entry takes – they *want* to be judged against the best in the world, just as Asian creatives want to be judged against the best at Cannes. Anything else could be seen as patronising. In a few years' time, they'll be teaching us Brits how to do evaluations better, faster and cheaper.

Notes

1. Quoted in Fletcher, W., *Powers of Persuasion: The Inside Story of British Advertising*, Oxford University Press, 2008.

Chapter 2

The new media communications model: a progress report

By Nick Manning
Chief Operating Officer, Ebiquity

In this newly digitised media world there is an Aladdin's cave of communications options available to advertisers and their agencies. For example, there are over 400 commercial TV channels to choose from, with the majority offering spot advertising, sponsorship, interactivity and advertiser-funded programming.

Then add in the fundamentals of spot length, channel mix, weight of ratings, flighting, regionality, and the variables of buying strategy (dayparts, day-of-week etc.) and the range of planning options is staggering.

That's just TV. If the internet, say, is then added to the mix, the planner potentially has thousands of websites to evaluate, with additional choices to make in display, search, aggregators and affiliates, content and social networking opportunities.

Of course, no one medium should be considered in isolation. What matters these days is the interrelationship between, in this example, TV and the internet, how they work together, the influence they have on each other, and their cumulative effect.

All this has to be considered, and that's before the media planner reviews the role of print media, radio, cinema, out-of-home, sports and music events, and the multiplicity of other ways to reach the public in order to influence awareness, attitudes and behaviour.

It's a great time to be a media planner, but it's not an easy time to be one.

Today's audiences do not meekly submit any longer to advertisers' attempts to connect with them. They are moving targets, flitting between devices, gladly accepting the media owners' offer to serve them the content they want, where they want it, at the time and on the platform of their choosing.

They can create their own media menus from a huge repository of sources, but the media planner has to create their advertising menu for them, finding apertures in their media lives to get the commercial message through.

Against this backdrop, the two key media planning principles of recent times are the recognition of the need to reach audiences through a range of 'touchpoints', influencing them across their chosen range of channels, and the need to engage with them in a way that encourages favourability rather than the interruptive model, which can have the opposite effect.

There is no question that this logic is correct: research proves that engaging an audience actively with 'permission' across a range of channels is clearly the best way to build a deeper relationship with a brand's consumers.

How the industry is shaping up

This year's IPA Effectiveness Awards offer us a fascinating insight into the extent to which these principles have been adopted within the industry, beyond the rhetoric.

The signs are good. Several papers stand out as examples of integrated media thinking across multiple media platforms, which created an interwoven depth and breadth of messaging to achieve the required effect.

Quite correctly, these campaigns were rooted in a profound understanding of the target audience, not just in outdated demographic terms, but through their lifestyles, behaviour, attitudes and media 'triggers' – the touchpoints that allow brands into their lives in an effective way.

Principal among these was the paper for Lucozade Sport. Against a backdrop of declines in penetration and usage, the brand needed to be reinvigorated in the face of competition from Coca-Cola's Powerade, and this was achieved in spades.

The Lucozade Sport team chose to focus clearly on subsets of the sports participant market, with in-depth research providing the basis for a fully thought-through media strategy, which majored on partnerships with the key media channels for runners, footballers and other serious sports participants. These were underpinned by carefully targeted mainstream media, promotional events and PR activities – a range of offline and online channels built into a total plan that achieved a stunning commercial result for the brand.

The Lucozade Sport entry was the most comprehensive in achieving engaging communications across a wide range of integrated channels. This campaign also proves that sharp communications thinking and execution can help advertisers build brands when budgets are limited.

Such a good case history was slightly diluted by the paper itself, which could have been clearer in making its case, but the quality of the work shone through the dense layout.

Another good example of integrated media thinking and execution came from Unilever's Dove, and it was notable from this and other entries that successful integrated campaigns can be created by multiple agency teams driven by a clear and simple strategy.

This case history, based around the 'Campaign for real beauty', has already become famous for its striking imagery, but less attention has been paid to the media component of its success.

Media was part of a broader-based 'contact strategy' embracing PR, events and promotions, and the Dove case also shows how 'big' media like TV and outdoor can have a significant effect by framing the debate.

The Dove campaign would not have been featured on 'Oprah' if it hadn't first been seen by the public in mainstream channels, proving (if proof were needed) that the established broadcast media are alive and kicking, and still have a propaganda effect that money can't buy.

The depth of research underpinning the Dove campaign was, in itself, breathtaking and the best evidence in all of the papers of how statistical rigour can be applied to a communications programme in a way that the main board of a large multinational company, as well as IPA judges, can understand and appreciate.

Being able to deliver an integrated communications strategy on an international level is a difficult task but one that Dove achieved, as did a much less famous case, De Beers, whose paper (Billion dollar idea) stood out as one of the surprise 'hits'.

This was one example where the perceived quality of the creative work was not a big element, but the critical success factor was the seamless way that product innovation was showcased through a wide range of advertising and sales platforms.

Almost uniquely, the De Beers case featured a strong 'trade' element (as this is critical in the diamond industry) and this was integrated into a range of traditional, but well-integrated, channels spanning advertising, PR, point of sale, promotions and events.

Like Dove, this was an example of an international, multi-platform marketing campaign driven from a central strategy, and the results were equally impressive.

Meanwhile, at the other end of the scale, there were three striking case histories from the public sector (Cabwise, Trident and Acquisition Crime), all of which were locally relevant.

All three made great use of location-based and ambient media to reach their audience at critical times ('moments of careless stupidity' in the case of Acquisition Crime) and in critical places (nightclubs in the case of Cabwise).

All three media strategies were built around consumer insights that were translated cleverly into media solutions that tapped into the lifestyles of the target audience.

Although the 'Crime' campaign was national, the 'test and control' methodology, used to measure its effect by matching local police areas, stood out as an example of best practice in testing strategies beyond conventional metrics.

Three other notable papers were from Audi, Marmite and Waitrose. While all are great examples of multi-platform planning, all three left the reader slightly short-changed on the metrics of success from the channels used.

The Audi paper was highly convincing in its breadth of media coverage, incorporating the traditional TV routes with interactive TV, mobile, podcasting and direct marketing elements.

The Audi Channel itself on digital satellite is a bold and inventive route to market, but there was little within the results to prove its worth, bar the one sentence which states that it has 'had a positive influence on potential buyers' decision making'.

The entry from Waitrose brought in interesting elements of interactive TV, advertiser-funded programming, online and direct mail. However, there was again little reference to the results of any of these initiatives, in media metrics terms or sales effect.

The launch of Marmite's 'squeezy' packaging was very nicely executed in media, recognising the role of brand advocates and involving the audience in online Marmite-squeezing competitions to mimic the creative work.

As with Audi and Waitrose, the cumulative effect of the activity produced great results, but didn't really say how.

This raises an interesting and highly topical point about the industry as a whole.

The big gap: media effectiveness and digitally driven case histories

All the case histories referred to in this chapter stood out as great examples of the new media thinking in terms of strategy and planning, and there is evidence that the multiple platform engagement model is beginning to take hold where it is relevant.

There were, however, two common, and interlinked, factors that united virtually all the papers from a media perspective. First, there was hardly any reference in any of the papers to *media* effectiveness. There was plenty of great work to prove that advertising drove business success, but virtually nothing that validated media's contribution to that success. The second salient theme was the relative absence of the specific contribution of digital media, and specifically the internet.

Most of the entries were firmly rooted in the traditional media world, with no entries at all majoring on digital media and very few providing any measure of interactive success.

Dealing first specifically with media effectiveness, this was mentioned only twice in all the papers reviewed, and in both instances the context was in pre-campaign strategy and planning. The advertiser (Unilever) was the same in both cases.

It is entirely possible to measure the business results of the different planning choices that can be made in media, and this is becoming increasingly important as the range of choices multiplies, and the means of measuring them improves via statistical techniques and interactive channels.

In today's tough business world, with the measurement of ROI mandatory rather than an optional extra, it is vital to measure the effect of routes-to-market individually and in combination.

Measurement of offline and online media effect can be conducted at any stage in the communications cycle as long as the right data exist, yet this subject is barely broached by any of the papers.

It is happily a long while since media was deemed to be an afterthought in the advertising process, and there is plenty of evidence of great media thinking to be found throughout the industry, as evidenced by these awards. However, this thinking is still primarily rooted in the generation of impact, appearance rather than effect, rather than the hard-edged business result that the advertiser is after.

The awards papers were generally highly convincing in their proof that the advertising 'worked' but media is an integral part of the advertising process, and therefore the choices made in media have an unquestionable impact on success.

After all, media is where the bulk of the money is spent. Typically, a TV campaign can cost £300,000 to make but £3m to show, so it must be important to measure the specific metrics of the media as well as the overall advertising effect.

So, why has the subject of media effectiveness not hit the top of the agenda, even though today's financially astute advertisers demand the rigour of ROI in everything else they do? The reasons for this are deep-seated. Media is still seen as a dark art, a riddle wrapped up inside an enigma, often clouded by jargon.

It is also often seen as something that is primarily bought, not planned. A lot of time and attention is devoted to measuring media pricing, but a lot less is dedicated to proving its payback to the advertiser. The media part of the equation is deemed to have done its job if it delivers the right number of eyeballs with market-beating economy.

In many advertiser organisations, media is increasingly seen as a procurement-led discipline, rather than one that adds real value to business results. If anything, the industry has gone backwards in this regard. This is surprising in that one of the great benefits of the digital media era is that data are both rich and fast, and are rapidly replacing traditional, and slow, consumer research as a place to start.

We are now able to read consumer behaviour in minute detail via a plethora of data sources, in offline and online channels, and we have the statistical techniques on hand to consolidate those data and plan accordingly.

The irony of this is that the exact modelling techniques used throughout the IPA papers to prove the effect of advertising can be applied to measure the effectiveness of the media used. In fact, the results do measure the media effect by default, but this is hardly ever broken out, and rarely are these techniques used to determine the optimal use of the budget at planning stage.

There is even less attention given to the ability of these techniques to determine the budget in the first place, something that is eminently achievable.

Even within agencies, there is some suspicion of 'black box' modelling techniques in relation to both the creative and media components of the marketing communications mix, based on the fear that science could rule over art and reduce agencies' scope for creativity.

Logically, there is no tension in this debate. The role of creativity in driving effectiveness is undisputed, and the IPA papers assert this on every page. A hugely impactful campaign built on a rigorous analysis of channel effectiveness gives the advertiser the best of both worlds.

It should be said that the majority of media agencies have responded to the effectiveness agenda by investing in modelling and ROI resources, but the evidence of this year's IPA papers is that little of this work is filtering through to these awards, and there appears to be less involvement by the media agencies in the proof of effectiveness this year than in previous years.

However, the media agencies are well placed to play a vital and dynamic role in the advertising industry's demonstration of its contribution to the business success of its paymasters. They have the advantage of operating across all platforms and in the vital areas of content, data and insight, and they have the techniques available to demonstrate the effect of their work.

To achieve this, the focus of the media industry needs to shift from the generation of audience impact to the generation of business effect, with the right ROI data to support the case. While this already happens in some instances, it is by no means the norm, and the current economic climate cries out for a more concerted effort in this area.

In these straitened times, advertisers are challenging the industry to give them the data-backed analyses they need to make informed decisions on communications strategy, before, during and after the planning cycle.

Digital media: the need for more case studies

Beyond the paucity of thinking in the media effectiveness field, the second major theme emerging from this year's awards was the surprising lack of entries where the internet and other interactive media played a significant role.

Some papers referred to YouTube viewings of TV-led executions, but this simply demonstrates that the old 'eyeballs' language is being used in respect of the new media.

The industry still seems to see digital media as somehow different to analogue media, even though the industry consensus would seem to suggest that this distinction has rightly disappeared.

There is plenty of other evidence of good work being created daily in the converged world of established and 'new' media, with the internet playing a vital role. While spending in the more traditional media stagnates as the economy slows, the internet continues to grow, driven by its proven effectiveness.

So it is surprising that there is so little material in these papers relating to the internet and the metrics that it can produce.

While there were some examples of offline and online integration, the balance was heavily weighted in favour of the traditional channels, and the internet was often an afterthought or used in a sales promotional way, rather than being an integral part of the campaign.

Perhaps the relatively low level of digital content was reflective of the industry's structures, which still tend to divide the world into 'old' and 'new', and also of the dominance of the Awards by the larger creative agencies.

The verdict: good progress with lots to play for

One of the key themes emerging from this year's Awards was the extent to which integration is pervading the industry's thinking, and there was strong evidence that success is being achieved in this area, sometimes overcoming the agency divide.

There is less evidence from the papers, however, that the integration of offline and online channels is being successfully achieved when it comes to evaluation of effects. There are undoubtedly good examples of this to be found elsewhere, but they are yet to find their way into the IPA Awards.

This will undoubtedly change as we move towards digital switch-over and the industry creates new structures for itself to bring the established channels closer to the newer ones, but it will take some pioneers to pick up the challenge of converting great work into awards.

So, from a media perspective, there was a lot of promise in this year's awards papers, especially in the area of cross-media integration and engagement.

However, in future awards papers it would be good to see more attention focused on media effectiveness, especially in the convergence of offline and online channels, and more papers that explore the undoubted contribution of the internet and other interactive media would be especially welcome.

Chapter 3

Judging the IPA Effectiveness Awards: the client perspective

Why I agreed to be a judge

By Jeremy Davies
Director of Brand and Communications, E.on

I answered with an instinctive and unequivocal 'Yes' when I was asked if I would judge this year's IPA Effectiveness Awards. From a client's perspective, these are the awards that matter: by reputation they are the most rigorous of their kind, focusing on actual business results, widely respected across all sectors, and reported and commented upon beyond the trade press. They are rightly taken seriously by most creative and media agencies because a successful entry confers lasting credibility, and by many clients because they provide a bank of best-practice case studies giving invaluable insight into the way to improve return on marketing investment. The industry and client judges are assembled from the great and the good of the agency, academic and business world. So it seemed foolish not to agree to be a judge.

As you would expect, the process of judging the entries is as rigorous as the awards themselves: two expert panels with vast experience and strong opinions scrutinise each entry, bringing their own understanding and perspectives to bear. At 4,000 words each (not including footnotes, charts and diagrams), this is quite a task: 50 cases were submitted in 2008. Fortunately, as a client judge you are somewhat sheltered from the volume of entries as each is sifted through by the industry panel before a limited selection are handed to the clients.

I think there are two real benefits to being a judge.

Breadth and depth in abundance

First, the ability to read the entries; this is, of course, available to anyone with the time to pick up a previous copy of this book or go to the IPA website, but with time always at a premium the advantage of being a judge is the discipline of having to read and analyse each one. As a collection, the entries offer an insight into diverse sectors, which is refreshing: as a client you spend your time focusing deeply on the detail of your own business and that of your immediate competitors, so the opportunity to look more broadly outside your particular sector, and share the problems and solutions of others, is both fascinating and educational.

This year's entries certainly didn't disappoint in terms of breadth of subject matter or robustness of evidence, taking us from Vietnam to south London, and involving Paddington Bear, Scottie dogs and grime music collectives, often backed up with impressive econometric models. However, the five entries awarded Gold stood out not only because they met the standard judging criteria but because of the confidence and passion with which they were written, and because the insight and ideas that were at their core were inextricably linked to the success of the business or cause. Ideas that seem simple and obvious are born of rigorous thinking, and it is impossible in the outstanding cases to imagine the idea disassociated from the organisation it embodies.

While there are obvious disadvantages to having to read a two-foot-high pile of case studies over the summer holiday period, these are outweighed by the fact that the majority of the cases are very readable, being clearly written and structured; it's worth remembering that the quality of the writing makes a real difference to the perceived strength of the entry. While 'clarity of the case' is just one of the seven judging criteria, in reality it is disproportionately important because a confusing and badly structured argument, or one overladen with irrelevant detail, is so much harder to wade through. Beyond clarity, the judges are asked to consider the scale of the task, the strength of the solution, the exploitation of communication channels and what new learning the entry brings. Overall, however, it is the scale of the effect and the strength of the proof that are looked at most closely; awards are given only to papers that conclusively prove that a campaign actually worked and provided a return on investment.

It is this last area that gives the IPA Awards their rigour, but also provides one of the biggest challenges for those writing an entry. Proof of business success requires evidence in the form of detailed data, and many businesses are hesitant about releasing data that can be scrutinised by competitors. There are clearly ways around this issue, such as using indexed and industry-standard data, but actual data will always be more compelling. For that reason, it is useful to ensure a client is fully engaged in creating an entry, so that the data are as good as they can be. It shows in an entry when the methods of proof have been thought about throughout a campaign rather than as an afterthought. Most client teams should be happy to support the process, given the need to prove a return on investment within the business, not to mention the cachet that an IPA Award can bring.

Having got the data, it's vital to remember that not everything that can be counted counts, and not everything that counts can be counted. Quantity of data is irrelevant: it's the quality and the relevance to the argument that matters. It's inevitable that there will be gaps or inconsistencies in the evidence, or areas that cannot be conclusively proven. Making measurable what isn't is difficult, but successful cases find imaginative and often circumstantial ways around this problem. Beyond that, it's up to the intuition and judgement of the judges to fill in any gaps.

A debate to relish

The second benefit of being a judge is the opportunity to debate your views with a group of fellow judges. Effectively locked in a room until the awards are made and the special prizes and Grand Prix allocated, the judges have surprisingly different perspectives from one another. Perhaps that's unsurprising given the different sectors and backgrounds that they are picked from, but a clear winner to one can be a loser for another. While a clearly structured, well-proven case with powerful results and strong return on investment will find unanimous support, in reality there are few of these and so the debate focuses on a majority that are subject to some very individual perspectives: each judge will bring to bear their own particular experience and preoccupations, pointing out different strengths and weaknesses. Often these can sway the room, especially where that experience is directly relevant. Judging the Effectiveness Awards is a fascinating and rewarding process, and you leave the judging room at the end of it feeling enriched by the efforts and knowledge of others.

Chapter 4

Payback calculations

How to make sure you get your sums right

By Les Binet
European Director, DDB Matrix

The IPA Effectiveness Awards exist to prove to the world that advertising (in its widest sense) really does work and can be an excellent way for a client to invest its money. So a crucial part of any winning entry has to be some measure of payback.

Yet IPA authors seem remarkably ill-informed about how to measure payback and return on investment (ROI). When Peter Field and I reviewed the IPA dataBANK for our book *Marketing in the Era of Accountability*, we found that, of the 880 papers submitted since 1980, only 39 actually calculated ROI correctly.

So how should you measure payback? Here's a brief guide to the calculations. For further details, see *Measuring Marketing Payback – a Best Practice Guide*, available online at www.IPA.co.uk.

There are three main steps to a standard payback calculation.

Step 1: Measure the incremental sales effect

The first step is to estimate the incremental sales generated by your campaign. To do this, you need to estimate 'base sales' – how much you would have sold without the campaign in question. Common methods include the following.

- **Extrapolating from a trend.** Sometimes you can estimate base sales by extrapolating from the pre-campaign trend. But you need to be sure that there were no other factors affecting sales during the period in question.
- **Test and control.** Alternatively, you may be able to find a group of people or products that was not exposed to your campaign. Comparing advertised regions with 'silent' regions is a classic way to estimate incremental sales.
- **Econometric modelling.** Econometrics is the most sophisticated measurement method. For further information see the IPA's *Econometrics Explained*, available at www.IPA.co.uk.

Step 2: Calculate net payback

The next step is to calculate the revenue generated for the client. Remember to take account of the retailer's cut:

Incremental revenue = Incremental retail sales value – Retailer cash margin

Next, calculate the contribution that those sales make to profit, taking account of any incremental costs incurred (materials, wages, etc.):

Incremental costs = Variable cost per unit × Incremental units

Subtracting these costs from the incremental sales revenue gives the marginal contribution to profit:

Marginal contribution = Incremental revenue – Incremental costs

Alternatively, rather than using unit costs, one can do exactly the same calculation using the *contribution margin*, if this is known. The calculation then becomes:

Marginal contribution = Incremental sales revenue × Contribution margin %

Finally, subtract the cost of the campaign to calculate the net profit it generates:

Net profit generated = Marginal contribution – Cost of campaign

The net profit generated is the ultimate measure of effectiveness, namely the measure of how much money the campaign made for the brand's owners.

Step 3: Calculate return on marketing investment (ROMI)

Net profit generated is the ultimate measure of marketing *effectiveness*. However, if you want to measure financial *efficiency*, then you need to calculate the ROMI:

ROMI = (Net profit/Cost of campaign) × 100%

In order to avoid confusion with other measures of financial return, such as return on capital employed (ROCE), we recommend that the term 'ROMI' be used rather than just 'ROI'.

ROMI is a useful measure, because it allows you to compare the efficiency of different campaigns with different budgets. It also allows you to compare the return from your campaign with the returns from other alternative investments. For instance, you might compare the return from advertising with the return you might earn from investing in a new factory, or from new product development (NPD), or from simply keeping the money in the bank and earning interest. This allows you to assess the *opportunity cost* of spending money on marketing.

Common mistakes

So why do so many IPA authors get these sums wrong? Here's a guide to the most common errors.

- **Failing to measure financial payback at all.** Some IPA cases fail to tackle the issue of financial payback at all, restricting themselves to intermediate measures such as awareness shifts or direct response rates. The worst of these add insult to injury by trying to pass these off as 'ROI measures'.
- **Confusing sales increases with incremental sales.** Measuring incremental sales is not the same as measuring sales growth. Sales may grow despite ineffective marketing (due to other factors). Effective marketing may not lead to growth (it might just slow a decline).
- **Treating all direct sales as incremental.** Sometimes it's possible to measure 'direct sales', namely sales to people who responded directly to your campaign. However, not all direct sales are incremental sales – some of those sales might have happened anyway. And not all incremental sales are direct – your campaign might be driving people to buy your brand in the shops as well.
- **Treating revenue as profit.** Marketing effectiveness is often assessed in terms of incremental *revenue* generated, rather than profit, usually because profit data are unavailable. This is perfectly valid, of course, but such measures should never be referred to as measures of 'payback' or 'ROI'. True payback calculations are based on incremental *profit*.
- **Using the wrong profit margin.** The only costs that should be subtracted when calculating payback are variable costs. Do *not* subtract fixed costs, otherwise you will underestimate the payback from your campaign. This means you should always use the 'contribution margin', not the 'net profit margin' that appears in the client's accounts. Using net profit margins will lead to a serious underestimate of payback.
- **Careless use of the term 'ROI'.** This term has a very precise meaning. The ROI is *not* the number of direct responses, the amount of PR coverage, the increase in brand awareness, nor even the amount of profit generated. It's the ratio of net profit generated to the amount invested, expressed as a percentage. To use the term in any other way is to make yourself look foolish.

Longer and broader effects

The basic calculations outlined above are fine for the simple marketing effects, but there are various 'longer and broader' effects that you may also wish to consider.

- **Supporting higher prices.** Rather than increasing volume, your campaign may be allowing the campaign to sell the same volume at a higher price. Measuring such effects is tricky, and may well require econometrics to measure price elasticity. However, the payback calculation is basically the same as before, except that the increase in sales value comes from higher prices.

■ **Reducing costs.** In principle, marketing might be used to reduce costs rather than increase revenue. For example, better marketing might help a manufacturer to negotiate better deals with suppliers, or to reduce the costs associated with staff recruitment and retention. Measuring such effects is hard, but the payback calculations do not change significantly, except that the incremental costs now become incremental cost savings.

■ **Creating options.** As well as increasing profits from existing products and markets, marketing might allow a brand owner to launch new products or enter new markets. In principle, the theory of financial options provides a way of quantifying the value created here, although in practice this is hard.

■ **Changing market expectations.** Marketing affects investors as well as consumers. By improving market expectations of a product or company's future performance, marketing may increase the financial value of a company and its brands. Again, quantifying the contribution of marketing here is hard.

■ **Reducing the cost of capital.** If your campaign causes the City to reassess your client's company, then one effect may be to reduce the cost of capital. Little research has been done on this effect, but the potential benefits for highly geared firms might be large. Measuring such an effect would be an interesting challenge for the marketing community.

Most of these effects are much more long term. When estimating *long-term payback*, bear in mind that you need to take account of the 'time value of money' – the idea that profits in the future are worth less than profits now. A campaign that generates £1m of extra profit immediately is better than a campaign that takes five years to generate the same profit. Managers and financiers deal with this by using *discounted cash-flow analysis*, and you should do the same. This is a very complex area – get your CFO to help you.

Chapter 5

Tales from the judging rooms

Experiences of judging an IPA Effectiveness submission vs writing one

By David Golding
Founding Partner, Adam & Eve, London

The overwhelming response whenever I've mentioned any involvement with the IPA Effectiveness Awards has always been 'Oh, you poor bastard.' If you're beavering away at the agency crafting your case surrounded by reams of data, your peers will regularly pity you. And the same applies to being a judge. As a large cardboard box arrived for me at Adam & Eve containing this year's entries, again I was bestowed the sympathy of my colleagues. This was, however, misplaced. Undoubtedly both entering and judging the IPA Effectiveness Awards is a significant commitment, but both are hugely rewarding experiences offering a great opportunity to learn more about client businesses, the power and importance of communications and, quite frankly, yourself.

In this short chapter I'm going to highlight my experiences having now been on both sides of the fence, and, I hope, give some guidance to future authors, and judges, on how to get the best from participating in the IPA Effectiveness Awards.

Authors want to win; judges want to learn

First off is a macro observation. Authors and judges both want to get something out of the time invested in this process. The authors want to win; the judges want to learn. It's striking how much the judges respect the authors and their entries. It's a far cry from the high-minded professors who marked our essays as lowly students. Rather this judging process is peer reviewing at its best, with each judge hoping to really learn something fresh about advertising and marketing. Get a judge to think about a subject in a way they haven't before and you'll be a long way towards achieving your goal of winning.

Authors think 'how big'; judges think 'how hard'

Related to this is another important difference between writing and judging: many authors are primarily concerned with how big a payback they can show was achieved. Judges, however, appear to be slightly less concerned by this. So long as a return on investment is shown, the judges often take a more qualitative stance and ask 'How hard was it to achieve this result?' In line with this overall desire to learn from the process, the judges were more inclined towards tough tasks tackled well, than easier tasks delivering stellar results. And stellar results carry with them another problem: they often feel intuitively wrong.

Authors think about the marketing world; judges think about the real world

Judges read all the papers with a bigger sense of 'the real world' than I had expected. If an argument or claim doesn't feel right it takes an awful lot of hard persuasion to help the judges accept it. This goes against the authors' mentality of finding ways to make the figures look as epic as possible. I'm not advocating a conservatism around the presentation of results, but I am suggesting that acknowledging a surprisingly high rate of success, rather than crowing about it, will help a lot.

Authors want to look different; judges want to know what they're looking at

Next up is trying to stand out. As an author I was aware that there was a way of writing a paper. This involved setting out the problem, describing the solution, putting in a media section written by the media agency (to show integration), show the results and then discount all other factors. And so as an author I always wanted to write entries in a different and fresh way. As a judge, however, the formula is so welcome. It helps navigate the papers and compare them against each other. Writing to a formula is boring only if the writing is formulaic too. Where the style is lively, a structured paper makes the judging a joy, and the scores so much higher.

Somewhat paradoxically, lively writing can often be let down by equally lively charts. Attempting to look clever with intricate graphs and models is something many authors love to do. But often judges struggle with this. They don't know the market like the author does and don't have the time and skills to decode complex illustrations. Instead the judges responded best to the entries with really simple, clear graphics that almost tell the story without the supporting words.

Authors think that God is in the detail; judges fear that's where the Devil can hide

While I'm on the subject of supporting your argument, it's worth knowing that the judges tend not to read the appendix in any great detail. The technical judges do, but the rest figure that the case and its merits stand on the main body of the entry.

So don't risk putting anything material into the appendix. Equally, there is a rather debilitating symptom that I call the 'burst appendix' where the author has loaded it with data and charts and graphs. The judges just wonder why. It raises suspicions and puts a lot of pressure on the technical experts to reassure the remaining group, which isn't a position you should get into.

Another expert I wasn't too aware of when I was writing entries is the City analyst that sits on the judging panels. This person reads the papers in a very different way to everyone else. They couldn't care less about the creative, the insight or the media deployment. But they are fascinated by the business problem. Articulating this well and upfront will have this lead voice shouting in your favour as the other judges debate the merits of the 'bus ticket' media you used in the north-east uplift area.

Authors think about lots of people when they write a paper but it's good if the judges are among them

So, as an author, when writing a paper don't just think of the glory, of pleasing your client and impressing your boss. Think of the judges, too. Think of how they will learn something from reading your paper; think how to ensure it sits happily within their 'real world'; think about keeping it lively but structured; think about how easy the graphs are to decode; and think about the business case and making it clear. And maybe think about becoming a judge yourself one day and seeing what you could learn from the best in business – the other judges and all the authors like you.

Chapter 6

The evolution of commercially effective communications

By Neil Dawson
Founder, Hurrell Moseley Dawson & Grimmer

The IPA Effectiveness Awards exist to celebrate and reward commercial payback for investment in marketing communications. The judging criteria demand a high-level of proof, making these Awards more rigorous than any other effectiveness scheme in the world. Twenty-eight years of competitions have yielded a databank of over 1,200 cases covering a myriad of problems, categories, audiences, creative ideas, channel selections and supporting evidence. All are united by the common cause of demonstrating that the investment made in communications is either profitable or has delivered value.

Ideas are at the heart of each of these cases. Creative communications ideas of extraordinary power. They are engines of growth and confidence. As a result brand owners enjoy longevity and stability of revenues and profits, the ability to plan a business, deploy assets and resources; and public services are able to change behaviour and attitudes for social and economic benefit.

Considered as a whole, the databank is a fascinating tale of the evolution of commercially effective ideas and our understanding of how they work. Each competition yields another snapshot of this evolution. In Darwinian terms we are reviewing the 'fittest' – those best equipped to survive and thrive whatever the prevailing conditions.

While there remains no universal formula for successful creative communications, this year's winners reveal several trends and success factors of broad relevance, as well as more 'micro' insights of value in specific situations.

Big Ideas Go Global

The Awards have consistently demonstrated the power of the 'big idea' to transform businesses and brands, with iconic UK cases such as Stella Artois's

'Reassuringly Expensive', Orange's 'The Future's Bright' and 'Your M&S'. This year's winners again demonstrate this, for the first time with cases that take big ideas onto the global stage.

Grand Prix winner Johnnie Walker and Silver winner Dove show how ideas can create 'bona fide' global icons, valuable additions to the IPA dataBANK which until 2008 contained just 10 multi-market or international cases. Both took declining franchises and transformed them via a powerful core idea flexible enough to adapt to local and organisational needs, working across markets and multiple channels. Each is built on human truths with universal resonance. Dove's quest to 'help more women feel more beautiful everyday' and Johnnie Walker's aim 'to inspire personal progress' are enduring, robust engines of global growth.

Sainsbury's 'Try Something New Today' is both an evolution and optimisation of big idea 'best practice'. The precision of the business objective of persuading shoppers to spend an extra £1.14 a trip, and the impressive application of the idea to both internal and external audiences, make its phenomenal success seem deceptively easy.

De Beers put game-changing ideas at the heart of their business via' Justifying Narratives', each creating emotional value in the form of a new role for diamonds in the lives of the owner. These informed product concepts, design, naming, consumer and trade communications to drive growth in the mature US market.

Multiple channels increasingly a success norm

Integration is now so much the norm that the term itself seems almost obsolete, with 'new' and 'old' media rapidly blurring into a single communications armoury. Creative ideas delivered across a scientifically selected and skilfully deployed range of channels are widely in evidence. Interruption and engagement channels are complementary tools rather than 'old' pitted against 'new' media. While use of a wide range of channels is no guarantee of success, there is strong evidence that intelligent, insightful channel selection is a key success factor.

TV remains the dominant medium, used in 22 of the 23 winners – unsurprising given its still unrivalled ability to bring reach and impact for mass-market brands (from supermarkets to fast food this continues to be a critical task). What is changing is the way in which TV is blended with previously 'supporting' channels.

This year's winners used on average six channels; in 2004 the corresponding number was four; back in 1990 the number was two. While driven in part by the explosion of channels available, there is clearly a corresponding cultural shift away from the historic 'silo mentality' of disciplines and channels. Media-led solutions are increasingly evident.

■ The long-running Anti-Crime campaign used a strong visual device to unify a range of messages across multiple crimes. Winner of the Best Media prize in both 2008 and 2006, TV was deployed for awareness; print and ambient targeted 'moments of careless stupidity'. These targeted areas included public transport, bars and nightclubs, garage forecourts, door hangers on student accommodation, and door-drops in high-risk burglary postcodes.

- Audi's growth as a prestige brand is supported by an innovative channel mix, consistently deployed. Each model launch combined advertising with an iconic communications innovation that entered popular culture: for the RS3 a special edition of *GQ*; for the Audi TT a Jimi Hendrix photographic exhibition.
- Lucozade Sport doubled sales with a decreased budget via a better conversation with a tighter audience, forensically targeting 'Competitive Warriors' with communications and partnerships tailored to different sports environments. Intelligent and innovative approaches to such diverse sports as football, running, rowing and hockey delivered coherence without resorting to the traditional integrated approach of 'one size fits all'.
- The Metropolitan Police's Trident campaign used a unique and diverse channel mix (from cinema and niche TV through to barber shops) to give its anti-gun message crucial credibility with a streetwise urban audience.

A significant caveat is the lack of specific focus on media effectiveness; for instance, the quality of evidence is low for the less established online and interactive channels. Too many winners describe intriguing strategies, creative and media approaches, only to disappoint with proof limited to the traditional components of their plan – the conventional tracking and modelling of (mainly) TV effects. A more coherent approach to media effectiveness across channels is required, both in the development of campaigns and their evaluation. (More on this later in Nick Manning's media perspective on the winners.)

Overcommitment overdelivers

There is much evidence here of the power of 'overcommitment' to a brand or consumer truth to deliver results in increasingly cluttered and undifferentiated categories.

Kentucky Fried Chicken ignored the temptations of attempting to re-present itself as a healthy option in an increasingly anti-fast food environment. Celebrating why people loved KFC in the first place led to a reversal of fortune.

Waitrose and Morrisons used truths of 'quality' and 'freshness' respectively to build distinctive and compelling territories. For Waitrose, this involved adding a layer of ethical value to the already established platform of 'Quality food honestly priced'. For Morrisons it meant focusing on its market-stall roots and its commitment to fresh food. This galvanised the organisation in the wake of the Safeway takeover and created competitive advantage.

As a much-loved (and much-hated) British institution, Marmite risked the wrath of its existing 'purists' by introducing the squeezy format. But maintaining its commitment to the provocative 'Love–Hate' strategy reassured fans that 'their Marmite' was still theirs.

Danone Activia took advantage of changed health claim regulations to focus single-mindedly on the unpleasant problem of 'bloating', resulting in sales growth of 459% in three and a half years. Communications driving this claim transformed a brand previously on a sales and penetration plateau, ranked only 16th in the market by value. Opportunistic overcommitment works too.

Public service: diverse paths to payback

Public service campaigns again feature heavily among the winners, helped by a strong effectiveness culture based on the obligation to demonstrate that public money is well spent. The effects of such campaigns can also often be easier to disentangle than, say, sales effects in a complex fmcg market where distribution, pricing, competitors and promotions will be muddying the water.

This year's winners include seven from the public service arena, and it is their diversity that particularly stands out. They can be loosely divided into three distinct camps.

No-spin wins

The introduction of electronic payments for social security and pension payments met with widespread public and media hostility. There was no personal incentive to switch nor would there be any penalty for refusal. Direct Payments succeeded by adopting a powerful 'spin-free' posture, with the conventional marketing approaches of persuasion and benefits eschewed in favour of simple, helpful information portrayed as neutrally as possible. This defusion of an emotionally charged issue led to an over-delivery on government targets, 95% switching within two years. There are echoes here of previous campaigns facing public hostility, most notably the resolutely spin-free introduction of the Congestion Charge (Gold winner in 2004).

Brand mnemonics

The Anti-Crime, CABWISE and Learndirect cases demonstrate the power of branding devices in public service campaigns. Each acted as shorthands for their respective services. CABWISE branding was deployed to dissuade women from using illegal minicabs and provide practical information on how to use the text service. Learndirect's jigsaw dramatises the incompleteness people can feel about their jobs and careers. This acted as a simple cipher for messages about the practical solutions to improving your prospects.

All the above draw heavily on the established practices of consumer marketing, where brand mnemonics are familiar vehicles to create consistent identities and provide 'nudges' to consumer behaviour and attitudes.

Confront the issue

Helmet-wearing in Vietnam, seatbelt-wearing in Ireland, and the Trident anti-gun campaign are perhaps closest to the archetypal public service campaign. For many issues, confrontation works – whether it is the stupid excuses for not wearing a crash helmet, the moral irresponsibility of failing to wear a seatbelt or the appalling consequences of gun crime. Each tackles a widely recognised negative societal issue via powerful imagery, dramatising the problem, and delivers a strong rallying call against it.

The small can survive and thrive

Since 1980 these Awards have consistently shown that limited resources are no barrier to commercial success. The special prize for Best Small Budget case (media spend of less than £1m) retains significant cachet in a competition where scale of effect is not an absolute but a relative measure.

Certainly creative ideas and content that genuinely engage are less reliant on big budgets and paid-for media than ever before: what more cost-effective approach than to get other people or channels to do your marketing for you, free of charge?

Take, for example, the reinvention of TV channel uktvg2 as Dave. The name and the supporting campaign created a distinctive identity and personality for what was previously another space on the ever-expanding electronic programme guide. Success was achieved without significant changes to content or programming strategy. Launch PR and the talkability effects of the campaign lead to the conclusion that a larger media spend would have been wasted. This share of mind delivered an additional 8 million viewers and £4.5m profit in the first six months.

Good husbandry of limited creative resources and media spend is the more familiar story of the Small Budget category. Radley shows how payback can be achieved in the world of fashion – not a common environment for rigorous communications evaluation. Radley's private equity ownership wanted rapid growth over three years: communications delivered this with added benefits. As well as increasing the rate of sales growth by a factor of 2.4, broader effects on company valuation and subsequent sale of the Radley brand were extraordinary. Thus the notoriously short-term world of fashion brings new learning about the long-term effects of communications.

Success: the long and the short of it all

The 2008 winners again prove that short-term and long-term effects need not belong to discrete or mutually exclusive communications activities.

Since becoming a specific focus of the Awards in 1990, 'longer and broader' effects demonstrated have included increasing shareholder value (Orange), improving the ability to command a price premium (BMW), and positive effects on employee morale (Tesco).

The importance of these effects for brands should not be underestimated. The long-term view is supported by evidence from the world of neuroscience that our decision-making processes are driven by 'hard-wired memories'. Brands become shorthands for decision making over time through repetition and consistent story-telling. This is what can lead to both immediate and long-term sales. Business success (and indeed survival) is dependent on both, and the most efficient way to do this is to create impacts that endure by getting into people's brains and staying there.

The Audi, Johnnie Walker, Dove and Anti-Crime cases already referred to show the power of ideas and communications campaigns to deliver on this. Two further

2008 examples are worthy of specific mention: Virgin Atlantic as an exemplar of long-term brand-building, and Motorola for its proof of advertising's long-term benefits relative to other marketing activity.

For more than 15 years Virgin Atlantic has consistently created a sense of 'Virginness' through all brand behaviours to drive preference and sales. A consistently irreverent tone and iconic use of channels strengthened Virginness. New destinations, product innovations and tactical messages were all short-term steps but an integral part of the 'long-haul' brand journey to success.

Motorola demonstrates advertising's enduring impact compared with short-term 'retail push'. In China the 'Moto Tribe' campaign grew market share from 13% to 20% in one year – a faster rate of growth than their global average, proving the value of communications over and above the new product effect. Within the marketing mix, advertising was shown through modelling to be the only activity with long-term effects (12 months per burst); other marketing activities had no effects after two months but half of advertising-generated sales effect comes from persistence beyond the first two months. While 'retail push' only talks to those actively looking for a mobile phone, advertising creates a dialogue with current and future buyers.

Many recently commenced campaigns featured here, such as Morrisons and KFC, have the mark of long-term potential – succeeding in the short term by taking a long-term view, creating long-term brand meaning while simultaneously achieving short-term goals of sales.

In conclusion

Ideas are at the heart of each of these cases. Creative communications ideas of extraordinary power. They are engines of growth and confidence. As a result brand owners enjoy longevity and stability of revenues and profits, the ability to plan a business, deploy assets and resources; and public services are able to change behaviour and attitudes for social and economic benefit.

So what conclusions can be drawn from the 'class of 2008'? What are the emergent trends and success factors? And what has been added to the sum of our knowledge?

There are some common 'evolutionary' threads of commercially effective ideas:

■ They transform brands and the organisations behind them. And, for the first time, we are witnessing hard evidence of their ability to do so on a global scale.
■ They work *both* in the short and long term to drive immediate results and deliver long-term benefits.
■ They work seamlessly across multiple channels – 'joined-up' creative and media thinking, reaching the 'tipping point' where what were previously divided silos are forming one single communications armoury.
■ They are unlimited by size of budget, only by the ambition and imagination of those deploying them.

- Those rooted in overcommitment to a brand or product truth are particularly potent.
- They work equally well for commercial and public service organisations, with the latter often learning from the former.

'Prevailing market conditions' have changed since the 2008 entries were submitted. A decade of growth and prosperity has been abruptly reversed by the global financial crisis. The economic and societal benefits of brands in providing stability and security will be of greater significance than ever. The value of creative communications ideas and media effectiveness will therefore not diminish, although specific ideas, strategies and tactics will evolve in response to the new environment. The IPA Effectiveness Awards and what they represent will be more important than ever.

Chapter 7

Effectiveness and digital media

How to avoid the trap of knowing the price of everything and the value of nothing

By Greg Grimmer
Partner, Hurrell Moseley Dawson & Grimmer

Cut once, measure twice …

As I approach this chapter and attempt to do justice to the given title in the IPA's most sacred tome I am reminded of the advice given to me very early in my media planning career by one of my first planning directors:

As soon as you spend it, measure it.

By measurement, the advice being given wasn't the counting of eyeballs (or indeed the extrapolation of panel data) but the creation of bespoke research to ascertain the positive effect (if any) of the actions of my colleagues. This simple and effective advice saw me through the first decade or so of my career in the halcyon days before media fragmentation, and certainly before the digital explosion that hastened the onslaught of the information age.

While it may seem difficult to believe for those of a more tender age, the paucity of information in media was a true phenomenon until at least the mid-1990s. Therefore the judicious use of simple quantitative data to ascertain the success and justify the continuation of media investment was a simple but useful lesson. Now, as we enter the second decade of the information age, I am reminded of one of my favourite Oscar Wilde quotes, now over one hundred years old but never more apposite:

The trouble is these days there is too little useless information.

Plus ça change ...

Within my new silo-free agency I was discussing this phenomenon with an account handler and a copywriter, and all of us were bemoaning the fact that our latest TV commercial wouldn't be judged for four to six months, while its online cousin was being judged by its click-through rate *one day* after launching. The availability of the data and those who receive it means that decisions are often made to change, stop or amend far quicker in online than in other media channels.

'Why did you change it? Because I can' should be the mantra to avoid.

We shouldn't however be surprised by this. It is within the professional lifetime of most people still working that decision making, amendment and approval have transferred from Royal Mail, to telephone, to fax, to email. A process that may once have taken weeks is now often actioned within hours (if not minutes). The future for the bright is digital. We must acknowledge this and it is a one-way street. There are no negative integers in binary.

So, we are stuck with a new marketing world that gives us great measurability and, crucially, immediate measurability.

Efficient use of effective media?

One of the much returned to debates in marketing strategy, forever highlighted by the always assertive Patrick Barwise, is that of *efficiency versus effectiveness*. This debate is never more relevant than in media investment targeting and deployment.

Online media (and specifically I will focus here on online media such as search PPC as opposed to the vague term 'digital media', which encompasses digital outdoor, digital TV, mobile etc., that have not benefited in the same way as online) are very in vogue due to their immediate measurability. They are also manipulated to become 'more' *efficient* through a combination of human and technology inputs. Indeed their *effectiveness* is also trumpeted due to the simplistic ROI that can often be shown in a dollar in – dollar out fashion.

This however is the nub of the issue. Online media are very good at counting.

E-commerce businesses make a science out of this methodology and indeed Google, as the world's largest, most powerful media owner, built its 'do no evil' empire out of this base simplistic counting process. We should not and indeed must not conclude that because we can count direct actions (even in dollars, pounds or euros), we are making a positive contribution to the effectiveness debate.

Are you affected (by online)?

The internet is now well into its second decade as a media and marketing tool. Yet looking at *Advertising Works* back copies you will find very few of the excellent and award-winning papers, which are able to show the effectiveness of the internet marketing that has been included within the featured campaign. Many talk about the effect, but the campaigns that have been *affected* by digital marketing are notable absentees. Now many naysayers will state that this is testament to the traditional advertising world's neglect of the online channel. This I believe would be a crass point of view harboured only by those who inhabit the small (padded?) cell and believe *only* digital channels can affect positive results.

The geek will inherit the Earth, but we will all become geeks. Digital natives (those who have been in or left in education since the mid-1990s) see no difference. What we are failing to do is determine the combined effectiveness of messages delivered within any channel that have a longer-term effect on consumers.

The first dotcom boom (1998–2001) was in reality a boom of online brands and properties that spent huge amounts of money in traditional media trying to ensure a piece of consumer mind-set for their particular piece of online land grab. The second dotcom boom (2005–2008) has been those dotcom survivors, and let us not forget lots of traditional media owners, benefiting from real advertisers transferring large portions of their advertising budgets to the online world.

Retail, Motors, Finance and Travel are categories that have embraced online as accountable media, but these are categories that have had things to count: shoppers, test drives, policies, flights. For all of these it is very easy to show that, within an efficiency hierarchy, online is working. Where the internet media owners have had fewer successes has been in the sectors of luxury goods and fmcg where the e-commerce marketplace is either frowned upon or controlled via powerful third parties.

Technology can hinder as well as help

Steps towards greater accountability within our new(ish) world have of course been taken, and digital evangelists will talk in educated tones at great length about cookie duration, post-click impressions, and behavioural targeting. While it is true that all these allow for longer-term effects of an initial commercial impression to be measured, all remain measures of increased accountability within the online channel, not within the wider media mix.

Now of course this is not a new issue. Television advertising has long dominated tracking research, and many will have wrestled with the problem of isolating radio or print advertising effects from a Millward Brown study. Millward Brown's sister company Dynamic Logic has attempted to make strong strides in this area to allow for multimedia modelling to be conducted, including the online advertising effect. But these research methodologies are too often overlooked in favour of the more direct counting methods of online evaluation, and if print, radio and outdoor are still struggling, online creativity (or lack of it) has only hampered the measurement of the online contribution further.

This is another aspect of the online accountability debate. Poor-quality online sales presentations to agencies and clients will often cite the amount of time that is spent consuming online media (20%-plus now in some demographics) but these studies, while accurate and fairly conducted, do not measure the *actual exposure to commercial messages* during that time and how this varies in comparison with other media. Last time I checked, 100% of exposure to outdoor was to commercial not editorial messages! Online advertising effectiveness suffers from the manner in which it is consumed and therefore the current deflation on impression delivered cost per thousands might well be for the long-term health of the business.

It's all about the idea, stupid

The creative debate is also one that is still in play. A worldwide creative director of a major network who shall remain nameless joked with me how one of his team had 'cracked the digital brief – by uploading the TV ad on to YouTube'.

Even those films that do achieve 'success' on YouTube achieve the same level of impact as an early peak spot on Central or the readership of the *Sun*. And then there is the debate over what this impact is worth.

A senior executive of a leading creative agency and eloquent supporter of effectiveness argued at a recent conference that:

> *Everyone knows a view on YouTube is worth five views on television.*

Well unfortunately of course we don't know this; it is a personal hypothesis and one I can counter with my own personal experience. I, like many, will have viewed the Guy Ritchie-directed Nike football film on YouTube, as it viralled its way round the industry. I saw, I liked, I logged in my neural networks. However, when the same ad appeared as first ad in break coming out of the Champions League semi-final I went further: I enjoyed the ad, encouraged others to share it, and eulogised about it (to this very moment it seems), but the in-situ effect outweighed the 'opt in' effect.

Online of course offers fantastic creative possibilities within text, video and interactive combinations of the two, and I firmly believe that the exploitation of this channel moving forward will help us with the accountability debate as it will be impossible to ignore. A piece of research I conducted among online evangelists produced a result of 37% unable to name a piece of online creativity they admired. The elimination of this factor must be a goal for everyone and is a factor of efficient levels of investment as well as effective creative.

We are stronger together

We must seek to look for measurement tools that get us away from online counting. Mixed retail models, brick and clicks won't go away: online communication does already have an effect in driving offline sales, plus long-term online sales will be as a result of many, not singular, commercial messages.

Econometric models for those who have the faith in data and budgets to afford them will normally provide some of these answers, but the wider advertising industry should also seek to positively discriminate the measurement of online's positive effects, as budgets now reach levels where the isolation of its effect (and oft its proximity to sale) can be a powerful defence of accountability. Moreover, the online industry must embrace multi-channel research work. The IAB has made excellent strides in this area and we must hope that the macro-economic conditions mean that we don't revert to counting actions and eyeballs, rather than measuring cause and effect.

SECTION 3

Gold winners

Chapter 8

Johnnie Walker

From whisky producer to global icon:
the story of 'Keep Walking'

By Steve Mustardé, BBH
Contributing author: Karl Weaver, Data2Decisions

Foreword

We would like to acknowledge the authors of past IPA and APG papers on Johnnie Walker, on whose insight and analysis this paper has drawn: Ashley Alsup, Dorothea Gartland, Orlando Hooper Greenhill, Ben King, Lisa Matchett, Aisling Ryan.

Editor's summary

This extraordinary paper answers one of the most significant questions asked of any marketing campaign – to reach across borders with a powerful, motivating and above all universal consumer insight. In doing so, a global campaign was able to transform Johnnie Walker from an ailing whisky brand into a global icon.

At the turn of the millennium, global research found that the concept of 'success' was no longer symbolised by material wealth but was increasingly linked to a desire for self-improvement. The most powerful expression of masculine success in the 21st century was 'progress'.

The brand icon of 'The Striding Man' was resurrected as this insight was expressed throughout the world by an injunction to 'Keep Walking'.

The campaign has run in 120 markets so far, and across the world in media including over 50 TV executions, more than 150 print executions, radio ads, websites, sponsorships, internal awards, consumer awards, and a charitable fund. It has succeeded in creating considerable consumer engagement and sales growth. Some eight years after it was launched, Johnnie Walker's communications campaign has grown sales by almost 50% and delivered in excess of US$2bn of incremental sales.

Introduction

As the 21st century brings the continents ever closer together, so more and more brands will assume a global footprint. Inevitably, their communications will adopt a similarly global remit.

Yet a glance at the IPA database reveals only seven case histories with which to illuminate the path towards global effectiveness. In the world of global advertising there are precious few travel guides.

The most commonly asked questions about planning, developing, managing and measuring global campaigns remain unanswered:

- What are the hallmarks of an idea that can transcend disparate geographies and cultures to captivate consumers worldwide?
- How can a brand establish a new campaign consistently across the world?
- How can a campaign be flexed to meet various geographical and organisational needs without losing focus?
- How might the returns on campaign budgets be expected to evolve over time?

In this paper we endeavour to answer these fundamental questions, and more, by documenting the fall and rise of Johnnie Walker, a brand whose global reach is matched by few others.

This is the story of a brand whose title, 'The world's most popular whisky', hid an unsettling sales decline, and the global campaign that returned it to winning ways: a campaign that transformed Johnnie Walker from a whisky producer alone, into a global icon brand. The campaign has run in over 120 markets worldwide and even now, more than eight years after its launch, drives impressive growth.

This is the story of 'Keep Walking'.

Background

In 1820, the regulars in John Walker's grocery shop had begun complaining about the whisky he stocked, its flavour apparently too challenging for their taste. So in a response typical of his determined opportunism he began blending his own whiskies in the shop's back room, confident that his expertise in blending teas would serve him well. So began the illustrious story of Johnnie Walker whisky (see Figure 1).

Figure 1: John Walker's 1820s grocery shop in Kilmarnock, Scotland

To readers in the UK, Johnnie Walker is likely to be known but not familiar. In global terms however, it is one of the most famous[1] and valuable brands[2] in any category. Sold in over 180 markets, it is the world's largest whisky brand by some margin, selling over US$4.5bn[3] worth of whisky in 2007. The brand's portfolio ranges from Red Label, the world's most popular whisky,[4] to Blue Label, one of the most expensive (see Figure 2).

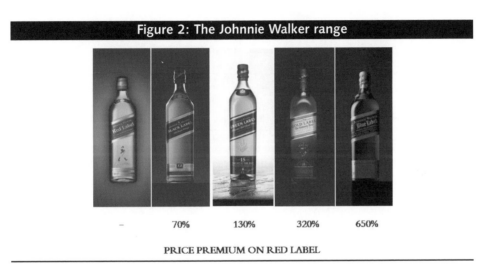

Figure 2: The Johnnie Walker range

| – | 70% | 130% | 320% | 650% |

PRICE PREMIUM ON RED LABEL

A brand in danger

In 1999, however, Johnnie Walker was on red alert. In the three years since 1996, volume sales had dropped 14%[5] (see Figure 3).

The brand was also steadily losing market share (see Figure 4) because of a complex set of brand and organisational issues.

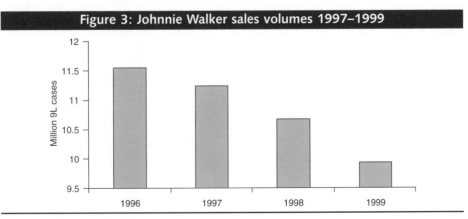

Figure 3: Johnnie Walker sales volumes 1997–1999

Source: Original UDV Pitch brief

Figure 4: Johnnie Walker volume share of Scotch 1997–1999

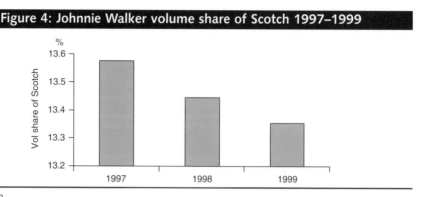

Source: IWSR

Johnnie Walker was still market leader in 1999 but that position was under threat. For a brand with such a proud past, the future was looking bleak. So in 1998 BBH was called to pitch for the business.

The brief from Diageo was twofold: to reverse the immediate fortunes of the brand in terms of sales; and to develop a future-proof, global communications strategy that would ensure sustained growth in all Johnnie Walker's markets and much-needed focus internally.

Understanding the problem

In the Scotch category, consumer choice is driven by brand affinity.[6] The Johnnie Walker brand, however, had become badly fragmented.

At a market level, local teams were empowered to respond to local issues, resulting in numerous unrelated campaigns in each market (see Figure 5).

At a product level, each variant was positioned and marketed separately. Inevitably, this variant strategy diverted support and investment away from the brand.

Figure 5: Between 1997 and 1999 at least 27 different campaigns existed for Red Label and Black Label

Johnnie Walker had become a disparate collection of products – it needed to become a single, powerful brand again.

> *Johnnie Walker was all over the place: it was a mess. In Europe it was open fires and comfy slippers, in Latin America a spirit for mixing at parties, in the US a premium brand and a status symbol in Asia.*

> Stephen Morley, Global Brand Director, 1999

Diverse markets, bold targets

The team identified two fundamental challenges:

1. Local market nuances

Each market's relationship with whisky was unique: consumer profiles varied in terms of age, mind-set, cultural diversity and economic prosperity. Whisky was drunk mixed in Spain, straight in the US, with guarana[7] in Brazil, or by the bottleful in Thailand.

Additionally, Johnnie Walker was known for its standard-priced Red Label in some markets but by the more premium Black Label elsewhere (see Figure 6). Our brand idea had to work in all these environments.

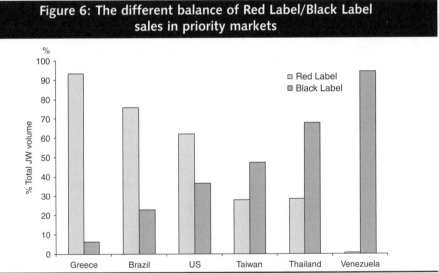

Figure 6: The different balance of Red Label/Black Label sales in priority markets

Source: IWSR

2. Ambitious growth targets

Furthermore, Diageo's brief targeted a return to aggressive growth. Such a turn-around in fortunes would require significantly stronger consumer engagement with the brand than it invited at the time, despite being the global market leader (see Figure 7). Clearly, being the preferred whisky was not enough: Johnnie Walker had to change the rules of the category and play a far greater role in consumers' lives.

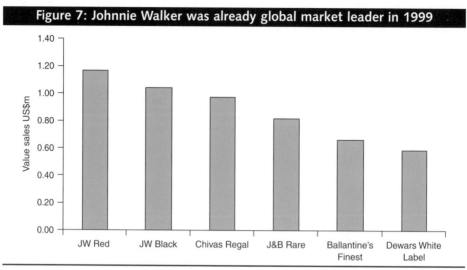

Figure 7: Johnnie Walker was already global market leader in 1999

Source: IWSR

The team understood that to overcome both issues would require a step-change in the way the brand communicated. Johnnie Walker had to be not just a whisky brand but a global icon brand.

I want Johnnie Walker to step out and lead the male target.

Alberto Gavazzi, Johnnie Walker Brazil

Understanding icon brands

The world's most iconic global brands have three key things in common:

1. *Fame* – they are branded with a universally recognised icon that is symbolic of everything they stand for.
2. *Resonance* – they are founded on a set of fundamental human values.

Apple opposes, IBM solves, Nike exhorts, Virgin enlightens, Sony dreams, Benetton protests … I believe Dan Wieden said that brands are not nouns but verbs.

Jean Marie Dru, *Disruption*, 1996

3. *Adoption* – they take on meaning outside their product or service categories: they are used by people to express themselves and signal their identification with those values.

For brands like Coke, Budweiser, Nike and Jack Daniel's, customers value the brands' stories largely for their identity value. Consumers flock to brands that embody the ideals they admire, brands that help them express who they want to be. The most successful of these become iconic brands.

Douglas Holt, *How Brands Become Icons*, 2004

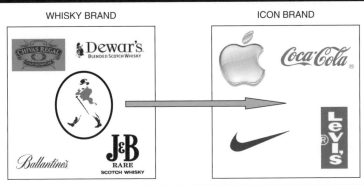

Figure 8: Johnnie Walker needed to move into the sphere of the icon brands

We needed to create these things for Johnnie Walker. Johnnie Walker had to become an icon brand (see Figure 8).

Identifying the values of Johnnie Walker

To qualify as a 'superbrand' you have to be at least talking about a brand that is definitive in its market, a brand which owns the emotional heartland of its category.

John Hegarty, Superbrands

The whisky category has always represented masculine success.[8] We knew that to walk away from these values would have been to ignore whisky's fundamental role in consumers' lives.

Global qualitative research was commissioned to understand the nature of masculine success at the dawn of the 21st century. We found an emerging trend – to men all around the world, success was no longer about material wealth or ostentatious displays of status. It was now an internal quality, about becoming a better man, having an unquenchable thirst for self-improvement. A man was judged a success not by where he was, but where he was going.

The most powerful expression of masculine success in the 21st century was 'progress' (see Table 1).

No one really grows from having a Mercedes or a beach house – it's about family, friends ... no one's ever done everything, never learnt it all.

Source: Male Venezuelan respondent, 50 years old

Each night I put my head on the pillow I'm not the same.

Source: Male Brazilian respondent, 30 years old

Progress was the insight with which Johnnie Walker would transcend market idiosyncrasies to inspire men throughout the world. In Diageo language, the brand's *Key Brand Benefit*, its statement of intent, became 'Johnnie Walker Inspires Personal Progress'.

Table 1: Success in the 21st century is about progress	
Success	**Progress**
■ Competitive: 'me vs others'	■ Me
■ Winning – public recognition	■ Taking part – experiencing
■ Material and monetary wealth, career and social status	■ Inner growth that can manifest outwardly
■ Richness via money	■ Richness via life
■ Tangible conclusion of a single-minded goal	■ Intangible progress of pursuing multi-faceted interests or ambitions
■ Achievement, accomplishment, victory, triumph	■ Development, growth, evolution, advancement
■ Finite – the 'arrival'	■ Infinite – the 'journey'
■ A full-stop	■ To be continued …

Source: DRSM Research, June 2000

The rebirth of an icon

We then needed to own this idea through a universally recognisable brand icon. The answer lay in the brand's history: the Striding Man.

Originally drawn on the back of a restaurant menu in 1908, the Striding Man represented the pioneering and entrepreneurial zeal of the Walker family (see Figure 9). It carried the strength of heritage but was inherently dynamic.

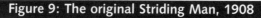

Figure 9: The original Striding Man, 1908

The Striding Man had been central to advertising that ran around the world[9] for 50 years (see Figure 10).

Figure 10: The Johnnie Walker historical global ads featuring the Striding Man

Recently, however, he had been left out of communications – the brand's forgotten hero. We wanted him to be the standard behind which the revitalised brand would march. This meant a change in prominence and direction: he would be at the heart of all communications and we would turn him around so he strode forwards, into the future (see Figure 11).

Figure 11: The new Striding Man

Inspiring personal progress

The Striding Man forged a deep connection between the universal human desire to progress and the Johnnie Walker brand. It was essential to be proactive, to inspire progress in our consumers not merely celebrate it in the brand. From this the campaign idea was born, encapsulated in the powerful exhortation 'Keep Walking' (see Figure 12).

Figure 12: The new brand campaign idea

We had a simple but challenging model for how this idea should engage consumers (see Figure 13).

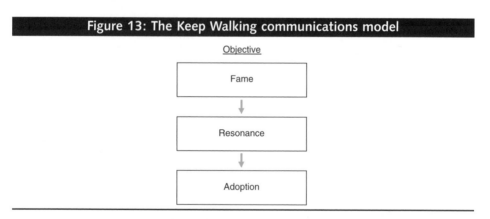

Figure 13: The Keep Walking communications model

The Keep Walking global campaign

Keep Walking has run in more than 120[10] countries over eight years, including over 50 TV executions, 150+ print executions, radio ads, websites, sponsorships, internal awards, consumer awards, even a charitable fund. £0.8bn had been spent on media between 2000 and 2007 – a considerably lower spend rate than other global brands.[11]

The core principles that guide brand media behaviour are to reinforce stature and to demonstrate pioneering spirit. Thereafter, media is managed at a local level, allowing these two principles to be exploited in the most appropriate way for the local media environment.

There have been two main phases:

- stage 1 – launching with focus and control
- stage 2 – expanding the idea with fresh expressions of progress and flexing it to accommodate specific local/business needs.

Stage 1: Launching with focus and control

At this early stage central control and consistency were essential in ensuring the idea was launched effectively. The same ads ran everywhere.

The TV campaign was based on individual 'walks' – stories of personal progress from celebrities and other inspiring individuals (see Figures 14 and 15). The print featured inspiring quotes relating to journeys of progress (see Figures 16 and 17).

Figure 14: The launch campaign, TV, *Keitel*, 2000–2002

Keitel walks in the Coliseum

He recalls his stage fright

His first time on stage in the 1970s

Feeling vulnerable and exposed. But he developed courage and overcame his fear

Harvey Keitel's walk

Keep Walking

Figure 15: The launch campaign, TV, *Baggio*, **2000–2002**

Baggio recalls the World Cup penalty
he missed in 1994

Four years later he chooses to take
another penalty

All eyes on him, he nervously goes for
the goal

Keep Walking

Figure 16: The launch campaign, print, 2000–2002

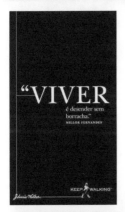

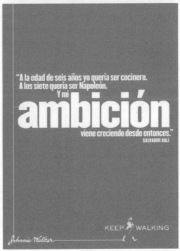

Figure 17: Print translations

Living is like drawing but without an eraser.

Millor Fernandes

Do not follow the beaten path. Leave it and make your own.

Muriel Strode

It's better to walk slowly than stop completely.

Anonymous

At the age of six I wanted to be a chef. At seven I wanted to be Napoleon. And my ambition has been growing steadily ever since.

Salvador Dali

Perfection is not waiting for the perfect moment.

Daniel Dantas

We evolved the campaign to lionise the Striding Man, showing him conquering challenges on his restless journey of progress (see Figure 18).

Figure 18: Global 'Icons' print, 2003 onwards

A pioneering media strategy amplified the message by placing executions in surprising and meaningful places, whether leaping across buildings or adjacent to relevant editorial content (see Figures 19 and 20).

Figure 19: Global print campaign, 2003 onwards

Figure 20: Global poster campaign, 2003 onwards

Stage 2: Expanding Keep Walking with fresh expressions of progress

The campaign developed from 'personal walks' to many expressions of progress, tackling different brand needs. At a global level we moved beyond the more literal 'walks' towards more surprising and arresting expressions of progress.

'Fish' (see Figure 21) reinforced the brand's pioneering credentials using the metaphor of man's evolution, to provoke men to 'Take The First Step'.

Figure 21: 'Fish', TV, global, 2002

Music throughout. Shoal of fish swim under water

Fish diving in and out of the ocean

They are not fish, but human beings

One man approaches the shore

We see him take the first evolutionary step

Keep Walking

'Painting' (see Figure 22) used a historical journey of progress through the world of art to support the brand's 'statusful' image.

Figure 22: 'Painting', TV, global, 2005

A figure escapes from Delacroix's *Battle of Taillebourg*

He rides a shield down the mountain of *Gaifu Kaisei* by Hokusai

Crashing into a picnic in Seurat's *Sunday Afternoon on the Island of La Grande Jatte*

Before exiting via the door in Magritte's *La Victoire*

We then see all the paintings in an art gallery and his journey

Keep Walking

'Android' (see Figure 23) took progress to its natural home, the future. The android character surprises by telling the viewer 'I am not the future, you are' before challenging you to do 'one great thing' in your life.

Figure 23: Android, TV, global, 2006

A man sits at the far end of a grand library

A close-up reveals he is in fact an android

He says 'I am not the future, you are'

'I can achieve immortality simply by not wearing out'

'You can achieve immortality by doing one great thing'

Keep Walking

The TV ad was accompanied by print (see Figure 24).

Figure 24: Android, print, global, 2006

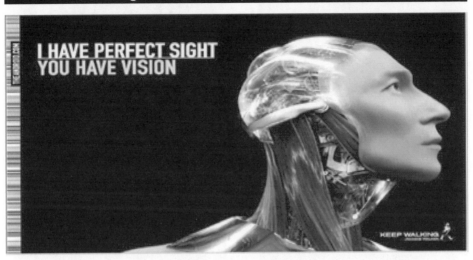

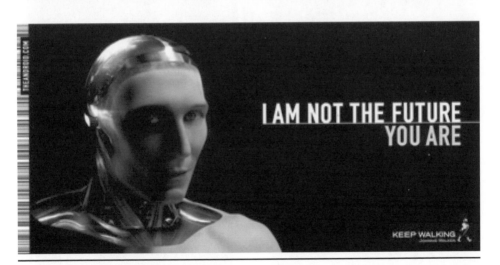

Stage 2: Flexing Keep Walking to accommodate specific local/business needs

At this point the campaign was broadened to accommodate specific market needs and to achieve more diverse business tasks. This helped the local markets feel a sense of ownership of the campaign.

All alcohol advertising in Thailand must have a socially beneficial message. 'Teacher' (see Figure 25) dramatised the positive effects of progress on an entire community.

Figure 25: 'Teacher', TV, Thailand, 2004

A successful pupil encounters his former teacher

His teacher speaks negatively of a company which is taking all the land

The teacher realises that he was a good teacher after all

And the pupil realises, to move forward you have to give something back.

Keep Walking

When launching the brand in an emergent China, Keep Walking again proved an excellent platform. The Chinese New Year provided a creative opportunity to celebrate the progress of an entire nation (see Figure 26).

Figure 26: Chinese New Year was a celebration of the progress of a nation, TV, China, 2006

Across the world people look to the East

They marvel at the coloured auras appearing

From Paris to Japan, people stare in awe

The lights are fireworks ushering in the Chinese New Year

People gather to celebrate the progress of China and its people as a man raises a glass of Johnnie Walker in celebration

Keep Walking

From 2005, Formula 1 sponsorship represented significant investment for Johnnie Walker. Keep Walking enabled the brand to maximise this opportunity by linking the Striding Man with Formula 1 drivers – the Striding Men of their sport (see Figure 27).

Figure 27: Announcement of the sponsorship of Team McLaren Mercedes, print/poster, global, 2005

'Dogfight' (see Figure 28) further strengthened the link between Johnnie Walker's progress values and the character of Formula 1 drivers by dramatising the stresses they endure throughout a race.

Keep Walking also allowed us to accommodate a responsible drinking message – an organisational imperative for a modern drinks brand (see Figure 29).

Over the last eight years Keep Walking has had numerous expressions. The foundation of a universal human truth and a powerful icon have enabled it to transcend geography, while allowing sufficient breadth to meet the variety of needs the world has thrown at it.

What happened as a result?

In the following sections we will show Johnnie Walker's performance in the eight years since Keep Walking launched.

Figure 28: 'Dogfight', TV, 2006

A fighter jet is in a dogfight

VO explains: 'In a dogfight the pilot experiences up to 5 G for over a minute'

Jet comes into land on the aircraft carrier

The jet touches down and turns into an F1 car

VO concludes: 'In a race an F1 driver experiences up to 5 G for over an hour'

Johnnie Walker sponsors McLaren Mercedes - Keep Walking

Figure 29: 'Control' delivered a responsible drinking message, TV, global, 2005

An F1 race track

And the dangerous turns of the track

There are 858 corners …

That's 858 chances to win or lose the race

Winners always stay in control

Keep Walking

The return to growth

Figure 30 shows the return to strong growth enjoyed by Johnnie Walker since the launch of Keep Walking – taking sales from 10.2m 9-litre cases in 1999 to 15.1m cases in 2007 – an increase of 48%.

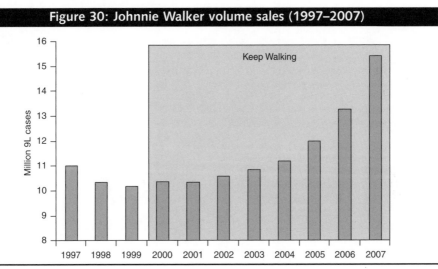

Figure 30: Johnnie Walker volume sales (1997–2007)

Source: IWSR

This increase in volume represented an increase in Johnnie Walker's volume share of Scotch of 3.9 percentage points (see Figure 31).

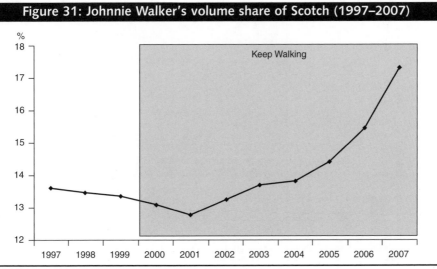

Figure 31: Johnnie Walker's volume share of Scotch (1997–2007)

Source: IWSR

Volume growth was accompanied by value growth from US$2.35bn to US$4.56bn between 1999 and 2007 – an increase of 94% (see Figure 32).

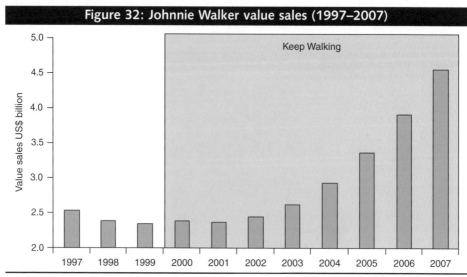

Figure 32: Johnnie Walker value sales (1997–2007)

Source: IWSR

This represented value share growth of 5.6% from 2000 to 2007 (see Figure 33).

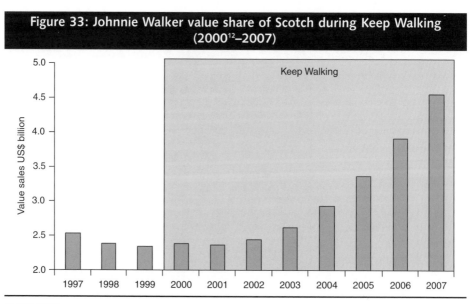

Figure 33: Johnnie Walker value share of Scotch during Keep Walking (2000[12]–2007)

Source: IWSR

Keep Walking's brand-centric approach allowed brand stretch into more premium segments. While Johnnie Walker's super-premium variants[13] accounted for only 4% of total volume sales in 2006, the campaign drove significant growth for those variants too (see Table 2).

Table 2: Volume growth of Johnnie Walker super-premium variants (1999–2006)			
Variant	Green	Gold	Blue
Growth vs 1999	607%	247%	607%

At the simplest level, these results show a reversal in the brand's fortunes in terms of volume, value and market share beginning at the launch of the Keep Walking campaign.

Additional effects

Organisational benefits

An aligned, adaptive organisation will typically outperform a non-aligned one by a factor of four times in revenue generation.[14] This need for alignment is particularly acute for a brand of Johnnie Walker's scale. Keep Walking has enabled the organisation to unite behind Johnnie Walker as never before.

Alignment among senior management

The organisational benefit of Keep Walking is endorsed at the most senior levels within Diageo.

> *Our brands are at their best when they have strong momentum – from consumers and from the organisation. Beyond the obvious strength of Keep Walking as a global positioning and advertising platform, it gave the organisation both clear direction and confidence they could get behind. The result has been accelerated growth that even now, eight years later, remains very strong and continues to outpace the category significantly. The campaign continues to be the springboard for fresh, engaging execution – a testimony to both the power and longevity of the campaign.*
>
> Rob Malcolm, President, Marketing, Sales and Innovation, Diageo

Alignment throughout the organisation

Equally importantly, alignment and energy were also created throughout the global Johnnie Walker community. To create a sense of ownership among the entire network of client and agency teams, workshops were held in Miami, Bangkok and London in 2000 (see Figure 34).

To understand the nature of the organisational effect we surveyed a broad spectrum of Diageo employees. We found that the effect of Keep Walking had been felt at all levels of the business.

Figure 34: Photograph from a Bangkok hotel roof as delegates of the 2000 Bangkok workshop unite to spell the words 'Keep Walking'

[In 1999] the brand was somewhat reviled in many markets, seen as unsexy and the strategy and growth drivers completely unclear. It is so easy to forget how this situation has been completely reversed. A huge amount has been achieved – more than for any other Diageo brand, I would say.

Global Marketing Manager, Survey of Diageo staff

I'm very excited and passionate about the company and the brand now, more confident and proud of what I do. What a company, what a brand!

Vlasta Blazek, UDV, Czech Republic, in *Brand Home Guest Book*, 2001

This new vigour went right to the heart of the brand, with the Striding Man now facing forward on the label of every bottle produced (see Figure 35).

Figure 35: The Striding Man now faced forward

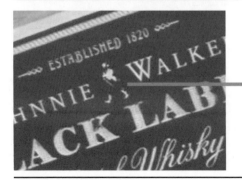

Financial stakeholder effect

Johnnie Walker is one of the most important drivers of shareholder value in Diageo's portfolio. An additional success of Keep Walking was to raise Johnnie Walker's profile with Diageo's financial stakeholders (Figures 36 and 37).

Figure 36: Positive mentions of Johnnie Walker in Diageo annual reports (1995–2007)

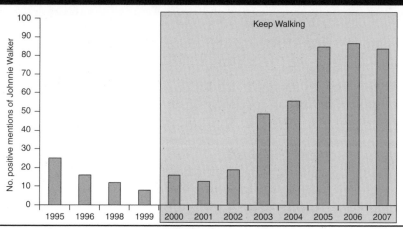

Source: Meta-analysis of Diageo annual reports 1995–2007

Figure 37: Positive Keep Walking references in Diageo annual reports (2000–2007)

2001 – The **Keep Walking** campaign launched in February 2001 was a <u>key driver of growth</u>.

2001 – Johnnie Walker volume grew 1%, with a 24% growth in Johnnie Walker Black Label **in response to the introduction of the Keep Walking campaign.**

2001 – The **successful introduction of the Keep Walking campaign** for Johnnie Walker led to a strong year.

2002 – Marketing spend on the GPBs (global priority brands) grew by 10%, **particularly behind the 'Keep Walking' campaign for Johnnie Walker.**

2003 – **The continued success of the 'Keep Walking' campaign** contributed to 40% volume growth in Johnnie Walker.

2004 – Johnnie Walker volume increased 3% **on strong advertising and promotion** in a declining whisky category.

2005 – **Successful advertising activities** drove Johnnie Walker growth of 6%.

2006 – Black Label has driven growth in China **supported by three new local advertising executions.**

2007 – **Johnnie Walker continued to demonstrate the success of its global campaign** with volume up 16% and net sales up 18%, benefiting from increased marketing investment especially in Latin America and South Africa.

Source: Diageo annual reports 2001–2007

We have demonstrated a significant turnaround in sales performance and a renewed alignment around Johnnie Walker within Diageo since the launch of Keep Walking. We will now demonstrate, beyond reasonable doubt, that communication is the key driver of this recovery.

Attributing the effect to Keep Walking

In this section we demonstrate that advertising was the key driver of Johnnie Walker's sales growth between 1999 and 2007. We do this in three ways:

1. We show that the advertising worked as intended with consumers.
2. Using a regional 'test and control' analysis we demonstrate that there were significant differences in performance between those markets that ran Keep Walking extensively and those that did not.
3. We eliminate, beyond all reasonable doubt, all other factors that could have contributed to sales performance over the period.

1. Advertising worked as intended

In this section we will show that advertising worked as intended at each stage of the communications model (see Figure 38).

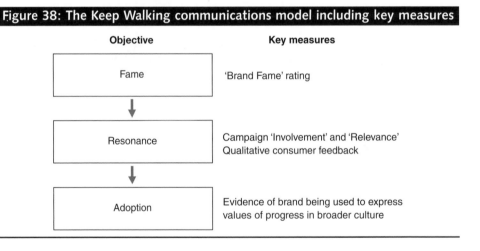

Figure 38: The Keep Walking communications model including key measures

Fame

The Research International 'Brand Fame' rating measures the percentage of consumers throughout the world who agree with the statement '[Brand logo] is one of the world's most famous logos'. In 2005 it showed the Johnnie Walker Striding Man to be equal to (and in some cases more famous than) the world's most established icon brands (see Figure 39).

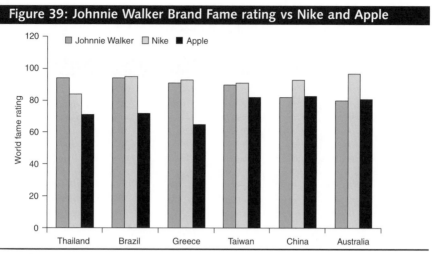

Figure 39: Johnnie Walker Brand Fame rating vs Nike and Apple

Source: Research International, November 2005

Resonance

To demonstrate the resonance of Keep Walking's message we have analysed Millward Brown's entire database of Johnnie Walker 'Link' advertising pre-tests. The 'Involvement' and 'Relevance' scores for every link test performed on a Keep Walking advert that eventually ran were included: 51 tests across 12 countries[15] stretching from 2002 to 2008 (2007 figures are excluded due to insufficient number of tests). This provides a reliable long-term, global measure of Keep Walking's resonance with consumers.

Keep Walking advertising has consistently achieved involvement scores well above country norms (see Figure 40).

Figure 40: Involvement with Keep Walking advertising 2002–2008

Source: Millward Brown: overview of all 51 Keep Walking link tests worldwide, 2002–2008 (insufficient data for 2007)

Figure 41 shows the extent to which the perceived relevance of Keep Walking's progress message has strengthened over time.

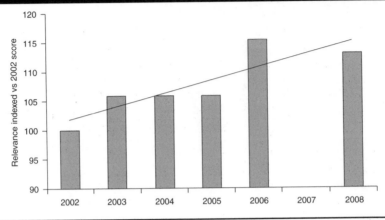

Figure 41: Relevance of Keep Walking advertising messages 2002–2008

Source: Millward Brown: overview of all 51 Keep Walking link tests worldwide, 2002–2008 (insufficient data for 2007)
Question: 'How relevant were the points made in the advert to you?'

Comments that reveal Keep Walking's sometimes profound resonance with consumers proliferate when researching creative materials across the world (see Figure 42).

The observations of our research partners

We've researched Keep Walking all around the world; and seen it galvanise Thailand in the wake of currency collapse, reinforce the pride in national progress of Brazil and China, provide role models for masculinity in the Middle East, and make America believe the dream can be real. This is a campaign that inspires men in a way that only very few brands can.

Chris Francis, Director, Flamingo International

Adoption

Joining the pantheon of cultural icons, [iconic brands] become consensus expressions of particular values held dear by some members of society.

Douglas Holt, *How Brands Become Icons*, 2004

As a result of Keep Walking, the Johnnie Walker brand has indeed become a 'consensus expression' of progress used by many cultures to signal their identification with those values.

In 2005, after the assassination of their Prime Minister, Rafic Hariri, the people of Lebanon took to the streets. To proclaim their resolve to the world as they struggled for a more peaceful future, they carried banners emblazoned with the words 'Keep Walking' and carrying a local pun on the name 'Red Label' (see Figure 43).

Figure 42: Consumer quotes from qualitative research

All Johnnie Walker ads, they have great meaning, they're big, we feel the luxury in them ... they're very beautiful, and a message, Keep Walking, there is hope ... I wait for their ads, they really penetrate our feelings.

Source: Creative Development research, Lebanon, 2003

Johnnie Walker became better in my eyes after this, it is trying to communicate with you, not just show you whisky. There is more than just a beautiful bottle, this is philosophy.

Source: Creative Development research, Russia, 2007

I think the last Johnnie Walker ad is really clever, whoever designed this ad has really gone beyond everything. Whenever I hear the music I rush in to the TV to see it again and again; most ads bore you after just once.

Source: Creative Development research, Greece, 2004

So often we are too scared to go for it and we need to be more confident in taking action, to be brave enough to do things. The biggest risk in life is not doing things. This campaign is about that confidence.

Source: Creative Development research, Spain, 2007

It makes me feel important – we're the future, we make our own decisions. It's powerful.

Source: Creative Development research, Brazil, 2004

It is thought provoking and makes you want to seek new horizons and new ways of life.

Source: Creative Development research, Lebanon, 2004

This is about daring, about having the confidence to move into your future. We all need encouragement to face our fears and make changes.

Source: Creative Development research, Spain, 2007

Constantly moving forward, despite adversity and hard times. Keep moving on through life. This relates to everyone.

Source: Creative Development research, US, 2007

At a March 2008 party conference, the leader of Greece's opposition, George Papandreou, proclaimed, in Greek, to party members 'We need to continue our pursuit until we achieve our goal' then exhorted, in English, 'Keep Walking!' (see Figure 44).

We even found instances of people permanently tattooing the Striding Man on their bodies![16] (See Figure 45.)

Keep Walking is one of the most prominent examples in the world today of a campaign that truly captivates consumers. So inspiring is its core message of personal progress to men around the world that the brand has come to mean something far more profound to them than a whisky producer alone. It is today a genuine global icon brand.

Figure 43: Banners carried in Lebanon

Figure 44: A newspaper article covering George Papandreou's speech

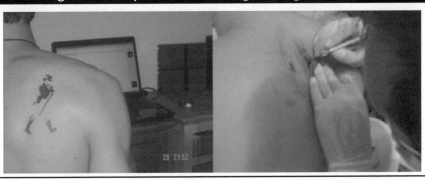

Figure 45: People are even having Striding Man tattoos

2. High/low Keep Walking market analysis

We have demonstrated that Keep Walking worked as intended in the hearts and minds of consumers to make Johnnie Walker a genuine global icon. It seems reasonable to assume this will also have had a material effect on buying behaviour. Here we give additional evidence suggesting that Keep Walking did indeed have a significant effect on Johnnie Walker's turnaround by comparing sales in those markets that invested most heavily in the campaign versus those that ran little or no Keep Walking.

This is not a perfect control, but having looked at certain key variables across the two samples we believe they are broadly comparable[17] and that any significant difference in sales results across the two is a robust further indicator of the effectiveness of the campaign.

In the absence of granular media data at market level we created the categories via a proxy measure based on the number of campaigns supplied by BBH. Table 3 shows the categories.

Table 3: Keep Walking categories	
High	**Low**
US	France
Greece	United Kingdom
Taiwan	India
Thailand	Japan
Brazil	Germany
Spain	South Korea
Australia	Canada
Mexico	Italy
Venezuela	Turkey
Dubai	Portugal
Lebanon	Czech Republic
South Africa	Denmark, Finland, Sweden, Norway
Colombia	Netherlands
Paraguay	Poland
Philippines	Switzerland
	Belgium/Luxembourg
	Canary Islands

**Figure 46: Volume sales in high and low Keep Walking categories
(1995–2006)**

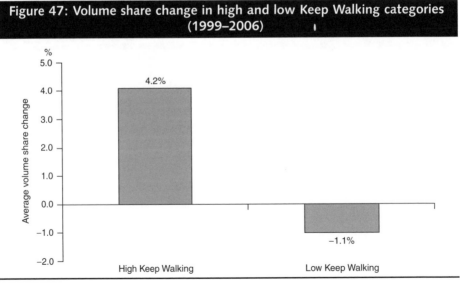

Source: IWSR

Figure 46 shows the high Keep Walking category performed significantly better than the low Keep Walking category. Figure 47 shows that, between 1999 and 2006,[18] the high markets increased their share of Scotch by 4.2% while the low markets lost 1.1% share. This 'test and control' further suggests that Keep Walking was a key driver of growth.

**Figure 47: Volume share change in high and low Keep Walking categories
(1999–2006)**

Source: IWSR

3. Removing other factors

We have demonstrated that Keep Walking works as intended with consumers and that there are material differences in sales performance between those markets that invested heavily in the campaign and those that did not. Here we will go on to demonstrate that there are no other factors that could have significantly affected Johnnie Walker's sales performance over the period to such a marked extent.

While variables may exist at a local level, which could potentially impact a campaign's effectiveness in one market, none of Johnnie Walker's markets accounts for a large enough proportion of total sales to significantly influence global performance (see Figure 48). Therefore, we will focus on global factors that could materially influence the global picture.

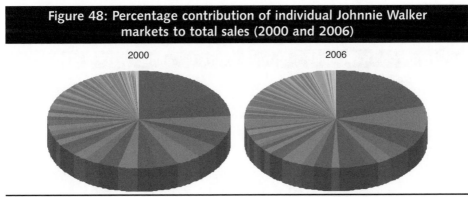

Figure 48: Percentage contribution of individual Johnnie Walker markets to total sales (2000 and 2006)

2000

2006

Source: IWSR

Market factors

At a global level, economic or population growth, or changes in consumer confidence could of course impact the growth of the Scotch category. However, when calculating the return on investment achieved by the campaign we will focus on Johnnie Walker's increased share of the Scotch category, thus discounting such category-level forces as drivers of growth.

Competition

The Scotch category became increasingly competitive throughout Keep Walking. Figure 49 shows the number of brand variants in existence growing throughout, while Figure 50 shows the category's simultaneous rise in advertising levels.

Throughout Keep Walking, competition from major competitors' global advertising campaigns has been unrelenting.[19] Thus, lightening competitive pressures can be excluded as possible drivers of Johnnie Walker's growth.

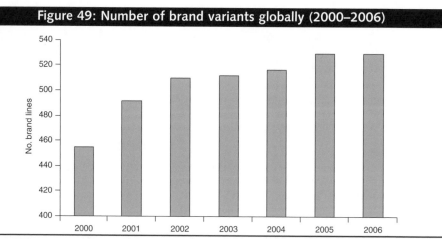

Figure 49: Number of brand variants globally (2000–2006)

Source: IWSR

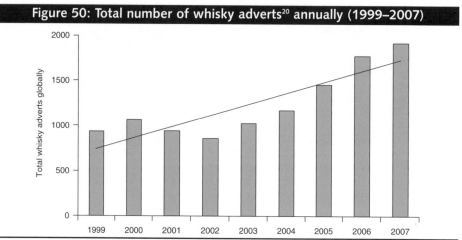

Figure 50: Total number of whisky adverts[20] annually (1999–2007)

Source: IWSR

Price

Table 4 demonstrates that Johnnie Walker actually increased price over the campaign period. Furthermore, this rate of growth was slightly faster than that of the category so we did not benefit from decreases in either absolute or relative price (see Table 4).

Table 4: Average price per case increase during Keep Walking

	Price per case 2000 (US$)	Price per case 2006 (US$)	% increase
Johnnie Walker	231	296	+28.1
Rest of Scotch	183	232	+26.2

Promotions

Local teams produce on-trade and off-trade promotions to push specific variants at the point of purchase. Investment in these programmes has remained at its pre-Keep Walking levels throughout the campaign and no local campaign could have significantly impacted the brand's global sales, so increased local promotional activity can be excluded as a potential driver of growth.

Other product variants

Green Label was relaunched[21] in 2004 but received minimal advertising support, focused mainly in Taiwan. Green Label sales accounted for only 2% of Johnnie Walker's value sales in 2006[22] so cannot be considered a key driver of total growth.

Distribution

We know that, with the exception of Russia and China, Johnnie Walker did not enter any significant new markets over the course of Keep Walking. We will remove China and Russia from our ROI calculations and by doing so exclude emerging market distribution as a possible driver of growth.

We also know that across Johnnie Walker's existing markets distribution remained static throughout Keep Walking. It has not been possible to find distribution data at a market level, leaving us unable to quantify this lack of change. However, we offer as support the experience of a Senior Brand Director who has worked on the campaign since its inception:

> *Johnnie Walker has always been a Global Priority Brand for Diageo, with strong distribution already in place in its markets when Keep Walking was introduced. With the exception of China and Russia coming into play, distribution has not changed significantly over the course of the campaign.*

> Peter Dee, Global Marketing Director, Diageo

Quantifying the effect of Keep Walking

In the previous sections we showed that Johnnie Walker's volume sales grew by 48% in the first eight years of Keep Walking – representing a 3.9% point share growth in the Scotch category. We have shown that this growth was driven by Keep Walking communications and that no other factor can be thought to have accounted for it. We now quantify the effect of the campaign.

Johnnie Walker's truly global presence makes the task of measuring the return from marketing particularly challenging. The ideal situation would be to have econometric models in each market and aggregate the result, but this is simply impractical given that the brand operates in over 180 diverse markets.

The next best option is to make a conservative judgement based on consistent data across the markets. The International Wine and Spirit Record provides such data at a variant, brand and Scotch Whisky sector level in terms of both volume and value. For the purposes of calculating the campaign's return on investment we have, for the reasons outlined above, excluded all sales and media spend data from China and Russia, but included total global sponsorship costs, which will cover those regions.

Figure 51 shows Johnnie Walker's share of Scotch whisky volume over the period 1997 to 2007.[23] Prior to the launch of Keep Walking there was a slow downward trend in volume share. If this rate of decline had continued, the volume share would have been 12.5% in 2007. However, the share achieved was in fact 16.8% (excluding China and Russia) (see Figure 51).

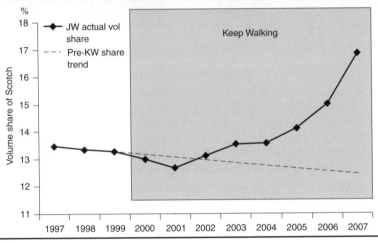

Figure 51: Johnnie Walker predicted vs actual volume share of Scotch (1997–2007)

Source: IWSR

The difference between the underlying share trend and share achieved is calculated each year and converted into sales revenue using Johnnie Walker's average price.

The price these additional cases commanded reveals that Keep Walking generated US$2.21bn of incremental sales.

This increased value was achieved through a total investment in the campaign of US$0.70bn (excluding China and Russia media spend).

Therefore the Revenue return of Keep Walking is 3.2 (see Table 5).

Table 5: Keep Walking financials (2000–2007)

Incremental value attributable to Keep Walking (excluding China and Russia)	US$2.21bn
Campaign spend including sponsorship, media, agency fees, production etc. (excluding China and Russia)	US$0.70bn
Revenue return	3.2

With a revenue return of 3.2 the gross profit made on Johnnie Walker whisky would need to be 32% or higher for the campaign to be considered profitable. Diageo's confidentiality policy prevents the release of profit margins; however, we can say that their actual gross profit margin is comfortably above 32%, meaning Keep Walking has been a profitable campaign for Diageo.

What can we learn from Keep Walking?

Through the story of Keep Walking we have championed the cause of global brand ideas, showing that to captivate consumers worldwide, brands must represent fundamental human values that unite, rather than try to reflect local market idiosyncrasies.

We showed how such campaigns must be controlled in their early stages, with focused creative work to ensure the idea takes root.

We then showed that broad, over-arching brand territories can offer sufficient flexibility to meet specific local and organisational needs, while maintaining focus on the core idea.

Keep Walking took some months for the immediate consumer plaudits to be reflected in sales, but once the idea gained traction it developed momentum on a global scale that today shows no signs of fatigue: patience was a profitable quality. Indeed, as the campaign continues, the return on media budgets increases year on year: Keep Walking's finest hour is yet to come.

Finally, the case of Keep Walking is clear evidence that ambitious communications ideas – ideas that seek to truly inspire and embolden their audiences – can revitalise sales, unify organisations and enable brands to play a far more meaningful role in consumers' lives than more conventional competitors. As a last demonstration of this, we offer a consumer's recent description of what the Keep Walking campaign meant to him:

> *We have to take advantage of everything we have, to enjoy everything and to give our maximum so we have no regrets when we die. We have to think we are on this earth to do something; it motivates me to be a better human being.*
>
> Source: Creative Development research, Venezuela, 2006

Notes

1. Source: Research International brand fame rating, 2005.
2. Source: Interbrand global brand valuation study, 2003.
3. Source: Impact databank.
4. Source: IWSR (International Wine and Spirit Record).
5. Source: Original UDV pitch brief.
6. A strong positive correlation exists between the statement '[XX] is a brand I relate to' and purchase intent.
7. Naturally occurring Amazonian plant extract, which is a stimulant.
8. Source: *Marketing to Men in the Millennium*, P. Assisotis and D. Jones, ESOMAR, 1998.
9. We believe that the early Johnnie Walker advertising is probably the first ever global advertising campaign.
10. Source: Diageo.
11. Source: *Advertising Age*, 14 November 2005: BMW US$505m, Nike US$343m, Heineken US$272m.
12. Scotch category value data were not available pre-2000.
13. Green Label, Gold Label and Blue Label.
14. Source: Heskett, Sasser and Schlesinger, The Value Profit Chain, 2003.
15. Markets included: Australia, Brazil, China, Colombia, Germany, Greece, Mexico, South Africa, Taiwan, Turkey, UK, US.
16. Note the Striding Man's left-to-right direction – a product of the Keep Walking era.
17. The high and low categories were found to be comparable in terms of their proportion of males aged 25+, weighted average growth in GDP per capita 1999–2007, size of the annual spirits market and size of the annual Scotch market.

18. Country-level sales data for 2007 were unavailable at the time of writing.
19. Ballantine's 'Go Play' (2002 – £80m/year) and 'Leave An Impression' (2007 – £27m/year); Chivas' 'The Chivas Life' (2003 – £69m/year).
20. Includes TV, radio, press, outdoor, cinema, internet and direct mail advertising.
21. Previously marketed as Johnnie Walker Pure Malt.
22. 2007 sales data at a variant level were unavailable at the time of writing.
23. 2007 data derived by applying Diageo's quoted 2007 growth figures to 2006 IWSR figures.

Chapter 9

Acquisition Crime

Cutting the cost of crime: how advertising turned a nation of victims into a nation of crime prevention officers

By Alice Huntley, RKCR/Y&R
Contributing authors: Sharon Sawers and Emma Roberts, The Home Office

Editor's summary

Theft costs British society an estimated £9.5bn per year. Many of these opportunistic crimes can be easily avoided if people take simple preventative measures. The challenge was to find a single campaign idea that could motivate a core target audience most at risk of crime and demonstrate measures they could take to prevent it. Using a single, humorous campaign idea, executed through TV, radio and print, the strategy was to dramatise how thieves saw their victims as stupidly careless. The campaign reduced the cost of crime to the taxpayer by £189m and generated payback of £14 per every £1 spent.

Introduction

Chances are that one in five of you reading this paper will be a victim of theft this year.[1]

Chances also are that you think there's not much you can do about it.

However, did you make sure all your doors and windows were locked before leaving the house this morning?

Do you remember to lock your car every time you stop for petrol? Honestly?

Do you ever leave your mobile phone on the table while you go to the bar for a drink, or talk on it while walking down the street at night?

If so, then you could make a difference to your chances of being a victim of crime. And a difference to the amount of crime in this country.

This is a story of how advertising got individuals who, like you, thought there was nothing they could do to bring the crime rate down. A story of how advertising turned a nation of potential victims into a nation of crime prevention officers.

This paper will show how a single, humorous campaign idea could tackle serious, multiple crimes; how the least empowered could become the most empowered; and how £13.5m of advertising money could reduce the cost of crime by £189m.

The cost of crime

Knife attacks and terrorism dominate the headlines, but these account for only a tiny percentage of crime.[2] Most crime is of a much less headline-grabbing nature: theft.

Britain's most commonly experienced crime is acquisitive crime, which accounts for half of all recorded crime[3] comprising:

- theft of, and from, vehicles (car crime)
- burglary
- theft from the person (robbery).

In 2003/4, there were 2.8 million incidents; over 4 million including unreported crime.[4]

The cost of acquisitive crime to British society is high: an estimated £9.5bn per year[5] – more than the annual turnover of British high-street giant M&S.[6] No value can truly be put on the emotional distress it causes to victims.

Reducing this cost to society is of paramount importance. While the media keeps us preoccupied with dramatic terrorism arrests, gruesome murders and high-end frauds, a quiet success story has been under way.

Government targets

In this context the government set an ambitious target to reduce acquisitive crime by 15% over four years.

A multi-faceted task

Tackling acquisitive crime is not simple, requiring efforts from multiple agencies. Most of the effort falls within the responsibility of government – investing taxpayers' money in schemes and systems that will help to reduce crime. Drug rehabilitation programmes, the police, the criminal justice system and street crime initiatives are key, as is liaising with industry to 'design out' the opportunity for theft, e.g. making immobilisers standard on all cars.

The role for communications

The vast majority of acquisitive crime is opportunistic: thieves seizing low-risk opportunities to take anything they can see that's worth taking.

It is *individuals* who inadvertently create these opportunities for easy theft – leaving doors and windows unlocked or open, and things on view. It is therefore *individuals* who have most power to reduce their risk of becoming victims of acquisitive crime. Getting people to take preventative measures in their everyday lives and reduce the opportunities for theft is a major part of the effort to reduce crime.

This is where communications can make a huge difference.

Past experience

We knew from past experience that communications could have an impact on a specific type of opportunistic crime. From 1997 to 2004 we[7] ran a highly successful campaign to help reduce vehicle crime. The campaign portrayed car crime from the point of view of the thief. It showed how shockingly quickly car theft happened, and over what shockingly tiny things – a leather jacket, a baby-changing bag, a handful of change. The lead TV ads were designed to make people despise rather than fear car thieves, and to resolve to not make it easy for them (see Figure 1).

Ambient media reminded people, in car parks and on parking meters, to be careful (see Figure 2).

The campaign successfully mobilised individuals to take preventative measures. Vehicle crime fell by 37%, and the campaign payback was estimated at 28:1.[8]

The new task: using a single campaign to tackle multiple crimes

The question was: could the same approach be extended successfully across other types of crime?

Strong evidence from strategic research suggested that burglary, robbery and car crime were driven by the same criminal behaviour – opportunism. Research with young offenders revealed that individuals carry out a variety of types of theft (burglary, vehicle crime or robbery), depending on what opportunities arise during the day.

> *If the car window's open and there's a handbag or mobile ... or there's a window or back door open and you can see the bag.*[9]

The opportunities that the offenders looked for were identical too (see Figure 3) – careless behaviour on behalf of their victims, such as unattended belongings, open windows, unlocked doors. The statistics are staggeringly high:

Figure 1: Vehicle crime prevention TV ad – car crime from the point of view of the thief

THIEF: This is a great place. It's really handy. Anything you want within easy reach, if you keep your eyes open.

Always something on special offer. Hello.

What's this rubbish?
MVO: They might think it's worth something. Never leave anything on show.
THIEF: Never mind, there's plenty more.
MVO: Don't give them an easy ride.

Figure 2: Example of vehicle crime ambient – car park barriers and parking tickets

Figure 3: Key unifying behavioural factors of acquisitive crime	
	Behaviour
Criminal	Opportunism
Victim	Carelessness

- although we'd reduced vehicle crime by 37%, even after nine years of advertising, a fifth of motorists still forget to lock the doors when they leave their car[10]
- in 30% of burglaries, burglars get in through an unlocked door or window;[11] there are no forced locks, smashed windows or kicked-down doors.

However, there was one crucial difference: the emotional impact. Getting your car stereo stolen is at worst a bit aggravating. But getting your mobile snatched from your hand is frightening. It takes time to feel safe again walking alone outside.[12] And the sense of intrusion and violation at being burgled can be overwhelming.

> *Every time I go in my front door I think 'have I been burgled again?' Every day my little girl thinks they are going to come back. Even if I am there, she still does not like me being on my own.*
>
> Lisa Stevens, burgled twice in three and a half years[13]

So whereas the vehicle crime campaign depicted car crime actually happening, it was not appropriate for advertising to further dramatise what it felt like to be robbed or burgled. The brief stipulated that communication must not increase fear among vulnerable segments of the population who live in fear of crime disproportionate to their risk, e.g. elderly people in rural areas.

It was clear we would have to find a new creative strategy – one that dramatised not what the criminal did but what people could actually do to stop him.

Across the audiences, the need is more for advice and guidance than for seeing depictions of crime and its consequences: people know what the results of theft will be – most have experienced it first or second hand; they need tips and reminders about minimising the risk.[14]

Communications model

The objectives for the campaign (Table 1) were to:

- empower – help people realise they can easily prevent themselves becoming victims
- equip – give them the tools (the knowledge) to do so.

While we needed a single idea that would work across all three crimes, each piece of communication would need to give different messages that were specific to each crime and context (Table 2).

Table 1: Communications model and evaluation criteria			
	Current	**Future**	**Evaluation**
Attitude	Powerless	Empowered	I can do a great deal to reduce my risk
Response	Clueless	Clued-up	Change in knowledge about how to prevent crime
Behaviour	Careless	Careful	Change in claimed/ actual behavioural practice

Table 2: Priority messages conveyed in advertising by crime type		
Burglary	**Robbery**	**Car crime**
Keep valuables hidden	Avoid using mobile in certain places	Don't leave belongings in car
Have window locks	Don't leave valuables unattended	Don't leave car unlocked
Shut windows when out	Make sure mobile not visible	Don't leave belongings on view

The target audience

Crime affects us all. As a population, we feel that it is on the increase. This is exacerbated by the media (see Figure 4).

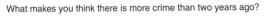

Figure 4: TV and newspapers feed sense that crime is on the increase

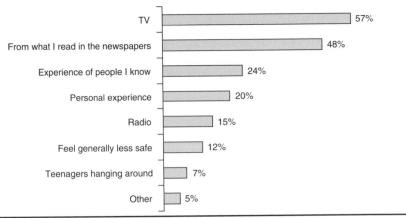

What makes you think there is more crime than two years ago?

- TV — 57%
- From what I read in the newspapers — 48%
- Experience of people I know — 24%
- Personal experience — 20%
- Radio — 15%
- Feel generally less safe — 12%
- Teenagers hanging around — 7%
- Other — 5%

Source: IPSOS MORI 2007.
Base: Those who say there is a lot more crime (1,191).

However, in truth, some people experience more crime than others. Young people living in urban areas are most at risk (see Figure 5).[15]

Figure 5: The campaign was designed to talk to everyone, with urban 16–34s as the core target

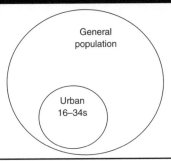

General population

Urban 16–34s

Why do urban 16–34s experience a disproportionate amount of crime?

In part, just because of where they live. They are often literally in the wrong place at the wrong time – surrounded by the urban deprivation that leads to high levels of crime.

But there are also psychological factors at play. Most of urban 16–34s have first- or second-hand experience of being a victim of theft. The result: crime seems inevitable and they feel powerless to prevent it; more powerless than most people (see Figure 6).[16]

If they want to do it they will, you can't stop them.[17]

Figure 6: Least empowerment among those most at risk

% Agree I can do great deal to reduce my risk of being a victim of [crime]

Robbery– mobile	15** / 25* / 31
Robbery– other	16** / 19* / 25
Vehicle crime	20** / 30* / 35
Burglary	20** / 29* / 32

■ Students
▨ Urban 16–34
☐ All respondents

0   10   20   30   40

Source: BMRB Tracking, Base: All respondents, Baseline 2004 (1084)
* = significant at 95% confidence   ** = significant at 99% confidence

The problem is, powerlessness leads to inaction, which only increases their likelihood of experiencing crime (see Figure 7).

We had to find a way to interrupt this cycle.

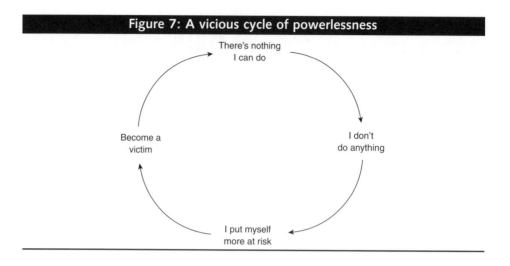

Figure 7: A vicious cycle of powerlessness

In pursuit of insight

The solution came from going back to the scene of the crime: ethnographic research in Manchester's Moss Side.

Moss Side is a classic example of a high acquisitive crime area. Unemployment is double the national average[18] and only 24% of dwellings are owner-occupied.[19] It has lots of cheap rental accommodation, popular with university students. Carefree, mobile-touting, laptop-owning young people live cheek by jowl with people desperate for some easy cash.

Sitting in the back of an unmarked police car, on a bright July morning, the robberies started to roll in over the intercom. There were too many, too fast. And they all seemed preventable.

The police greeted the 'regulars' – teenage robbers of both sexes in uniform dark hoodies[20] – clocking them, letting them know they'd been clocked.

And then we saw their potential victims: students, romantically dressed in brightly coloured ponchos, blithely twirling their expensive handbags as they chatted on their mobiles and strolled down some of the most notorious streets in the UK, bullet marks still grazing the sides of the terraced housing.[21]

A thief could simply walk or cycle by, and just lift the phone, or the bag, from their hands. In the words of the young robbers, these students were 'easy pickings'. So easy in fact, it was 'almost as if they were asking to have their stuff nicked'.[22]

This was true for other kinds of theft, and not just in Moss Side.[23] Speaking to the real specialists – young offenders – confirmed our thinking.

They regaled us with tales of their exploits. What struck us was their amused incredulity at the careless 'stupidity' they encountered. This carelessness supplied them with a regular source of income (see Figure 8).

People are always going off for the weekend or whatever and forgetting that they've left the windows open.

Figure 8: Signs of easy pickings

- visibly unrepaired burglar alarms
- handy ladders kept outside the house or in unlocked sheds
- easily accessible windows left open or unlocked
- houses regularly left unlocked during school runs
- mobiles left on pub tables while their owners go to the bar
- cash, bags, jackets left on show in cars
- car stereos put away in unlocked glove compartments
- cars left unlocked on forecourts while owners pay for petrol.

I try back doors mid-afternoon when few people are about and if anyone answers I say I'm looking for 'John'.

I found £4,000 in a fridge once, in a sandwich box. And I've found it in biscuit tins, under mattresses and under beds.

If you see an opportunity you just take it.[24]

You can usually find up to 20 grands' worth of gear just inside someone's front door. This is where they dump their bags, laptops, briefcases, which all contain phones, credit cards and money. Not to mention the keys to their car.[25]

The insight

The fact that people were being 'carelessly stupid' was the insight we needed for a new creative brief; a way to get our target to understand how ridiculously easy they made it for thieves – and how ridiculously easily they could change that.

The creative proposition was therefore directed at the advice we had to communicate:

You can *so* easily reduce your chance of being a victim of crime.

The idea

The creative idea was to humorously dramatise people's carelessness.

The ads depicted people 'selling' their house, car and phone to a likely-looking thief, advertising all the ways they had made it easy for him to steal, leading to the endline:

Don't advertise your stuff to thieves.

Two aspects made this creative idea stand out:

1. It was very funny. This was highly innovative. Few government campaigns use humour – much less crime prevention campaigns. Creative development research (Figure 9) demonstrated how powerful a tonal platform this was. Humour helped not just to engage but to change our target audience. By laughing at observational humour people admit their own foibles and are more likely to make changes.

   [The ads] highlight people's stupidity without making them feel stupid.[26]

Figure 9: Creative development research confirmed the strength of the idea

- An effective means of attracting and sustaining attention; amusing, but not inappropriately so; humour understood as means of engaging interest.

- Use of people obviously failing to take precautions is effective; this is clearly someone acting foolishly – not to be taken literally but a device to demonstrate risks many of us take.

- If it does make people feel stupid, this is thought not a bad thing by those who like the idea – we need to understand how easy we make it for criminals.

- Well regarded for large number and wide range of tips on reducing crime; all scripts have numerous examples, most seem useful.

Source: Cragg Ross Dawson Acquisitive Crime Campaign Creative Development Research September 2004

2. It was highly practical. By compiling all the carelessly stupid things people do that make themselves 'easy pickings', the ads showed what people could **do** to prevent crime. The ads were full of advice (see Figures 10–13).

Media strategy

Media fell into two main types: awareness building and reminder activity (see Figure 14). The role for awareness media was to establish the campaign idea and to get people to appreciate that they could be careless sometimes. Everything else had to remind them not to be careless when it really mattered – at the key places and key times when they are most at risk.

The awareness strand was broadcast media bought in the four TV regions that experienced the majority of acquisitive crime.

The 'moments of careless stupidity' strand was highly innovative and very complex. It was designed to reach people at the precise moment when they were most at risk: from students staggering home from a night out to commuters rushing to work, and from school children flashing their mobiles on the way to school to motorists filling up at petrol stations. Each region received a unique mix of media and crime focus according to risk.[27] This set a high bar for the econometric analysis but was very effective at getting to crime where it actually happened.[28]

Media and creative quickly became inseparable, and included the following.

Robbery

Transport links are high-risk areas for robbery,[29] so advertising in and around bus and tube stations was critical (see Figure 15). This was supported by stunts where men dressed as robbers used megaphones to 'advertise' careless commuters who were displaying their valuables. The story was picked up in *Metro* and the

Figure 10: 'Don't advertise your stuff to thieves' TV and press

Advertising House 30-second spot

A couple take a young bloke around their house as if they were selling it.

It's a great location, nice and quiet.

Original front door. Should open with a good kick.

Don't worry about the alarm; it hasn't worked for years.

No padlock.

All our valuables are easy to find.

Look, it's like a giant cat-flap.

So what do you reckon, interested?

VO: *Don't advertise your house to burglars.*

Figure 11: Advertising car 30-second TV spot

A man shows two guys around his car as if he were selling it.

It goes well, you'll love it.

Alloys are worth a few quid.

Normally there's a bit of spare change in here.

Coat on the back seat.

And as always, the stereo's in here.

The keys are on a table by the door. You can reach them with a stick, right?

So what do you think lads, fancy it?

VO: *Don't advertise your car to thieves.*

Figure 12: Advertising phone 30-second TV spot

A man in a pub 'sells' his phone

Oi! Over here.

Here it is, colour screen, camera, Internet . . . like it?

If you want it, I'll leave it on the table when I go to the bar. You can grab it then . . . or

. . . you can wait for me outside. I always call the missus on my way home.

You'll see me coming a mile off, all lit up like a Christmas tree!

VO: *Don't advertise your phone to thieves.*

Figure 13: Easy Pickings ad

Figure 14: Media strategy

Awareness	TV/radio
Reminder 'Moments of careless stupidity'	Print and ambient

Figure 15: Tube stations, tube panels, ATMs and bus stops

Evening Standard, amplifying the message to commuters across London (see Figure 16).

Nights out are key times of vulnerability, when students are often a bit worse for wear. We placed ads in pub washrooms, fast-food outlets, and on kebab wrappers and pizza boxes (see Figure 17).

Figure 16: PR 'Swag Man' event picked up by *Metro* and *Evening Standard*

Figure 17: Reaching students on nights out

Burglary

Figure 18 shows the warnings used in high-risk areas.[30]

Vehicle crime

Figure 19 shows the ad warnings used on petrol nozzles and on car park barriers. Figure 20 shows the timing of the six bursts of activity. So what happened?

Figure 18: Door-drops in high-risk burglary postcodes, and door hangers in student accommodation

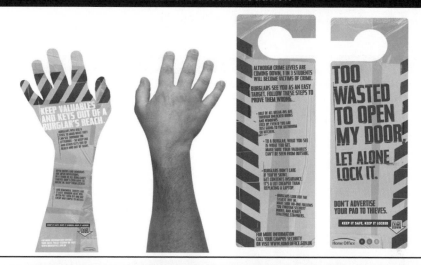

Figure 19: Petrol nozzle and car park barrier warnings for careless motorists

Figure 20: Simplified media schematic

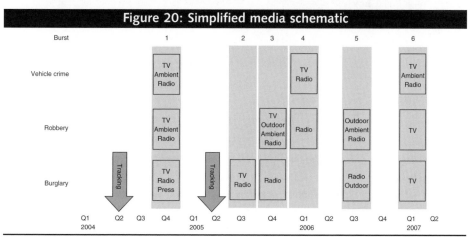

Source: British Crime Survey 2002–2007

Crime fell

The target of 15% reduction in acquisitive crime was surpassed. By 2007, acquisitive crime had fallen by 19% (see Figure 21).

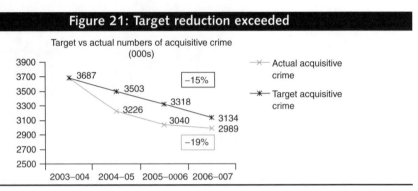

Figure 21: Target reduction exceeded

Source: British Crime Survey

Crucially, given the new strategy of combining all three crime types into one campaign, the reduction in crime was evident across all three crime types (see Table 3).[31]

Table 3: Crime fell across all three crime types

	2003/4 (000s)	2006/7 (000s)	% decline
Burglary	943	726	−23
All vehicle thefts	2,121	1,689	−20
Robbery	623	574	−8
Total acquisitive	3,687	2,989	−19

Source: British Crime Survey

It is our contention that communications played a significant role in these reductions. We will show that:

- people *remembered* the advertising
- the advertising made them feel *empowered* to prevent crime
- this is because it gave them an improved understanding of *how* to prevent crime
- people claimed the advertising made them more likely to change their behaviour
- they did change their behaviour (after just one burst of advertising)
- econometric modelling has helped us to quantify the contribution that advertising made in terms of the actual cost of crime.

People remembered the advertising

Tracking was carried out in just two waves: a baseline measure in April 2004 and a post measure in spring 2005 following the first burst of the campaign.[32] Results were so strong that The Home Office decided not to invest in further waves of tracking.[33] Given that there were five further bursts, final measures are likely to have been even higher (see Figure 22).

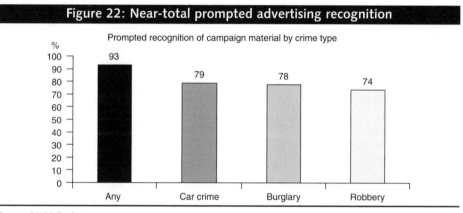

Figure 22: Near-total prompted advertising recognition

Prompted recognition of campaign material by crime type

Source: BMRB Tracking
Base: All respondents, spring 2005 (1056)

Car crime had already enjoyed £21.4m of advertising so we expected levels of car crime advertising awareness to remain high. However, there were substantial increases in awareness of the 'new' crime types now covered by the campaign (Figure 23).

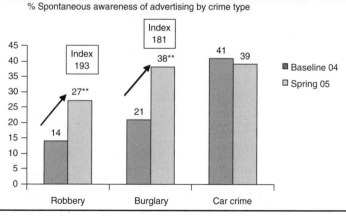

Figure 23: Spontaneous awareness of advertising about new crime types almost doubled

% Spontaneous awareness of advertising by crime type

Source: BMRB Tracking
Base: All respondents, spring 2005 (1056)
* = significant at 95% confidence, ** = significant at 99% confidence

Advertising made people feel more empowered

People got the message – that just doing simple things could reduce their risk of being a crime victim (see Figure 24).

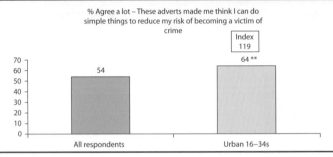

Figure 24: People understood the advertising was encouraging them to do simple things

% Agree a lot – These adverts made me think I can do simple things to reduce my risk of becoming a victim of crime

Source: BMRB Tracking
Base: All respondents, spring 2005 (1056)

By spring 2005, 35% more urban 16–34s and 11% more total respondents thought they could do a great deal to reduce their risk of acquisitive crime (see Figure 25).

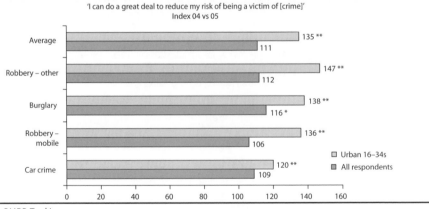

Figure 25: Crucially, advertising actually made people feel more empowered, with biggest increases seen among the core target audience of 16–34s

'I can do a great deal to reduce my risk of being a victim of [crime]'
Index 04 vs 05

Source: BMRB Tracking
Base: All respondents, baseline 2004 (1084), spring 2005 (1056)
* = significant at 95% confidence, ** = significant at 99% confidence

Students were a key sub-target for robbery. Together with urban 16–34s, having been less empowered than the population in general, they became more empowered. The number of empowered students more than doubled (see Figure 26).[34]

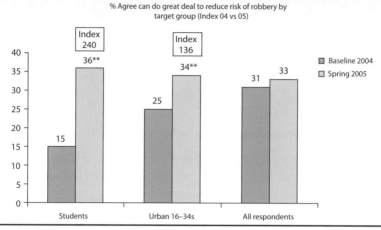

Figure 26: For some crimes, the least empowered were now the most empowered

Source: BMRB Tracking
Base: All respondents, spring 2005 (1056)
* = significant at 95% confidence, ** = significant at 99% confidence

People understood how to reduce their risk

People's belief that they could reduce their risk of being a victim of crime improved because they understood how to reduce their risk (see Table 4).

Table 4: People more equipped to prevent crime

Increase in spontaneous awareness of key crime prevention message
Index 04 vs 05

Burglary	Index	Robbery	Index	Car crime	Index
Keep valuables hidden	156**	Avoid using mobile in certain places	130*	Don't leave belongings in car	121**
Have window locks	113**	Don't leave valuables unattended	128**	Don't leave car unlocked	111**
Shut windows when out	111**	Make sure mobile not visible	107	Don't leave belongings on view	106

* = significant at 95% confidence, ** = significant at 99% confidence

These uplifts were higher among those aware of the advertising (see Figure 27).

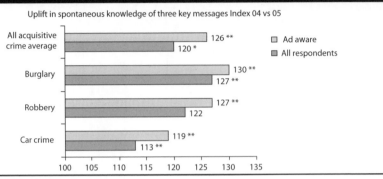

Figure 27: Those aware of the advertising saw most increase in knowledge about how to prevent crime

Uplift in spontaneous knowledge of three key messages Index 04 vs 05

Source: BMRB Tracking
Base: All respondents, baseline 2004 (1084), spring 2005 (1056)
* = significant at 95% confidence, ** = significant at 99% confidence

People claimed the advertising would affect their behaviour

Figure 28 illustrates how people claimed the advertising would affect their behaviour.

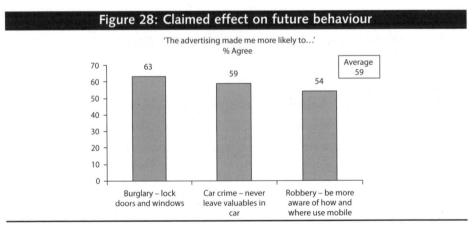

Figure 28: Claimed effect on future behaviour

'The advertising made me more likely to...'
% Agree

Source: BMRB Tracking
Base: All ad-aware respondents, spring 2005 (894)

And it did!

After just one burst of advertising there was the beginning of evidence that people had already started to change their behaviour (see Figure 29).

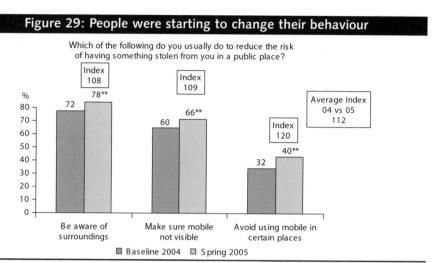

Figure 29: People were starting to change their behaviour

Which of the following do you usually do to reduce the risk
of having something stolen from you in a public place?

Source: BMRB Tracking
Base: All respondents, baseline 2004 (1084), spring 2005 (1056)
** = significant at 99% confidence

Summary of tracking vs communication model

The campaign had delivered on all elements of the communications model after just one burst (see Table 5).

	Current	Future	Evaluation
Table 5: Changes evaluated			
Attitude	Powerless	Empowered	I can do a great deal to reduce my risk
			+ 11% total population
			+ 35% ** urban 16–34s
Response	Clueless	Clued-up	Change in knowledge about how to prevent crime
			+20% ** total population
			+ 26% ** among ad aware
Behaviour	Careless	Careful	Change in claimed/actual behavioural practice
			59% agree ads made them more likely to take preventative measures
			+12% ** average improvement in actual behavioural practice after just one burst of advertising

** = significant at 99% confidence

What would the results have been like after bursts two, three, four and five? We think the econometrics tells that story.

Isolating the effect of communications

As shown earlier, acquisitive crime fell 19% over the campaign period. Many factors will have contributed to this reduction, so to evaluate what part communications played we needed to find a way to isolate its effect.

Developing a methodology

Isolating the effect of communication in this context is not straightforward. Factors influencing crime levels are far-reaching and many are reported infrequently or prove difficult to quantify. Louise Cook described the task as 'the most complex and challenging project we have ever worked on'.[35]

The selected methodology worked on the basic premise of comparing acquisitive crime reduction in regions that received high-level advertising spend, with acquisitive crime reduction in regions that had received low-level advertising spend. If the campaign had been effective, one would expect the region with a higher spend to have seen a bigger reduction in acquisitive crime than the region with a lower spend.

This approach had a distinct advantage over other methodologies because it enabled us to discount the effect of any factors that would impact on all regions equally. For example, any change to the proportion of young males in the population, shown to influence crime levels,[36] would impact both regions equally and could not therefore account for the variation in crime reduction between the two.

Other macro factors that might affect crime, such as national events or steps increasingly taken by car and mobile phone manufacturers to 'design out' crime, are also factored out in this way.

However, simply comparing high-spend regions with low-spend regions would not be a robust analysis, because factors other than communication could have influenced the crime levels in one or other of the regions. For example, if the region with higher advertising spend also had a younger age profile of cars on the road, a greater relative decrease in crime could be a result of superior car security not communications. Therefore, to isolate the effect of communications from other influencing factors, we needed to ensure that the regions we compared shared similar characteristics. In other words, we needed to make sure we were comparing apples with apples.

The process of matching regions was complex. It started with the 43 police regions in England and Wales. Each region was classified on a range of dimensions, shown in Table 6.

Table 6: How regions were classified for analysis	
Recorded crime statistics	Data from each region had to be consistent in order to be comparable
Crime profile	The police force groups regions according to the prevalence and nature of crime and their approach to tackling it
Socio-economic factors	Similar socio-economic factors relevant to the crime in question were taken account of, including percentage of people living in social housing, age of vehicle, since newer vehicles have superior security, etc.
Correlation with TV regions	In order to establish whether a police region had received high- or low-weight media spend, we needed to overlay TV regions and eliminate any police regions that bridged more than one TV region

Source: Holmes and Cook

Through this process a proportion of regions was eliminated from the analysis. The remaining regions were paired, then analysed to assess the impact of communications.

In total we identified 28 'matched pairs' where we could isolate the effect of a single media type on a single crime type, e.g. TV, radio, outdoor. Each of these comparisons will hitherto be referred to as a model.

This built upon a tried-and-tested methodology.[37]

Quantifying the effects of advertising on acquisitive crime

To demonstrate this methodology in action we will show the results we found from just one model that looked at TV advertising and its effect on reducing robberies.

A police force in the east of England was paired with another police force for robbery and the ratio of robberies modelled. The change resulting from communication can be derived directly from the model and then translated into a given number of crimes saved, in this case 780 robberies over a two-year period, representing 18% fewer robberies than would otherwise have occurred (see Figure 30).

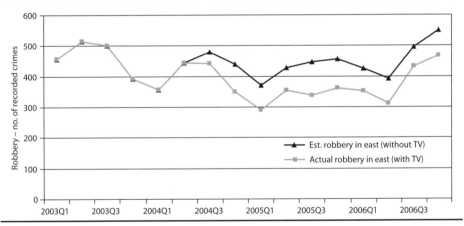

Figure 30: The reduction in robberies in police force in east of England resulting from TV activity[38]

Source: Holmes and Cook Figures 23–26

Ideally, we would quantify the reduction in acquisitive crime that could be attributed to the campaign across England and Wales in a similar chart. However, the complexity of the evaluation (28 models, three crime types, four different media solutions) means that we will never get the 'tidy' econometric results one would expect for fmcg.

What we can show, though, is the nature and scale of effects for those areas we were able to model. We have a very consistent pattern of results across all 28 models, which provides compelling evidence that all three strands of the campaign did indeed reduce crime levels.

Table 7: Proportion of models identifying communication reducing the levels of crime at which it was aimed			
	Robbery	Burglary	Vehicle crime[39]
TV	4/4	4/4	8/8
Outdoor	4/5	No burglary outdoor	4/4
Radio[40]	3/3	1/1	2/2
Ambient	Not able to measure separate effects of this. Potentially included in outdoor estimates		

Source: Holmes and Cook

Table 7 shows that 27 out of 28 models clearly identified particular TV, outdoor or radio messages as reducing the levels of the crime type at which they were directed.

In only one case, of outdoor on robbery, was an effect not measured.

The econometrics were also able to evaluate how long the effects of the campaign lasted by medium (see Table 8).

Table 8: Length of effect by medium	
TV	Six months or more
Outdoor	Three to six months
Radio	Shorter than three months

Source: Holmes and Cook

Return on investment

How do we measure the savings of reduction in crime?

The Home Office estimates the cost of individual crimes based on a number of key measures including policing, insurance costs, Criminal Justice System time and loss to individuals.[41] Different acquisitive crimes have different associated costs (see Table 9).

Table 9: Estimated cost per crime[42]	
Crime	Estimated average cost per crime (£)
Robbery	7,282
Burglary	3,268
Theft from vehicle	858
Theft of vehicle	4,138

Source: Holmes and Cook

How did we calculate this campaign's ROI?

In total, acquisitive crime fell by 19% across the period of the campaign (see Table 10).

The total budget for this campaign was £13.5m.

Table 10: Crime rates			
Crime	2003/4 (000s)	2006/7 (000s)	% decline
Burglary	943	726	–23
All vehicle thefts	2,121	1,689	–20
Robbery	623	574	–8
Total acquisitive	3,687	2,989	–19

Source: British Crime Survey

In order for the campaign to have paid back this investment it would have had to account for a 0.28% reduction in each crime type for a full year. Given the robbery example detailed earlier in Figure 30 (an 18% reduction, which was not untypical of the robbery results), percentage reductions were coming in well above this.

However, rates of return differed by crime type and by police force. Robbery, with the highest cost per crime, not surprisingly produces the greatest benefit, followed by vehicle theft and then burglary.

To reach an absolute ROI figure we compiled a large matrix of the ROI effects by police force for each crime type and for each medium successfully evaluated. Any that were clearly untypical of the general pattern of results were discarded. (This tended to be ones where communication had been unbelievably effective!) This then provided us with a general overview of how each piece of activity had worked and the average levels of ROI. Next we compared these with the general scale of any displacement.[43] This gave us a net estimated ROI for each crime type and each medium. These were then weighted together by relative media weight to provide an estimate of overall payback for the campaign as a whole. Although there were some halo effects from crime to crime, these were not included in the ROI figure as our estimates of them were less consistent.

By this calculation, for every £1 spent on TV and outdoor, £19 was saved. If we take account of the costs of the other media for which we don't have quantification, then the payback for the campaign as a whole is 14:1. This is conservative, as it is based on the lowest estimate for each medium and does not include any halo effect.

When the vehicle crime campaign was evaluated in 2004, potential effects on other crimes were acknowledged but not looked for. Thus for this campaign to achieve a return of 14:1 from simultaneous reductions in three crime types is an outstanding result.

Taking this ratio, then, overall the campaign accounts for at least £189m reduction in the cost of crime (see Table 11).

Table 11: Summary of payback	
Total campaign spend	£13.5m
Conservative estimate of payback per £1 spent	£14
Minimum reduction in cost of crime attributable to campaign	£189m

*With closer scrutiny on value for money and ROI, the econometrics has really
helped us secure funding for crime communications next year.*

Sharon Sawers, Head of Marketing and Strategy, The Home Office

Summary

Acquisitive crime costs Britain £9.5bn a year. Between 2003 and 2007 Britain
experienced a 19% reduction in the number of acquisitive crimes committed –
that's 698,000 fewer crimes,[44] and a saving to the taxpayer of £1.3bn.

Econometric analysis demonstrates that this was in part due to a new
communications campaign that embraced the whole of acquisitive crime – the first
time that a single campaign idea has been used to tackle multiple crime types.

The strategy built on the back of the highly successful Vehicle Crime campaign
– encouraging people to take preventative measures against opportunistic theft
from vehicles.

Burglary and robbery were equally opportunistic – and preventable, if people
could just be made to take simple preventative measures. The challenge was to find
a single campaign idea that could span all three crime types, and that could
motivate a core target most at risk of crime, who were apathetic and unaware of
what they could do to mitigate their risk.

Ethnographic research on the streets of Moss Side provided the inspiration for
a strategy that reflected the way offenders really see their victims: as so careless
they deserve to be robbed. By dramatising this carelessness in a humorous way, the
campaign, 'Don't advertise your stuff to thieves', found a way to empower and
equip this difficult target audience to take preventative measures. In doing so, it
turned a nation of potential victims into a nation of crime prevention officers.

Conservative estimates from econometric analysis suggest that the campaign
ROI was at least 14:1. This means the campaign reduced the cost of crime in
Britain by a minimum of £189m, accounting for 15% of the total £1.3bn saved
through the overall reduction in crime. The real percentage is undoubtedly much
higher.

Notes

1. British Crime Survey 2004.
2. Out of 5.6m offences in 2006 only 0.013% (765) were homicides, even including the victims of the July 7th
   bombings. A worst-case scenario estimate of 60,000 knife-related crimes in 2006 would put knife crime as only
   1% of all crime. Source: Research Development and Statistics (CRCSG) The Home Office, in *Telegraph* article
   on 'The vagaries of knife crime statistics', 20 March 2007.
3. The Home Office, *Crime in England and Wales 2003/4.*
4. British Crime Survey 2004.
5. Estimated costs per crime are: burglary £3,268, robbery £7,282, theft from vehicle £858 and theft of vehicle
   £4,138. In addition to costs to the criminal justice and health systems the estimates also take into account
   insurance, recovery of property, and physical and emotional impact on direct victims. Source: *The economic and
   social costs of crime against individuals and households 2003/04*, The Home Office online report 30/05.
6. M&S 2007 turnover was £8.6bn. Source: www.M&S.com.
7. For the rest of this paper, 'we' refers to a joint team from RKCR/Y&R and The Home Office. MEC was involved
   for the first year of the campaign.
8. 'Crime doesn't pay ... but advertising to stop it does' – IPA Gold Winner 2006.
9. IFF Research with Opportunistic Offenders, August 2004.
10. TNS Vehicle Crime Tracking Study, June 2004.
11. www.crimereduction.gov.uk, 2004.

12. The increased emotional cost of robbery is reflected in the estimated cost of crime: robbery is by far the most 'costly' crime, estimated at £7,382 per crime vs £858 for vehicle crime. Source: *The economic and social costs of crime against individuals and households 2003/04*, The Home Office online report 30/05.
13. Taken from BBC News Online article 'Burglary victims speak out', 9 January 2003.
14. Cragg Ross Dawson, Creative Development Research, Sept 2004.
15. Source: The Home Office, based on analysis of Acorn groups against the British Crime Survey. Urban 16–34s are 50–200% more likely to be victims of robbery, burglary or car crime vs the general population.
16. Throughout this paper (e.g. as in Figure 6), ** indicates a significant difference at the 99% confidence level and * indicates at the 95% confidence level.
17. Qualitative research into perceptions and fear of crime, CML Research, January 2007.
18. 2001 UK census. Moss Side has 7.9% unemployment vs UK average of 3.3%.
19. Compared to a national average of 70%. Source: UK Census 2001.
20. Deliberately worn to make identification difficult.
21. Police working in Moss Side carry bullet-proof vests, as did we during the ethnographic research.
22. Ethnographic research in Moss Side, 2004.
23. We conducted similar research in Salford and Southwark, in addition to speaking to a wide range of police officers from other forces.
24. IFF Research with Young Offenders, 2004,
25. Taken from interviews with police officers in Notting Hill, 2004.
26. Steve Stretton, Private view, *Campaign* magazine, autumn 2004.
27. For example, London accounts for 45% of all robbery (source: British Crime Survey 2007) and received 50% of the robbery budget. The overall budget split by crime type was based on difficulty of task and level of prior support, and equated to vehicle crime 25%, robbery 40% and burglary 35%.
28. Econometricians Holmes & Cook were involved in the media planning stage to help ensure there was at least some possibility of comparative analysis from an econometric point of view.
29. Source: Street Crime Initiative Crime Density Analysis in Brent, January to June 2003.
30. The burglary door-drop informed people about a new technique thieves were using – 'fishing' through the letterbox for car keys and house keys, which many people keep within easy reach of their front door, and using them to burgle their house and then drive off in their car.
31. Declines for total acquisitive crime, burglary and vehicle theft are all significant at a 95% confidence level. The decline in robbery was an achievement given that, over the period in consideration, funding was diverted away from the critical anti-robbery Street Crime Initiative. NB: What we refer to as robbery within this paper is referred to by the British Crime Survey as 'theft from the person'.
32. See media schematic, Figure 20.
33. Research was conducted with adults aged 16+ in the four main TV campaign regions of London, HTV, the Midlands and the North. Half the interviews were with the key target group of 16–34s; the final data were reweighted back to the natural profile.
34. The same pattern was true for other crime types (i.e. students showed the greatest increase in empowerment), although not quite to the same levels.
35. This was a complex piece of analysis and there is insufficient space within the body of the paper to discuss it in anything but the most cursory detail. The analysis was carried out by Holmes & Cook, and was discussed at all key stages with The Home Office. It is based on data from the first three years of the campaign.
36. Young men make up a large proportion of vehicle theft offenders and crime levels are shown to be directly related to the proportion of young men in the population at the time.
37. This methodology had been used successfully to isolate the effect of the Vehicle Crime campaign, which won an IPA Effectiveness Gold in 2006. Furthermore, when the National Consumer Council reviewed the evaluation of a range of government communication campaigns it cited the Vehicle Crime analysis as 'exemplary'.
38. The models were actually constructed using monthly recorded crime data, i.e. the analysis is based on far more data points than shown here. As only quarterly data are routinely published, that is what is shown here.
39. Theft from vehicles and theft of vehicles were modelled separately, hence higher number of models.
40. It was most difficult to find police forces who matched on macro factors but had different radio levels.
41. Economic and Social Cost of Crime against Individuals and Households, 2003/2004.
42. The Home Office online report 30/05.
43. Displacement effects are where one crime is reduced but other crime types increase as a result.
44. British Crime Survey 2002/3 survey data vs 2006/7 survey data. Combined figures for burglary, vehicle-related thefts and theft from person.

Other companies involved in campaign: Media company: Mediaedge:cia

Chapter 10

Dave

Now everyone has a mate called Dave

By Hannah Yelin and Jonathan Wise, Red Bee Media
Contributing authors: Clare Phillips and Mills Willis, Red Bee Media, and Emma Boston, Uktv

Editor's summary

This is a paper that demonstrates a fresh approach to the marketing of a TV channel. As the number of digital TV channels has grown, very few demonstrated a desire to really stand out in the increasingly cluttered EPG. However the re-branding of Uktv G2 to Dave broke many conventions of TV channel marketing and produced breakthrough results.

Rebranding the channel away from the customary bunch of letters and numbers that populate the digital TV landscape helped Dave immediately signal that it was a channel that was different. It was a channel with a real personality and that personality was designed to chime with a clear target audience of 16–44-year-old men, with the promise of 'witty banter'. On top of this, the communications promoted the overall channel rather than just individual programmes.

This communications campaign took Dave off the TV and onto the streets through innovative PR stunts and high-impact large-scale outdoor advertising across the UK's major cities, making the brand's arrival unmissable.

It's success attracted an additional eight million viewers and generated a payback of £2.99 for every £1 spent.

Meet Dave

This is the remarkable story of how a tiny, underperforming channel with a modest communications budget can get noticed overnight.

Before the coming of Dave, when a TV channel wanted to reinvent itself, or become more successful, it changed its programming.

Yet here is a story that evidences the power of branding. Uktv reinvented its channel Uktv G2 as Dave and within one month increased audience share by 35%. In its first three months it attracted an additional 8 million viewers to the Uktv network and in six months delivered £4.5m profit.

All brands want to stand out in a crowd. But in the TV world the crowds are massive and many digital channels appear anonymous and lost. Yet Dave demonstrates that brilliant branding of attractive content can turn just another face in the crowd into the centre of attention.

This paper is relevant and instructive to all, particularly suppliers of content, from terrestrial broadcasters to online content providers. This paper reveals that rebranding need not mean the junking of content or a wholesale change in programming strategy. By intelligently defining and packaging a channel's content, by identifying a channel's emotional role in people's lives, and by selling the idea of a channel and not just the individual programmes, it is possible to create a channel that stands out, gets noticed and attracts viewers in their millions.

The British television market is fiercely competitive and oversupplied

The arrival of digital television is changing Britain – changing its viewing habits, its tastes, its experiences, even its bedtime. It is a revolution:

> Digital switchover is one of the biggest public projects in the postwar era. It's been compared to decimalisation and North Sea gas conversion. It affects virtually every UK household.

> Digital UK Annual Review, 2006/7

Switchover will be complete in 2012, but we are already witnessing a huge appetite for more TV channels as digital penetration reached 89% in March 2008.

Viewers' demand has been more than matched by media owners' desire to launch more channels. In 20 years, 497 new channels have been introduced – a 12,525% increase. As a result, the average number of channels a person watches increased from four to 30.

TV remains a popular pastime. On average, people spend more time watching TV than in paid employment;[1] however, average weekly hours viewed have remained static. As a result, average viewing per channel declined from 6 hours 18 minutes to 50 minutes – an 87% decline.

The combination of huge increase in supply and static demand means achieving growth has become a formidable task. Indeed, Uktv 's multi channel (MC) competitors have all seen decline in the last year (see Figure 1).

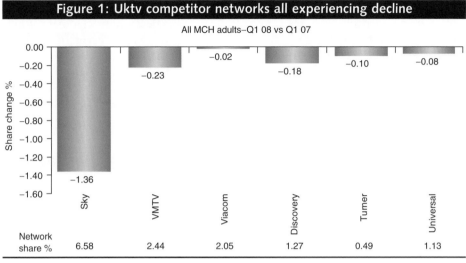

Figure 1: Uktv competitor networks all experiencing decline

All MCH adults–Q1 08 vs Q1 07

Network	Sky	VMTV	Viacom	Discovery	Turner	Universal
Share change %	-1.36	-0.23	-0.02	-0.18	-0.10	-0.08
Network share %	6.58	2.44	2.05	1.27	0.49	1.13

Source: BARB; Q1 08 vs Q1 07

Uktv's opportunities for growth declined

Uktv is a joint venture between BBC Worldwide and Virgin Media, funded by spot advertising and subscription. It operated a successful growth strategy of introducing new channels that have access to the BBC archive. By 2007, Uktv had a portfolio of ten channels and seven '+1' channels (see Figure 2).

However, by 2007 access to channel spaces was severely constrained. Sky was not opening any more spaces for channels and demand for Freeview capacity so

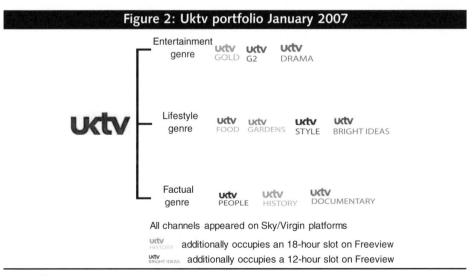

Figure 2: Uktv portfolio January 2007

Entertainment genre: uktv GOLD   uktv G2   uktv DRAMA

Lifestyle genre: uktv FOOD   uktv GARDENS   uktv STYLE   uktv BRIGHT IDEAS

Factual genre: uktv PEOPLE   uktv HISTORY   uktv DOCUMENTARY

All channels appeared on Sky/Virgin platforms

uktv HISTORY additionally occupies an 18-hour slot on Freeview

uktv BRIGHT IDEAS additionally occupies a 12-hour slot on Freeview

Source: Uktv

greatly outstripped the limited supply that price became prohibitive, increasing from £3m per year in 2003 to £12m in 2006 for a single 24-hour channel.[2] While Uktv's aggressive growth targets remained, its previously successful growth strategy was no longer going to work.

This resulted in a sudden plateau in growth of Uktv viewing (see Figure 3). Having launched no new channels since 2005, Uktv faced added pressure from terrestrial channels investing heavily in digital extensions of their core brands.

Figure 3: Plateau in Uktv share growth

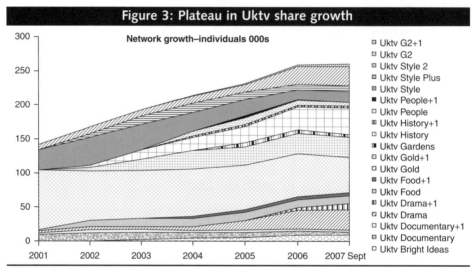

Source: BARB

Freeview offered some hope

A strategic review of the business identified that we could grow by rearranging our existing slots. At this point, the Uktv Freeview slots broadcast Uktv History and Uktv Bright Ideas, channels that didn't offer optimum advertising audiences. Looking at the portfolio, profitable growth could come from attracting more 16–44 ABC1 males. Uktv G2 was identified as offering the biggest potential because of its mix of content (see Figure 4).

The decision was made to take Uktv History's Freeview slot and substitute Uktv G2 in its place. The date for change was set as October 2007.

The story could have ended there. A straight swap would grow Uktv G2's audience with access to 3.2 million additional, valuable 16–44-year-old males.

However, the set viewing target demanded that this wouldn't be enough. The five-year objective was set for Uktv G2 to become the number one digital channel for men aged 16–44. An ambitious target for a repeats channel given this position is currently held by Sky Sports 1 – a channel driven by the £669m deal for Premiership Football rights.[3]

Figure 4: Uktv G2 featured a multi-genre mix of programming

Music shows, e.g. TOTP2

Sketch shows, e.g. Catherine Tate

Factual entertainment, e.g. Top Gear

Reality shows, e.g. Dragons' Den

Quiz shows, e.g. QI

Movies, e.g. Almost Famous

Adventure, e.g. Ray Mears

Sitcoms, e.g. Red Dwarf

How could Uktv G2 increase its share?

We needed to increase Uktv G2's audience. Dramatically.

The challenge was that traditional techniques of boosting channel growth were unavailable to us.

- Launching a '+1' creates additional viewing opportunities but Uktv G2 had already done this in Pay and couldn't in Freeview as there were no available slots.
- Cross-promotion from terrestrial channels to digital sister channels is another method for attracting larger audiences. Terrestrial broadcasters have grown their digital channels through heavy promotion on the main channels, compounded by their incumbent size and top positions in the programme Guide. However, Uktv channels are available only on digital platforms. Uktv G2 had no terrestrial big sister channel to send viewers its way.
- Programming is a primary driver of viewing for any channel. A common channel strategy is putting the majority of budget behind one high-profile 'brand-defining' acquisition or commission then promoting this heavily to bring in viewers (see Table 1).

However, in this area again we were inhibited given the high cost and our restricted budget (see Table 2).

Table 1: Digital channels spend a high percentage of their advertising budget promoting one show			
Channel	Total recorded off-air spend for year (£)	Programme with largest off-air spend	Amount spent on that programme (£)	% of total off-air spent on that programme
Virgin1	615,397	Sarah Conner Chronicles	553,528	90
E4	980,479	Skins	838,716	85
FX	480,428	Dexter	289,966	60
More4	676,768	Trial of Tony Blair	385,484	57

Source: Adynamics, April 2008

Table 2: High cost of programming on digital channels					
	Channel	Name of show	Reported cost per episode (£)	Number of episodes	Cost of series (£m)
1	E4	Skins	250k	9	2.25
2	More4	Blunkett: A Very Social Secretary	1.5m	1	1.5
3	Virgin1	Sarah Conner Chronicles	450k	9	4.05
4	ITV2	Secret Diary of a Call Girl	250k	8	2
5	Sky One	Lost series 2	909k	22	20
6	Sky One	Prison Break	500k	13	6.5

Sources: 1–4, industry estimates; 5, *Brand Republic*, 04/02/08; 6, *Media Guardian*, 05/06/07

Looking at the conventions of competitors who follow this strategy we took three learnings:

1. If the programme airs one episode each week, we would be promoting one hour out of the available 126. It seemed to neglect so much of what we offer.
2. Even if viewers watched that particular show, this doesn't necessarily translate into them staying on our channel after it finished (see Figure 5).
3. Building association between programme and channel is difficult. Channels outbid each other for returning series, bringing the danger that launch spend becomes wasted as viewers follow the series to another channel. Not an effective strategy in a market littered with programmes that move between TV channels and VoD (video on demand) services with little discernible benefit beyond short-term impacts (see Table 3).

The three traditional tools for channel growth were unavailable to us. Absence of alternative resources meant we would have to make more efficient, creative use of our existing resources. We decided to find a way to make the programming we already had, which should have been performing well given its quality, work much harder.

Figure 5: One key acquisition does not lead to sustained growth

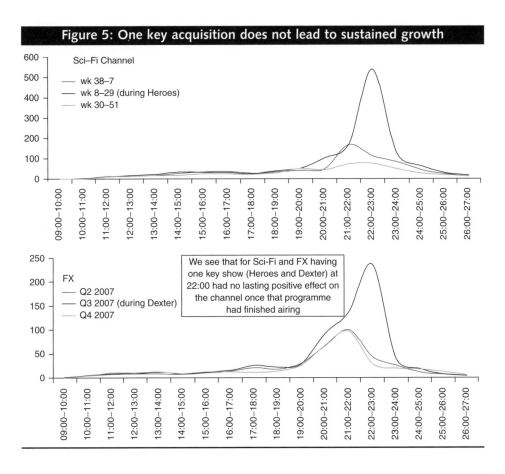

We see that for Sci-Fi and FX having one key show (Heroes and Dexter) at 22:00 had no lasting positive effect on the channel once that programme had finished airing

Table 3: 'Promiscuous programmes'

Name of show	UK channel it first appeared on	Has subsequently appeared on
Never Mind the Buzzcocks	BBC2	VH1, TMF, Dave
Lost	Channel 4	Sky One
24	BBC2	Sky One
Heroes	Sci-Fi	BBC2
Dexter	FX	ITV1
Prison Break	Five	Sky One, Uktv Gold
Sex and the City	Channel 4, E4	Paramount, fiver
Everybody Hates Chris	Five	Paramount Comedy
The Simpsons	Sky One	Channel 4
Robot Wars	BBC2	Five, Sci-Fi, Challenge, Sky One, Sky Two, Sky Three
Scrapheap Challenge	Channel 4	Discovery UK
Air Crash Investigation	Five	National Geographic

Where would budget generate greatest return?

Lastly, we had our £1.5m budget, extremely modest for the TV market. The question was how best to spend it. In television, £1.5m buys three episodes of a US acquisition, 90 minutes of commissioned drama, or 19 30-second primetime terrestrial ad spots. However, these are not business-transforming solutions.

Our budget had to be spent effectively, cleverly and innovatively. We were looking for a huge return from a small investment. We identified that the best – in fact the only – area to spend our budget to enable the channel to realise its potential was to create a channel brand that stood out from the crowd.

Uktv G2 was a weak brand, lost and invisible

With competition growing exponentially, having stand-out and a clear offering was crucial. This meant Uktv G2 was not in a good place.

■ it didn't stand out – despite four years in the market (see Figure 6)

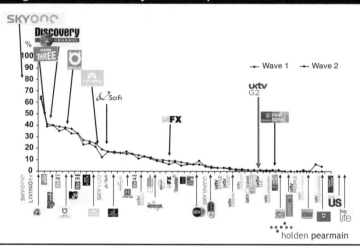

Figure 6: Uktv G2 only had 2% spontaneous awareness

Source: Uktv and Virgin Brand Tracker – QA1: Wave 1 (Base: 2,614), Wave 2 (Base: 2,587)

■ it didn't even stand out for those who were actually watching the channel (see Figure 7)
■ the name confused viewers (see Figure 8)
■ while good quality, the vast majority of Uktv G2's programmes were repeats, with stock favourites like *Red Dwarf* originally screened over 20 years ago.

Figure 7: Uktv G2 suffers highest misattribution

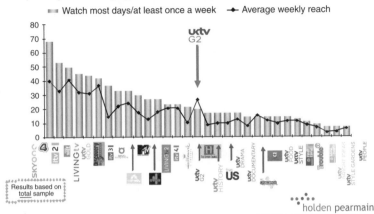

• People tuning in to Uktv G2's programmes, aren't aware they are watching them on Uktv G2

■■ Watch most days/at least once a week → Average weekly reach

Results based on total sample

holden pearmain

Source: BARB Nov–Jan 2006/7 – Pay TV 16–64 Adults, 1 minute reach
Uktv and Virgin Brand Tracker – Wave 2 (Base: 2,587), QA3

Figure 8: The name was confusing

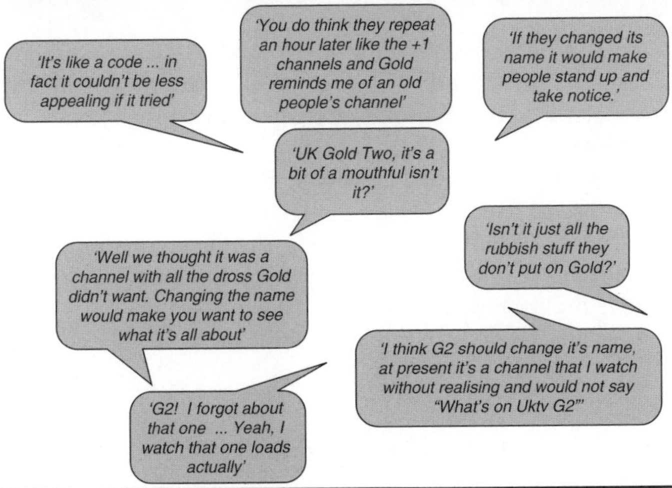

'It's like a code ... in fact it couldn't be less appealing if it tried'

'You do think they repeat an hour later like the +1 channels and Gold reminds me of an old people's channel'

'If they changed its name it would make people stand up and take notice.'

'UK Gold Two, it's a bit of a mouthful isn't it?'

'Well we thought it was a channel with all the dross Gold didn't want. Changing the name would make you want to see what it's all about'

'Isn't it just all the rubbish stuff they don't put on Gold?'

'I think G2 should change it's name, at present it's a channel that I watch without realising and would not say "What's on Uktv G2"'

'G2! I forgot about that one ... Yeah, I watch that one loads actually'

Source: Results of qualitative research conducted by Uktv Planning & Research and Qmedia in May 07

Uktv G2 had no presence and no new programmes. In a congested market, it had no personality and no clear role in people's lives. It was unsurprising that viewing figures were lacklustre. We had to create standout in one of the most competitive markets in the world, yet we were starting from a very poor place (see Figure 9).

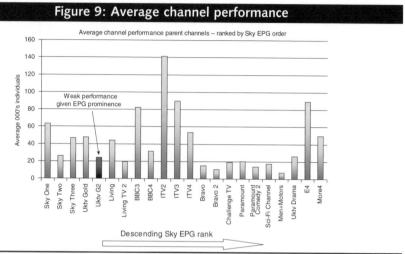

Figure 9: Average channel performance

Average channel performance parent channels – ranked by Sky EPG order

Source: BARB – 15 July to 14 October 2007 (pre-Dave)

Create a powerful brand

With our small marketing budget, we could not push individual programmes. Instead our strategy had to focus on building viewers' relationship with the channel as a whole.

We had to break from conventional thinking and its focus on programming. We believed we should radically alter our channel brand into something viewers wanted to spend time with. A brand with personality appealing to the 16–44 upmarket male demographic.

We had to offer these valuable viewers a brand that would help navigate the congested TV landscape by clearly signalling what it stood for.

By focusing on the channel brand, not the programmes, we could build something more ownable and long term that we could control, not just for the life cycle of particular programmes.

We summarised our strategy in three key areas on which our channel brand had to deliver.

1. give the channel personality:
   ■ define what we offer, change the name and the on-screen presentation
2. fulfil a role in people's lives:
   ■ understand how people would use and relate to what we offered
3. find a compelling way to promote the channel:
   ■ based on the above and not individual content.

Defining what we offered

We had a range of quality programmes, but no homogeneous genre, which made communicating what we offered extremely difficult. However, research identified the root of our programming – 'Intelligent, Irreverent Humour' (see Figure 10).

Figure 10: Commonality in Uktv G2's programming

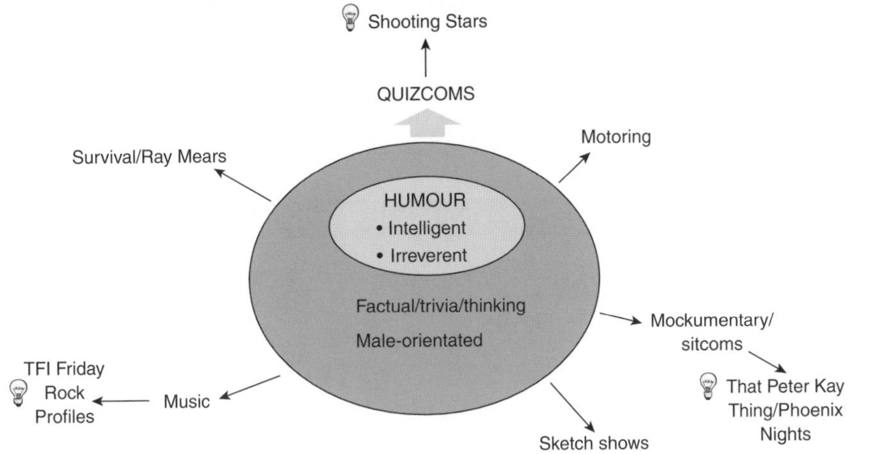

Source: Qmedia March 2007

Further investigation helped us understand why. This content satisfied a fundamental male need: having a laugh with other men.

Role in viewers' lives

Men being men, they would more often than not rather be down the pub with their mates! Sadly, this isn't always an option, especially once demanding jobs or families are involved. So they miss the bonding backchat they are used to having over a few pints.

The breakthrough came when we realised, for fans of Uktv G2, it wasn't merely a TV channel but a surrogate for being down the pub with their amusing mates. And for them it didn't feel like a poor substitute as here their mates were Stephen Fry and Paul Merton. The channel was a 'place' to spend quality time with very funny men.

Proposition

From our understanding of what purpose the channel served and the type of content it showed, we were able to generate a compelling expression of the channel's focus:

The Home of Witty Banter

Personality

We felt confident we had an interesting way to sum up the channel's role – what its programming always offered, not just what its lead programme offered. Armed with this, we needed to consider two critical factors: the channel name and the way it presented itself.

Channel name

In crowded markets, powerful branding and evocative brand names influence consumer choices. However, the TV market has been slow to respond to this opportunity. Long-established broadcasters are reluctant to change their naming model and, as such, many channels and their new terrestrial extensions adhere to the traditional 'network-and-numeral' strategy (see Figure 11).

Figure 11: Network-and-number naming strategies

Even newer channels often follow a predictable genre-based approach, at the expense of personality and originality (see Figure 12).

Figure 12: Functional naming at the expense of originality

Overturning conventions

Looking at Uktv G2's name, it adhered to typical TV naming conventions. Worse still, the meaning of 'G2' was unclear, and it could even be seen as derogatory, with some consumers believing Uktv G2 denoted a second-best version of Uktv Gold!

What's in a name?

Uktv G2, then, doesn't scream Witty Banter; it doesn't suggest the content; and it fails to give the brand any personality. It was clear we needed a new name – but what? The brief was:

- drop Uktv
- avoid letters and numerals
- have real standout and personality.

We generated a long list that offered different routes (see Table 4).

Table 4: Potential names	
Route	**Example name**
'Suggestive' names	'Grrr', 'Edge'
'Signposts'	'Comedy', 'Mentertainment'
'Idea' names	'Shed', 'Dave'

Research showed 'idea' names attracted interesting responses, with Dave in particular inspiring excitement:

Those that were convinced were passionately convinced ... it took a person to get behind it [Dave] and sell it to others.

Qmedia, March 2007

This was exactly what we were looking for – a distinctive, personality-laden name that could engender real passion. Dave harnessed the audience insight that people could treat the channel as a friend and Dave gave that friend a real personality. Research also showed that the name appealed across social groups, sexes and ages: 'Everyone's got a mate called Dave.' Furthermore, Dave is a name with comedy credentials befitting the humorous content – Baddiel, Gorman, Radio 1's Comedy Dave, etc.

We felt we had something powerful. No UK channel had called itself a first name. *Ever.*

How it presented itself

The Home of Witty Banter became the brief's proposition (see Figure 13).

Figure 13: The brief

Synopsis
This is the Home of Witty Banter. Alternative, smart, funny and quick witted. Like being down the pub with the funniest, smartest version of your own mates. It gives you a new angle on things and makes you feel part of the banter. Imagine your local with Paul Merton, Jeremy Clarkson and Johnny Vegas as barflies.

Audience
Blokes who like a more varied and substantial diet than stereotypical male media fodder. They appreciate wit and intelligence and something a bit subversive, that gives them social currency. They've got partners, families, careers – lots going on. They need an entertainment channel that allows them to retreat into a world that is just for them. They go out with their mates a couple of times a month, even once a week, but meanwhile our brand offers a little bit of male camaraderie and stimulation every day. It's a faithful mate that they can rely on for a bit of a laugh.

Tone of voice
Smart, funny and a bit alternative. The opposite of mainstream tits n ass parody, monster truck 'for men' stereotypes and grrrr TV. More 'Stephen Fry', less 'Bernard Manning'.

The creative invention came straight from our insight – people treated the channel as a 'place' to spend time with witty men (see Figure 14). Rather than present Dave as a person, Dave could be a 'location'.

Figure 14: The creative

We created a different world. *Peter's Friends* meets *The Life Aquatic*, subverting expectation through highly visual communication.

Idents depicted a weekend in 'The World of Dave' with unusual situations and stories. From arrival, to dinner, to departure, nothing is what it seems. All around are rich visual ephemera: gilt frames, stuffed giraffes, building a sense of place. Thus, the world of Dave was born – a stately gentlemen's club where (as in its programming) quirky, unexpected things happen. A unique, compelling, adventurous and ever-evolving brand.

Launching the new brand

We couldn't legally call the channel 'new' because, technically, it wasn't – it was a rebrand. However, we gave it the excitement and momentum of a true launch. TV launches differ from others, our main weapon being our on-air presence. As well as creating a brand that infused everything on the channel, we announced our rebrand with an off-air campaign that went hand in hand with PR maximising free media coverage of the launch.

Given our strategy was creating buzz and salience with our innovative name, our media choice was to concentrate the entire media budget into a tightly focused two-week outdoor burst. High-impact, large-scale back-lit sites emblazoned Dave across the UK's major cities, making its arrival unmissable.

New approach to channel promotion

Exactly what to communicate off-air was a challenging question. We knew that, although our content was largely repeats, it was good quality and well-liked, but it hadn't been performing well enough on the channel.

However, now we also knew that, with 'The Home of Witty Banter', we had a strong rationale to tie any range of our content back to the idea behind the channel. Our off-air campaign reinforced this: 'Imagine your local with Paul Merton, Jeremy Clarkson and Johnny Vegas as barflies.'

By combining the well-known faces from Uktv G2, the creative placed programmes in the quirky 'World of Dave'. It showed Dave chose to screen these programmes because they reflected our personality. This enhanced perceptions of repeat content, conferring Dave's point of view on these shows.

The channel was no longer merely a receptacle for its content. Our programmes, which people had seen before, were collectively building and solidifying what Dave stood for. To launch with no new programming – the very same programming that hadn't previously performed – was bold. But we believed that the combined effect of well-known wits in the context of the new Dave brand could be more potent to viewers than new, expensive programmes (see Figures 15–19).

Figure 15: Combined talent in off-air launch reflected the Dave personality, rather than any one programme

Figure 16: Media plan and spend

	8 Oct	15 Oct	22 Oct	29 Oct	5 Nov	12 Nov	19 Nov
London Underground 48 sheets							
London Underground tube card panels							
National 96 sheets							
National 6 sheets							
London premier, portrait and platinum panels							
Key city landscape backlights							
National press (colour pages)							

Spend
Identity
Creative fees and production:
£561,000
Off-air launch
Outdoor media spend: £591,831
Press media spend: £273,169
Production: £85,000
£950,000
Total: £1,511,000

Figure 17: We had an integrated PR campaign

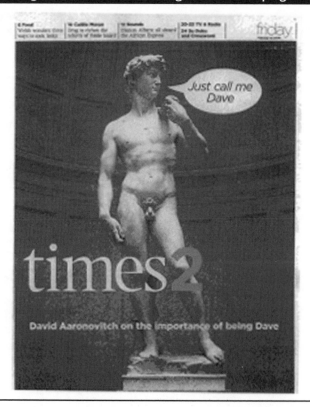

Figure 18: We had the building wrapped

Figure 19: We even had a marching band!

Calculating results

We have an advantage in demonstrating effectiveness with some certainty because in Pay homes (cable or Sky) the before and after effects are clear as nothing else changed on the channel other than the rebrand from Uktv G2 to Dave.

However, just looking at Pay does not take the rebrand effect within Freeview into account. As Uktv G2 had never previously been on Freeview, we need to deduce how much of Dave's success is attributable solely to the rebrand.

We examine the results in two ways: the creation of a powerful channel brand and marketing's return on investment.

The rebrand surpassed its objectives

1. A rebrand that gets noticed (see Figure 20).

Figure 20: Outdoor and press campaign seen and noticed

Out of home campaign appears to have been a success/noticeable; tube/billboards both referenced.

Qmedia qualitative research, November 2008
(NB: No advertising tracking data exist)

2. **Grow awareness of the new brand (see Figure 21).**
   This is ahead of competitors More4, BBC4, ITV3, MTV1 and Bravo.

Figure 21: Spontaneous awareness increased dramatically

%
35
30
25
20
15
10
5
0
Spontaneous awareness
32%
2%
Uktv G2 (pre-rebrand)
Dave (post-rebrand)

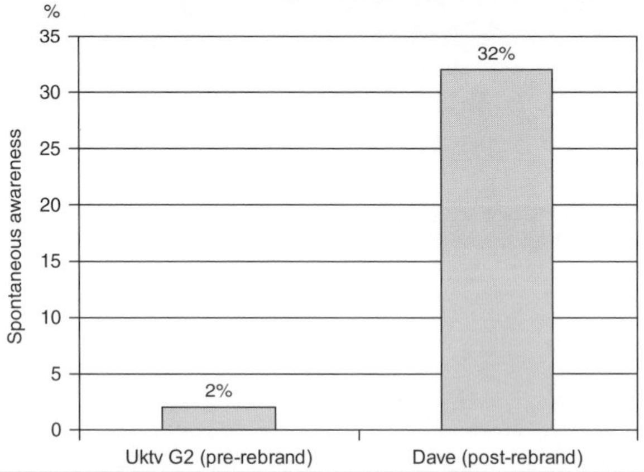

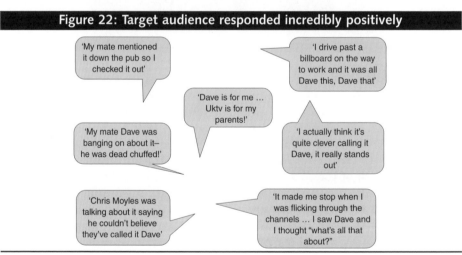

Source: Uktv and Virgin Brand Tracker, Jan–Apr 07 and Nov 07

3. **A brand with strong appeal for our target (see Figure 22).**

Figure 22: Target audience responded incredibly positively

'My mate mentioned it down the pub so I checked it out'
'I drive past a billboard on the way to work and it was all Dave this, Dave that'
'Dave is for me ... Uktv is for my parents!'
'My mate Dave was banging on about it– he was dead chuffed!'
'I actually think it's quite clever calling it Dave, it really stands out'
'Chris Moyles was talking about it saying he couldn't believe they've called it Dave'
'It made me stop when I was flicking through the channels ... I saw Dave and I thought "what's all that about?"

Source: Qmedia qualitative research, March 2008

4. **Create buzz: get the channel talked about (see Figures 23 and 24).**
5. **Attract more 16–44 men to the channel.**
   We successfully drove viewing among our target (see Figures 25 and 26).
6. **Increase the amount of time that our target spend viewing the channel (see Figure 27).**

Figure 23: Launch PR circulation

There were 93 million opportunities to see and hear about Dave on the day of launch

Source: Durants

Figure 24: Rebrand created talkability and brand advocates

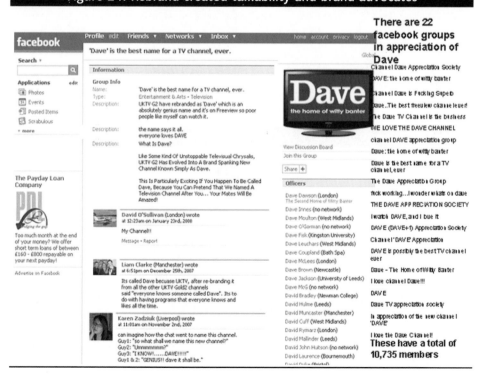

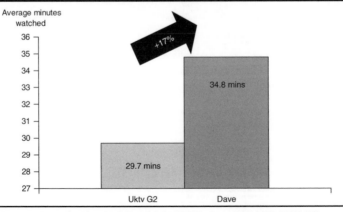

Figure 25: A 67% uplift in reach

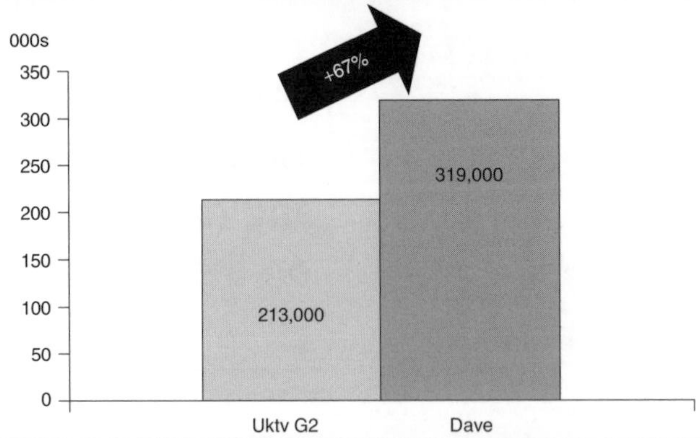

000s

+67%

319,000

213,000

Uktv G2   Dave

Source: BARB, ABC1 men 16–44 for Uktv G2 (16/10/06–31/03/07); Dave (15/10/07–31/03/08)

Figure 26: 71% uplift in share in Pay TV

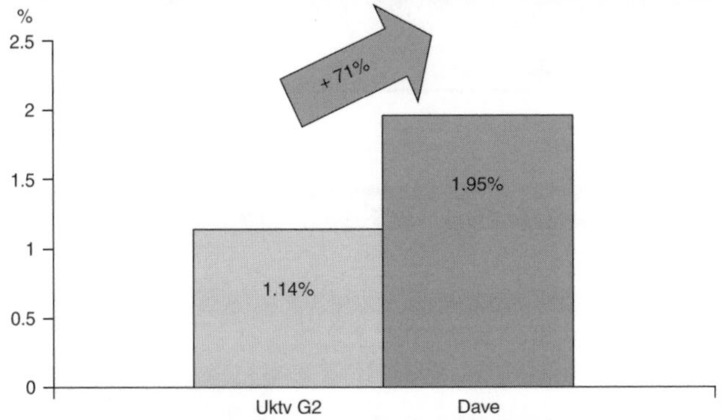

%

+71%

1.95%

1.14%

Uktv G2   Dave

Source: BARB, ABC1 men 16–44 for Uktv G2 (16/10/06–31/03/07); Dave (15/10/07–31/03/08)

Figure 27: Average minutes watched on the channel in Pay increased by 17%

Average minutes
watched

+17%

34.8 mins

29.7 mins

Uktv G2   Dave

Source: BARB, ABC1 men 16–44 for Uktv G2 (16/10/06–31/03/07); Dave (15/10/07–31/03/08)

7. Drive viewing of all our programmes, not just of one or two key slots (see Figure 28).

Ranking (000s)	Programme	Uktv G2 (000s)	Dave (000s)	% difference
	Figure 28: Viewing increased significantly for nearly all programmes			
1	Ray Mears' Extreme Survival	27	76	179
2	Red Dwarf	65	136	110
3	Motoring Duels	41	82	100
4	The Fast Show	43	77	79
5	Top Gear	81	135	67
6	Never Mind the Buzzcocks	81	134	65
7	QI	140	227	62
8	Big Train	32	50	57
9	Have I Got News For You	90	140	55
10	Dead Ringers	63	96	53
11	Bottom	76	106	39
12	I'm Alan Partridge	57	79	37
13	Billy Connolly's World Tour of New Zealand	121	156	29
14	Totally Viral	37	46	25
15	Billy Connolly's World Tour of Australia	97	111	15
16	The Catherine Tate Show	130	147	13
17	Mind, Body and Kick Ass Moves	36	40	11
18	Harry Enfield's Television Programme	71	77	9
19	They Think It's All Over	66	70	6
20	Ray Mears' Bushcraft	48	51	5

Source: BARB

Our top 20 programmes saw an average audience increase of 51%.

8. **Make viewers feel proud to be part of Dave.**

People became such passionate advocates of Dave that they now significantly overclaimed their viewing (see Figure 29).

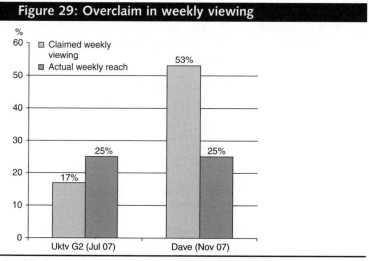

Figure 29: Overclaim in weekly viewing

- Claimed weekly viewing
- Actual weekly reach

Uktv G2 (Jul 07): 17%, 25%
Dave (Nov 07): 53%, 25%

Sources: Uktv and Virgin Brand Tracker; actual weekly reach; BARB Pay 16–64 adults. 1 minute reach

Long-term business objective

This was to become the number one non-terrestrial channel among our target audience. Five months in, we already share this position with the incumbent Sky Sports 1 (see Table 5).

Table 5: Dave is joint number 1 MC channel amongst target audience

	16-44 Men - Multichannel								
	Pre 5.5 months					5.5 months since launch			
	Channels	TVR	Share	000s		Channels	TVR	Share	000s
1	BBC1	1.725	16.93	92	1	BBC1	2.003	17.79	114
2	ITV1	1.232	12.09	66	2	ITV1	1.363	12.11	78
3	CH4	0.863	8.47	46	3	BBC2	0.812	7.21	46
4	BBC2	0.7	6.86	37	4	CH4	0.804	7.14	46
5	Five	0.388	3.81	21	5	Five	0.418	3.72	24
6	Sky Sports 1	0.291	2.86	16	6	Sky Sports 1	0.32	2.84	18
7	E4 Total	0.284	2.79	15	7	Dave Total	0.31	2.79	18
8	ITV2 Total	0.231	2.27	12	8	E4 Total	0.296	2.63	17
9	BBC3	0.203	2	11	9	ITV2 Total	0.246	2.19	14
10	Sky One	0.182	1.78	10	10	Sky One	0.206	1.83	12
11	Sky Sports News	0.154	1.52	8	11	BBC3	0.198	1.76	11
12	Film4 Total	0.122	1.19	6	12	Sky Sports News	0.158	1.4	9
13	Uktv Gold Total	0.114	1.12	6	13	More4 Total	0.144	1.28	8
14	More4 Total	0.113	1.1	6	14	UKTV Gold Total	0.122	1.08	7
15	Living Total	0.109	1.07	6	15	Cbeebies	0.119	1.06	7
16	ITV4	0.106	1.04	6	16	Film4 Total	0.119	1.06	7
17	Cbeebies	0.094	0.92	5	17	ITV4	0.114	1.01	6
18	Paramount Total	0.094	0.92	5	18	Paramount Total	0.097	0.86	6
19	Dave Total	0.094	0.92	5	19	BBC News	0.096	0.85	5
20	BBC News	0.092	0.91	5	20	Living Total	0.091	0.81	5
21	Sky Sports 2	0.085	0.84	5	21	Sky Three	0.084	0.75	5
22	Sky Three	0.085	0.83	5	22	Sky Sports 2	0.083	0.74	5
23	ITV3 Total	0.068	0.66	4	23	Virgin1	0.079	0.7	4
24	Sky News	0.066	0.65	4	24	ITV3 Total	0.076	0.67	4
25	Sky Two	0.066	0.64	4	25	BBC4	0.069	0.61	4

Source: BARB

Calculating marketing's return on investment

The appropriate 'currency' to use for our calculations is impacts. An impact is one person watching one ad once. If there are six ads in a break and the whole break is viewed, that's six impacts. So the more people viewing the channel, the more impacts there are.

Impacts determine advertising revenue. They represent the number of people watching a particular ad. The commercial value of impacts is calculated by multiplying the number of impacts by the cost per thousand of reaching those people. This gives the advertising revenue.

Providing short- and long-term payback figures

1. Results to date (October 2007–March 2008)

This six-and-a-half-month period represents the time period for which we have actual in-market data.

2. Prediction of future impacts (2008–2012)

Uktv works on a five-year planning cycle, thus we can extrapolate from in-market data the rebrand's financial impact over five years.

Impacts resulting from the rebrand results to date (October 2007–March 2008)

Calculating the impacts generated by the Dave rebrand in Pay is straightforward: we can clearly see the before and after effects.

However, calculating the results of the rebrand in Freeview is more complicated since the channel never existed on the platform prior to becoming Dave.

Our methodology (Figures 30–34) enable us to calculate the total number of impacts attributable to the rebrand.

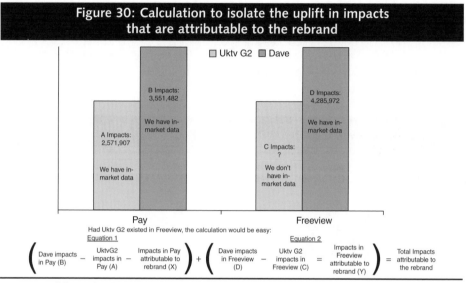

Figure 30: Calculation to isolate the uplift in impacts that are attributable to the rebrand

Source: IDS; all figures for Uktv G2, October 2006–March 2007; all figures for Dave, October 2007–March 2008

But there are complications in estimating the size of Uktv G2 had it aired on Freeview (see Figure 31).

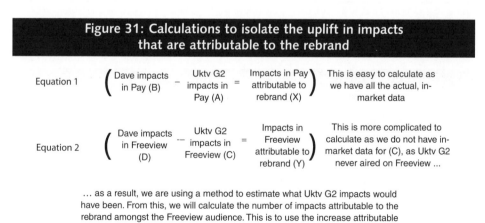

Figure 31: Calculations to isolate the uplift in impacts that are attributable to the rebrand

Equation 1
$$\left(\text{Dave impacts in Pay (B)} - \text{Uktv G2 impacts in Pay (A)} = \text{Impacts in Pay attributable to rebrand (X)} \right)$$
This is easy to calculate as we have all the actual, in-market data

Equation 2
$$\left(\text{Dave impacts in Freeview (D)} - \text{Uktv G2 impacts in Freeview (C)} = \text{Impacts in Freeview attributable to rebrand (Y)} \right)$$
This is more complicated to calculate as we do not have in-market data for (C), as Uktv G2 never aired on Freeview ...

... as a result, we are using a method to estimate what Uktv G2 impacts would have been. From this, we will calculate the number of impacts attributable to the rebrand amongst the Freeview audience. This is to use the increase attributable to the rebrand in Pay and apply it to Freeview

Calculating the impacts in Pay attributable to the rebrand (see Figure 32).

Figure 32: Equation 1

$$\left(\begin{array}{ccc} \text{Dave} & \text{Uktv G2} & \text{Impacts in Pay} \\ \text{impacts in} & - \text{ impacts in} & = \text{attributable to} \\ \text{Pay (B)} & \text{Pay (A)} & \text{rebrand (X)} \end{array} \right)$$

$$\frac{3,551,482}{\text{(B)}} - \frac{2,571,907}{\text{(A)}} = \frac{979,575}{\text{(X)}}$$

Source: IDS; all figures for Uktv G2, October 2006–March 2007; all figures for Dave, October 2007–March 2008

Applying the increase attributable to the rebrand in Pay and applying it to Freeview (see Figure 33).

Figure 33: Using the increase attributable to the rebrand in Pay and applying it to Freeview

Step 1:
$$\left(\frac{\text{Dave impacts in Pay (B)}}{\text{Uktv G2 impacts in Pay (A)}} \right) = \text{Index attributable to the rebrand}$$

$$\left(\frac{3,551,482 \text{ (B)}}{2,571,907 \text{ (A)}} \right) = 1.381$$

Step 2:
$$\left(\frac{\text{Dave impacts in Freeview (D)}}{\text{Index attributable to the rebrand}} \right) = \text{Impacts we would have seen if Uktv G2 had existed on Freeview}$$

$$\left(\frac{4,285,972 \text{ (D)}}{1.381} \right) = \frac{3,103,528}{\text{(C)}}$$

Step 3:
$$\left(\begin{array}{c} \text{Dave impacts} \\ \text{in Freeview (D)} \end{array} - \begin{array}{c} \text{Impacts we would have} \\ \text{seen if Uktv G2 had existed} \\ \text{in Freeview} \end{array} \right) = \begin{array}{c} \text{Impacts attributable to} \\ \text{the rebrand on Freeview (Y)} \end{array}$$

$$\left(4,285,972 \text{ (D)} - 3,103,527 \text{ (C)} \right) = \frac{1,182,444}{\text{(Y)}}$$

Source: IDS; all figures for Uktv G2, October 2006–March 2007; all figures for Dave, October 2007–March 2008

Returning to our original equation, which we can now complete (see Figure 34).

Figure 34: Total number of impacts attributable to the rebrand

So, pulling it all together and reprising our initial equation ...

Equation 1

Equation 2

$$\left(\begin{array}{ccc} \text{Dave impacts} & \text{Uktv G2} & \text{Impacts in} \\ \text{in Pay} & - \text{ impacts in} & = \text{Pay attributable} \\ \text{(B)} & \text{Pay (A)} & \text{to rebrand (X)} \end{array} \right) + \left(\begin{array}{ccc} \text{Dave impacts} & \text{Uktv G2} & \text{Impacts in Freeview} \\ \text{in Freeview} & - \text{ impacts in} & = \text{attributable to} \\ \text{(D)} & \text{Freeview (C)} & \text{rebrand (Y)} \end{array} \right) = \begin{array}{c} \text{Total Impacts} \\ \text{attributable to} \\ \text{the rebrand} \end{array}$$

$$\left(\frac{3,551,482}{\text{(B)}} - \frac{2,571,907}{\text{(A)}} = \frac{979,575}{\text{(X)}} \right) + \left(\frac{4,285,972}{\text{(D)}} - \frac{3,103,528}{\text{(C)}} = \frac{1,182,444}{\text{(Y)}} \right) = 2,162,019$$

Total number of impacts on Dave	Total number of impacts on Dave attributable to the rebrand	% of total impacts on Dave attributable to the rebrand
7,837,454	2,162,019	27.6%

Source: IDS; all figures for Uktv G2, October 2006–March 2007; all figures for Dave, October 2007–March 2008

In terms of the ad sales market there is a 'lag' – between the time impacts are recorded and when they can be monetised – that exists in the market. Despite this, we can calculate the advertising revenue as a result of the impacts generated by the rebrand. If the number of impacts we can attribute to the rebrand is 2,162,019 we can multiply this by the CPT (cost per thousand). Due to confidentiality we are unable to publish the Dave CPT and are therefore using our sales house (IDS) average (£2.77) instead. Therefore the gross advertising revenue attributable to the rebrand = £5,989,000.

Costs

While there are mechanical costs for a channel transmitting on Freeview, these costs would have been incurred as a result of Uktv G2 moving on to the platform. As a result, it is not applicable to include them as a cost of the rebrand. Further, due to the nature of the television market, there are no incremental costs of sales to consider. In fact, the only incremental cost that can be associated with the rebrand is the cost of executing the initial rebrand itself.

This cost, which includes both creative agency fees to produce the Dave idents, OSP (on-screen presentation) and above-the-line advertising materials, as well as the above-the-line media spend, is £1,511,000.

Payback – results to date

If we subtract the costs (£1,511,000) from the advertising revenue attributable to the rebrand (£5,989,000), we arrive at the profit contribution of £4,478,000 attributable to the rebrand or, for every pound spent on the rebrand, a return on investment of £2.99.

Payback – five-year forecast

In considering the five-year forecast, all new programming would still have been commissioned and acquired had the channel still been named Uktv G2 and so the only costs to take into consideration are the continuing marketing costs of Dave. These are costed at £14.14m over the period. Therefore, using the same mean average (27.4%) increase attributable to the rebrand, we see that, for the five-year forecast, the rebrand equates to a profit of £9.8m.

Additional economic benefits

While the profit driver for Dave is impacts, an important factor for the channel is its relationship with the media agencies who buy the advertising on behalf of advertisers. It's important that Dave is seen and heard, and is on their considera-tion and recommendation list. What we have seen among this group is that the rebrand has had a transformative effect. They are far more considerate of the channel as a key tool to attract the difficult-to-reach, yet highly valuable young upmarket men (see Figure 35).

Another source of revenue for Dave is that of sponsorship. Again, we see the dramatic effect that the rebrand has – resulting in the recent deal with Cobra beer (see Figure 36).

Figure 35: Positive impact of Dave for media agencies

'A refreshing example of how to re-brand a TV channel and certainly the most successful re-branding to date. In the past, TV buyers looked at Uktv G2 as another station in an extremely cluttered market but Dave, having capitalised on the Freeview surge, is now a must have for any male TV brands – the likes of E4 and ITV2 watch out as they are no longer guaranteed positions 1 and 2 in the multi-channel hierarchy. Despite the combination of old school entertainment and established content Dave's schedule appears fresh and original and there is always something to watch ... long may Dave continue to provide a channel that reaches out to those elusive younger upmarket males'.

Ben Chesters, TV Group Director (Scottish & Newcastle Account), Starcom Mediavest

'I, along with the rest of the industry, have been astonished at how successful the rebranding of Uktv G2 to Dave has been. Quite simply the rebranding has seen the channel elevated from being "just another satellite channel" to one of the jewels in Uktv's crown. It is now an essential part of any schedule targeting those elusive young and upmarket viewers, delivering in both quantity and quality of audience.'

Luke Duffy, Carat

Figure 36: Positive impact of Dave on developing commercial partnerships

'Approaching brands on behalf of Uktv G2 to discuss partnership opportunities was always a challenge for the simple reason that no-one knew what it was. Making approaches on behalf of Dave could not be more different. Marketers for major brands immediately know Dave and have an understanding of its personality and positioning as well as its programming. People in the past who were reluctant to even take our calls are now eager to explore ways we can work together. The shift in awareness has been truly phenomenal'.

Elaine Robertson, Managing Director, Mediator

'As one of the UK's fastest growing UK beer brands, its is really important for Cobra to continue to find new ways of engaging with our target audience of 28–34-year-old men. Our sponsorship of Dave will give us exactly that opportunity, allowing us to reach a high proportion of our core consumers on a daily basis and become associated with quality TV programming.'

Will Ghali, Marketing Director, Cobra Beer

However, before the rebrand can claim credit for the increased advertising revenue, we must consider other factors that could have been responsible for the uplift in the growth.

1. Was it new programming?

Some 87.3% of content on Dave since launch was broadcast on Uktv G2. The 12.7% 'new' content from the BBC archive would have appeared on Uktv G2 anyway, as rights deals require a minimum of 90 days to clear. This content was added to the stocklist before rebranding. The only exception is *World Rally Championships* (WRC), which launched in January 2008. But this aired three months after the rebrand launch date.

Lastly, the strongest Dave programmes are largely Uktv G2 titles that greatly increased their audience because of the rebrand (see Figure 37).

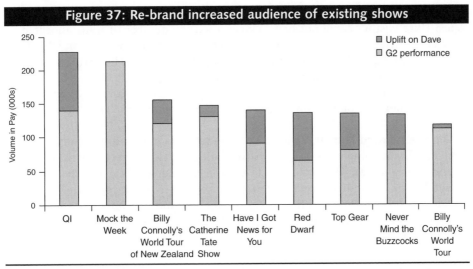

Figure 37: Re-brand increased audience of existing shows

Source: BARB

2. Was the Freeview audience a better match for Dave?

If the Freeview audience matched Dave's target audience profile better than the 'Pay' audience who could access Uktv G2, this could have aided the channel's Freeview launch. However, the Freeview audience are demographically less likely than their Pay counterparts to be predisposed towards a channel targeted to ABC1 males aged 16–44. This made it harder to reach our target audience. Rather than being a factor contributing to the channel's success, the profile of the new audience was a challenge the rebrand successfully overcame (see Figure 38).

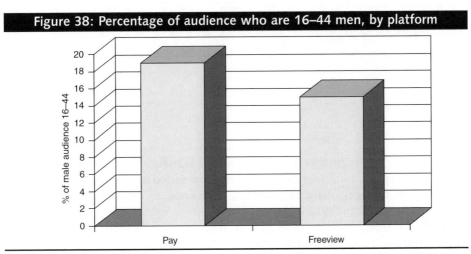

Figure 38: Percentage of audience who are 16–44 men, by platform

Source: BARB

3. Was it the result of increased on-air promotion?

When Uktv History came out of Freeview peak, the number of trails allocated to the channel swapped with Dave. Therefore Dave's allocation went from Uktv G2's six promos per month to Dave's nine – a straight swap with History.

However, despite an increase in promotion on air, these trails are only communicating with an audience who were already on the channel. We know that the Dave rebrand brought in 8m new viewers from outside the Uktv network.[4]

4. Did the rebrand launch coincide with beneficial competitor activity?

Had significant competitors recently dropped out of the market, this would have provided a ready audience that could have increased viewing. On the contrary, Dave's launch coincided exactly with that of Virgin1, a direct competitor.

This was a real threat to the success of the rebrand and unfavourable market conditions for launch; however, the rebrand withstood this competition to witness sustained growth at a much stronger rate than Virgin1 (see Figure 39).

Figure 39: Dave witnessed sustained growth against key competitor launching at the same time

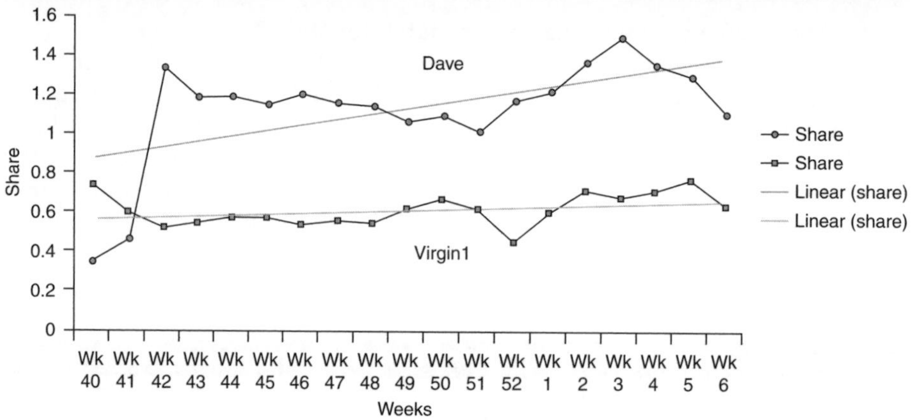

Source: BARB

Conclusion

This is a remarkable case that demonstrates how branding alone was a more potent and effective engine for growth than any tried and tested market convention. It has already delivered real financial payback, amounting to £4.5m additional profit within the first six months of relaunch. The return on investment is a healthy £2.99 for every £1 spent. It is a case of a little voice that used creativity and strategic insight to make a big noise; that came from relative obscurity to be the best in its class in a fiercely competitive market.

Notes

1. Average time spent watching TV per day: 4 hours 48 minutes (all UK adults post 16). Source: BARB. Average time spent in paid employment per day: 2 hours 50 minutes (all UK adults post 16). Source: Office of National Statistics, *The Time Use Survey* 2005, published August 2006.
2. Competition Commission.
3. *Daily Telegraph*, 13 April 2008.
4. BARB/Infosys.

Chapter 11

KFC

Finger lickin' good results: how celebrating taste reversed the fortunes of KFC

By Ed Booty and Jude Lowson, BBH
Contributing authors: Debbie Williams, KFC, and
Patricia McDonald, BBH
Consultant: Paul Dyson, Data2Decisions

Editor's summary

It is so often a case that marketers and agencies are praised for the speed and creativity with which they respond to emergent market trends. This, however, is a paper that demonstrates considerable success through sticking to what the brand has always offered, in the face of counter-trends.

In 2005, as health concerns mounted among the general public, KFC was losing penetration, sales and market share. The communications challenge was therefore to attract back lapsing users. The immediately appealing solution would have been to present KFC as new, improved and healthier. This was certainly the approach taken by key competitors such as McDonalds. Instead, KFC and its agency BBH, decided that rather than surrender the core appeal of their product – its great taste – they would celebrate it.

KFC demonstrated its strength in the core promise of the category, rather than hide behind a veneer or healthier claims. The results of this counter-intuitive approach were startling. Fortunes turned around almost immediately with sales and share value returning to growth.

Using a combination of measures, this paper demonstrates how KFC's commitment to great fast-food helped generate significant incremental sales, returning over £4 for every £1 spent on advertising.

Introduction

This is the story of a dramatic revival in the fortunes of one of the nation's best-known fast-food brands. It is a revival against all the odds, and a revival achieved by going against every received wisdom in the category.

In 2005, things looked bleak for KFC. The 'health agenda' reached critical mass, with relentless media commentary around child obesity and the 'fast food nation'. Consumers, inspired by the likes of 'Dr' Gillian McKeith and Jamie Oliver, viewed Turkey Twizzlers, burgers and fried chicken with profound suspicion. Consumers were moving away from fast food, resulting in declining market penetration, share and sales for KFC.

The immediately attractive solution was to embrace a new, healthier positioning, with advertising communicating the health credentials of the brand. However, KFC defied convention by unashamedly celebrating the irresistible taste of its core fried chicken products. Rather than remind people of all the health concerns that had turned them away from fast food, KFC opted to remind people of why they loved it in the first place.

We will demonstrate that this counter-intuitive approach led to an almost immediate reversal in sales performance. We will show that consumers returned to the brand in greater numbers and bought more chicken than ever before. We will show that KFC bucked all category trends to deliver both sales and share growth in a potentially disastrous market context. We will link this turnaround inextricably to advertising and demonstrate an ROI of over 1:4.5.

This paper is about a brand facing a perfect storm, the likes of which few ever experience. However, there are learnings beyond the fast-food industry for every brand. This is a story about simplicity and focus amid temptation to diversify. It is about brand confidence, and about keeping your head when all around are losing theirs.

Background

KFC[1] is the original chicken fast-food brand. It was founded (in Kentucky) by Colonel Harland Sanders in 1945. KFC is now owned by YUM! International, based in Dallas, but to this day serves its famous Original Recipe chicken made with 11 herbs and spices.

The brand arrived in Britain in 1965. It now has a national turnover in excess of £650m a year.[2]

Its main competitors need little introduction: McDonald's is the dominant force in the market with more than 1,000 outlets,[3] followed by Burger King. The branded fast-food market is worth over £3.6bn annually.[4]

Fast-food brands had enjoyed strong growth throughout the 1990s, but by 2005 the outlook appeared to be very different.[5]

Market conditions

In 2005, fast-food brands became public enemy number one; the health debate stopped quietly simmering and began to truly boil over. Jamie Oliver began his quest to rid the nation's schools of Turkey Twizzlers. 'Dr' Gillian McKeith reminded the public that they were what they ate. Morgan Spurlock ate nothing but fast food for 30 days, documenting the results in the film *Super Size Me* (see Figure 1).

Figure 1: UK – Fast-food nation

Source: Various

Figure 2: Media focus on health

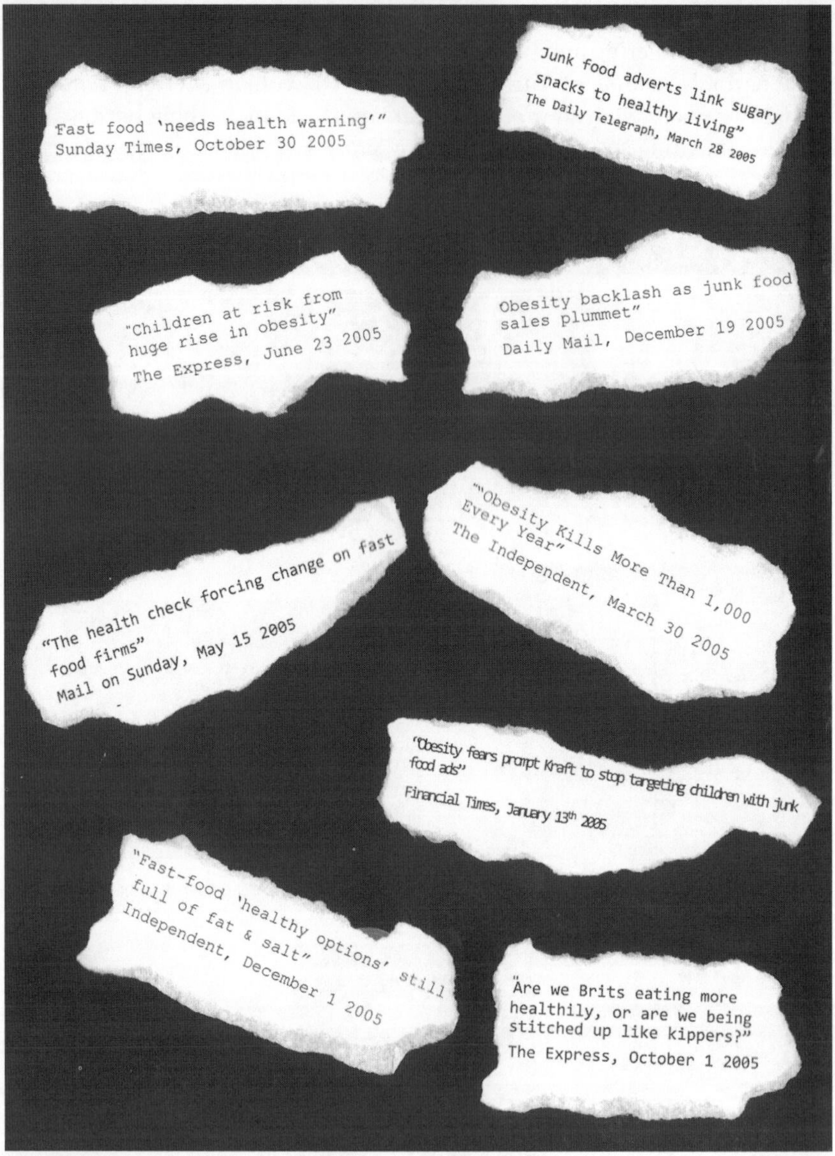

Fast food 'needs health warning'"
Sunday Times, October 30 2005

Junk food adverts link sugary
snacks to healthy living"
The Daily Telegraph, March 28 2005

"Children at risk from
huge rise in obesity"
The Express, June 23 2005

Obesity backlash as junk food
sales plummet"
Daily Mail, December 19 2005

"The health check forcing change on fast
food firms"
Mail on Sunday, May 15 2005

"'Obesity Kills More Than 1,000
Every Year"
The Independent, March 30 2005

"Obesity fears prompt Kraft to stop targeting children with junk
food ads"
Financial Times, January 13th 2005

"Fast-food 'healthy options' still
full of fat & salt"
Independent, December 1 2005

"Are we Brits eating more
healthily, or are we being
stitched up like kippers?"
The Express, October 1 2005

Source: Reuters

The media began a crusade against 'junk' and fast food, and consumers became increasingly health aware (see Figure 2).[6]

Consequently, consumers began to move away from the idea of fast food as a whole. However, it was fast-food brands[7] on which the debate focused and who suffered most (see Figure 3).

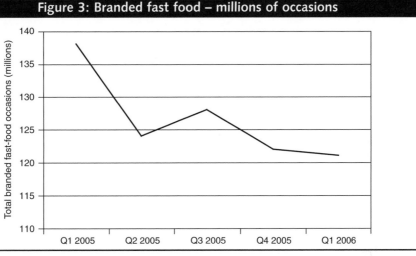

Figure 3: Branded fast food – millions of occasions

Source: Brand Image Tracker Report, Conquest Research. Hereafter referred to as 'BIT Report, Conquest'

Business challenge

This harsh environment had dire implications for KFC. Penetration was falling rapidly as consumers stayed away from a demonised market (see Figure 4).[8]

This decline was particularly steep among family users (see Figure 5).

Youth[9] penetration was also dropping (see Figure 6). In addition to the new health agenda, people were faced with a proliferation of choice on the high street, with brands such as Subway and Pret A Manger[10] in rapid growth. KFC was slipping out of the repertoire of this notoriously fickle audience.

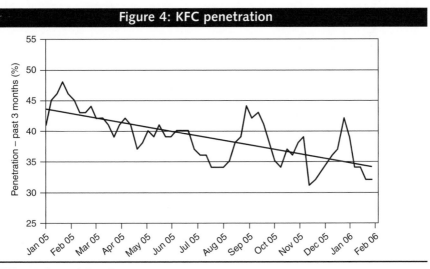

Figure 4: KFC penetration

Source: BIT Report, Conquest. Base: Pop

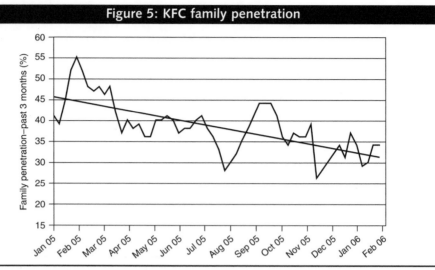

Figure 5: KFC family penetration

Source: BIT Report, Conquest. Base: Families

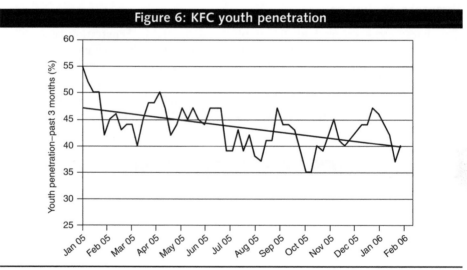

Figure 6: KFC youth penetration

Source: BIT Report, Conquest. Base: Youth

Together, these two audiences account for 89% of KFC's sales.[11]

Declining penetration among them was leading to a serious overall decline in value sales.[12]

Weekly average value sales[13] per store were £2,000 lower in Q1 2006 than they had been in Q1 2005 (see Figure 7). A weekly per store average decline from £17,500 to £15,500 equates to an average of £625,000 in lost revenue for KFC every week.

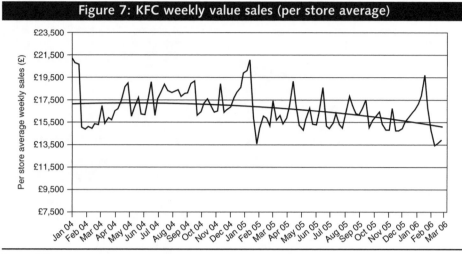

Figure 7: KFC weekly value sales (per store average)

Source: KFC

To reverse this decline and return to value sales growth, KFC needed to bring lapsed users back to the brand.

More specifically, KFC needed to increase penetration for the two core audiences, namely families and youth (see Figure 8).

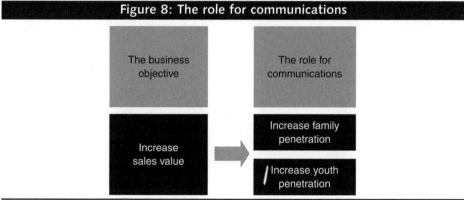

Figure 8: The role for communications

Source: BBH

Strategic solution

Competitor behaviour

Faced with the same problem, KFC's competitors tried to lure lapsed consumers back to the category by presenting themselves as a healthy option.

Despite being brands famed for (and dependent upon) selling burgers and chips, the category's advertising was suddenly awash with salad and packets of fruit (see Figure 9).

Figure 9: Competitor health-focused communications

Source: Xtreme Information

It was an understandable response, but one that lacked credibility for consumers:

You've decided to go to McDonald's. Why would you buy chopped up apple?!

C1 Mum, Bristol, Leading Edge qualitative research, 2006

Turning convention on its head

KFC too needed to regain lapsed users. Pretending to be something KFC was not would have clearly lacked conviction. But what would motivate people to return to KFC?

An alternative approach was needed. The answer was surprisingly simple.

Fast food tastes good

The obesity debate had given consumers a new awareness that a diet heavily dependent on 'fast food' was not healthy. However, this didn't mean they wanted total abstinence from their favourite food. Although they might be indulging less often, when they did they wanted proper indulgence. They didn't want fast food to be 'good for you'. Consumers choose fast food because it tastes good.

In chasing the health agenda, KFC's competitors were turning their back on what people know and want from fast food: taste and indulgence.

KFC tastes especially good

There's something especially compelling about the taste of KFC's Original Recipe:

> *You can't make it yourself and competitors can't get close.*
> C1 Mum, New Malden, Leading Edge qualitative research, 2006

Love of KFC's unique taste unified all consumers. Once the desire for KFC is sparked, there is nothing else that will satisfy the urge.

Our strategy: putting taste at the heart of communications

KFC chose therefore to showcase great-tasting food at the heart of communications – to remind consumers of what makes KFC truly unique.

This was a radical step. While KFC's competitors attempted to embrace healthy eating trends, KFC repositioned itself around an unashamed celebration of taste. In so doing, KFC would remind lapsing users of what they loved and missed about the brand. KFC needed to create pure food desire for our audience; to spark that unique and irresistible KFC craving. Celebrating the core chicken product also allowed KFC to remind people that, while not the healthiest option, KFC is made with real chicken.

Audience segmentation

Great taste was identified as the most motivating brand truth among consumers as a whole. Until now, communications had addressed them as a homogeneous group, but the brand's two key consumer groups actually had very different needs and hence a different relationship with the brand. Communications were realigned to acknowledge and exploit these differences under the overarching banner of taste.

Families are the key driver of value sales, spending significantly more per transaction.[14] The youth audience is the driver of volume sales,[15] but they are relatively low spenders. To drive value sales, families became our primary audience.

1. Targeting families

Mums are the key decision makers at family dinners. KFC acts as an economical and convenient way to feed hungry mouths, but they had been lapsing from the brand in large numbers. Feeding the kids had become a fraught and guilt-ridden experience. Mums wanted to feel that someone understood and empathised with the realities of feeding a young family.

In order to bring mums back, KFC needed to remind them what was great about the brand. It had to make them feel good about buying it by demonstrating how it suited their lifestyle and aspirations. It had to be something they could relate to, empathise with and feel positive about purchasing.

2. Young adults

Young adults are frequent purchasers of fast food, but with the increased presence of new brands, were also drifting away from KFC.

Their mealtimes are less formally defined than those of families; they're impulsive eaters, snacking whenever they're hungry. They follow their cravings and aren't brand loyal – constantly looking for novelty and variety.

KFC needed to create a sense of constant novelty and excitement, so that when hunger struck, it would be met with an irrepressible urge for KFC.

In summary, the objectives for communications were threefold:

1. overall to create food desire and remind people of what they love about KFC
2. to evoke a new empathy with mums
3. to prompt a craving for KFC with the youth audience by creating a sense of novelty and excitement about the brand.

See Figure 10.

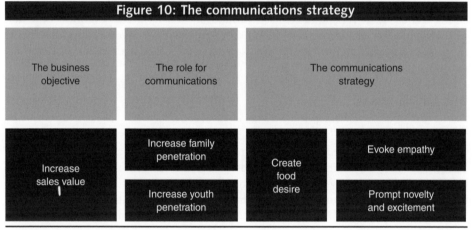

Figure 10: The communications strategy

The business objective	The role for communications	The communications strategy

| Increase sales value | Increase family penetration | Create food desire | Evoke empathy |
| | Increase youth penetration | | Prompt novelty and excitement |

Source: BBH

Implementing the new approach

Media

Having established specific target audiences, Walker Media was responsible for developing a highly focused media strategy designed to connect with our two separate audience groups. Rather than fragmenting our spend across multiple channels, we focused on the two most relevant channels (see Figure 11).

This strategy was not about an overall increase in share of voice; due to increased competition, KFC's SOV actually declined slightly over the period. It was about a more focused and targeted use of the budget available.

Mums

Mums are keen viewers of evening television, so primetime TV was used to create the desired emotional connection at a time when dinner is on their mind (see Figure 12).

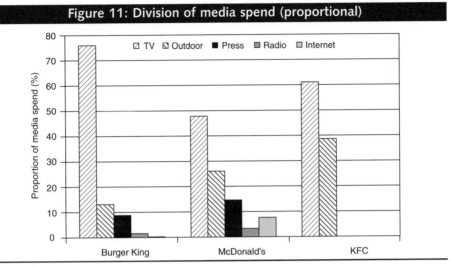

Figure 11: Division of media spend (proportional)

Source: Walker Media/Nielsen

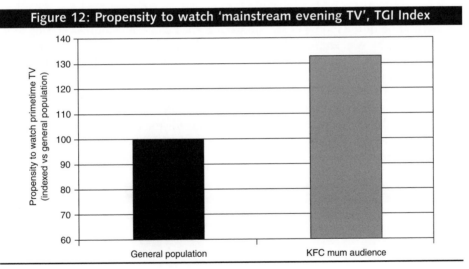

Figure 12: Propensity to watch 'mainstream evening TV', TGI Index

Source: TGI

Youth

Posters became the lead medium for targeting young adults, who are frequently out and about and hungry. Investment in outdoor enabled KFC to create a craving at the point of purchase.

Media was bought in close proximity to stores, meaning this craving could be acted on at once (see Figure 13). This activity was supplemented by limited, highly targeted TV.

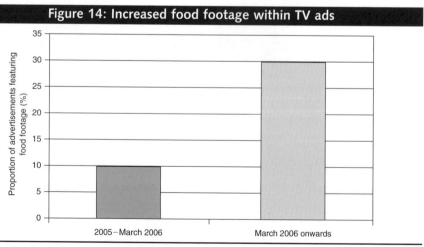

Figure 13: Proportion of media spend on outdoor, average monthly %

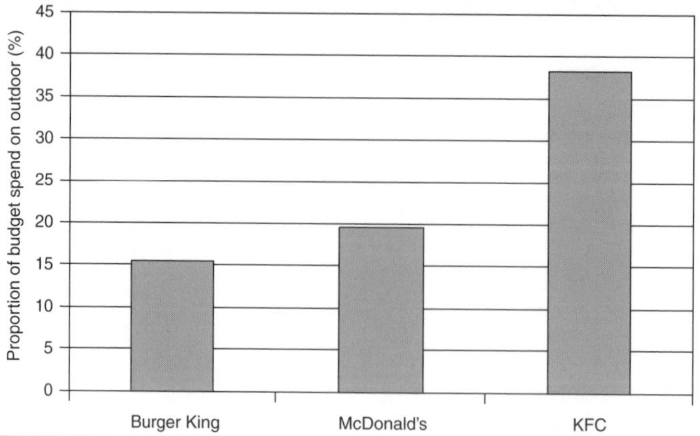

Source: Walker Media/Nielsen

Creative work

1. **Celebrating the food.** Primarily, our creative work became an unashamed celebration of the food KFC is famous for: fried chicken. Mouth-watering food photography was employed across TV and posters (see Figure 14). The food had to look delicious and to dominate the commercial. The chicken was handled with the skill and devotion usually reserved for a Hollywood star.

2. **Mums.** To build that all-important sense of empathy, advertising delivered a slice of recognisable family life – communicating real and familiar truths that would build a sense of warmth and relevance for the brand. We wanted mums to recognise their own lives and emotions in the ads. Everyday family life became the setting, and casting was similarly down to earth.

Figure 14: Increased food footage within TV ads

Source: Xtreme Information

3. **Youth.** Appetising products were put at the heart of posters to spark a craving with this impulsive audience. The result was loud, proud and appetising. The posters created a sense of news around the food, each celebrating a single piece of product news.

The new campaign broke in mid-March 2006.

Examples of advertising: families

Figures 15–18 show examples of the advertising directed at families.

Figure 15: Copycat – Mum's Night Off – February 2007

Little girl hoovers around her mum, 'Lift up!'

Little girl takes the washing out of the machine, 'I've been on my feet all day'.

Family sitting around the table eating KFC. *VO: Give Mum a break with the KFC Mum's Night Off Bucket.*

VO: Six pieces of original recipe popcorn chicken, fries, sides . . .

. . . drink and Rolo ice cream.

'Best get on with the washing up then.'

VO: And disposable plates and cutlery. The KFC Mum's Night Off Bucket.

Figure 16: Henry – Deluxe Boneless Box – October 2006

Little girl puts the crusts on Henry's plate.

She then puts her egg on his plate, 'Here you go Henry, you like the white bits'.

Family look at her expectantly, 'No, Henry doesn't like boneless chicken'.

VO: The KFC Deluxe Boneless Box, eight original recipe mini breast fillets.

VO: Two regular popcorn chickens, fries, large sides, Pepsi and a choice of dips all for only £12.99.

VO: Kids won't leave a thing.

Figure 17: DVD – Variety Bucket – April 2007

'What about that?'

'Dad, I'd rather watch paint dry.'

VO: We all know families can't always agree so the KFC Variety Bucket has . . .

VO: . . . four pieces of original recipe chicken, four pure breast mini fillets . . .

VO: . . . popcorn and fries, just £9.99.

'It's a film!' 'A book!' 'Two words!'

VO: The KFC Variety Bucket – pleasing everyone just got easier.

Figure 18: Are we there yet? Family Feast – November 2006

'Are we there yet?'

'Are we there yet?'

'Yes! We're there!'

VO: The KFC Family Feast, eight pieces of succulent chicken . . .

VO: . . . four fries, a bottle of Pepsi and 2 large sides.

VO: The perfect way to end a family day.

Examples of advertising: youth

Figure 19 shows examples of advertising aimed at the youth market.

Figure 19: Examples of posters from the campaign

Commercial results

Our objectives were clear. KFC needed to return to value sales growth by bringing lapsed users back to the brand. Specifically the campaign had to result in:

1. **Increased penetration with the family audience.** The return of the high-spending family audience was to be crucial to KFC's resurgence. Penetration among families increased significantly throughout 2006 and 2007 (see Figure 20).
2. **Increased youth penetration.** Penetration also recovered among the youth audience (see Figure 21).

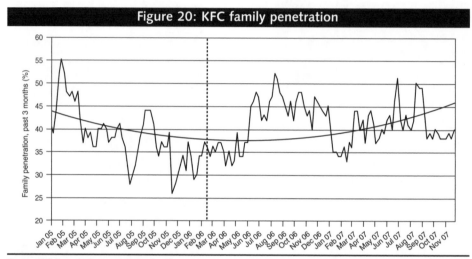

Figure 20: KFC family penetration

Source: BIT Report, Conquest. Base: Families

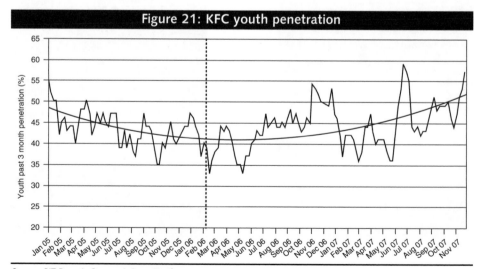

Figure 21: KFC youth penetration

Source: BIT Report, Conquest. Base: Youth

As a result of enticing high-spending families back to the brand, we also saw a sharp increase in average transaction value, which rose more than 10% in the campaign period (see Figure 22).

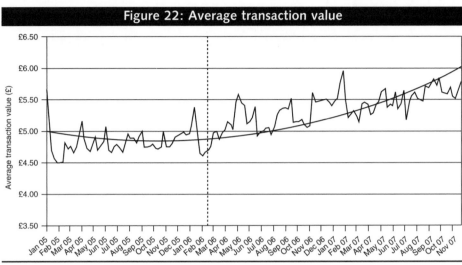

Figure 22: Average transaction value

Source: KFC

As a result, value sales increased significantly (see Figure 23).

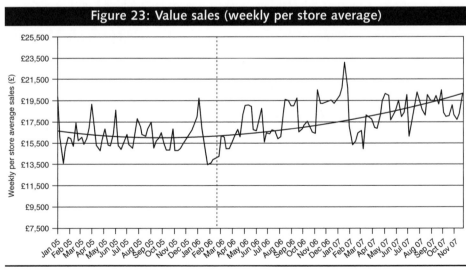

Figure 23: Value sales (weekly per store average)

Source: KFC

Share also increased, demonstrating that KFC's success bucked the trend for the category (see Figure 24).

Figure 24: KFC's share of occasions, total fast food

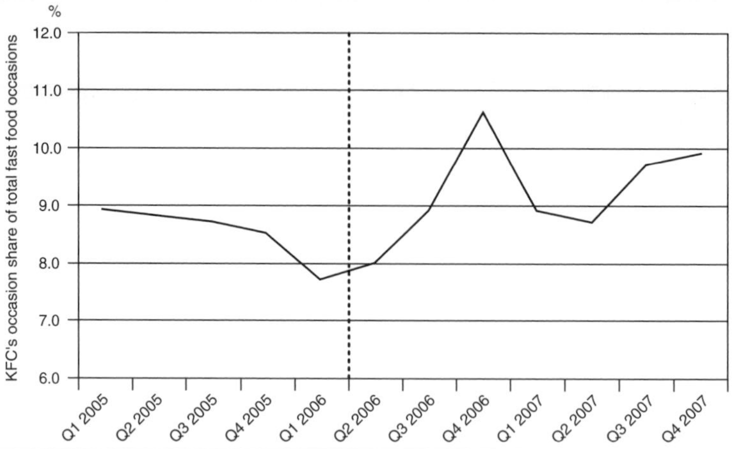

Source: BIT report, Conquest, KFC

The impact of advertising

We have demonstrated a sharp turnaround in the fortunes of KFC concurrent with the change in advertising strategy. We will now demonstrate that advertising was the key driver of this reversal of fortune and that the growth cannot be accounted for by any other variables. We will demonstrate this in three ways:

1. by demonstrating that advertising worked exactly as intended with our target audience
2. by quantifying or eliminating all other variables that could have contributed to sales growth over the period
3. by using econometric modelling to precisely identify and quantify the contribution of advertising to KFC's total sales over the period.

The advertising worked as intended

We have already demonstrated that the necessary changes in consumer behaviour took place in order to return KFC to growth. Both families and youth returned to the brand in significant numbers. We will now demonstrate that advertising worked as intended to create the attitudinal changes that prompted this return.

The objectives of the advertising were threefold:

1. to create food desire
2. to evoke a new empathy with families
3. to prompt a craving for KFC with the youth audience by creating a sense of novelty and excitement about the brand.

1. Creating food desire

The campaign had to remind consumers of the great taste of KFC chicken and to bring KFC to front of mind with lapsed users.

Perceptions of KFC's food versus that of its competitors rose dramatically across all audiences (see Figure 25).

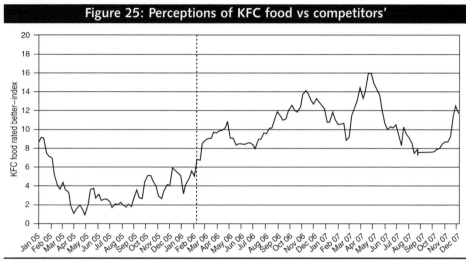

Figure 25: Perceptions of KFC food vs competitors'

Source: BIT report, Conquest

Advertising during the campaign was more successful in communicating that 'KFC has delicious-tasting food' (see Figure 26).

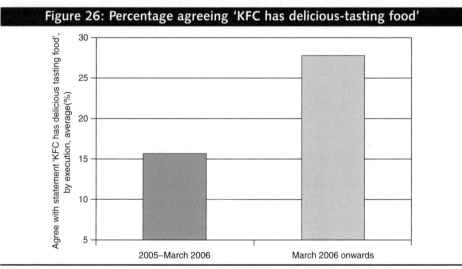

Figure 26: Percentage agreeing 'KFC has delicious-tasting food'

Source: BIT report, Conquest. Base: Fast food users aware of KFC advertising

KFC evolved from being one of a host of 'also-ran' competitors to being a clear second favourite in the market, gaining on McDonald's (see Figure 27).

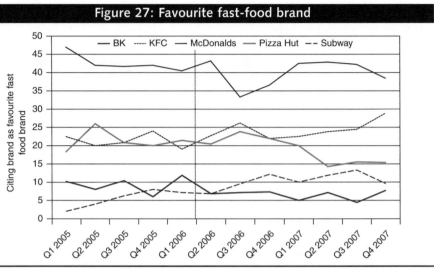

Figure 27: Favourite fast-food brand

Source: BIT Report, Conquest

2. Evoking a new empathy with families

Our goal with this audience was to create a new empathy with the brand.

The new campaign was significantly more successful in creating empathy than the previous advertising (see Figure 28).

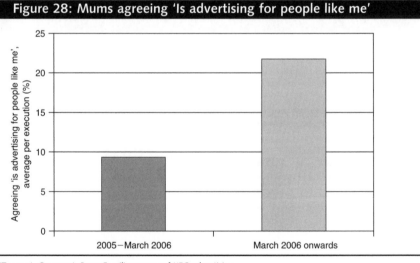

Figure 28: Mums agreeing 'Is advertising for people like me'

Source: BIT report, Conquest. Base: Families aware of KFC advertising

Moreover, the strategy worked: the more we managed to evoke empathy in the TV executions, the more mums were compelled to go to KFC (see Figure 29).

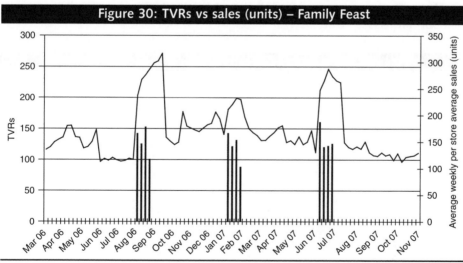

Figure 29: Correlation between empathy and compulsion to visit KFC for mums

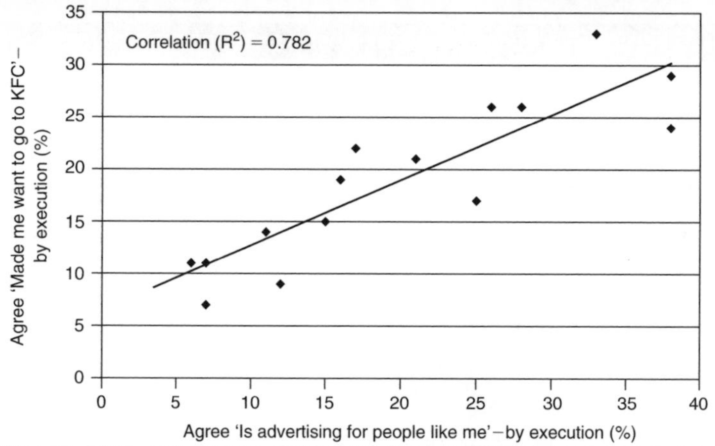

Correlation (R^2) = 0.782
Agree 'Made me want to go to KFC' – by execution (%)
Agree 'Is advertising for people like me' – by execution (%)
0
5
10
15
20
25
30
35
40

Source: BIT Report, Conquest. Base: Families aware of KFC advertising

Consequently, when ads targeting families were aired, sales of the product in question rose significantly (see Figure 30).

Figure 30: TVRs vs sales (units) – Family Feast

TVRs
Average weekly per store average sales (units)
0
50
100
150
200
250
300
350
Mar 06
Apr 06
May 06
Jun 06
Jul 06
Aug 06
Sep 06
Oct 06
Nov 06
Dec 06
Jan 07
Feb 07
Mar 07
Apr 07
May 07
Jun 07
Jul 07
Aug 07
Sep 07
Oct 07
Nov 07

Source: KFC and Walker Media

3. Prompting a craving for KFC among the youth audience by creating a sense of novelty and excitement

With the youth audience, KFC needed to create a sense of novelty and excitement about the products, which would prompt an insatiable craving for KFC and maintain brand interest versus distracting new competitors.

The posters were highly impactful and attention grabbing, exceeding recognition norms for the medium (see Figure 31).

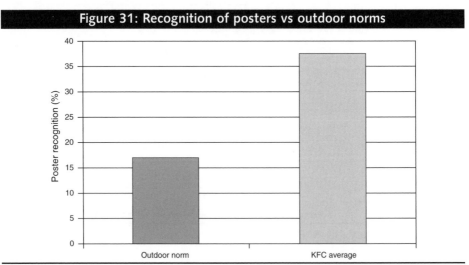

Figure 31: Recognition of posters vs outdoor norms

Source: BIT report, Conquest. Norm: Conquest Outdoor Normative database, Conquest. Base: Youth

They were also inextricably linked to KFC, with branding far in excess of outdoor norms (see Figure 32).

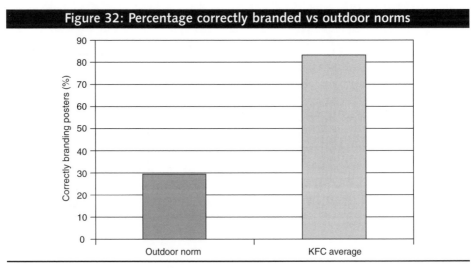

Figure 32: Percentage correctly branded vs outdoor norms

Source: BIT report, Conquest. Norm: Conquest outdoor normative database, Conquest. Base: Youth

Advertising in the campaign period communicated a renewed sense that KFC's food was more 'new and different' (see Figure 33).

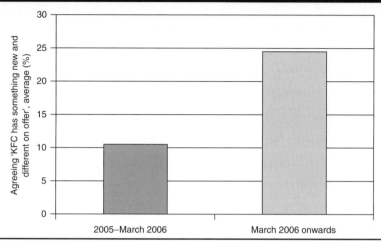

Figure 33: Youth agreeing 'KFC has something new and different on offer'
– average, per execution

Source: BIT report, Conquest. Base: Youth recognising ads

Again, the advertising worked as intended: the more a poster prompted a sense of excitement and difference around the products, the more motivated the audience was to visit KFC (see Figure 34).

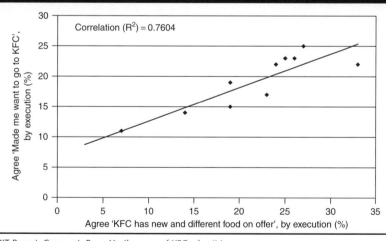

Figure 34: Correlation between novelty/difference and compulsion to visit KFC for youth

Source: BIT Report, Conquest. Base: Youth aware of KFC advertising

Finally, when posters targeting youth ran, sales of the product in question rose dramatically (see Figure 35).

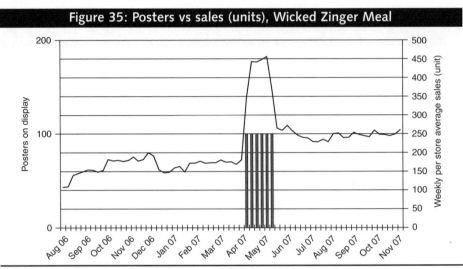

Figure 35: Posters vs sales (units), Wicked Zinger Meal

Source: Walker Media/KFC

In summary, we can demonstrate that advertising worked as intended across all the key measures to shift consumer perceptions of KFC and drive purchase intent (see Table 1).

Table 1: Advertising worked as expected	
Communications objective	**Result**
To create food desire	Improved taste perceptions vs competitors
	Advertising strongly communicates 'KFC has great tasting food'
	Brand popularity grew
To evoke a new empathy with mums	The advertising prompted a stronger sense of empathy
	When mums empathise with the advertising, they are more compelled to visit KFC
	Sales of advertised core products peak when advertising is on air
To prompt a craving for KFC among the youth audience	The posters achieved high recognition and branding scores among the target audience
	The advertising prompted a stronger sense of novelty and difference
	When the advertising prompts a sense of novelty and difference with youth, they are more compelled to visit KFC
	Sales of advertised core products peak when posters are up

We will now go on to demonstrate that no other factors could have been responsible for KFC's recovery, by quantifying or eliminating all other variables that could have impacted KFC sales over the period.

Eliminating other variables

Clearly, a number of other factors could have impacted on KFC sales over the period. In order to isolate the impact of advertising, we have examined all other factors that could have had an impact. In most cases, we will demonstrate that their effect is negligible. Where an effect is present, it has been quantified or eliminated using a combination of econometric modelling and other data. We will examine variables in four key areas, from micro – effects of KFC's own marketing strategy – to macro – effects in the broader socio-economic environment:

1. KFC's business
2. competition
3. the wider market
4. the broader socio-economic environment.

1. KFC's business

(a) *The food*

■ **Did food quality and taste improve?**
KFC's food quality did not change during this period; the Colonel's secret blend of 11 herbs and spices, the core of the recipe, has remained unchanged since the brand's inception. The taste and quality of chicken remained constant.[16]

■ **Did the product range increase?**
The total number of products on offer did not alter significantly between 2005 and 2007. The product range is continuously being slightly adapted; however, there was no significant change in this period.[17]

■ **Did KFC offer more and better new products?**
While advertising did drive perceptions of novelty, this is the effect of improved communication, not a material improvement in NPD.

KFC operates a nine-window promotional calendar with limited time offers every year, often featuring simple flavour variants or new bundles of pre-existent products. However:

- the rate at which new products entered the KFC menu remained constant[18] versus 2005
- the quality of the new products remained constant; new products are tested independently, prior to launch; the pass thresholds of testing remained constant, with 'Purchase Intention' and 'Appeal' averages remaining constant both prior to and during the campaign
- the effect of limited time menu additions on sales mix has been accounted for in the model.

(b) *Price*

KFC did not discount price in 2005 or 2006–2007.[19]

(c) *Distribution*

■ **Did KFC open up more stores?**
KFC opened up new stores, but these sales results are not included in the per-store averages. All sales data referred to in this paper relate to existing stores only.

■ **Were stores open longer?**
KFC's opening hours remained 11am–11pm throughout the period.[20]

■ **Did KFC stores improve?**
Store refreshes and refurbishments did take place over the period. By analysis of sales performance at a store-by-store level we have been able to isolate and quantify the impact of refurbishment.

Overall perceptions of the stores remained constant (see Figure 36).

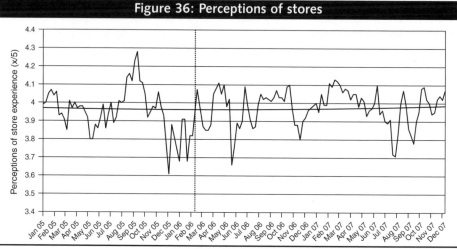

Figure 36: Perceptions of stores

Source: BIT Report Conquest. Base: KFC users

■ **Did KFC's media spend increase dramatically?**
While KFC's media spend grew slightly, its share of voice actually shrank from 22% to 18% as competitor spend increased disproportionately (see Figure 37).

■ **Public relations**
KFC did not invest in any active PR activity between 2005 and 2007, so coverage was low. Due to the health debate, the PR KFC did receive was overwhelmingly negative. The influence of PR on sales can only be considered to be adverse (see Figure 38).

2. Competitor activity
■ **Was KFC simply the beneficiary of a decline in McDonald's reputation?**
Supersize Me, the documentary whose maker and star ate nothing but McDonald's for 30 days, was released in 2004.

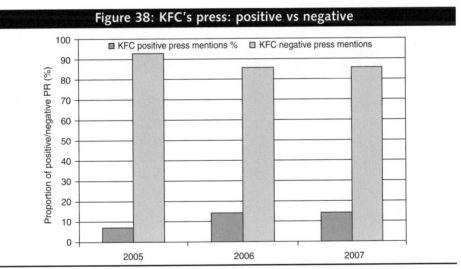

Figure 37: Share of voice – KFC vs competitors

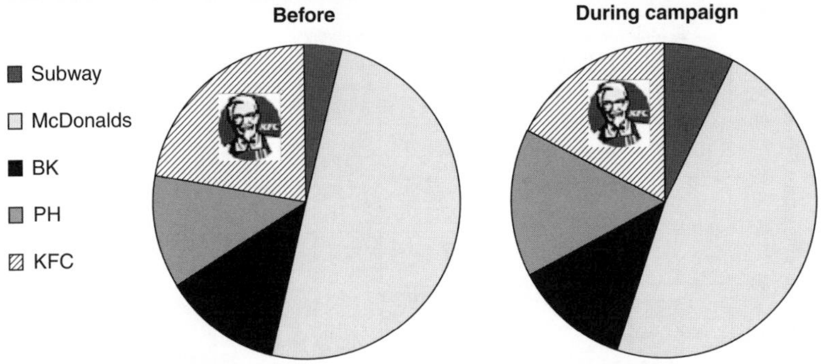

Before　　　　　During campaign

- Subway
- McDonalds
- BK
- PH
- KFC

Source: Walker Media

Figure 38: KFC's press: positive vs negative

■ KFC positive press mentions %　□ KFC negative press mentions

Proportion of positive/negative PR (%)

2005　　2006　　2007

Source: Reuters

However, the majority of negative press following the film attacked fast food as a whole – affecting the whole category equally, not just McDonald's.

Anti-McDonald's activity was a fraction of the overall press related to fast food and healthy eating. Of all the press articles about junk food in 2005–2007, only 3.2% directly mentioned McDonald's.[21]

KFC was not the beneficiary of increasing negative sentiment towards McDonald's. The balance of positive and negative press about McDonald's remained constant prior to and during the campaign (see Figure 39).

KFC consumers' relationship with McDonald's became only very slightly weaker in this period (see Figure 40).

Figure 39: McDonald's press: positive vs negative

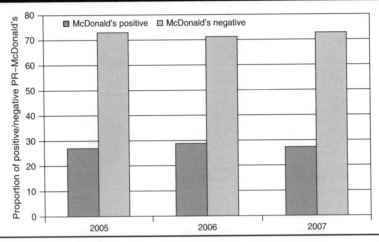

Source: Reuters

Figure 40: McDonald's penetration among KFC users

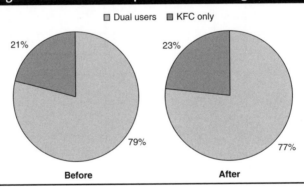

Source: BIT report, Conquest

■ Did KFC's competitors' prices increase?

We do not have rolling price data for competitors. However, we know that there were no significant increases in KFC's competitors' prices that could have benefited KFC. Competitors did run a number of price and sales promotions during this period, with competitions, offers and discounts (see Figure 41). Overall, average spend remains static over the period (see Table 2).

Table 2: Average spend per head

	2005	2007
Burger King	£3.97	£3.91
McDonald's	£4.01	£4.00

Source: Post Purchase User Survey, Conquest

Figure 41: Selected competitor price promotions

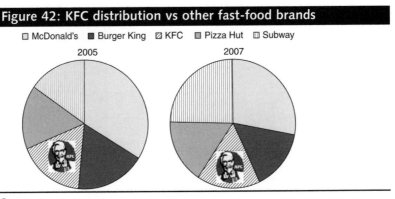

Source: Xtreme Information

■ **Did KFC's competitors' products get worse?**

KFC's competitors' core offerings remained constant, without significant alterations to their core burger and chicken ranges. They did significantly extend their range of products with additional healthier items.

■ **Did competitor distribution decline?**

The number of McDonald's outlets declined marginally over the period, but the rapid expansion of Subway and Pizza Hut meant that KFC's share of outlets remained the same (17%) (see Figure 42).

Figure 42: KFC distribution vs other fast-food brands

☐ McDonald's ■ Burger King ▨ KFC ▤ Pizza Hut ▥ Subway

2005   2007

Source: Mintel/KFC

3. The wider market context

■ **Was KFC a beneficiary of category recovery?**

KFC grew share as well as sales, showing that it was not simply a beneficiary of category growth. Within total fast food, the branded fast-food segment (McDonald's, Burger King, etc.) continued to decline, with KFC proving a notable exception (see Figure 43).

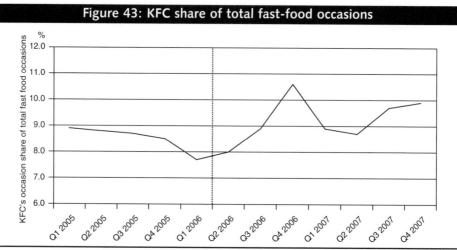

Figure 43: KFC share of total fast-food occasions

Source: BIT Report, Conquest, KFC

■ **Did chicken become more popular than other meats?**

The nation's taste in meat type did not alter significantly in this period. Occasions involving other meats grew slightly, while chicken remained constant (see Figure 44).

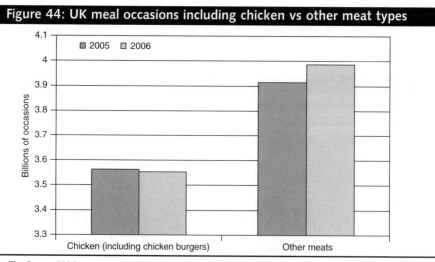

Figure 44: UK meal occasions including chicken vs other meat types

Source: *The Grocer*, 2006

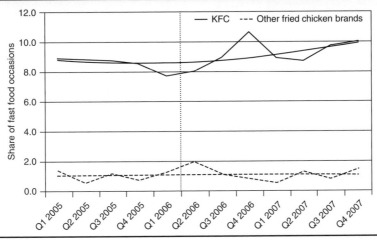

Figure 45: KFC occasion share vs other fried chicken occasion share (share of fast-food occasions)

Source: BIT report, Conquest

More specifically, within the branded fast-food market, fried chicken brands other than KFC experienced no upturn in use (see Figure 45).

■ **Were consumers less concerned about healthy eating?**
As discussed, there was an ongoing trend towards healthy eating throughout this period, and away from fast food. This trend continued throughout the entire period covered, and continues to gain momentum to this day (see Figure 46).

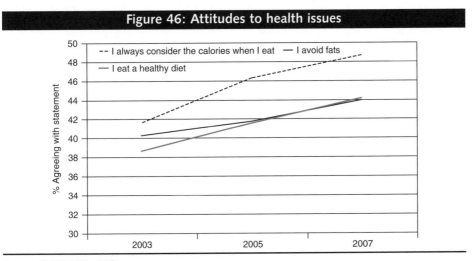

Figure 46: Attitudes to health issues

Source: GB TGI, 2003–2007

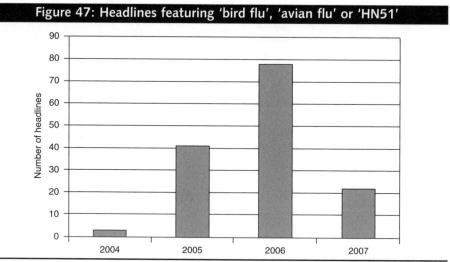

Figure 47: Headlines featuring 'bird flu', 'avian flu' or 'HN51'

Source: Reuters

■ **Were sales recovering from a downturn caused by bird flu?**

Bird flu arrived in the news in 2004. There was a marked increase in the amount of news coverage this epidemic received throughout 2006 when the disease arrived in the UK. This was coincident with an increase in sales of KFC (see Figure 47).

Moreover, fast-food consumers were largely unconcerned by avian flu, so any effect would have been marginal.[22]

4. Socio-economic factors

These slow-moving factors affect the entire category equally, so KFC's share growth suggests minimal impact. Moreover, there is no significant change in key factors over the period 2005–2007.

■ **Affluence**

The rate at which personal disposable income grew remained largely constant between 2002 and 2007 (see Table 3).

Table 3: Annual growth in personal disposable income (PDI) and consumer expenditure (CE)

	2002	2003	2004	2005	2006	2007
% growth in PDI	1.9	2.7	2.1	3.5	1.3	0.9
% growth in CE	3.5	3.0	3.5	1.6	2.0	2.5

Source: Mintel

■ **Demographics**

The demographic balance of the nation did not alter significantly over the campaign period, in fact the potential buying audience shrank slightly (see Table 4).

Table 4: Millions of Britons in core audiences			
	2003	**2005**	**2007**
C1C2DE Mums	7.04	7.09	6.97
C1C2DE Youth	5.67	5.69	5.66

Source: TGI

We have quantified or eliminated all other factors that could have affected KFC's sales over the campaign period. We will now go on to precisely quantify the contribution of advertising to total brand sales.

Econometric modelling

Econometric modelling has been used to identify and accurately quantify the effect of advertising on KFC sales in the campaign period. Rich data are available only for company-owned stores, so the model uses these stores as a proxy for the brand as a whole. Company-owned stores account for 41% of total brand sales, so this represents a robust data set.[23]

After taking account of other important factors – price, competitor activity, store refurbishments, promotional windows and seasonality – advertising effects can be identified as a significant driver of overall sales value.

The fit of the model is excellent, with an R^2 figure of 97.1%, indicating that all major variations in sales have been accounted for (see Figure 48).

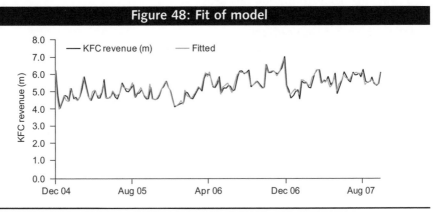

Figure 48: Fit of model

Source: Data2Decisions

Quantifying the effect of advertising

The effect of advertising was quantified by setting the advertising input in the model to zero; this shows what sales would have been without advertising support, but with all other factors being equal. The difference between these two lines represents the total effect of the campaign (see Figure 49).

Figure 49: Sales with and without advertising 2006–2007

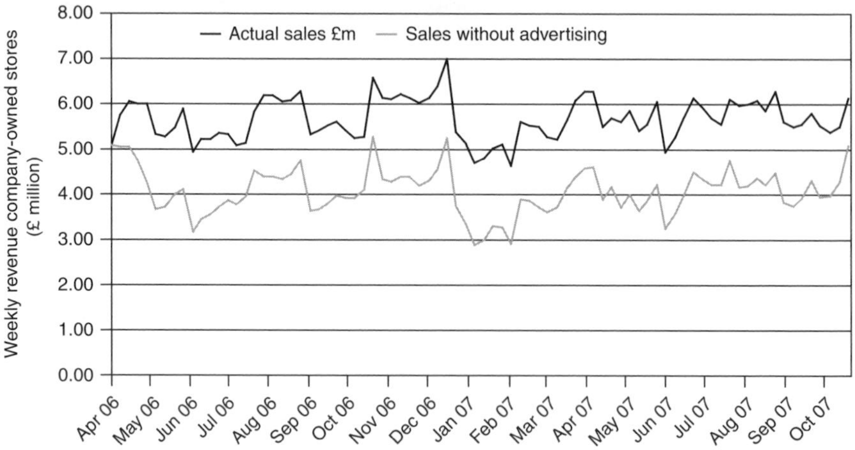

Source: Data2Decisions

As KFC is a retail brand and advertises continuously, advertising from the previous campaign ran throughout 2005 and in the first three months of 2006. This would have had a residual effect on sales for a short time after it had come off air. To ensure that we are accurately quantifying *only* the effect of the new campaign, we have eliminated this effect and quantified the effect only of those GRPs running from April 2006 onwards.

Isolating the advertising effect

Using this approach we can establish that value sales are *£134.5m* higher in KFC-owned stores than they would have been had we not advertised over the campaign period.

Total KFC sales

In order to obtain a total figure for incremental sales generated by advertising for the entire system (both company- and franchisee-operated stores) we need to scale up the company incremental sales.

Company-operated stores account for an average of 41% of total revenue.[24] There is no reason to suspect that franchisee-operated stores will react any differently to company-operated stores in terms of their response to advertising. The two store types are indistinguishable to consumers, offer the same products and have the same in-store displays.

Therefore, the total incremental sales attributable to advertising over the campaign period across the total portfolio are *£328.05m*.[25]

Demonstrating payback

As econometric modelling demonstrates, advertising is responsible for *£328.05m* in incremental sales over the campaign period.

Total marketing costs over the campaign period are £36.42m (media spend was £32.5m;[26] production costs and agency fee come to £3.92m).[27]

Thus revenue ROI for this campaign is:

$$\frac{£328.05m}{36.42m} = 9.01$$

We will now demonstrate that KFC's investment paid back handsomely in incremental profit.

Incremental sales do not incur fixed costs.[28] We will therefore use gross margin in quantifying the additional profit generated by advertising. For confidentiality reasons we are unable to release the exact KFC margin; however, the category average gross margin is 62.5%.[29] This includes costs of goods, and the nominal increases in distribution and energy costs incurred through additional sales.

Applying this figure gives us profit before marketing costs of £205.03m. Marketing costs are £36.42m. Therefore incremental profit after costs amounts to £168.61m (see Table 5).

Table 5: Incremental net profit by advertising	
Incremental sales generated by advertising	£328.05m
Incremental profit generated by advertising	£205.03m
Advertising costs	£36.42m
Incremental net profit generated by advertising	£168.61m

$$\frac{168.61m}{36.42m} = 4.63$$

Hence, each £1 that KFC invested in advertising delivered an incremental profit of £4.63. In the context of past papers, this is a very high level of ROI (see Figure 50).[30]

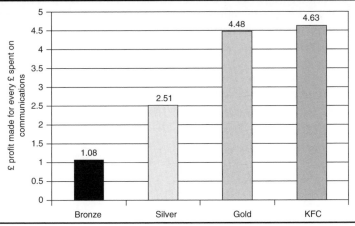

Figure 50: Average of papers explicitly revealing profit ROI, 2002, 2004, 2006

Source: *Advertising Works*

Summary

This is a paper that demonstrates how, even in the most disastrous market circumstances, a brand can thrive by remaining true to its core values and core competence.

In 2005, KFC faced a declining market, public mistrust and an angry media. The brand was rapidly losing penetration, sales and share. By 2007 the brand had reversed its fortunes and won renewed favour. KFC's turnaround has become an exemplary case study within the global corporation and the competition. By the end of 2006 McDonald's publicly conceded it was making a U-turn in its image,[31] with a back-to-basics approach that bore uncanny similarities to KFC's. This is not a scenario the most optimistic observers would have foreseen in 2005.

We have demonstrated that advertising worked exactly as intended to drive lapsed users back to the brand. We have quantified or eliminated all other factors that could have been responsible for the turnaround in brand fortunes. Using econometrics we have quantified additional revenue generated by advertising as £328.05m and demonstrated an ROI of 1:4.63.

Few brands ever experience such an assault on their entire category; nevertheless, there are learnings with broader relevance for marketing as a whole.

Conclusions and broader learnings

'To thine own brand be true'

Our competitors were never really credible as purveyors of salad greens. While our competitors became mired in apologetic concessions to the health agenda, KFC held its nerve and maintained its self-belief. Rather than trying to change its spots (or its feathers), KFC continued to unashamedly celebrate its fried chicken product and remind consumers of what they loved about the brand.

The power of ruthless simplicity

It would have been all too easy to get drawn into shoehorning additional messages into KFC communications. By focusing ruthlessly on our core objectives – taste, family empathy and youth innovation – we delivered communications that performed exactly as we needed them to.

KFC reaped the benefits of defying category convention by going on to achieve category-defying sales performance. Above all, this paper is a reminder of the power of courageous communications thinking. It's easy to be brave when you're on top. It's more important to be brave when times are hard. As talk of economic slowdown continues apace, this is perhaps the most salient lesson for the industry today.

Notes

1. All brand communications are centralised. Franchisees and Kentucky Fried Chicken Ltd jointly fund brand activity, and likewise both parties share profits. So, for the purposes of this paper it is unnecessary to distinguish between these groups. This is the story of the KFC brand as a whole, and the value advertising has delivered to its respective stakeholders. Company stores account for 41% of the total estate and revenue.
2. Source: KFC.

3. Source: Mintel.
4. Source: Mintel, Burgers and Fried Chicken Report, March 2008.
5. This paper focuses on the effects of advertising between March 2006 and December 2007; 2005 will be referred to by way of comparison. Issues of data availability do not permit us to continue into 2008.
6. Mintel British Lifestyles Report, 2006.
7. The fast-food market encompasses a plethora of outlets – from fish and chips, Indians, supermarkets, cafés and pubs. However, within this, the nearest competition are fast-food brands, such as McDonald's or Pizza Hut. Their products and prices are most comparable and, more importantly they are grouped together in the minds of consumers. Therefore this paper uses the term 'fast-food brands' to refer to this subset.
8. Penetration refers to 'past three months penetration'. Annual penetration approaches 100%, and thus is a highly unresponsive measure. Hence this is a more accurate measure of brand usage.
9. Aged 16–24.
10. Source: BIT Report, Conquest – branded sandwich chains experienced a 7% rise in penetration over the second half of 2005 (Q3 05/Q1 2006), indexing particularly highly against KFC users.
11. Source: KFC.
12. Value sales are a much more accurate measure of business health in fast food, as volume sales fail to capture the enormous variation in the value of individual units. For example, Toasted Twister retails at £2.69, whereas a Family Feast retails at £9.99 but also counts as one unit.
13. Sales breakdowns are all 'per store averages' as opposed to aggregated totals. This measure is a more accurate reflection of changes in sales, as it eliminates any variation in the number of stores.
14. Average family spend is £13.58 – 2.84 times that of youth (£4.77). Source: KFC.
15. Buckets and 'high end' products accounted for 25% of the sales mix in 2005. Source: KFC.
16. Only grade 'A' chicken was used.
17. Standard deviation = 5, mean = 105.
18. Source: KFC.
19. Source: KFC.
20. Source: KFC.
21. Source: Reuters.
22. Average level of concern 2006–2007, 2.3% (BIT Report, Conquest).
23. Source: KFC.
24. Source: KFC (data 2001–2007).
25. £134.5 million/0.41.
26. Walker Media.
27. Our confidentiality agreement prevents us from breaking down this figure further.
28. *Advertising Works 15*, Andrew Sharp article.
29. HM Customs & Revenue Tax Report.
30. *Advertising Works 15, 13, 11*.
31. Source: *Marketing* magazine , 25 October 2006 – 'McDonald's gets back to basics'.

Other companies involved in campaign: Media company: Walker Media.

Chapter 12

Sainsbury's

How an idea helped make Sainsbury's great again

By Tom Roach and Craig Mawdsley, AMV.BBDO
Contributing author: Jane Dorsett, AMV.BBDO

Editor's summary

This is a wonderful case of a focused business problem leading to a brilliant business driving idea. 'Do the maths' is an often used phrase in US films but less so in advertising agencies. However, that's exactly what AMV.BBDO did and the outcome was spectacular. The challenge was clear – deliver £2.5bn extra sales. This huge figure is too large to help inform the creative process. However, it would become more instructive when broken down into what it means in the real world. With 14 million transactions a week and three years to achieve the sales target, it was a simple calculation to say that Sainsbury's needed to earn an extra £1.14 for every shopping trip.

The challenge was that shoppers had developed ingrained behavior at their supermarket. They shopped on auto-pilot. This 'sleep-shopping' needed to be interrupted. And that's exactly what the idea – 'Try something new today' – was designed to achieve.

'Try something new today' became a powerful organising thought, guiding not just communications, but store design, merchandising and product innovation. Following the launch of the idea, Sainsbury's experienced ten consecutive quarters of sales growth, with over half of that coming from existing customers.

The advertising alone has been proven to have driven £550m in incremental sales over two years, with that figure boosted to £1.9bn when combined with all the in-store 'try ideas', putting the three-year £2.5bn target well within reach.

Introduction: putting a value on an idea

This case goes further than showing that advertising can 'work', that it can deliver profitable returns, or that integrated communications can work more effectively still. And to our knowledge it contains an element that is a first for an IPA case.

It isolates the value of an *idea* – as distinct from the value delivered by the advertising that *carried* that idea.

In so doing it gets to the heart of our evolving role as an industry – creating business-changing ideas that deliver value to our clients and their shareholders – and answers a question we all too rarely ask: how much is the idea we have planned, created and executed actually worth to our client's business?

It tells the story of how that idea did its work so successfully because of its fitness for purpose. *Try something new today* was created with a specific business objective in mind: to help Sainsbury's deliver an additional £2.5bn in revenue.

And it shows that this idea delivered value by changing how Sainsbury's operates from the inside, not simply by changing how it communicates to the *outside*.

The value of the idea? £550m in increased revenue over two years.

First, some history.

A retailer in trouble: 2004

In 2004, Sainsbury's was seen by many as a troubled business with its glory years behind it.

Asda overtook Sainsbury's in July 2003 to become the number two in UK grocery retailing,[1] with like-for-like sales[2] for the financial year 2003/04 declining by 0.2%.[3]

Enter a new Chief Executive, Justin King (see Figure 1).

Figure 1: Extract from BBC News website

His task could not have been clearer: to turn the troubled supermarket around.

Justin King's first move was to undertake a review of Sainsbury's entire operation, which resulted in his recovery plan entitled 'Making Sainsbury's Great Again'.

The recovery plan: phase 1

The plan had at its heart a goal to drive a sales-led profit recovery with a target of £2.5bn additional sales over three years.[4]

It was based on a simple strategy: to deliver great products at fair prices to all.

The plan identified two major barriers to delivering this goal, which would need urgent attention: availability and pricing.

Availability, or rather *un*availability, was identified as Sainsbury's number one issue.[5] Figure 2 was Justin King's way of highlighting the issue at Sainsbury's AGM in July 2004.

Figure 2: Customer letter highlighting problems of unavailability

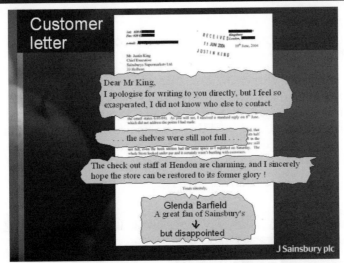

The second barrier to achieving the goal was pricing: by 2004 prices had become uncompetitive as shown by *The Grocer* magazine's survey on pricing (see Table 1).

Table 1: Pricing survey

October 2004 *Grocer* 100 basket price	Sainsbury's	Competitor average
	£178	£173

From October 2004 to September 2005, 3,000 extra store colleagues were hired,[6] 6,000 prices cut and availability was improved.[7]

These initiatives had a positive effect: Sainsbury's delivered two quarters of modest like-for-like sales growth (of 1.7% and 1.3% respectively) following three consecutive quarters of decline[8] (Figure 3).

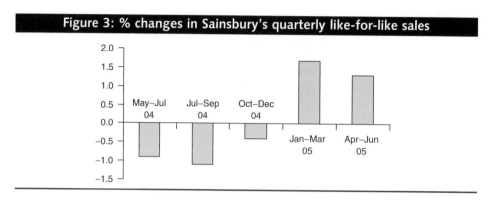

Figure 3: % changes in Sainsbury's quarterly like-for-like sales

Phase 1 of the recovery: advertising's contribution (2004 to August 2005)

The as yet unchanged advertising campaign was not a major factor in driving the initial returns to quarterly sales growth seen by the business in early 2005.

Sainsbury's advertising underwent no major changes during this period. Jamie Oliver continued to be used in TV advertising to reinforce Sainsbury's quality credentials. He was used only in TV, with campaigns in other media created in isolation, linked only loosely by the passive slogan 'Making life taste better' (see Figure 4).

Figure 4: Examples of campaign media

The sales effects of the Jamie Oliver TV campaign are confidential; however, we can reveal that it was continuing to deliver sales at levels worthy of many award-winning IPA cases but at seriously declining levels of payback since 2001[9] (see Figure 5).

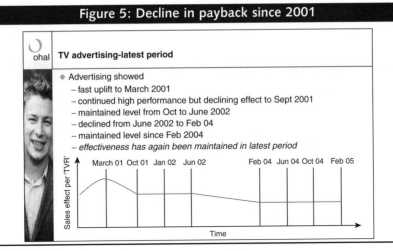

Figure 5: Decline in payback since 2001

ohal — TV advertising-latest period

◆ Advertising showed
 – fast uplift to March 2001
 – continued high performance but declining effect to Sept 2001
 – maintained level from Oct to June 2002
 – declined from June 2002 to Feb 04
 – maintained level since Feb 2004
 – *effectiveness has again been maintained in latest period*

In 2004, before the basics had been fixed, the existing advertising was at best only mitigating the overall declines.

So in early 2005 when the only changes had been to pricing and availability, and the business began to see modest quarterly growth, the unchanged advertising was not fuelling the recovery: fixing the basics was doing the hard work.

Communications would need to be fundamentally re-engineered to play a role in the recovery and help deliver the £2.5bn of extra sales demanded by the business plan.

Phase 2 of the recovery: a new brand idea

The problem creativity would need to help solve was clear: £2.5bn extra sales. But this initially proved too big a problem to be a useful input into the creative process.

Previously communications had been used to get people to 'switch' to Sainsbury's – to win shoppers. But the days when people chose one shop once a week were gone: everybody has a repertoire of grocery shops these days. Consistent with Justin King's belief at the time that the recovery would be led by existing shoppers spending more, we reframed the role for communications as being about winning more pounds per trip.

This led to an astonishingly simple analysis of the objective. With 14m transactions a week and three years to achieve the goal, we calculated that we would need to earn an extra £1.14 for every shopping trip:

£1.14 × 52 weeks × 3 years × 14m customers = £2.5bn

This transformed the role for communications:

- from *Helping deliver £2.5bn extra sales*
- to *Getting shoppers to spend a little extra.*

This unlocked the £2.5bn problem so that creativity could be used to help solve it. An unimaginably daunting objective was transformed into something as tangible and approachable as it is possible to imagine; £1.14 became the foundation-stone of an idea (see Figure 6).

Figure 6: £1.14 became a fundamental concept

The new idea

Our new idea was built on three insights:

1. *Brand insight.* Sainsbury's role is to offer great everyday food to all.
2. *Internal business insight.* Sainsbury's needed shoppers to spend an extra £1.14 for every shopping trip.
3. *External customer insight.* We're all sleep-shopping, buying the same products week in week out,[10] eating the same old meals for lack of inspiration. We dramatised this for colleagues by releasing a man in a gorilla suit into a store and filming the results: shoppers were in too much of a rut to notice (see Figure 7).

Figure 7: Dramatisation of sleep-shopping

The new brand idea was born (see Figure 8).

> ### Figure 8: The new brand idea

The idea was created to change behaviour first and position Sainsbury's as a store of ideas second (unlike most retailer brand ideas, which are primarily about positioning the brand).

It was designed to help inspire 150,000 colleagues to deliver extra spend from customers. In communications it was designed to give people simple food ideas (easy-to-remember tips such as 'Try nutmeg on your spag bol' or 'Try hot cross buns in bread and butter pudding' – try it, it's lovely).

Try something new today was created to inspire people to try simple food ideas and, in so doing, earn a little extra spend from them every time they shopped. If people who didn't come every week also came a few more times, so much the better.

The idea inspired change in the business from the inside out

Try something new today is not an advertising idea but a business idea that started its work by catalysing change throughout the business.

The huge role Sainsbury's 150,000 instore colleagues would need to play in delivering *Try* was recognised from the start. At launch, training helped them understand their role in giving customers ideas, and samples of ideas were distributed to all of them. The idea of *'earning the £1.14'* became common currency internally, helping store managers think about how to bring the idea to life instore.[11]

Try something new today spearheaded a cultural shift internally, becoming a rallying cry for the importance of innovation throughout the organisation.

It was instantly recognised by Sainsbury's as a powerful lever to change the way the business works and so help deliver the required step-change in sales performance:

> *... the relaunch of our brand supported by 'Try something new today' ... marks the next stage of our recovery plan and has also kick-started a change in the way we work, which is essential if we are to sustain our early progress.*[12]

> Justin King, 2005

Figure 9, a slide from Justin King's presentation to City analysts in October 2005, describes how the idea inspired change throughout the business.[13]

Figure 9: How the idea inspired change throughout the business

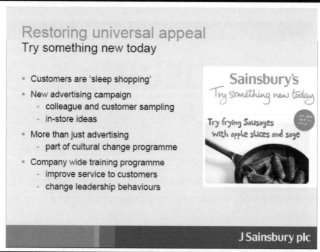

Sainsbury's board committed to creating an environment in which new ideas can flourish, where colleagues are encouraged to create new ways of working and failure is not feared. '*Try something new*' became one of six leadership behaviours identified for Sainsbury's store managers.

Try inspired thousands of colleagues to try something new, such as '*email free Wednesdays*' to encourage communication in person,[14] '*Supply something new*', a scheme to encourage the discovery of local suppliers, and '*Scan School*' a double-decker bus training centre that visits stores to train check-out colleagues[15] (see Figure 10).

Try inspired behavioural change in Sainsbury's colleagues first, and customers second.

Figure 10: 'Scan School', a double-decker bus training centre

The idea changed the way we communicated with customers

We transformed the store, distributing tip cards featuring simple food ideas (Figure 11) via displays in store entrances (Figure 12). Since September 2005, over 200 million tip cards have been distributed in stores, featuring 325 different ideas.[16] We place tip cards of ideas near featured products and POS throughout stores (Figure 13).

Figure 11: Tip cards

Figure 12: Typical tip cards display in store entrance

Figure 13: POS featuring food ideas to try

TV advertising gives customers new ideas to try. With its focus on food ideas, *Try* allowed us the flexibility not to use Jamie Oliver if the circumstances demanded it: since launch, of the 51 TV executions we have created featuring food ideas, 31 did not feature Jamie (see Figure 14).

Figure 14: Not all TV ads featured Jamie Oliver

Magazine advertising features ideas, not just products (see Figure 15).

Figure 15: Magazine ads offered ideas

Sainsbury's ITV Drama Premiers sponsorship has featured 77 ideas. Radio ads featuring deals also feature ideas – 112 to date. Weekly offers advertising in the national press includes ideas where possible. The three-weekly door-drop leaflet of offers features ideas – 45 to date (see Figure 16).

Figure 16: Offer leaflets also give ideas

The company website, www.sainsburys.co.uk, now features 3,500 ideas and a forum for customers to share their own.

Direct mail now includes ideas, and a new lifestyle magazine called *Fresh Ideas* was created, which contains many food ideas and is mailed to Nectar card users.

The idea allowed media money to be spent more efficiently

The beauty of *Try* in media terms is its power and flexibility – allowing budgets to be spent more efficiently and media to be deployed without constraint.

Dramatic increases in the total market's media spend in the period were met, not with extra media fire power, but with the extra fire power of the idea.

Media spend was reduced in *Try*'s launch year, which, coupled with a greatly increased total market spend, resulted in a decrease in share of supermarket spend year on year from 23% to 20%. In *Try*'s first two full years, Sainsbury's share of spend further reduced, down to 19%[17] (Figure 17 and Table 2).

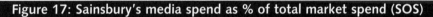

Figure 17: Sainsbury's media spend as % of total market spend (SOS)

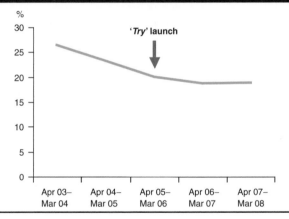

Table 2: Share of spend

	Year 1 pre-Try Apr 03– Mar 04	Year 2 pre-Try Apr 04– Mar 05	Try launch year Apr 05– Mar 06	Year 1 post-Try launch Apr 06– Mar 07	Year 2 post-Try launch Apr 07– Mar 08
Total market spend	190,825,797	229,263,519	261,989,660	296,880,511	344,633,340
Sainsbury's spend	50,345,684	52,857,599	52,422,595	55,516,647	64,702,663
Sainsbury's share of spend	26%	23%	20%	19%	19%

The idea's flexibility means it can be deployed in any media: it is as suited to a door-drop as a 60-second TV commercial.

Furthermore, as we'll see, its power outside paid-for media (tip cards, instore POS) means it can even deliver extra sales for 'free'.[18]

The idea inspired change in people's minds

Every piece of qualitative research we undertake on the idea reminds us afresh of *Try*'s power, which it derives from the universal and never-ending nature of its core customer insight: people are sleep-shopping and need ideas, however small, to inspire them.

One researcher had this to say:

> *Try has never faltered in its power because it's rooted in a true understanding of the realities and the needs of the shopper. It is greeted with powerful recognition, welcome and interest by shoppers, it comes from an unbeatable combination of understanding a real, major and never-ending need, and provides a real, fast and economical integrated solution ... It is one of the best ideas I've researched in nearly 40 years of researching – one of advertising's true really big ideas.*
>
> Clive Gabriel, Gabriel Ashworth Research and Consultancy

In research, customers always talk about the idea with a strong recognition of the need it fulfils: their need for ideas to inspire them beyond their narrow repertoire of meals[19] (see Figure 18).

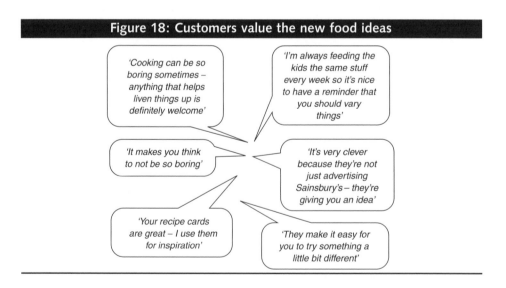

Figure 18: Customers value the new food ideas

'Cooking can be so boring sometimes – anything that helps liven things up is definitely welcome'

'I'm always feeding the kids the same stuff every week so it's nice to have a reminder that you should vary things'

'It makes you think to not be so boring'

'It's very clever because they're not just advertising Sainsbury's – they're giving you an idea'

'Your recipe cards are great – I use them for inspiration'

'They make it easy for you to try something a little bit different'

Figure 19 shows responses to recent TV executions in the campaign.[20] Note just how happy customers are to say they act on the ideas we give them – striking given most consumers' usual insistence that they're never influenced by advertising.

We believe this is because the idea isn't seen as advertising to be filtered out, but as a useful service worth *tuning in to*.

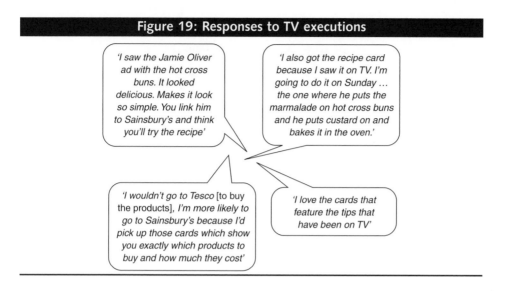

Figure 19: Responses to TV executions

'I saw the Jamie Oliver ad with the hot cross buns. It looked delicious. Makes it look so simple. You link him to Sainsbury's and think you'll try the recipe'

'I also got the recipe card because I saw it on TV. I'm going to do it on Sunday ... the one where he puts the marmalade on hot cross buns and he puts custard on and bakes it in the oven.'

'I wouldn't go to Tesco [to buy the products], I'm more likely to go to Sainsbury's because I'd pick up those cards which show you exactly which products to buy and how much they cost'

'I love the cards that feature the tips that have been on TV'

Pre-testing and tracking of the 51 TV commercials aired since September 2005 show a consistently strong communication of *'Sainsbury's is always coming up with new ideas'* – a key brand measure for Sainsbury's given the idea's role in positioning Sainsbury's as an innovative, imaginative and helpful store (see Figure 20).

Figure 20 also shows the close correlation between agreement with this statement and with 'this advert would tempt me to try this product' – a strong indication that giving people new food ideas is a powerful way of driving purchase intention.[21]

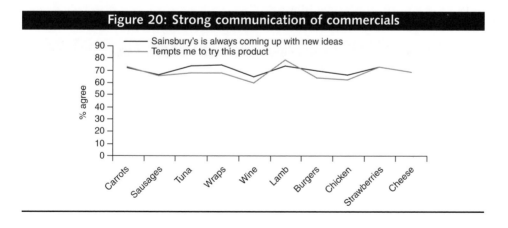

Figure 20: Strong communication of commercials

In line with our brand objectives, key brand image measures, stable in the months prior to *Try*'s launch, immediately began to rise post-launch, until they settled in mid-2006 at new, higher levels[22] (see Figure 21).

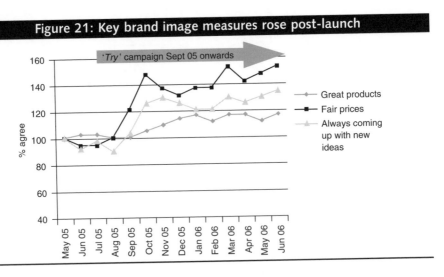

Figure 21: Key brand image measures rose post-launch

'Try' campaign Sept 05 onwards

Legend:
- Great products
- Fair prices
- Always coming up with new ideas

The idea inspired behaviour change in millions of people

The most interesting change that the idea has resulted in is not in people's minds (in brand image, perception, equity or whatever conceptual brand model you subscribe to) but in people's *behaviour*.

The tips we give people have a very clear and direct link to sales.

The very first idea used in advertising led to an explosion in nutmeg sales from 1,400 jars a week to 6,000 a week.[23] And nearly every tip advertised since then has delivered increased sales. Tip cards instore open up a new way of driving sales: in grocery retail these are traditionally driven by promotions or extra shelf space.

Table 3 shows a selection of weekly volume sales uplifts for individual products featured in advertising and on tip cards.[24]

Table 3: Sales uplifts	
Product	**Weekly % sales change**
Mangoes	+400%
Parsnips	+257%
Sausages	+168%
Apples	+154%
Mackerel	+113%
Pears	+105%
Kidney beans	+59%
Feta cheese	+49%

Since the launch of the idea, 200m tip cards have been distributed. Around 10m Sainsbury's shoppers claim to have picked one up.[25]

Over 8m shoppers (50% surveyed) claim to use Sainsbury's food ideas, with around 4m (26%) claiming to do so at least once a month and just under 1.5m (9%) using them at least every two weeks[26] (see Figure 22).

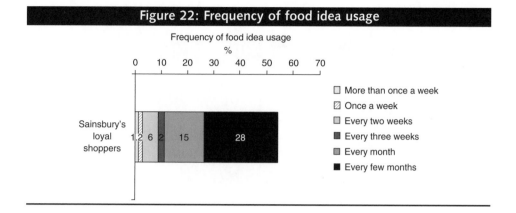

Figure 22: Frequency of food idea usage

In addition, some visible chart labels: Sainsbury's loyal shoppers — 1.2, 6, 2, 15, 28. Legend: More than once a week; Once a week; Every two weeks; Every three weeks; Every month; Every few months.

Around 3.5m claim to have shared a tip card with another person:[27] tip cards have become a viral carrier of the food ideas they feature.

While we have no data on whether competitors receive sales boosts from the tips we broadcast, qualitatively we've learned people much prefer to come to Sainsbury's rather than a competitor to buy the ingredients because of the presence of the cards:

> *I wouldn't go to Tesco [to buy the products], I'm more likely to go to Sainsbury's because I'd pick up those cards which show you exactly which products to buy and how much they cost.*[28]

Table 4 shows the pure sales-driving power of tip cards. The idea on the left received heavy-weight TV and press support in April 2008[29] and unsurprisingly delivered strong weekly sales uplifts. The idea on the right was displayed instore but received no media support: the tip card and POS alone were responsible for the strong sales uplifts on the burger ingredients.[30] Neither idea featured any ingredients on special offer[31] (see Figure 23).

Table 4: Tip cards drive sales uplift

Tip card with ad support		Tip card without ad support	
Meatballs idea	Sales uplift	Burger & wedges idea	Sales uplift
Coarse-cut beef mince	243.3%	Baking potatoes	26.9%
Spaghetti	34.8%	Lean steak mince	74.2%
Spring onions	10.9%	Burger buns	55.2%
Standard tomatoes	10.2%	Crunchy salad	37.3%

In addition, the idea has opened up new channels of communication, enabling Sainsbury's to use the internet for community, not just commerce, with sainsburys.co.uk becoming a place for users to share food ideas. Since October 2005, the community area (Figure 24) has received 1.5m[32] unique visits (20,000 a week) with no advertising support.

GOLD   Advertising Works 17

Figure 23: Tip cards with and without TV support

Figure 24: Sainsbury's online forum

The idea inspired existing shoppers to spend more

Data outlining average basket size is highly sensitive so we are not able to reveal the additional spend per basket that the idea generated.

However, we can show that sales growth for 2006 and 2007 was driven primarily by existing customers spending more at Sainsbury's, consistent with the primary communications objective. Table 5 shows the source of sales growth for the first two full financial years of *Try*'s existence.[33]

Table 5: Sales growth for first two years of *Try* campaign			
	Existing customers spending more	Spend gained from competitors	Customers adding JS to repertoire
Sainsbury's incremental sales Growth Q1 2006 to Q4 2007	52%	43%	6%

The idea inspired millions of lost shoppers to return to Sainsbury's

Sainsbury's also began to win back shopping trips from lost customers as soon as the campaign launched.

Over the first two quarters of the campaign (October 2005 to March 2006) Sainsbury's attracted an additional 1m weekly customers, bringing total weekly transactions to around 16m.[34] These additional transactions represented weekly spend from previous Sainsbury's shoppers being won back.[35]

By March 2008, Sainsbury's was handling 16.5m weekly transactions,[36] peaking during Christmas week 2007, when weekly transactions totalled 21.5m[37] – the greatest number in any week in Sainsbury's history.

Justin King made it clear from the start that while winning extra spend from existing customers would be the focus of the recovery, winning back lost shoppers was likely to follow should this primary aim be achieved.[38] His prediction proved correct.

The idea inspired people to try new Sainsbury's stores

The idea also applies perfectly to the behaviour change required by local communications (outdoor, local press, leaflets and DM), where inspiring people to try newly launched stores is the role for advertising (see Figure 25).

> As a creative idea and concept it is almost perfect for store development launches where the very essence of our communications is to encourage people to try something new ... in that respect it has been a huge success.
>
> Sainsbury's Local Marketing Manager

Figure 25: The *Try* idea transfers perfectly to advertising new stores

The idea helped Sainsbury's deliver ten consecutive quarters of sales growth

The idea was launched in September 2005, towards the end of three quarters that had seen Sainsbury's return to modest growth. Growth immediately accelerated, and Sainsbury's has subsequently seen ten more consecutive quarters of sales growth[39] (see Figure 26).

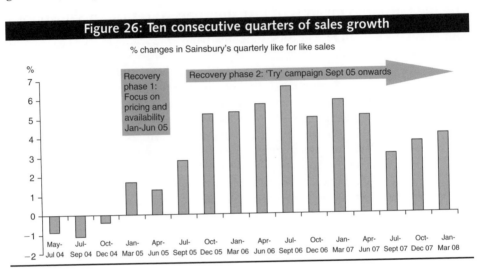

Figure 26: Ten consecutive quarters of sales growth

% changes in Sainsbury's quarterly like for like sales

The idea helped deliver Sainsbury's £2.5bn revenue goal

Sainsbury's announced in January 2008 that the £2.5bn revenue goal had been achieved three months ahead of schedule[40] and, by March 2008 (the original deadline), the total revenue increase stood at £2.7bn (see Figure 27). *Try something new today* was created to help deliver this goal and was implemented by a business that believed it could do so.[41]

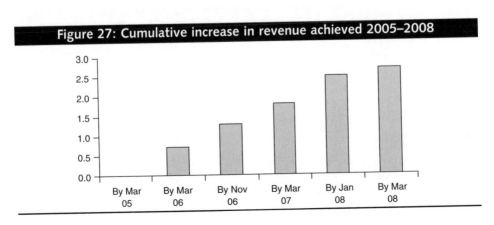

Figure 27: Cumulative increase in revenue achieved 2005–2008

The idea did not deliver the £2.5bn in additional sales on its own, and to claim so would be unfair: it was the inspiration and the perspiration of 150,000 Sainsbury's colleagues that did that.

The idea revitalised the efficacy of Sainsbury's TV advertising

While advertising is only one aspect of this case, one of the effects of the idea has been to restore its effectiveness.

At Sainsbury's we have employed ongoing econometric modelling through OHAL since the early 1990s, allowing us to isolate advertising returns.

Prior to the launch of *Try*, we had seen gradual, but inexorable declines in the ROI from TV advertising. In common with other long-running campaigns, its effectiveness was greatest at the beginning. So, by 2005, the TV advertising ROI was far lower than it had been when Jamie Oliver was first used[42] (see Figure 5).

This changed with *Try*. TV advertising ROI was restored as the idea enabled us to breathe new life into executions featuring Jamie Oliver (20 executions) and allowed us to create even more compelling executions that did not feature Jamie (31 executions).

This effect was achieved at no extra cost: TV commercials cost no more to produce post-*Try* than they did pre-*Try*.

The latest modelling data to December 2007 estimates that the TV campaign has made a sales contribution of £1.35bn since the campaign launched in September 2005.

Given a media spend of £55m[43] the TV campaign ROI since *Try* has been £24.55 per £1 spent.

Sainsbury's marginal profit is too sensitive to be revealed here. The IPA recommends the use of industry-standard marginal profit figures of 25% for grocery retailers, so for the purposes of all of our profit calculations we have applied this notional marginal profit figure.

Using a margin of 25%, TV advertising has therefore delivered £6.14 profit per £1 spent – equating to £337.5m profit since the campaign launch, or £2.9m profit per week to the bottom line.

The idea's value has been an additional £550m over two years

This case puts a value on an idea, as distinct from the value delivered by the advertising that *carried* the idea – to our knowledge a first for an IPA case.

> *Econometric modelling has enabled OHAL to isolate the sales effect of the* Try *idea as a distinct impact from the sales effects of the* Try *advertising campaign. The impact manifested itself as a step-change in base level sales occurring in the months following* Try's *launch that can only be explained by the idea's implementation.*
>
> Source: OHAL

Try something new today delivered this effect by generating accelerated revenue growth for the supermarket as a whole, irrespective of the effects it achieved through advertising activity: it is not simply a campaign effect by another name

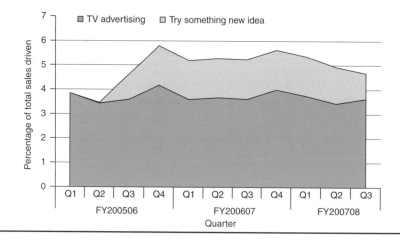

Figure 28: Sales contribution of TV advertising and the Try something new idea

and is quite distinct from the enhanced sales effects of the *Try* TV advertising discussed in the preceding section (see Figure 28).[44]

This *Try idea* effect has been calculated by OHAL as £550m in increased revenue in just over two years.[45]

In other words, *Try* led to behaviour change, unrelated to media spend, which had a massive impact on sales.

The *Try* idea has therefore delivered around £137.5m profit in two years, or £1.2m profit per week to the bottom line.

We are unable to deliver a standard return on investment for the *Try* idea as the incremental costs of delivering it have been negligible.[46]

However, if we combine the separate *TV advertising* and *Try idea* sales effects, incremental revenue totals £1.9bn across two years, a return of £34.55 per £1 spent.

The combined effect of TV advertising and the *Try idea* effect has delivered £475m profit over the course of the campaign, or £4.1m profit per week to the bottom line (Table 6).

Table 6: Combined profits from *TV advertising* and *Try idea* effect

	TV campaign Sept 2005 to Dec 2007 (£)	Try idea effect Sept 2005 to Dec 2007 (£)	Combined TV + Try idea effect (£)
Sales ROI	24.55:1	N/A	34.55:1
Total sales effect	1.35bn	550m	1.9bn
Profit ROI	6.14:1	N/A	8.64:1
Total profit	337.5m	137.5m	475m
Profit per week	2.9m	1.2m	4.1m

Eliminating other factors

OHAL's model analyses a comprehensive range of internal, competitive and external factors that we can eliminate as factors explaining either the sales contribution of the TV campaign or the *Try* idea effect:

- stock availability
- pricing vs competitors
- Sainsbury's media spend
- competitor media spend
- direct marketing and door-drops
- coupons at till
- climate
- special events (e.g. World Cup)
- Active Kids voucher collection scheme
- Comic/Sports Relief sponsorship
- new stores, extensions and refurbishments
- competitor openings/closures
- pay-day.

Conclusion

Through the IPA Effectiveness Awards, the IPA seeks to push the boundaries of our knowledge and understanding of how communications work. The greatest IPA cases are those that help answer the key challenges facing the industry at that moment in time.

This case does both.

By isolating the value delivered by an *idea* – as distinct from the value delivered by the communications that *carried* that idea – it pushes the boundaries of our learning.

And at a time when we seek to prove our worth beyond advertising as the creators of ideas that deliver value for our clients' businesses, *Try* provides compelling evidence.

We have isolated the value of an idea beyond its value in advertising – £550m in revenue over two years.

We have shown that it is an idea that worked from the inside out: inspiring Sainsbury's colleagues first and Sainsbury's customers second.

And that it helped Sainsbury's achieve a remarkable recovery by helping deliver £2.5bn in increased revenue, £1.14 at a time.

> Try something new today *is much more than a slogan. The spirit and success of the campaign has inspired our entire business, and customers love it too.*[47]
>
> Justin King

Notes

1. TNS measured Asda's market share at 17.0% to Sainsbury's 16.2%.
2. Like-for-like sales are used as a measure of underlying growth in the business because they exclude the effect of new store openings, refurbishments and extensions (i.e. they show year-on-year sales changes in comparable stores).

3. J Sainsbury trading statement, March 2004, quoting TNS sales data. Sainsbury's financial year runs April to March.
4. 'The purest measure of customer satisfaction will be increased sales and we believe plans outlined today will grow sales by £2.5 billion.' Source: J Sainsbury business review, 19 October 2004. See www.jsainsbury.co.uk.
5. 'Availability is the number one performance issue for Sainsbury's and a significant detractor to recent sales performance. Customers have too frequently been unable to complete their shop.' Source: J Sainsbury business review, 19 October 2004. See www.jsainsbury.co.uk.
6. Source: J Sainsbury business review, 19 October 2004. See www.jsainsbury.co.uk.
7. Whereas in June 2004 around one in ten items was unavailable, by June 2005 this had reduced to only around one in 20. Source: Justin King comment on First Quarter Trading Statement conference call with city investors, June 2005. See www.jsainsbury.co.uk.
8. Source: J Sainsbury First Quarter Trading Statement, June 2005. See www.jsainsbury.co.uk.
9. Details of the ROI of the Jamie Oliver TV campaign are confidential.
10. Shoppers buy only around 150 or so products from stores, which stock 30,000+. Source: Sainsbury's Customer Insights.
11. If you spot the store manager next time you're in Sainsbury's, see what he or she has to say about 'the £1.14'.
12. Source: Justin King quoted in J Sainsbury Pre-Close Second Quarter Trading Statement for 16 weeks to 8 October 2005. See www.jsainsbury.co.uk.
13. A PowerPoint slide from Justin King's presentation to city analysts as part of the Interim Results Announcement for the 28 weeks ending 8 October 2005. See www.jsainsbury.co.uk
14. 'We've applied the thinking behind "Try Something New Today" to the way we work. For example, we now have an "email-free day" in our store support centre to encourage colleagues to get up from their desks and communicate in person.' Source: J Sainsbury Annual Review and Summary Financial Statement 2006; www.jsainsbury.co.uk.
15. Excerpt from Justin King's statement in J Sainsbury Annual Review 2006: 'My Board colleagues and I also piloted a two-day training course focused on embedding new ways to lead our business, and helped to then deliver that training to 1,000 of our managers from stores and central teams. They, in turn, are delivering that training to a further 9,000 managers. We try to be innovative with training and development, and our Scan School is an example of that. The school is actually two specially fitted double-decker buses that visit our stores to train our training colleagues.' Source: www.j-sainsbury.co.uk.
16. Individual tip cards have print runs of 400k to 1m depending on predicted popularity. Sainsbury's had tried distributing tip cards before; for example, a lamb recipe card had accompanied a Jamie Oliver Easter TV campaign in 2002. Prior to 2005, however, they had only ever been used tactically and intermittently; never before had they been seen as an important strategic pillar to be used permanently and on such a scale.
17. Source: ACNielsen.
18. Additional printing costs for tip cards and POS are negligible.
19. Sources: various qualitative research projects commissioned in 2007 and 2008 by Sainsbury's Customer Insights team and undertaken by Gabriel Ashworth Research, Added Value and Razor Research.
20. Sources: various qualitative research projects commissioned in 2007 and 2008 by Sainsbury's Customer Insights team and undertaken by Gabriel Ashworth Research, Added Value and Razor Research.
21. Data from a selection of TV commercials pre-tested in 2006–07 using TNS/Sainsbury's TV ad pre-testing methodology.
22. Sainsbury's brand image tracking data. Source: Ipsos-MORI.
23. Sainsbury's sales data – weekly volume sales vs a weekly average of the previous 10 weeks' sales.
24. Sainsbury's sales data – weekly volume sales vs a weekly average of the previous 10 weeks' sales.
25. Source: TNS/Sainsbury's internet panel.
26. Sainsbury's Consumer Insights omnibus survey, November 2007.
27. Source: TNS/Sainsbury's internet panel.
28. Razor Research qualitative study April 2008.
29. As part of the 'Feed your family for a fiver' campaign.
30. Sainsbury's sales data – weekly volume sales vs a weekly average of the previous 10 weeks' sales.
31. The 'Feed your family for a fiver' campaign did not feature offers – all products were at their standard price for the duration of the campaign so a change in price was not the driver of the volume uplifts on the meatballs or burger idea.
32. Source: Sainsbury's online team. The ideas forum receives 100 posts a week from visitors, around half of which are posts containing visitors' own food ideas.
33. Source: TNS till roll data. Changes in TNS's data collection methodology mean that data for the first two quarters of the *Try* campaign and pre-*Try* are not directly comparable to the data shown (till roll data for FY 2006 and FY 2007).
34. Source: Sainsbury's Fourth Quarter Trading Statement for 12 weeks to 25 March 2006 reported that 'over 16 million customers are now shopping in our stores each week, an additional one million in the last six months'. See www.jsainsbury.co.uk.
35. On a conference call with investors on 25 March 2006, Justin King revealed the source of the 1m additional transactions: 'We are switching from all our major competitors. But as I have said before, that is very largely that

most of our customers have historically spent quite a bit of their spend elsewhere and we are winning that lost spend back.' Source: www.jsainsbury.co.uk.

36. Source: J Sainsbury's Fourth Quarter Trading Statement for 12 weeks to 22 March 2008. See www.jsainsbury.co.uk. It is interesting to note that this increase of 2 million transactions over three years is the same as the increase in customers over a four-year period claimed by Tesco in its IPA Effectiveness case of 2000.

37. Source: J Sainsbury's Third Quarter Trading Statement for 12 weeks to 29 December 2007. See www.jsainsbury.co.uk.

38. In October 2005's trading statement, Justin King summed up Sainsbury's position as follows: 'Encouraging current customers to complete more of their weekly shop with us again is key to reaching our sales growth target but we also believe lapsed and new customers will be attracted by the progress we have made.' Source: www.jsainsbury.co.uk.

39. Source: TNS, data published in Sainsbury's quarterly trading statements, www.jsainsbury.co.uk.

40. Source: J Sainsbury's Third Quarter Trading Statement for 12 weeks to 29 December 2007. See www.jsainsbury.co.uk.

41. Sainsbury's company news, 19 September 2005: 'The [communication] plans take Sainsbury's into the next stage of its Making Sainsbury's Great Again recovery programme ... the changes are the most significant in the company's 136-year history and are key to the company's target to grow sales by £2.5 billion by March 2008.' Source: www.jsainsbury.co.uk.

42. Details of the ROI of the Jamie Oliver TV campaign are confidential.

43. Source: PHD Media.

44. It is important to note that the *Try* idea effect is not simply a campaign effect by another name, as OHAL derived it not from a media spend variable – all of which have been isolated and excluded before determining the sales contribution of the idea – but from a step-change variable, a base level shift in the model. 'The measure of the *Try something new* idea is very strong, and the variable itself is not highly correlated with other variables in the regression matrix.' Source: OHAL.

45. September 2005 to December 2007.

46. Implementation costs have largely been print costs for tip cards, store signage and POS display.

47. Justin King statement from Sainsbury's Annual Review and Summary Financial Statement 2006. Source: www.jsainsbury.co.uk.

Other companies involved in campaign: Media Agency: PHD; Econometrics Marketing Consultancy: OHAL.

SECTION 4

Silver winners

Chapter 13

Audi

Firing up the quattro: how Audi accelerated into the 21st century

By Ed Booty, Rachel Hatton, Dan Hauck and Adam Knight, Bartle Bogle Hegarty

Editor's summary

Over the last eight years, Audi in the UK has produced some of the most creative and innovative communications in the automotive sector. This paper shows they have also been among the most effective.

At the turn of the new millennium Audi had ambitious targets for the UK market, aiming to accelerate sales growth, break out of third position in the premium sector and ultimately challenge BMW for leadership.

This period saw a return to 'Vorsprung durch Technik' as a consistent brand line and a theme for the whole communications strategy. It is this philosophy of a relentless desire to challenge and evolve that inspired Audi to radically change the way in which it uses communications, using leading models to emphasise credentials in design, performance and engineering and launching the Audi TV channel as a one-stop-shop for all things Audi.

Over the period Audi's performance in the UK outstripped the rest of Europe (which ran different communications) in terms of awareness, brand consideration and ultimately sales performance. This difference formed the basis of an ROI calculation for the UK advertising of £7.50 for every £1 spent. And while BMW still outsell Audi, the brand is now firmly in the number two spot and rising fast.

Any motor advertising that breaks the mould of the traditional car commercial, with its laboured shots of leather interiors, alloy wheels and sleek bodywork, is to be welcomed. Clearly a supporter of this philosophy, Audi has made a point of applying creative thinking in the development, not only of its cars but also to its marketing.

Source: *Superbrands Volume VI*

Introduction

This is the story of how Audi went from being the understated alternative to Mercedes and BMW, to become the fastest-growing brand in the prestige car sector – muscling past Mercedes and now chasing BMW for leadership of the sector.

Over the last eight years, Audi's sales and share growth have accelerated dramatically. This paper will show how in 1999 Audi initiated a radical overhaul of its communications strategy. This helped to fuel this unprecedented growth, culminating in over a billion pounds of added revenue.

We will show how the enduring spirit of the brand, *Vorsprung durch Technik* – the relentless desire to challenge and evolve – has inspired Audi to behave as a leader across all its communications. It has prompted Audi to change the way in which it uses communications to influence brand image and purchase behaviour.

Since the turn of the millennium, Audi has produced some of the most innovative, and we will show, effective communications the automotive sector has seen.

Background

Vorsprung durch Technik

Like 84% of the UK population, you're probably familiar with the phrase '*Vorsprung durch Technik*'. Even if you don't speak German, the phrase probably evokes a strong sense of technological expertise and precision engineering.

Vorsprung durch Technik literally means 'progression through technology'. It is the philosophy that has inspired Audi since 1899, and symbolises its relentless pursuit of innovation and superior performance.

Since 1982, this philosophy has also been the driving force for Audi's communications.

Building the Audi brand: 1982 to 1999

Hard though it is to believe now, in the early 1980s Audi had a very low profile. Initially, communications were designed to establish our identity, building our German engineering credentials and distinctive brand voice, 'Villas' being the most famous example of this (see Figure 1).

From 1995 to 1999, our communications positioned Audi as the antithesis to the overt ostentation of BMW and Mercedes – an understated choice for people confident enough to follow their own path. 'Number One' best exemplified this attitude (see Figure 2).

Figure 1: Villas

'Every year the Schmidts, the Mullers and the Reinharts drive to their holiday villas. The Schmidts' car is rather slow and noisy...'

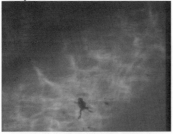

'The Mullers' drive a big thirsty car...'

Shot of frog in an unused swimming pool

The Reinharts drive an Audi 100. A car so aerodynamic it is capable of 125 miles per hour. Yet, at a steady 56 it slips along quietly for over 750 miles on one tank full of petrol."

'So when they arrive they'll need another holiday to get over this one.'

Local woman shakes still locked up Villa doors

'Which is probably at a petrol station somewhere between Munich and Marbella..'

Local man walks away from empty villa, phone rings unanswered

'And the moral of the story is, if you want to get on the beach before the Germans, you had better get an Audi 100.'

Cut to shot of two Audi cars

'Vorsprung durch Technik, as they say in Germany.'

Figure 2: Number One

VO: 'I've always been very competitive . . . [but I don't want to hear that, do I?] It's how I got where I am.

Sarcastically 'money can't buy happiness . . .'

'At the end of the day you've got to look after no. 1 to survive'.

'Yeah, the right car is important to me – I think that it does impress people . . . Money is nothing to be ashamed of' if you've got it – flaunt it.'

'The places you go, the clothes you wear, the people you're seen with . . . the car you drive'

Salesman: 'What do you think?' Main guy: 'Not really style – know what I mean'.

By the end of the last millennium, Audi was a fully fledged member of the prestige car club. It was seen as a breath of fresh air compared to the stuffy Mercedes and the brash BMW. However, despite solid sales growth, Audi remained resolutely number three in the market, behind its longer-established rivals (see Table 1).

Table 1: Audi's 1999 market position		
Brand	**Share of sector (%)**	**Position in sector**
BMW	39.41	1st
Mercedes	39.23	2nd
Audi	21.37	3rd

Source: VAG

Establishing Audi's leadership

The business challenge

Audi AG[1] had ambitious targets for the UK market. The aim for the new millennium was to step up a gear and overtake the competition. This would mean accelerating sales growth, and winning market share so that Audi could break out of third position and ultimately challenge BMW for leadership of the sector.

The implications for communications strategy

To achieve our ambition of overtaking BMW, we needed a radically different approach to communications. We needed to position Audi as the leading prestige brand.

Our communications over the previous four years had overtly positioned Audi as a more understated alternative: the brand to choose if you didn't want a BMW or a Mercedes. We had defined Audi by what it wasn't.

The brand now needed to be positive and bold about what it stood for. Audi needed to assert its leadership credentials: to set the category agenda, rather than subvert it. We needed to move from understatement to a more overt statement of intent.

It was time for a new phase in Audi's communications strategy (see Figure 3).

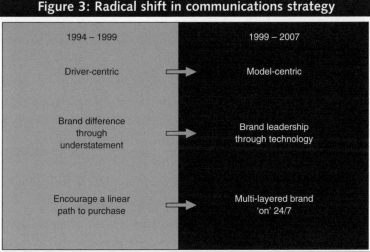

Figure 3: Radical shift in communications strategy

Source: BBH

Leadership in communications: 'Vorsprung durch Technik' redux

At this point, we realised that leadership is part of Audi's DNA. The restlessness and innovation embodied by *Vorsprung durch Technik* are defining characteristics of leadership.

Vorsprung durch Technik was to become the skewer for everything we did. It returned to centre stage in our creative executions but, more importantly, it became the spur for more radical communications thinking.

There were three key elements to our communications strategy:

1. Showcase leading models

Instead of supporting every new model launch, we took a decision to focus our fire-power on Audi's most prestigious models: its C and D segment cars, the A6 and A8; its sports coupés, the TT and the R8; and its performance models, the RS4 and RS6.

Our objective was to turn the cars into icons (see Figures 4–6).

Figure 4: R8 Text ad

Now listen to it.
Text R8 to 86100.

2. Demonstrate leadership through market-leading innovation

Communications needed to confidently assert Audi's product advantage. We didn't just want to show that Audi cars were technically better. We wanted to show Audi's superiority as a total package. Consequently we developed communications to highlight different aspects of Audi's holistic product philosophy. Our historic narrow focus on technological advantage broadened to encompass Audi's commitment to design, performance and innovation.

Our campaigns were planned to engage across multiple touchpoints – from television ads, print and digital channels, right through to retail communications.

Design

Our aim was to iconise unique elements of Audi design: the four rings, the front grille, the LED day running lights (see Figures 7 and 8).

Figure 5: RS 4 'Wings'

Figure 6: TT quattro

Figure 7: Rhythm of Lines

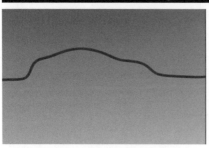

Calming piano music plays. A green line creeps onto the screen. It ebbs and flows and then makes a car-like shape before flowing away.

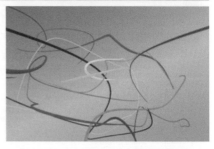

The piano music becomes more intense and a cello joins in. More lines flow around the screen apparently randomly. At this point it could be seen to resemble the boot of an Audi.

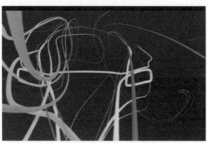

The cello and piano now play together as the colour scheme changes. Lines flow faster and the front of an Audi can be made out.

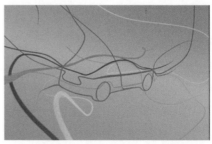

More stringed instruments join in. The lines more obviously start to make the shape of the Audi A5 model.

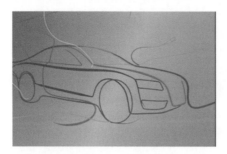

The music builds to a crescendo and the shape of the Audi A5 becomes clear.

The music slows down and we see the endline 'A rhythm of lines. The new Audi A5'

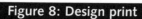

Figure 8: Design print

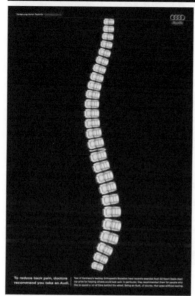

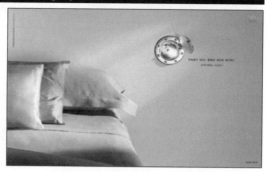

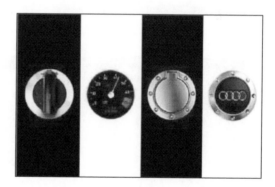

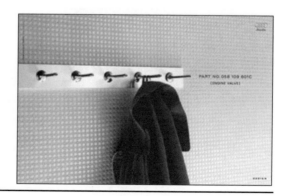

Performance

We dramatised Audi's performance credentials in an understated intelligent way, rooting our communications in proprietary Audi technology, such as quattro and Dynamic Ride Control, as showcased in 'Bull' and 'Wakeboarder'. The most recent expression of performance featured the R8 (see Figures 9–11).

Figure 9: Bull

Dramatic/dark music and light - slightly disturbing, night time

Man watches as Bull is released into ring

Bull leaps around in wild untamed manner with rider struggling to stay on

Man manages to stay on the bull throughout

Bull stands as if respecting the rider

Cut to shot of RS 6

Figure 10: Wakeboarder

Wakeboarder's cord goes tight

Wakeboarder does a number of tricks

Cruises behind car elegantly

Corners on board using his hand

Jumps an abandoned shipwreck
and lands jump

Car comes to stop - wakeboarder stares at car
adoringly, puts board in boot of car

Innovation

We highlighted Audi's continuing commitment to engineering innovation – from specific technologies, such as FSi direct injection, to Audi's approach to product development (for instance, the fact that in creating the latest A6, Audi filed more patents than NASA has ever done) (see Figures 12 and 13).

Figure 11: R8 Construction

Ticking clock music as lights in the
factory come on and show single car
in factory workshop

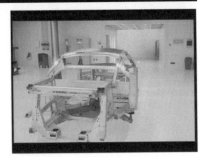

Beep beep music starts as car is
being welded

Images of car being painstakingly
constructed with every part
laboured over

Intricate measurements of the car
using lasers

Main body of car is added and car is
completed with 360 degree shots of it
completed

Front shot of R8, car lights go on,
white end line... 'the slowest car
we've ever built'

Figure 12: Fish

Music plays. An Audi drives through London at night. It stops at a pedestrian crossing.

A giant fish then pulls up alongside the car. When the light changes both the car and the fish move off.

The camera then shoots from the Audi driver's POV as we see they are surrounded by fish. A stingray floats through a tunnel.

There is a shot from above and we see that the Audi is the only car on the road. It appears that every other car in London has been replaced by a fish.

We see out the Audi from the driver's POV again. At a petrol station there are lots of fish being filled up at the pumps, as if they were cars.

As the Audi drives off into the night we see the tagline:

'FSI from Audi. A petrol engine without a drink problem'

Figure 13: Satellite

Changing weather, volatile/unsettled/changing conditions
VO: Combination of languages speaking over one another

Camera zooms out from earth into the stratosphere
VO: Mixture of languages continues

Cut to ground control screen

Parachute opens and heads into the abyss

Cut to another ground control screen

Cuts to sea, car dives underwater towards the camera

3. Leading communications innovation

The most profound change to our communications strategy concerned our approach to creative and channel thinking.

We observed that the way people buy prestige cars was radically changing. Ten years ago, the average prestige buyer would think seriously about cars only once every three years, when their car needed replacement.[2] We now found that prestige new car buyers were 'always on': always aware of the market, always researching their options, and using a plethora of media to do it. We were now in an age of casual consideration.

'Always on' car buying had two big implications for our channel thinking.

We were now in a world where brand image could be equally influenced by product placement in movies, user-generated content on YouTube, Jeremy Clarkson's latest rant: in effect these are brand communications. So we couldn't just be an advertiser. Our communications would need to lead popular culture: to invite participation and create debate.

We also needed to *lead buyer behaviour*. With no significant increases in overall communications budgets, and an increasingly fragmented media environment, we would need to pull people through from consideration to conversion more efficiently.

Leading popular culture

We explored leading brand behaviour in sectors outside our own. Brands such as Nike and Apple don't just advertise. They create experiences and content for people to engage with.

We set ourselves the challenge of becoming content creators. In the years since 2000, Audi has gone from pure advertiser to creator of prestige brand content. It's been a music brand, a curator, a publisher. We've created content that has shown people what Audi's 'Vorsprung' philosophy means in the context of contemporary culture.

For the launch of the RS6 in 2003, Audi created an edition of *GQ* magazine: the 'Power Edition' featuring modern icons of power – including the A6 (see Figure 14).

Figure 14: *GQ* Power Edition

Our campaign for the original Audi TT revealed that it had been designed under the influence of Jimi Hendrix. A key strand of activity was an Audi-curated Hendrix photographic exhibition (see Figure 15).

For the launch of the new TT, Audi turned music label, offering contemporary versions of classic tracks, with its TT Remastered campaign (see Figure 16).

For the launch of the new A6, Audi offered a trip to space as part of its Patents campaign (see Figure 17).

Figure 15: Hendrix Exhibition

Figure 16: TT Remastered

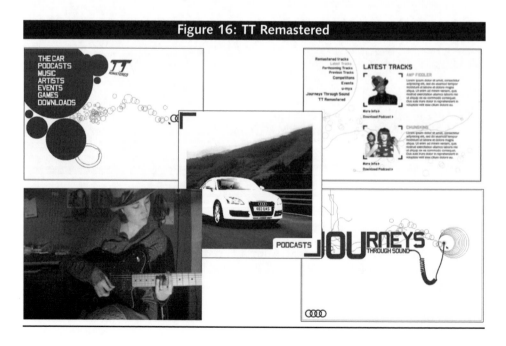

Figure 17: A6 Patents campaign

Audi has become a magazine publisher in its own right, offering a high-quality four-monthly magazine to customers.

Leading buyer behaviour

In response to the 'always on' buyer, we developed an 'always on' channel strategy.

Traditional advertising moved from a burst approach to a more continuous approach, with more efficient targeting allowing us to extend our campaign presence over longer periods.

We increased our commitment and investment online. Increasingly, www.audi.co.uk functions as a virtual dealership, enabling customers to research and configure their perfect Audi. Rich media content enables people to engage more deeply with the Audi brand (see Figures 18 and 19).

Our most radical innovation was to develop the Audi Channel, a 24-hour TV channel available on the Sky Digital platform, and latterly on www.audi.co.uk. It was the first brand-owned TV channel in the UK.

The Audi Channel was designed to create a rich experience for prospective customers at any time of day, at any point in the purchase process, without having to set foot in a dealership. Through a continually refreshed suite of bespoke programming, the Audi Channel has allowed potential customers to obtain

Figure 18: www.audi.co.uk

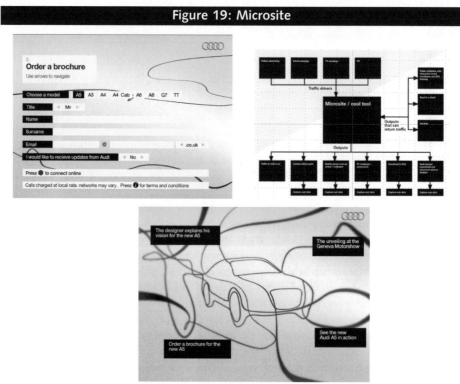

Figure 19: Microsite

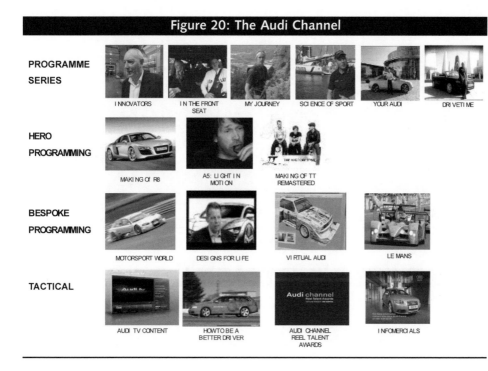

Figure 20: The Audi Channel

PROGRAMME
SERIES

INNOVATORS · IN THE FRONT SEAT · MY JOURNEY · SCIENCE OF SPORT · YOUR AUDI · DRIVE TIME

HERO
PROGRAMMING

MAKING OF R8 · A5: LIGHT IN MOTION · MAKING OF TT REMASTERED

BESPOKE
PROGRAMMING

MOTORSPORT WORLD · DESIGNS FOR LIFE · VIRTUAL AUDI · LE MANS

TACTICAL

AUDI TV CONTENT · HOW TO BE A BETTER DRIVER · AUDI CHANNEL REEL TALENT AWARDS · INFOMERCIALS

engaging and in-depth information on Audi's cars, the Audi brand and Audi's motor sport credentials (see Figure 20).

Summary

Audi's long-term business objectives were to overtake BMW as the leading prestige car brand in the UK.

Our communications needed to position Audi as a leader. We did this in three ways: by showcasing our leading models, demonstrating leadership in design philosophy and leading communications innovation.

We will now go on to show how our approach has paid dividends for Audi in terms of business results.

Sales results: 1999–2007

Between 1999 and 2007 Audi volume sales in the UK increased dramatically, culminating in the sale of its millionth car in 2007 (see Figure 21).

Audi's volume growth rate during the period has far exceeded the growth rate of the market (see Figure 22).

As a result, Audi has dramatically increased its share of overall market volume (see Figure 23).

This growth has been driven primarily by Audi's core models – the A3, A4 and A6 – which have all steadily built share (see Figure 24).

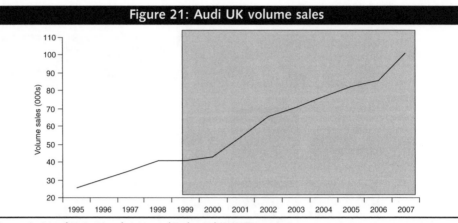

Source: Society of Motor Manufacturers and Traders Ltd (SMMT)

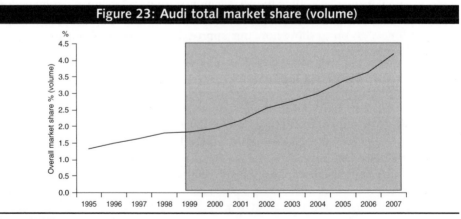

Source: SMMT

Figure 24: Audi core models share of prestige market

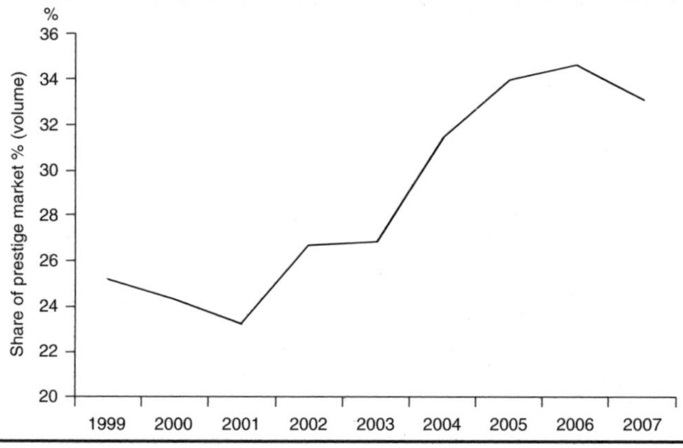

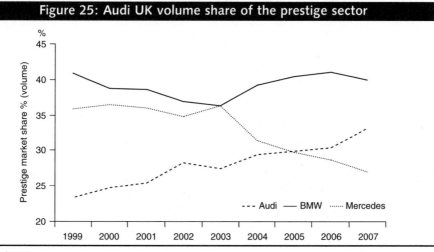

Source: SMMT

When we look at this growth in the context of the prestige sector it becomes even more impressive. Audi's volume growth has been the strongest of the sector over the last eight years (see Figure 25).

Figure 25: Audi UK volume share of the prestige sector

Source: SMMT

When set specifically against its key competitors – BMW and Mercedes – Audi has clearly outperformed the more established prestige marques (see Figure 26).

This growth success has led some to predict that Audi will overtake BMW within the coming years.

Audi set to overtake BMW as the UK's premium marque.

Source: *Marketing Week*, 2008

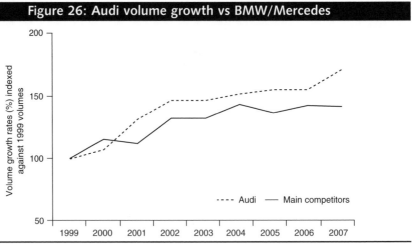

Figure 26: Audi volume growth vs BMW/Mercedes

Source: SMMT

Demonstrating the contribution of advertising

The success of Audi over the last ten years has been exceptional. Clearly, this success has been the result of a number of factors, including our communications. We will now prove that communications have played a significant role in the success of the brand in the UK.

We will do this in three ways:

1. by showing that Audi's success cannot solely be explained by other factors, either in Audi's marketing mix, or in the wider environment
2. by showing that this success has been driven by improvements in Audi's image in the UK relative to Europe
3. by demonstrating that, in the UK, Audi's communications have worked as intended to drive brand image.

As further evidence, we will also show that Audi communications have become more efficient over time, as a result of our numerous media innovations. Finally, we will show that Audi communications have had a positive impact on key influencers in the car-buying process.

Audi's success cannot solely be explained by other factors

We will now show that the remarkable success in the UK cannot be attributed to the following factors:

1. improved product
2. reduced prices
3. increased customer incentives
4. improved distribution
5. growth in the prestige sector
6. reduced competition in the prestige sector.

1. Improved product

Audi's product range has improved and expanded since 1997. However, the same improved and expanded product range has been sold in other European markets, and Audi's sales have grown faster in the UK than in the brand's other four major European markets (see Figure 27).[3] Therefore, it is clear that improved products are not the only reason for Audi's success.

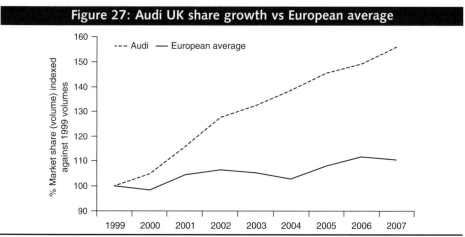

Figure 27: Audi UK share growth vs European average

Source: SMMT, Euromonitor

2. Reduced prices

Audi has maintained its price premium against the total car market over the last eight years, so reduced prices cannot account for Audi's success (see Figure 28).

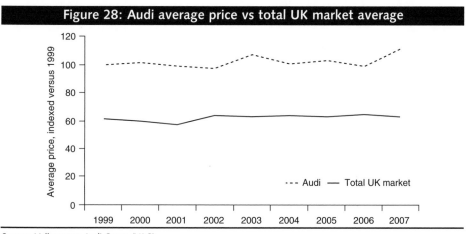

Figure 28: Audi average price vs total UK market average

Source: Volkswagen Audi Group (VAG)

Audi's price has always been a little lower than its main rivals, BMW and Mercedes. This positioning has been consistent over time; in fact, Audi's relative price has increased in the most recent campaign period (see Figure 29).

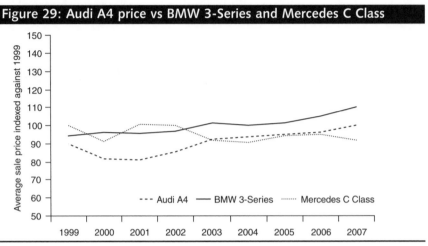

Figure 29: Audi A4 price vs BMW 3-Series and Mercedes C Class

Source: VAG

3. Increased customer incentives
Audi has continued to offer lower levels of incentives (the percentage of people who are offered financial incentives to purchase) than its competitors (see Figure 30).

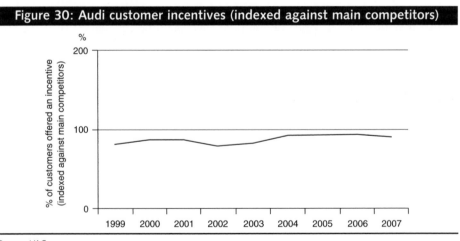

Figure 30: Audi customer incentives (indexed against main competitors)

Source: VAG

4. Improved distribution
The number of Audi dealerships in the UK had fallen between 1999 and 2007. Audi's increased sales are therefore not the result of increased distribution (see Figure 31).

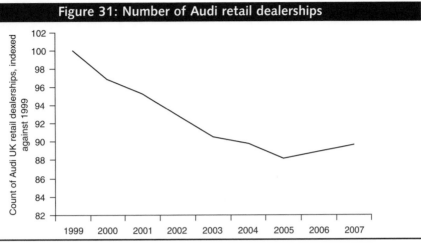

Figure 31: Number of Audi retail dealerships

Source: Audi UK

The Audi network does however remain strong and highly efficient. So, despite decreased numbers, it remains a highly effective organisation.

Moreover, Audi's rate of sale in the UK has risen faster than rate of sale in the other European markets. This suggests that demand for Audi has increased faster in the UK than in the other major European markets (see Figure 32).

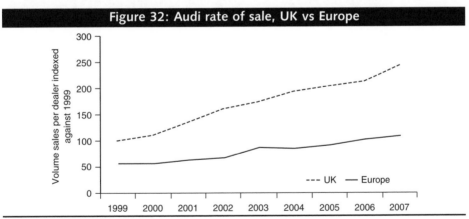

Figure 32: Audi rate of sale, UK vs Europe

Source: SMMT, Euromonitor, Audi UK

5. Growth in the prestige sector

The prestige sector in the UK has grown over the last eight years. But, as we have demonstrated, Audi's share of the prestige sector has also grown. This shows that the growing demand for prestige cars cannot explain Audi's growth.

In addition, the prestige market in Europe has grown at a similar rate to the UK, so Audi's relative success in the UK is not the result of a faster-growing prestige market (see Figure 33).

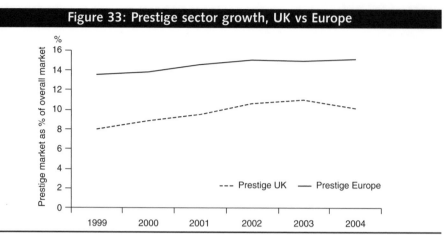

Figure 33: Prestige sector growth, UK vs Europe

Source: Primary – *Premium Power: The Secret of Success of Mercedes-Benz, BMW, Porsche and Audi*, 2005, by Philipp G. Rosengarten and Christoph B. Stuermer; Secondary – SMMT

6. Reduced competition in the prestige sector

During the period, BMW and Mercedes have continued to extend and expand their ranges (see Figure 34).

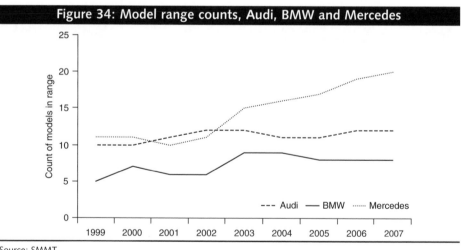

Figure 34: Model range counts, Audi, BMW and Mercedes

Source: SMMT

Equally, Audi's share of voice has not increased significantly during the time period (see Figure 35).

It is worth noting that Mercedes sales have undoubtedly suffered over recent years and Audi overtook Mercedes in terms of share within the prestige sector in 2005. However, Audi's sales since 2006 have not been disproportionately drawn from Mercedes (see Figure 36).

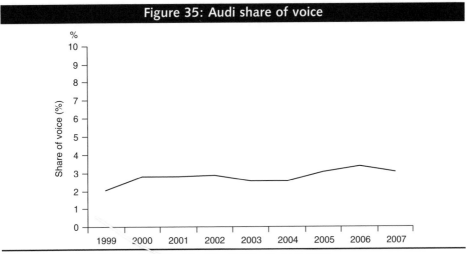

Figure 35: Audi share of voice

Source: Primary – Audi UK; Secondary – *The Advertising Statistics Yearbook*, 2007

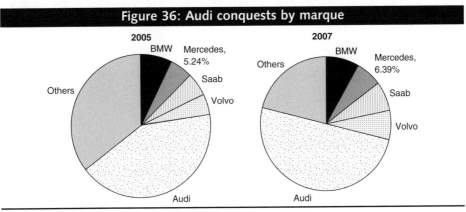

Figure 36: Audi conquests by marque

Source: VAG

We have shown that Audi's sales growth in the UK cannot be solely attributed to improved product, and that price, distribution and market factors also do not account for Audi's success.

Improvements in Audi's image in the UK relative to Europe

We will now go on to show that Audi's success in the UK (relative to the rest of Europe) is the result of Audi's stronger brand image.

In the period 1999–2007, we have specifically sought to position Audi as:

■ a technically advanced brand
■ a performance brand
■ a brand with well-designed products
■ a prestige brand.

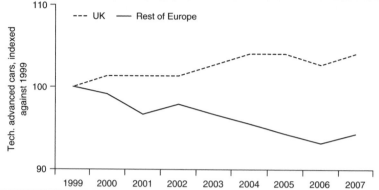

Figure 37: Audi image measures UK vs Europe: technically advanced

Source: Audi AG Brand Tracking Study, Image und Bekanntheits
Base: All new car buyers

Figure 38: Audi image measures UK vs Europe: good performance

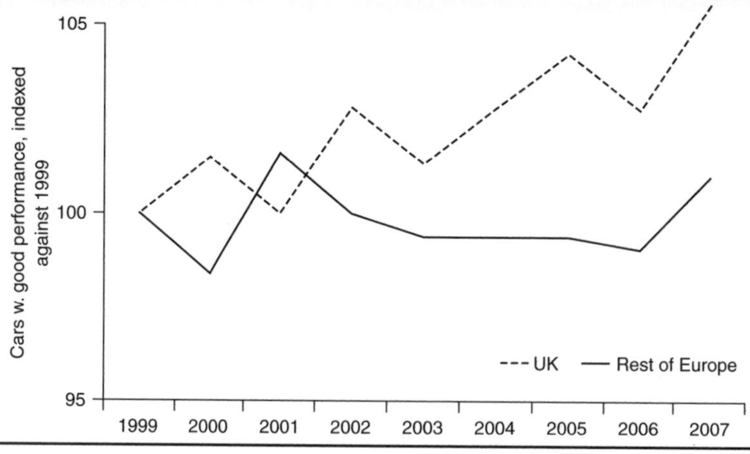

Source: Audi AG Brand Tracking Study, Image und Bekanntheits
Base: All new car buyers

When we look at corresponding image measures we can see improvements, relative to Europe, on the specific image dimensions we have targeted (see Figures 37–40, Note: The closest proxy to design that we have is 'well styled'.)

Overall, we can see a strengthening in Audi brand image relative to the rest of Europe (see Figure 41).

This suggests that the relative strength of Audi's sales in the UK can be attributed to relative improvement in brand image. We will now go on to show how communications have improved Audi's brand perceptions in the UK.

Figure 39: Audi image measures UK vs Europe: well styled

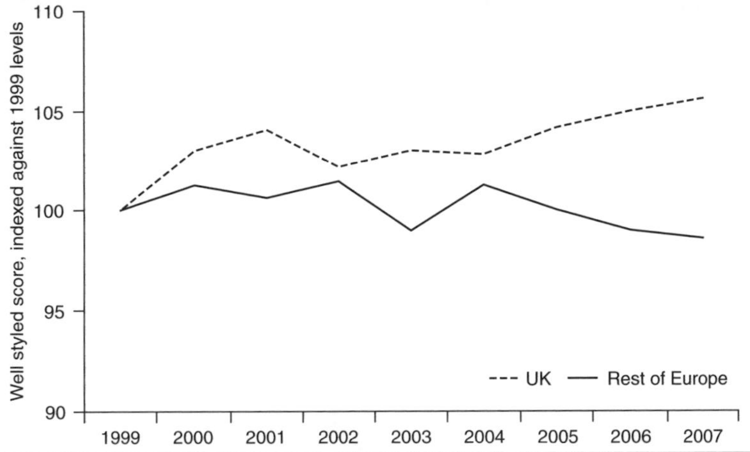

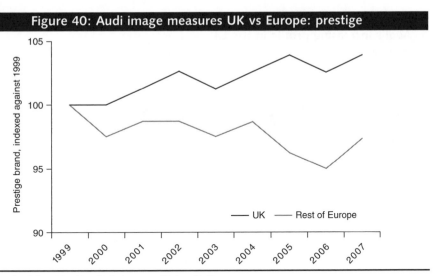

Source: Audi AG Brand Tracking Study, Image und Bekanntheits
Base: All new car buyers

Figure 40: Audi image measures UK vs Europe: prestige

Source: Audi AG Brand Tracking Study, Image und Bekanntheits
Base: All new car buyers

Audi's communications have worked as intended to drive brand image

We will show that:

1. communications have helped build Audi's profile in the UK
2. communications have established *Vorsprung durch Technik* as a famous and meaningful brand property for Audi
3. communications correlate with changes in brand image
4. communications correlate with uplifts in brand desirability and consideration.

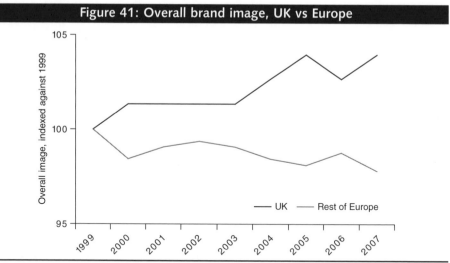

Figure 41: Overall brand image, UK vs Europe

Source: Audi AG Brand Tracking Study, Image und Bekanntheits
Base: All new car buyers

1. Audi's increasing profile in the UK

Awareness of Audi's advertising has steadily increased during the time period (see Figure 42).

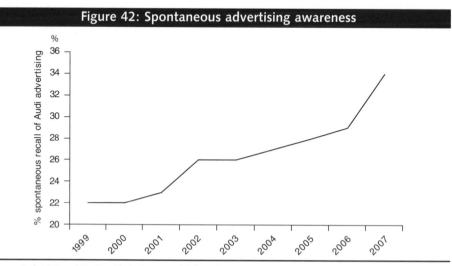

Figure 42: Spontaneous advertising awareness

Source: Audi AG Brand Tracking Study, Image und Bekanntheits
Base: All new car buyers

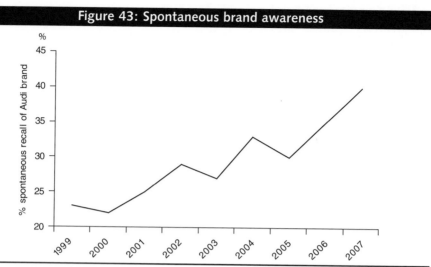

Figure 43: Spontaneous brand awareness

Source: Hall & Partners Brand Tracking Study; Simpson Carpenter Brand Tracking Study
Base: All new car buyers

Audi's brand awareness has also grown strongly over time (see Figure 43).

This growth in brand awareness has helped it become one of the most iconic brands in the UK (see Table 2).

Table 2: Coolest brands in the UK

Sector	Coolest brand
Fashion	Diesel
Drink	Stella Artois
Technology	Bose
Venue	London Eye
Motor	Audi
Music artist	The Streets
Director	Quentin Tarantino
Author	JK Rowling
Businessman	Sir Richard Branson
Celebrity	Johnny Depp
Uncoolest celebrity	Jordan

Source: Superbrands Limited/Brand Council of the UK, 2004

And, within the prestige market specifically, Audi's presence has grown (see Figure 44).

2. *Vorsprung durch Technik* is a famous and meaningful brand property
Vorsprung durch Technik has become one of the most widely recognised advertising ideas in the UK, with over 84% awareness. Its fame has continued to grow over the last ten years (see Figure 45).

Figure 44: Audi's share of prestige PR

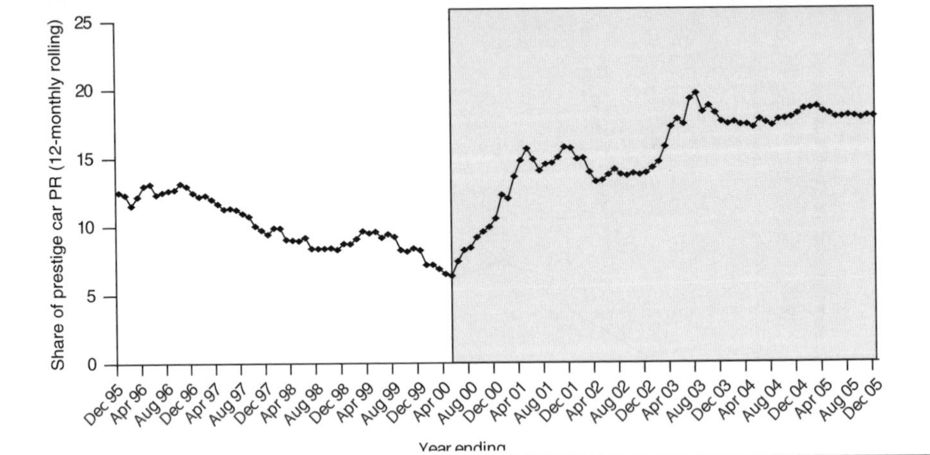

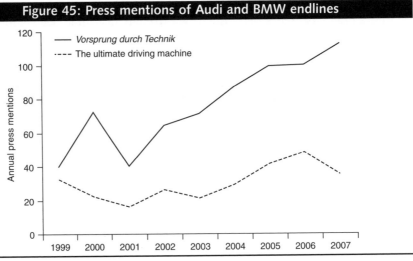

Source: Factiva

Figure 45: Press mentions of Audi and BMW endlines

Source: Factiva

It has entered into the British vernacular, often parodied in music, film and journalism (see Figure 46).

Despite the fact that people rarely know what it literally means, it has created a rich set of consumer associations (see Figure 47).

Take the slogan 'Vorsprung durch Technik': we may not understand it, but nevertheless it is unashamedly German which triggers engineering quality and performance. It uses the word 'Technik', which equates with scientific expertise; and because it is not translated it suggests sophistication and confidence.

Source: Robert Heath, *The Hidden Power of Advertising*

Figure 46: *Vorsprung durch Technik* as part of popular culture

Vorsprung durch Techno

Joe Queenan revels in the electrifying banality of
Kraftwerk. Has any pop act ever been more German?

Friday February 22, 2008
guardian.co.uk

Kraftwerk in inaction

'Vorsprung
durch
Terry'
as we say in England

Vorsprung Dyk Technik

Paul van Dyk *remixes* 92-98

Vorsprung durch Becknik
(AS THEY SAY IN MADRID AND HERTFORDSHIRE)

The Sun - 9th July 2003

Source: *The Sun* newspaper, 2006, 2003, and other sources as above

Figure 47: Consumer understanding of *Vorsprung durch Technik*

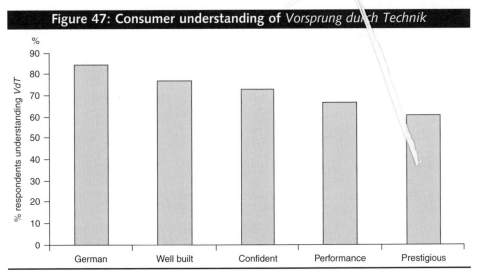

Source: Hall & Partners, Brand Tracking Study 2003

3. Communications correlate with changes in brand image

As intended, brand perceptions of Audi have improved versus our key competitors in the UK (see Figure 48).

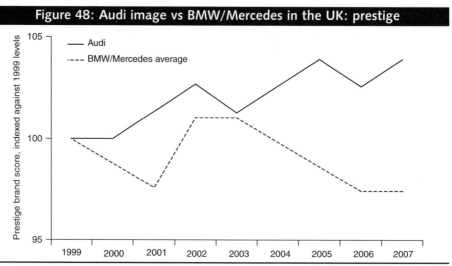

Figure 48: Audi image vs BMW/Mercedes in the UK: prestige

Source: Audi AG Brand Tracking Study, Image und Bekanntheits
Base: All new car buyers

We do not have continuous tracking data covering the period 1999–2007. However, when we look at image measures over the 2000–2003 period, we can see how these have consistently shifted in line with communications activity (see Figures 49 and 50).

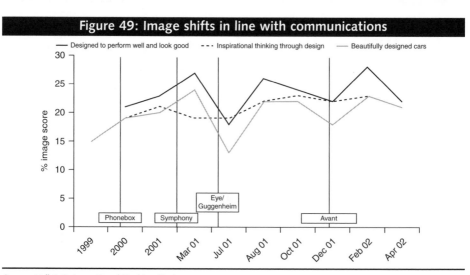

Figure 49: Image shifts in line with communications

Source: Hall & Partners, Brand Tracking Study
Base: All new car buyers

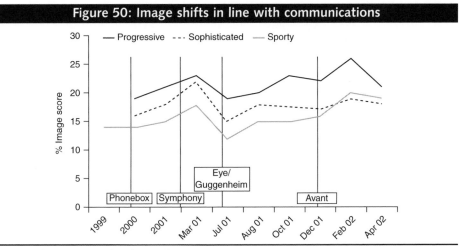

Figure 50: Image shifts in line with communications

Source: Hall & Partners, Brand Tracking Study
Base: All new car buyers

For this period, we can also compare perceptions of those who have seen the advertising with those who have not. This clearly demonstrates how effectively the key messages were communicated (see Figures 51–53). Note that these data are based on non-Audi drivers.

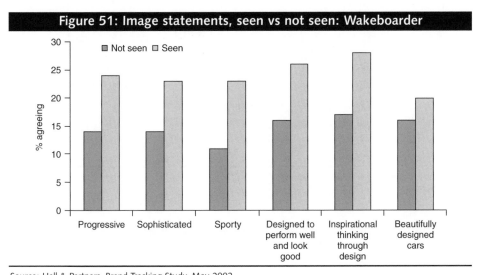

Figure 51: Image statements, seen vs not seen: Wakeboarder

Source: Hall & Partners, Brand Tracking Study, May 2002
Base: All new non-Audi-owning car buyers

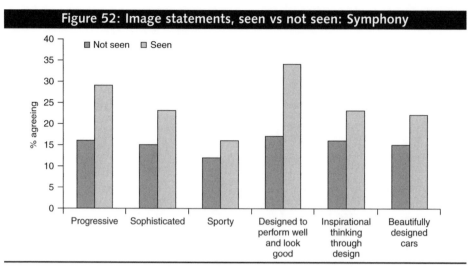

Figure 52: Image statements, seen vs not seen: Symphony

Source: Hall & Partners, Brand Tracking Study, March 2001
Base: All new non-Audi owning car buyers

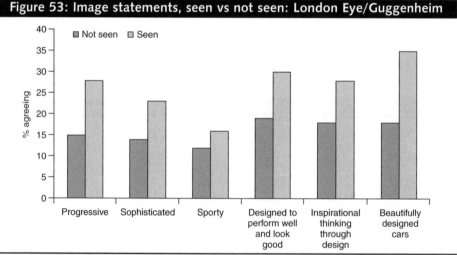

Figure 53: Image statements, seen vs not seen: London Eye/Guggenheim

Source: Hall & Partners, Brand Tracking Study, March 2001
Base: All new non-Audi owning car buyers

4. Communications correlate with uplifts in brand desirability and consideration

Brand consideration has increased steadily over the time period (see Figure 54).

Again, for the 1999–2003 phase, we can isolate the effect of communications on consideration by comparing viewers and non-viewers of the executions (see Figure 55).

For 2003–2007, we can see a direct correlation between consideration and communications (see Table 3).

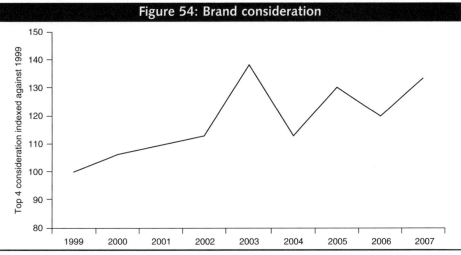

Figure 54: Brand consideration

Source: VAG

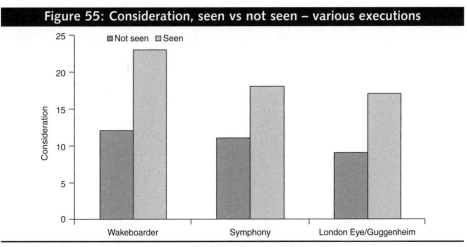

Figure 55: Consideration, seen vs not seen – various executions

Source: Hall & Partners, Brand Tracking Study, May 2002, August 2001, March 2001
Base: All new car buyers

Table 3: Serious brand consideration

Creative	Date	Consideration pre-exposure	Consideration post-exposure	Change
A8 'Test'	September 2004	14	18	29
A6 'Letters'	November 2004	12	20	67
RS4 'Spider'	November 2005	16	18	13
A6 'Satellite'	October 2006	17	20	18
A5 'Rhythm of Lines'	July 2007	18	23	28
R8 'Construction'	November 2007	19	24	26

Source: Simpson Carpenter Brand Tracking Study, July 2004–December 2007
Base: All new car buyers

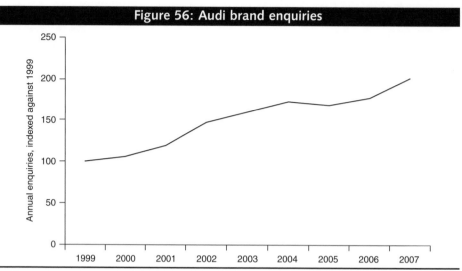

Figure 56: Audi brand enquiries

Source: Audi UK

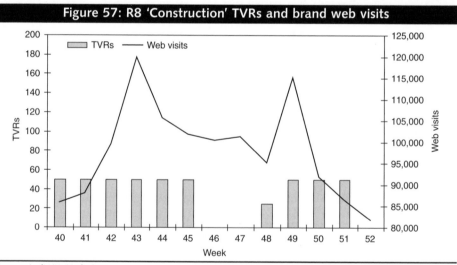

Figure 57: R8 'Construction' TVRs and brand web visits

Source: Audi UK, MediaCom

Overall enquiries have increased over time (see Figure 56) and again, we can see a clear correlation between uplifts in enquiries and communications activity (see Figure 57).

Further evidence of advertising effect

Increasing communication efficiency

Taking the category lead in media has reaped huge rewards, with our communications becoming more efficient over time.

Figure 58: Recognition, enjoyment and distinctiveness ad diagnostic scores

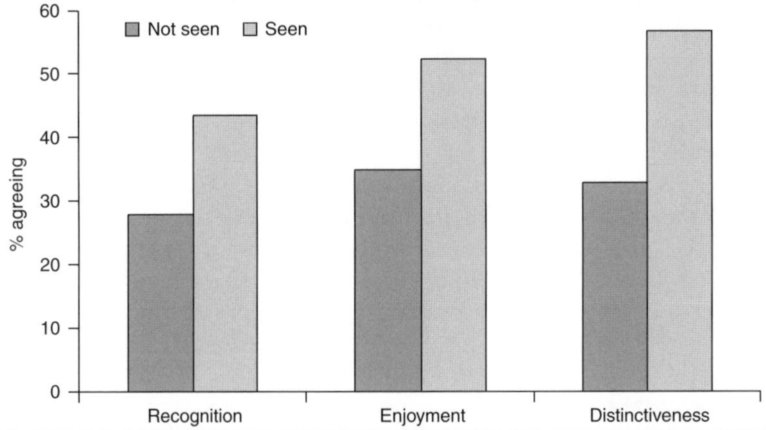

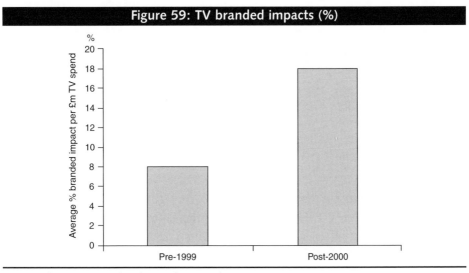

Source: Hall & Partners, Brand Tracking Study, various dates
Base: All new car buyers

TV ads have been consistently well recognised, cutting through the clutter (see Figure 58).

As a medium, TV has become more efficient at generating advertising awareness (see Figure 59).

Each digital campaign has produced high levels of engagement. Campaign microsites have gained unprecedented numbers of unique viewers.

Interactive TV (i-TV) has consistently outperformed the norms for the medium. For example, the A6 Satellite campaign achieved a 2.2% response rate versus an

Figure 59: TV branded impacts (%)

Source: Hall & Partners, Brand Tracking Study, various dates
Base: Prestige car buyers

industry norm of 0.96%, while the A5 Rhythm of Lines campaign achieved 171,000 household interactions, making it the third most successful i-TV campaign within the automotive sector.

Mobile has been equally effective. Within two weeks of the R8 campaign breaking, some 30,000 people had downloaded the ringtone. Of these, 93% were unknown to Audi, showing the effectiveness of the communications as a prospect-generating tool.

Innovative uses of content have also made a real impact. Over 60,00 people downloaded the tracks produced for the TT Remastered campaign, while the podcast was the most successful motoring podcast on iTunes during the campaign period, beating BMW, Porsche, Honda and *What Car?*

Our direct marketing activity has consistently registered higher than average response rates and has increased its efficiencies over time (see Figure 60).

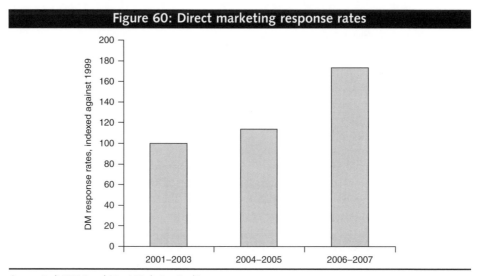

Figure 60: Direct marketing response rates

Source: Audi UK Internal Direct Marketing Tracking

The Audi Channel has proven to be an effective medium for engaging prospects. It has had an excellent reception and a positive influence on potential buyers' decision making.

As a consequence of this increased efficiency over many channels, overall marketing spend per car sold has significantly reduced over the last ten years (see Figure 61).

Positive impact on other key influencers

Audi communications have had a positive impact on key influencers in the purchase process.

First, our communications have been consistently well regarded by Audi dealers. Audi dealers' perceptions of Audi marketing in the UK have steadily improved over time (see Figure 62).

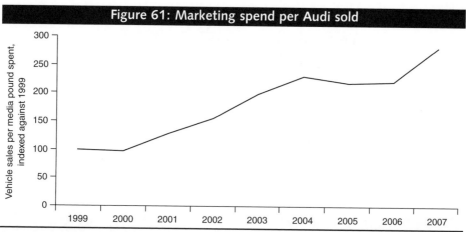

Figure 61: Marketing spend per Audi sold

Source: SMMT, Audi UK

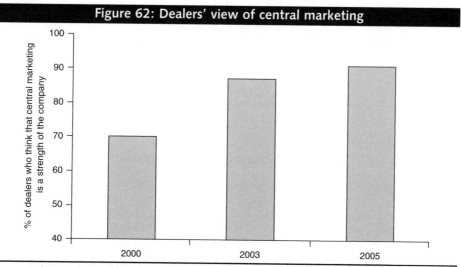

Figure 62: Dealers' view of central marketing

Source: Audi UK Dealer Satisfaction Questionnaire

Second, our communications have generated real traction, with considerably higher engagement online than our competitors (see Table 4).

The ads are not only viewed again and again, they are also talked about. They have generated over 1.3 million mentions within blogs. Below is a selection of what people have said.

This is an admittedly very cool new ad for Audi ...

The latest Audi advert a real killer.

There's no doubt it's a winning ad ...

Ultra Cool 2009 Audi RS6 Gymnastics TV Advert.

Two Great Audi Ads We Never See in the USA.

It's an Audi ad. It's beautifully shot. Audi drivers will love it, partly because the car looks stunning but mostly because it will make them feel slightly superior.

My award for the most impressive ad on right now would be the Audi (RS4) advert. It's dark, creepy and beautifully shot … The advert ends with spider's webs spelling out Vorsprung Durch Technik. Very impressive.

The RS4 TV ad really really kicks serious arse.

Source: Various online automotive blogs

Table 4: Car advertising YouTube views		
Brand	Creative	Views
Audi	R8 Slowest Car We've Ever Built	776,000
Audi	RS6 Gymnasts	114,000
Audi	A5 Rhythm of Lines	105,000
Audi	Audi 100 CS (1986) Ski Jump	94,000
BMW	It's only a car	84,767
BMW	See how it feels	78,854
Audi	RS4 Bull	70,000
Mercedes	Alonso vs Hamilton	20,851
Mercedes	Every owner has a history	13,008

Source: YouTube

Summary and quantifying the effect of communications

We have demonstrated that Audi's share of the car market has grown substantially faster than in the other four European markets. We have demonstrated that this cannot be the result of improved product, distribution, pricing, economic or competitive factors.

We have shown that Audi's brand image in the UK has improved relative to the other major European markets. We have shown that communications have been responsible for driving Audi's brand image, and we will now go on to quantify the effect of these communications.

To do this, we will compare Audi's UK performance between 1999 and 2007 against the aggregated performance of the other major European markets. Variations in product range, pricing strategy, media spend and distribution have been broadly similar over time. The only significant difference has been communications.

We can calculate the volume that Audi would have gained had it followed the same share growth as the rest of Europe. The difference between this figure and the actual sales figure is the incremental volume gain from UK communications.

This represents approximately *50,030 extra cars sold*, which equates to additional revenue for Audi of £1.29 billion. Communications spend for the period was £172m. This means that every £1 spent on communications produced £7.50 in extra revenue.

For communications to have paid back it would require the profit margin to exceed 13%. For confidentiality reasons, we are unable to disclose profit margins here, but we can say that communications have more than paid for themselves.

We should also consider that this figure takes into account only the additional effectiveness of communications in the UK versus other markets, rather than the total effectiveness of communications in the UK, which is likely to have been considerably higher, especially given the high adstock that such a long-running brand like Audi will have. This shows just how profitable Audi's communication strategy of the last decade has been.

Conclusions and learning

'*Vorsprung durch Technik*' is undoubtedly an extremely powerful and enduring brand idea for Audi.

This paper shows how we have derived additional value from this idea using it as the inspiration for how we behave, not just what we say. *Vorsprung durch Technik* was the spur to developing a radical communications agenda in response to a fundamental shift in the way people were buying prestige cars. In a world where how you behave is increasingly important in defining a brand's image, advertisers need to ensure that their brand ideas can genuinely inspire relevant and different brand behaviour.

This paper also highlights an emerging role for brand content. We often define this in terms of adding richness, deepening engagement or extending dwell time with an idea. This paper shows that brand content can increase efficiency. The Audi Channel now acts as a 'one-stop shop' for all things Audi, allowing people to interact with the brand at their convenience, 24/7.

This paper suggests that advertisers should be seeking to gain efficiencies as they create a broader palette of brand communications, not just extra richness.

Notes

1. The global Audi corporation.
2. Source: Advantage Research, 2003.
3. Audi's new models are launched at similar times across its major European markets, with a consistent pricing strategy and mix of engines. Major communication campaigns across Europe align behind these model launches. Local markets have the flexibility to run communications that are relevant to their consumers. They also have the flexibility to specify options packages at a local level.

Other companies involved in the campaign: Media company: MediaCom

Chapter 14

Danone Activia

The value of letting the product shine

By Jeremy Poole, RKCR/Y&R
Contributing author: Joanna Bamford, RKCR/Y&R

Editor's summary

This paper demonstrates how Activia went from a niche player worth £26.3m a year to a brand with sales over £120m in just three and a half years. Launched in 1999, Activia is unique for being a yoghurt containing a probiotic culture that has digestive benefits. Using a testimonial approach in its core TV campaign to discuss digestive discomfort, the product benefit was delivered sensitively and appropriately. The success of the campaign produced a short-term incremental profit of £29.9m, and also generated payback of £3.03 per every £1 spent.

Introduction

A good advertisement is one which sells the product without drawing attention to itself.

David Ogilvy

This is a simple story.

But it's a simple story with an impressive ending.

It is the story of how Activia went from a niche player worth £26.3m a year to a brand with sales of over £120m in just three and a half years.

It is a story of how a tried-and-tested communications convention proved to be the most appropriate way to talk about a sensitive issue.

It is the story of advertising that generated more incremental profit than the total value of the brand before the campaign began.

Sometimes it really is as simple as allowing the product to shine.

Activia circa September 2004

Activia was launched in 1999.[1] It is a great-tasting yoghurt with a difference: it contains a probiotic culture that has digestive system benefits.[2]

But due to Clearcast (formerly BACC) restrictions on making digestive claims, it was positioned as a general 'feel good' yoghurt.[3]

By September 2004, Activia was worth £26.3m but ranked only 16th in the market by value. Moreover, it looked as if Activia had reached a natural plateau. Sales volume and penetration had remained largely flat since the beginning of 2003. (See Figure 1 for sales in first year of launch.)

Turnover in the yoghurt aisle is high with around 150 new variants a year and aggressive promotional support. Staying still is suicide.

Activia was marooned. It urgently needed to regain momentum.

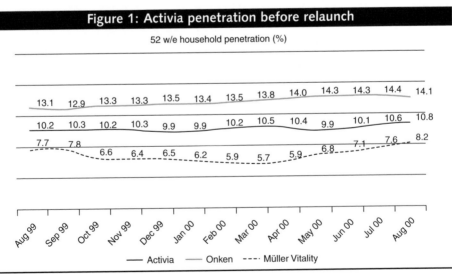

Figure 1: Activia penetration before relaunch

52 w/e household penetration (%)

Source: ACNielsen Homescan Sept. 2003–2004

Same product. New news

In mid-2004 we received good news.

On receipt of further clinical evidence, the Clearcast finally agreed we could make a more specific digestive health claim on TV:

> *Activia is scientifically proven to help improve digestive transit when eaten every day for 14 days.*

Or, not to sugar-coat it, when your digestive system is a little sluggish, Activia helps reduce the time it takes for your food to come out.

This was a breakthrough. Used right it could recast Activia from a general feel-good yoghurt into a brand with a specific and highly differentiated digestive health claim to give it renewed sales impetus.

The opportunity

Slow digestive transit means decomposing food ends up hanging around inside us for longer, leading to discomfort, heaviness, constipation and various unpleasant side-effects such as flatulence.

Clinical studies indicate that digestive transit is generally longer in women than men. Indeed Activia's 2004 U & A indicated that nearly two-thirds of the female population in the UK, close to 15 million women, self-diagnosed digestive system problems (see Figure 2).

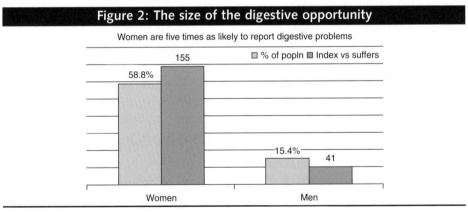

Figure 2: The size of the digestive opportunity

Women are five times as likely to report digestive problems

☐ % of popln ☐ Index vs suffers

Base: 604 aged 16+. Source: TNS U&A – June 2004

It's not an issue women talk about with men. But it is something women talk about among themselves, and tips for healthy digestion fill women's magazines (see Figure 3).

So we found ourselves with a big opportunity to talk to a huge target audience about a unique product. It should have been plain sailing but, as always, it wasn't quite that simple.

Figure 3: Digestion articles in women's press

The barriers

Research indicated we had to overcome three challenges:

Yoghurt per se is not on the digestive health radar

Perversely, by honing our benefit, we increased our competition. The brand no longer just competed with other natural health yoghurts but also with any product considered effective as a remedy for digestive discomfort.

Because women don't perceive digestive discomfort as a true medical condition, they typically don't take medicine to treat it, preferring a variety of preventive measures (mint tea, bran etc.).

Within this wider category, the competition was strong and yoghurt was way off the pace. Yoghurt featured at 13th on the list of products believed to be able to help with digestive discomfort, and only 9% believed a yoghurt with bifidus (a probiotic) would help (see Figure 4).

However, the remedies above us on the list (fibre, fruit and vegetables etc.) had been established as good for digestion for years and had the force of received health wisdom behind them.

This was a real issue. We couldn't afford to become the yoghurt that owned the addressing of digestive discomfort, while ignoring that consumers believed that more fresh fruit and veg was likely to work better.

Activia was perceived as generic 'feel good' yoghurt

Given its historic positioning, it was no surprise that people associated Activia with a general 'feel good' benefit. More worryingly, Activia was thought to reduce cholesterol almost as much as to address digestive discomfort (see Figure 5).

Figure 4: Products believed to combat digestive discomfort effectively

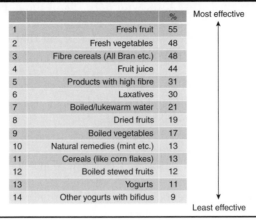

		%
1	Fresh fruit	55
2	Fresh vegetables	48
3	Fibre cereals (All Bran etc.)	48
4	Fruit juice	44
5	Products with high fibre	31
6	Laxatives	30
7	Boiled/lukewarm water	21
8	Dried fruits	19
9	Boiled vegetables	17
10	Natural remedies (mint etc.)	13
11	Cereals (like corn flakes)	13
12	Boiled stewed fruits	12
13	Yogurts	11
14	Other yogurts with bifidus	9

Most effective ↑ Least effective ↓

Base: 604 aged 16+. Source: TNS U & A – June 2004

Figure 5: Activia brand image – June 2004

% agree with statement

Feel better	31%
Great tasting	29%
Help with digestive discomfort	18%
Reduce cholesterol	15%

Base: Female yoghurt buyers 25+. Source: Millward Brown – June 2004

More fundamentally Activia sat behind general organic yoghurts in terms of a link to a digestive system benefit (see Table 1).

Table 1: Digestion credentials – June 2004

Brand	Helps keep your digestive system healthy (%)
Rachel's Organic	61
Yeo Valley (Organic)	55
Activia	54

Base: Female yoghurt buyers 25+. Source: Millward Brown tracking – June 2004

Indeed, on consumers' list of any products believed to be effective for digestive problems, Activia languished at 15th, with only 7% of the population believing it could help.

So our second major issue was that we had a brand that wasn't linked to our product benefit in consumers' minds.

A sensitive and stigmatised area

In qualitative research we soon found out that digestive discomfort was a sensitive area with a keenly felt emotional dimension:

> *I feel like an elephant walking down the street.*
>
> Source: Clarity Qualitative Research – June 2004

And, perhaps more fundamentally, it's a problem that causes unfortunate side-effects that for women are socially unacceptable:

> *Women don't have wind so that's what makes you feel more embarrassed.*
>
> Source: Clarity Qualitative Research – June 2004

So any brand that clumsily tackled the issue risked stigmatising and alienating users:

> *You'd end up hiding this under the cabbages with the tampons and the condoms.*
>
> Source: Clarity Qualitative Research – June 2004

It was clear the communications tone of voice would have to navigate a delicate path through the issue.

The communications challenge

Given the brand's position in the market, the focus for marketing was on recruitment of new users. To do this, the role for advertising was clear:

1. Create and take leadership of a new sector: the yoghurt digestive health sector.
2. Build belief in Activia's digestive health efficacy vs broader remedies.
3. Do it in a way that overcomes the sensitivities of the audience.

A defining insight

The digestive system is only vaguely understood:

> *... what happens when your food gets stuck in your stomach and you can't digest it.*
>
> *If the food I've eaten hasn't agreed with me I feel that the entire process in my body has been interrupted, but by eating something healthy I turn that around and return my system to how it should be.*
>
> Source: Hauck Qualitative Research – April 2003

What consumers did understand and were able to articulate in acute detail was how they felt when their digestion wasn't working properly:

Like somebody has got a pump and pumped you up.
I feel fat, fatigued, farty and uncomfortable.
I feel grumpy, bloated like a big grumpy fish.

Source: Hauck Qualitative Research – April 2003

We needed to find a way of cutting through the vaguery surrounding the issue to sum up the physical and emotional effects of the slow transit consumers felt.

Through qualitative research we found that the term 'feeling bloated' tapped in to the effect of slow digestive transit and really resonated with women. It was easily understood and it was how women (not their doctor) described the problem.

'Bloating' is the most common catch-all symptom, and can be coupled with
'uncomfortable' to imply both physical and emotional symptoms

Source: Clarity Qualitative Research – June 2004

It was also a term that didn't exist in the category. No other brand was talking about feeling bloated. This was our opportunity – we could create and own a new marketing language. Activia could own the physical and emotional effects of feeling bloated.

The creative brief

The brief was simple:

- Speak to the 15 million women who suffer physically and emotionally with feeling bloated.
- Relaunch Activia with a unique product claim, scientifically proven to help.
- Because of the sensitivities of the issue, be empathetic, supportive and understanding.

The creative solution

The solution was to use a tried and tested testimonial approach – initially in the form of 'Mother & Daughter', but since evolved to include celebrity interviewing testifiers, multiple testifiers, pairs of friends, single testifiers, slice-of-life testifiers, studio and in-home settings (see Figure 6).

The central tenet of the advertising has been to let real women tell the Activia story in their own words.

This felt right for three reasons:

Leveraging the richness of consumer language

It would have been all too easy to describe feeling bloated in overly scientific language, which would underplay the emotional significance of the problem:

Sounds like it's made in a French laboratory.

Source: Link Consumer Strategies – August 2003

Figure 6: Stills from Activia Advertising 2004–2008

Shelley
from Tunbridge Wells

Equally, an advertising idea that overdramatised bloating could have oversimplified or trivialised the issue:

> *It's gimmicky, difficult to understand.*
>
> *It's a bit slapstick … gauche.*
>
> *It's making fun of a potentially highly embarrassing predicament.*
>
> Source: Clarity Creative Development Qualitative Research – June 2004

The testimonial approach simply allowed us to describe the symptoms with all the richness of real consumer language.

Letting the product shine

If a product is genuinely good and unique in its category, perhaps the best thing is to let it speak for itself.

Testimonials were a simple way of doing this, mirroring the evangelism new users expressed:

> *You'd feel as if your food has gone through your system … And after I had finished my Activia I didn't have any for a week and immediately I started feeling that feeling again … now I wouldn't be without it … It definitely worked for me.*
>
> *I wasn't expecting anything to be honest with you and I didn't think it would work but it did work and I was amazed.*
>
> Source: Activia Qualitative Research – Movement, July 2007

But we also had years of received wisdom about effective remedies for digestive discomfort to subvert. It was vital to put the consumer straight on how and where Activia works.

Other female-focused sectors (such as beauty and haircare) faced similar challenges. So we borrowed the convention of the 'cut-away demo' to give the brand a sense of expertise and reassurance that Activia would work as the advertising promised (see Figure 7).

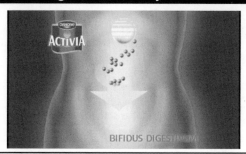

Figure 7: Cut-away demo

The demo provides an essential and credible explanation of what Activia does – sufficiently scientific to be efficacious, but not blinding with science.

Source: Hauck Qualitative Research – March 2005

The female grapevine

Research indicated women take advice and support on issues of this nature from a network of other women who also suffer. Testimonials allowed us to tap in to the female grapevine and replicate the natural warmth, empathy and support in communications:

What works well for this approach is the intimacy of the message. It's seen as friendly, confidential advice from one woman to another.

Clarity Qualitative Research debrief – June 2004

In summary

Figure 8 gives a diagrammatic representation of the Activia communications model.

A simple, volume-building media strategy

You might expect a sensitive subject like digestive discomfort to be handled through sensitive, intimate media. But the imperative driving media choices was to turn Activia from a niche to a mass-market brand. For that, we needed big, mainstream, mass media.

Hence 95% of spend has been on TV, buying a broad audience of ABC1 35–54-year-old women (the demographic where digestive issues are most prevalent). The mass, public nature of TV made it all the more important that our advertising felt supportive, empathetic and, crucially, did not embarrass women (see Figure 9).

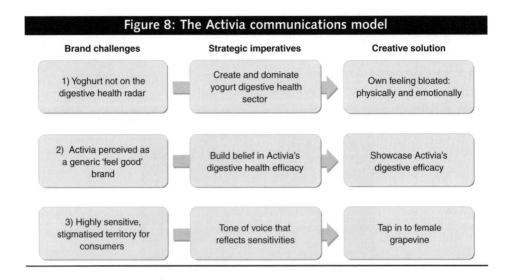

Figure 8: The Activia communications model

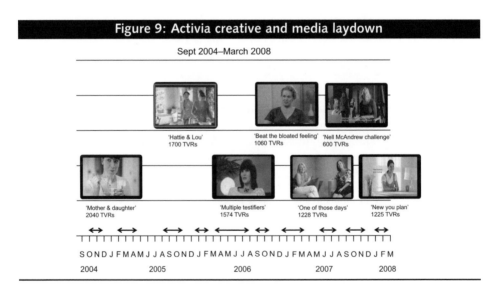

Figure 9: Activia creative and media laydown

What happened?

Storming sales

Activia experienced an immediate and dramatic sales uplift, and continues to enjoy impressive growth. Activia has seen a phenomenal 459% increase in value sales from £26.3m to £120.6m in just three and a half years (see Figure 10).[4]

From an overall position of 16th in the market in September 2004 Activia has become, by a considerable margin, the second biggest brand in the market (see Figure 11).

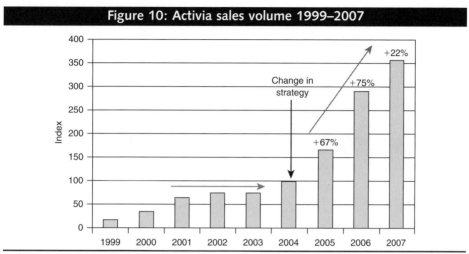

Figure 10: Activia sales volume 1999–2007

Base: Ex-factory volume sales. Source: Danone UK

Figure 11: Top 10 chilled yoghurt and dessert brands (Sept. 2004 vs Jan. 2008)

MAT value sales – Grocery multiples

Sept 2004		Jan 2008	
Müller Corner	£172.1m	Müller Corner	£178.3m
Müller Light	£129.4m	Activia	£120.6m
Actimel	£82.0m	Actimel	£99.6m
Petits Filous	£61.2m	Müller Light	£94.5m
Ski	£53.3m	Petits Filous	£80.5m
Weight Watchers	£52.6m	Yeo Valley	£64.5m
Yeo Valley	£47.6m	Müller Vitality	£56.2m
Cadbury	£45.7m	Cadbury	£53.7m
Munch Bunch	£41.1m	Weight Watchers	£48.3m
Shape	£40.7m	Yoplait Wlife	£37.6m
Activia	£26.3m		

Source: ACNielsen Scantrak

The success story of the category

In 2006, Nielsen indicated that Activia was responsible for nearly 50% of all growth in the £1.9bn Chilled yoghurts and desserts market. And throughout 2007 Activia has remained the strongest contributor to category growth (+33% in July, and +24% at year end).

One of the fastest-growing brands in Britain

In 2006, a year after the advertising relaunch, 77% year-on-year growth propelled Activia into the top 100 UK fmcg brands, placing it ahead of such stalwarts as Heinz Tomato Ketchup, Daz, Kellogg's Crunchy Nut Cornflakes and Anchor.[5]

In 2006 Activia was the second fastest-growing fmcg brand in the country. In 2007 it was the fifth fastest-growing brand (see Table 2).

Table 2: Fastest-growing Top 100 fmcg brands (all sectors)			
2006	**% change**	**2007**	**% change**
1. Innocent	+139	1. Innocent	+45
2. Activia	+77	2. Cravendale	+31
3. Uncle Ben's	+32	3. Cathedral City	+29
4. Fairy Laundry	+28	4. Uncle Ben's	+27
5. Tropicana	+27	5. Activia	+26

Source: *Checkout Magazine*/ACNielsen
Base: Nielsen sample includes grocery multiples, co-ops, forecourts, off-licences, symbol groups, independents and other impulse

As *Checkout Magazine*, which publishes Nielsen's Top 100 Grocery Brands survey, observed:

> *Activia yoghurt is a prime example of an established brand that has found its market and enjoyed a huge sales boost as a result.*

Why has Activia been so successful?

Since Activia relaunched in 2004, there has been a step-change in consumers' relationship with the brand, which correlates closely with their response to the new advertising.

> *We've always known there was a big market, but up until a couple of years ago we hadn't found the right message for the consumer. The product hasn't changed. We've just found the right way to promote it.*
>
> James King, Danone Category Strategy Manager (quoted in *Checkout Magazine*/Nielsen's survey of the Top 100 fmcg brands)

Awareness built rapidly

Although the advertising did not break any conventions, women noticed it. After the first burst, 55% of female yoghurt buyers were aware of the campaign. At the same time, brand awareness, already fairly high, jumped by 13 percentage points to 79% (see Figure 12).[6]

The 'new' digestive benefit was clearly communicated

After the first burst, 76% of our audience agreed that the advertising contained new information. Crucially, this wasn't just vague 'feel good' information, but clearly related to Activia's 'new' digestive benefit (see Figure 13).

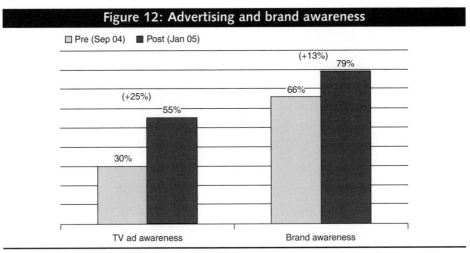

Figure 12: Advertising and brand awareness

□ Pre (Sep 04) ■ Post (Jan 05)

TV ad awareness: 30%, (+25%) 55%
Brand awareness: 66%, (+13%) 79%

Source: Millward Brown. Base: Female yoghurt buyers, 25+

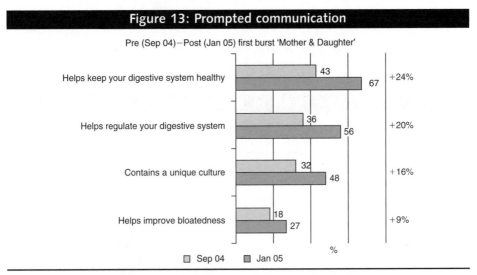

Figure 13: Prompted communication

Pre (Sep 04)–Post (Jan 05) first burst 'Mother & Daughter'

Helps keep your digestive system healthy: 43 / 67 — +24%
Helps regulate your digestive system: 36 / 56 — +20%
Contains a unique culture: 32 / 48 — +16%
Helps improve bloatedness: 18 / 27 — +9%

□ Sep 04 ■ Jan 05

%

Source: Millward Brown. Base: Female yoghurt buyers, 25+, who have seen the advertising

Moreover, the specificity of this benefit felt significantly different to the more general benefits claimed by other yoghurt brands (see Figure 14).[7]

Activia's 'new' digestive benefit wasn't just different, it was believable

After the first burst of advertising, 67% of our audience agreed that 'the points made in the advert were believable'.[8]

> *It's actually being truthful isn't it? It's not promising you miracles as soon as you eat one. It's being very realistic.*

265

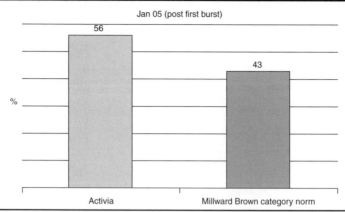

Figure 14: 'The ad contained different information to other yoghurt brands'

Jan 05 (post first burst)

Source: Millward Brown. Base: Female yoghurt buyers, 25+, who have seen the advertising

I like it 'cos you do learn from other people. It's like hearing it from a friend.

Female yoghurt buyers, Hauck Qualitative Research – June 2005, January 2006,
March 2006

As time (and the campaign) progressed, the credibility of our message stuck and Activia began to own its digestive benefit (see Figure 15).

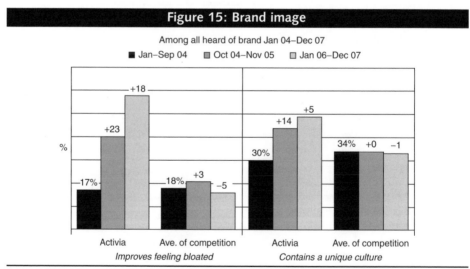

Figure 15: Brand image

Among all heard of brand Jan 04–Dec 07

■ Jan–Sep 04   ■ Oct 04–Nov 05   ☐ Jan 06–Dec 07

Source: Millward Brown. Base: Female yoghurt buyers, 25+, average includes all other yoghurt brands

From belonging to a set of brands who all could have laid claim to digestive health benefits, Activia now stands 48 percentage points ahead of its nearest rival on this dimension. The gap grew very rapidly at relaunch and has been consolidated ever since (see Figure 16).

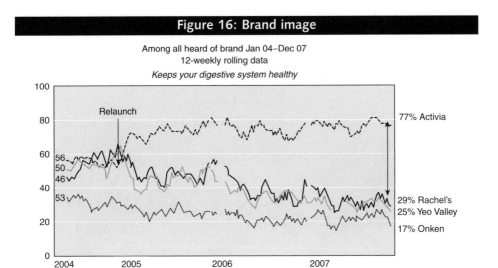

Figure 16: Brand image

Among all heard of brand Jan 04–Dec 07
12-weekly rolling data
Keeps your digestive system healthy

Source: Millward Brown. Base: Female yoghurt buyers, 25+

But perhaps the most impressive thing is that Activia isn't just ahead of its yoghurt competitors: it has jumped up the list of any products that consumers believe tackle digestive discomfort.

In 2004, Activia was languishing in 15th place. By September 2006, it had jumped to sixth place (see Figure 17) – a shade less efficacious than laxatives!

Activia saw by far the biggest increase in perceived efficacy of any product on the list over the two-year period, dramatically ahead of other yoghurts (with or without bifidus) (see Figure 18), further demonstrating how strongly Activia is

Figure 17: Products believed to combat digestive discomfort effectively – 2006

Most effective ↑

		%
1	Fresh fruit	54
2	Fresh vegetables	45
3	Fibre cereals (All Bran etc.)	40
4	Fruit juice	38
5	Laxatives	27
6	**Activia**	**25**
7	Products with high fibre	22
8	Boiled/lukewarm water	20
9	Dried fruits	19
10	Boiled vegetables	19
11	Other yogurts with bifidus	15
12	Yoghurts	14
13	Cereals (like corn flakes)	13
14	Natural remedies (mint etc.)	12

Least effective ↓

Source: TNS U & A – Sept 2006. Base: 604 aged 16 yrs+

Figure 18: Products believed to combat digestive discomfort effectively

Growth 2004–2006

+18% Activia

+6% Yoghurt with bifidus

+3% Yoghurt

+2% Boiled vegetables

Fresh fruit

Boiled water

Dried fruits

Cereals

Boiled fruit

−1% Natural remedies

−3% Fresh vegetables

−3% Laxatives

−6% Fruit juice

−8% Fibre cereals

Source: TNS U & A – Sept 2006. Base: 604 aged 16 yrs+

differentiated vs its competition – and indicating that this is very clearly an Activia, rather than a market, effect.

The advertising built affinity with the brand, despite its sensitive subject matter

The tried-and-trusted testimonial style ensured that a potentially embarrassing message was not delivered in a way that alienated women; indeed it built closeness and trust. Pre and post the first burst of advertising there was a 64% increase in people seeing Activia as a brand 'for someone like me' and a 61% increase in people seeing it as a brand they trusted (see Figure 19).

Figure 19: Brand closeness

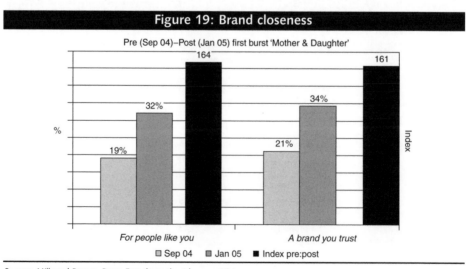

Pre (Sep 04)–Post (Jan 05) first burst 'Mother & Daughter'

For people like you: 19% (Sep 04), 32% (Jan 05), 164 (Index pre:post)

A brand you trust: 21% (Sep 04), 34% (Jan 05), 161 (Index pre:post)

□ Sep 04   ■ Jan 05   ■ Index pre:post

Source: Millward Brown. Base: Female yoghurt buyers, 25+

As with consumers' understanding of Activia's rational benefit, their emotional faith in the brand has been consolidated over time. It is testimony to the ability of the campaign to discuss an embarrassing subject matter in an unembarrassing way that half of women who buy yoghurt are now prepared to 'go public' and say that Activia is a brand 'for people like me' (see Figure 20).

Figure 20: Brand closeness

Source: Millward Brown. Base: Female yoghurt buyers, 25+

In summary: how the advertising changed consumers' relationship with Activia

Figure 21 illustrates diagrammatically the communications effect.

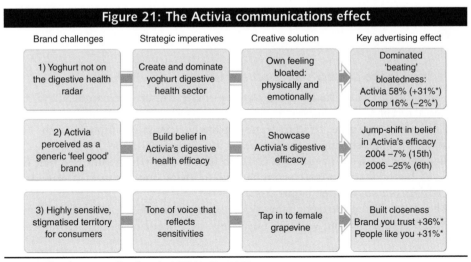

Figure 21: The Activia communications effect

Brand challenges	Strategic imperatives	Creative solution	Key advertising effect
1) Yoghurt not on the digestive health radar	Create and dominate yoghurt digestive health sector	Own feeling bloated: physically and emotionally	Dominated 'beating' bloatedness: Activia 58% (+31%*) Comp 16% (−2%*)
2) Activia perceived as a generic 'feel good' brand	Build belief in Activia's digestive health efficacy	Showcase Activia's digestive efficacy	Jump-shift in belief in Activia's efficacy 2004 −7% (15th) 2006 −25% (6th)
3) Highly sensitive, stigmatised territory for consumers	Tone of voice that reflects sensitivities	Tap in to female grapevine	Built closeness Brand you trust +36%* People like you +31%*

Source: Millward Brown tracking from Sept 2004 to Dec 2007

The relationship between advertising and trial

Activia now sits in a quarter of the nation's fridges, a phenomenal growth of 15 percentage points over the period since relaunch – an extra 4 million buyers for the brand in just three and a half years.

There is strong evidence to suggest that the advertising has been central to this growth in penetration.

The advertising is highly persuasive

The combination of a powerful rational benefit and the ability to build strong affinity with the brand made the advertising incredibly persuasive – significantly more so than Millward Brown (which tracked the campaign) typically sees (see Figure 22).[9]

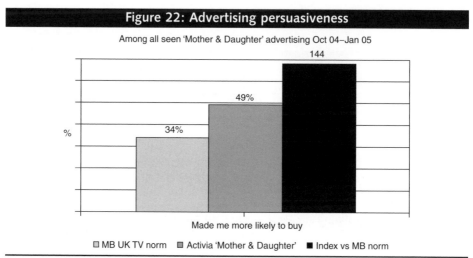

Figure 22: Advertising persuasiveness

Among all seen 'Mother & Daughter' advertising Oct 04–Jan 05

Source: Millward Brown. Base: Female yoghurt buyers, 25+

Advertising is the primary source of recommendation

The advertising is consistently cited as the primary source of recommendation. In the most recent U & A Survey, in September 2006, 77% of Activia buyers said they'd been introduced to the brand through recommendation – with 67% identifying TV advertising as the source of the recommendation.

Juxtapose this with an earlier U & A (in June 2004), which indicated that only 20% of buyers had Activia recommended to them and no one identified TV advertising as a source (see Figure 23).

The testimonial advertising is working exactly as intended: it has tapped in to the female grapevine and worked, effectively, as a word-of-mouth recommendation.

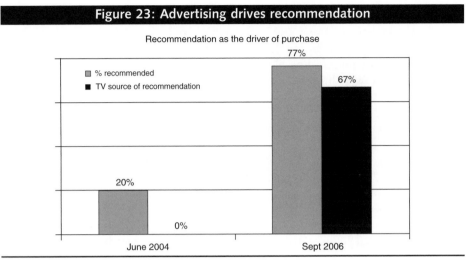

Figure 23: Advertising drives recommendation

Recommendation as the driver of purchase

Source: TNS U&A – Sept 2006. Base: Activia buyers aged 16 yrs+

Advertising periods correlate closely with penetration gains

Later in the paper, econometric analysis will isolate the precise role of advertising in driving Activia's sales explosion. However, there is a remarkable degree of consistency between periods of advertising and increases in household penetration (see Figure 24).

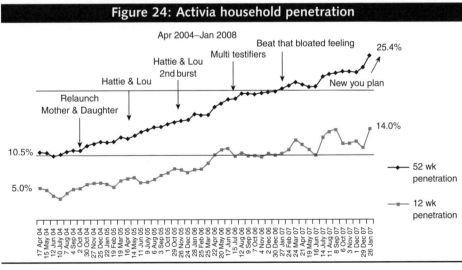

Figure 24: Activia household penetration

Source: ACNielsen Homescan

In summary

Between September 2004 and 2007, Activia invested around £15m in advertising.

We've shown how the brand has created and owned the new yoghurt digestive health sector by owning feeling bloated.

We've seen how telling the Activia story through the voice of the consumer jump-shifted Activia up the efficacy ladder, rising from a lowly 15th to sixth on the list.

We've demonstrated how tapping in to the female grapevine built trust in the brand.

The evidence indicates this was a significant factor in driving trial and contributing to Activia's outstanding sales growth.

But how significant?

First, we looked at the likely impact of factors other than advertising on Activia's growth.

Second, we used econometric modelling to help us answer the question.

The role of other factors in driving Activia's growth

Factors that don't appear to have been significant in Activia's growth

1. An increased interest in health

There is no doubt that attitudes are changing towards health. But this is a longer-term trend than the period with which we are concerned. In fact, there has been little change in the proportion of people saying they should do a lot more about their health over the period of the campaign (see Table 3).

Table 3: Attitudes to health 2003–2007				
	2003[10] (%)	2005 (%)	2007 (%)	2003–2007 (% pt change)
Agree:				
I should do a lot more about my health	52.8	54.6	53.8	+1.0

Base: adults aged 15+. Source: TGI UK

Juxtapose the one percentage point change in people saying they should do more about their health with the 15% increase over the same period in Activia household penetration and it is clear that something else is driving the growth.

2. An increase in digestive issues

U & A data suggest an increase in digestive issues is not the case. The proportion of women in September 2004 who suffer from digestive discomfort was 58.8%; in 2006 it was 59.1%.

Activia's new campaign was solving a problem that already existed. In any case, we have seen that prior to the campaign, women would resort to many other remedies (fruit, fibre cereals etc.) before they'd reach for Activia.

3. Greater interest in functional foods

Between 2004 and 2007, Mintel estimates the functional food market grew by 70%, to be worth £613m per year. But Activia alone accounted for 40% of this growth. Take Activia out and functional food growth looks more pedestrian.

4. A sector effect

Activia sits in the 'natural health' sector of the market (which includes organic and probiotic yoghurts). Value sales in this sector grew by 75% between 2004 and 2007, but once you take Activia, which grew by 459%, out of the equation the growth becomes somewhat less spectacular. It is Activia that is driving the sector, not the other way around (see Figure 25).[11]

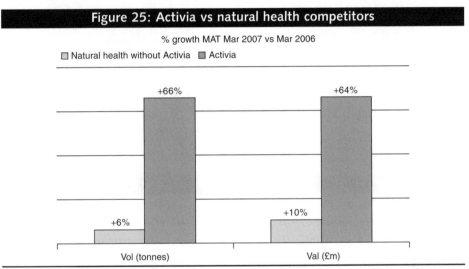

Figure 25: Activia vs natural health competitors

% growth MAT Mar 2007 vs Mar 2006

☐ Natural health without Activia ■ Activia

Source: ACNielsen Scantrak

5. Product formulation

As we have explained, the product formulation has stayed the same. What's changed is the way we communicated its benefit.

6. Price

Activia's price has also remained relatively constant over the advertising period (see Table 4).

Table 4: Activia price per kg			
Index (1999 = 100)			
1999	100	2004	116
2000	110	2005	116
2001	113	2006	114
2002	116	2007	119
2003	110		

Source: Danone

7. Packaging
Give or take a couple of pantone colours, Activia's packaging has remained largely the same (see Figure 26).

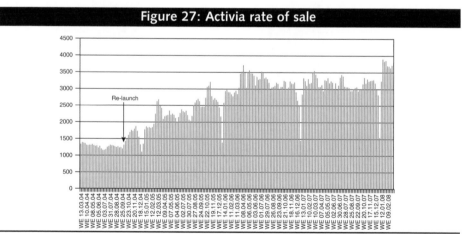

Figure 26: Packaging has not really changed

2004   **2007**

8. Distribution
Weighted distribution has stayed largely static at around 88%.[12] It is rate of sale, rather than distribution, that has increased dramatically over the period (see Figure 27).

Figure 27: Activia rate of sale

Source: ACNielsen Scantrak

Factors, other than advertising, that have played a significant role in Activia's success

1. Increased facings and SKUs
Activia has benefited from increased facings and increased SKUs. Clearly these have helped with shelf presence and given consumers greater choice. Econometric modelling[13] attributes 34.7% of Activia's volume sales during the period of the campaign to these factors.

2. Promotions

As with any fmcg category, promotions play an important role in driving sales. In Activia's case, modelling shows they accounted for 22% of its volume sales over the period of the campaign.

However, econometric modelling also shows that advertising has accounted for the lion's share of Activia's remarkable success.

The significance of advertising in driving Activia's growth

Econometric modelling confirms the critical role of advertising in Activia's growth.[14]

Advertising led the growth

The model identifies TV advertising as the number one driver of sales, accounting for nearly half of all volume sales from October 2004 until March 2007 (see Table 5).

Table 5: Key drivers of total Activia volume sales, October 2004–March 2007	
Driver	**% sales**
1. TV advertising	45.1
2. Base/facings/increased SKUs	34.0
3. Promotions	22.0
4. Other advertising	0.3
5. Other factors	0.3
6. Sampling	0.1
7. Seasonality	−2.4

The contribution of advertising amounts to 34,823 additional tonnes, or, at an average retail price of £2.60 per kg, £90.54m incremental revenue.

This under-reports the effect of the campaign since we only have econometric analysis for the first 30 months of the campaign to March 2007. There are nine further months of activity (23% of the total campaign period), which we have not been able to include in this analysis.

Advertising has already been extremely profitable

First, we looked at money in the bank. We will come on to look at profitability over the longer term.

Danone typically models the ROI of its advertising over the short term, so we will look at the effect of advertising over the 12-week period since it aired.

Confidentiality prevents us from publishing actual gross profit. Hence we have used a typical margin for this category as a proxy to help us establish whether the advertising was profitable for Danone. OHAL's experience in this category and fmcg indicates that it is reasonable to assume a gross profit margin of 33%.

On this basis, by the end of March 2007 Activia advertising had generated £29.9m incremental profit from a £15.6m media and production spend.

So every £1 spent on advertising has already generated £1.92 in gross profit.

Perhaps the best way of appreciating the scale of this effect is to remember that Activia's total annual sales revenue by September 2004 (£26.3m) was less than the short-term profit derived from the campaign (£29.9m).

The new campaign has been over twice as profitable as previous Activia advertising

There has been a step-change in return on advertising investment since the relaunch. The new advertising has been, on average, two and a half times as efficient as previous Activia advertising (see Figure 28).

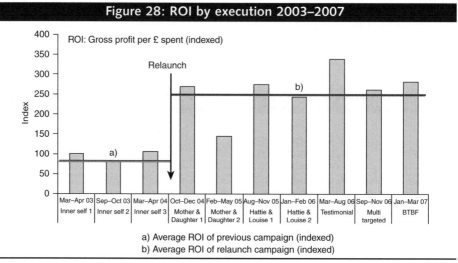

Figure 28: ROI by execution 2003–2007

a) Average ROI of previous campaign (indexed)
b) Average ROI of relaunch campaign (indexed)

Source: OHAL econometric model

The full value of the advertising

The £29.9m profit we have discussed underestimates the full value of the Activia campaign to Danone:

■ because it covers only the first 30 months of the campaign (we've not attempted to project the findings of the model, but as advertising content and media spend has remained consistent across the campaign, we'd expect to see similar levels of return per pound spent)

■ because it accounts only for the effect of each TVR over the period 12 weeks from airing; in fact, the effect of Activia lasts much longer than this; because Activia is so good (and unique) both in digestive efficacy and taste, once consumers try it they tend to convert to become loyal buyers (see Figure 29).

To reflect this we asked OHAL to model the total effect of the £15.6m advertising and production spend from October 2004 to March 2007, taking into account its full long-term effect.

On this basis, the model shows that advertising will generate £143m of revenue over its full life. This is a revenue return of £9.17 revenue for every £1 spent.

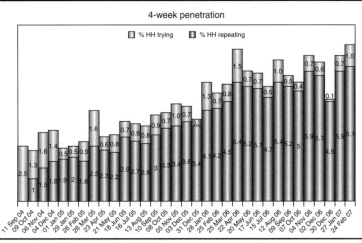

Figure 29: Trial and repeat of Activia since relaunch

Source: Nielsen Homescan Panel, August 2004–February 2007

On the basis of a 33% profit margin, over its full life the advertising will deliver an incremental gross profit to Danone of £47.19m.

This is a return of £3.03 gross profit for every £1 spent and is almost twice the value of the brand just before the campaign began.

That's the value of letting the product shine through.

Notes

1. It competes in the huge Chilled yoghurts and desserts market, which includes everything from luxury organic yoghurt to children's chocolatey desserts. It is a huge market, worth around £1.9bn a year.
2. The probiotic culture is called Bifidus Acti-regularis, known to scientists as Bifidobacterium animalis DN-173 010.
3. Clearcast ruled that Danone hadn't achieved sufficient depth of proof of clinical effect. Hence from launch to September 2004, Activia made a more general claim: 'Activia helps you feel good on the inside, which shows on the outside.'
4. We have used ex-factory sales as this is the only measure we have that goes back as far as 1999, when Activia was launched.
5. Source: Nielsen. Danone was worth £98m by value (+77% vs 2005), Heinz Ketchup was worth £97m (+4% vs 2005), Daz was worth £85m (flat vs 2005), Kellogg's Crunchy Nut Cornflakes was worth £79m (+13% vs 2005), Anchor was worth £75m (+1% vs 2005).
6. We just show response to the first burst of the campaign for simplicity and because this is when the major jump in awareness, understanding and affinity took place. Thereafter, the advertising consolidated this position.
7. MB UK Norm refers to all TV ads in Millward Brown's database, whatever the category. Obviously the question varies according to the category in question; for example, 'The ad contained different information to other car brands'; 'The ad contained different information to other bread brands.'
8. Source: Millward Brown, Jan 2005. Base: Female yoghurt buyers, 25+.
9. As before, the Millward Brown norm is for all TV ads tested, not just those in this category.
10. 2003 is the full year prior to the advertising relaunch in September 2004.
11. Table 3 shows Activia growth vs direct competitor growth from 2006 to 2007. Unfortunately we are unable to calculate this for previous years as the sales data for competitor brands are no longer available from either Danone or Nielsen.
12. Source: Nielsen.
13. OHAL.
14. OHAL built the model. Danone updates it on an annual basis. The last update was up to March 2007. The next update is not until May 2008.

Chapter 15

De Beers

Billion dollar ideas

 By Ian MacDonald, JWT

Editor's summary

This paper is not about communications, it is about the ideas that inform them and all other parts of the business. De Beers was challenged in 2000 with a slowing global economy and demand for diamond jewellery – a challenge that was not going to be solved by a surge in engagement rings. The solution was to create ideas that attached new meaning to the gift of love, such as the Right-Hand Ring, which allowed women to express love of their own unique style/spirit. The result was an invigoration of the market through three new ideas creating US$18.8bn in incremental sales, and generated payback of US$4 for every US$1 spent.

Introduction

This is a paper about love.

Actually, it's a paper about ideas that facilitate and symbolise love in its beautiful and glorious complexity. These ideas are not just advertising and communication ideas, although they do inform them. These are business ideas.

This paper tells the story of how JWT and De Beers created powerful ideas that drove dramatic growth within a troubled diamond jewellery market.

The value in these ideas is that they inspire trade and consumers alike to think and act differently in relation to diamonds.

This paper is also about the power of strong partnerships. Significantly, these ideas were born of an uninterrupted long-standing (over 40-year) partnership between client and agency, the two sharing the origination and development of them.

By stimulating the mature US market, by talking to committed diamond jewellery owners and using the power of communication and trade, we created almost US$19bn in retail sales. It will come as no surprise that this created a significant payback.

In short, this paper is a little different. It aims not to measure the return from a single piece of advertising or communications but rather to establish the importance and effectiveness of truly original ideas and detail their profitability to the business.

Background

De Beers is one of the most famous names in diamonds, mining and selling them as rough, unpolished gems since 1888.

Rough diamonds follow a long and complex journey through the hands of cutters, polishers, wholesalers, manufacturers and retailers, until eventually reaching a woman's finger, wrist or neck (see Figure 1).

Figure 1: The flow of diamond value

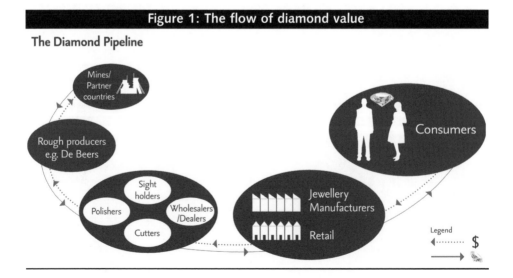

The Diamond Pipeline

Diamonds are precious because of their beauty, history and cultural associations; however, this is also a threat as they have no functional role. Like all products without a tangible benefit, consumers can abandon them in difficult times.

Additionally, mining diamonds is expensive and time-consuming. Developing a mine to its early stages of productivity takes many years and costs billions of dollars, with no guarantee of success.

De Beers' role is unique in the world of marketing – it mines diamonds and markets them to consumers. What it provides are ideas and communications, but no more. It relies on other people – manufacturers, wholesalers and retailers – to make and sell 'things' (see Figure 2).

Figure 2: De Beers stimulates consumer demand

The Diamond Pipeline

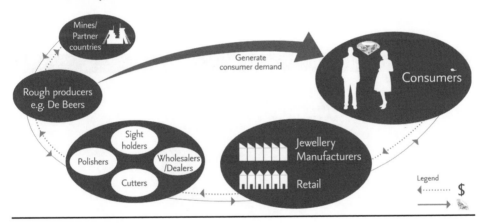

The rough problem

Our story begins in 2000 at a time when De Beers faced many challenges.

The Asian market crash in 1997 hit a number of diamond jewellery markets such as Japan (the world's second largest market), Thailand, Malaysia and Indonesia (see Figure 3).

By 2000 it was clear this was not a short-lived slump; three years later Thailand sales had not recovered, while Japan's continued to fall.

The new millennium also brought unprecedented competition in the supply of rough diamonds. The mining activities of other companies, such as Rio Tinto, and the prospect of fluctuation in Canada's output, created the prospect of increased supply coinciding with a possible collapse in consumer demand.

This was not only De Beers' problem but a problem for much of sub-Saharan Africa. Many countries – such as Botswana – partner with De Beers, relying upon stable and increasing diamond revenues to create long-term country plans.

De Beers recognised the danger and carefully considered its options. To compensate for the fall in Asia and to continue global growth, De Beers decided to focus on the US market, the only option with necessary scale (see Figure 4).

Figure 3: Asian markets fall amid economic crisis

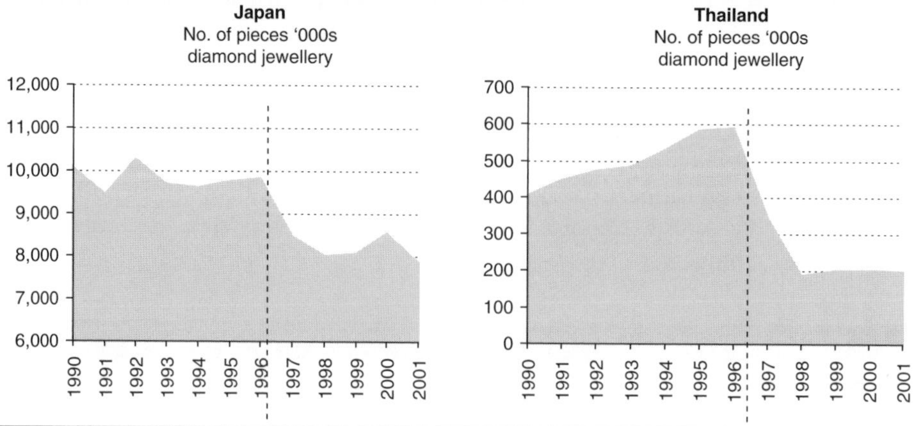
Japan
No. of pieces '000s
diamond jewellery
12,000
11,000
10,000
9,000
8,000
7,000
6,000
1990
1991
1992
1993
1994
1995
1996
1997
1998
1999
2000
2001
Thailand
No. of pieces '000s
diamond jewellery
700
600
500
400
300
200
100
0
1990
1991
1992
1993
1994
1995
1996
1997
1998
1999
2000
2001

Source: Commissioned research: Total Market Study

Figure 4: The US – the world's largest market

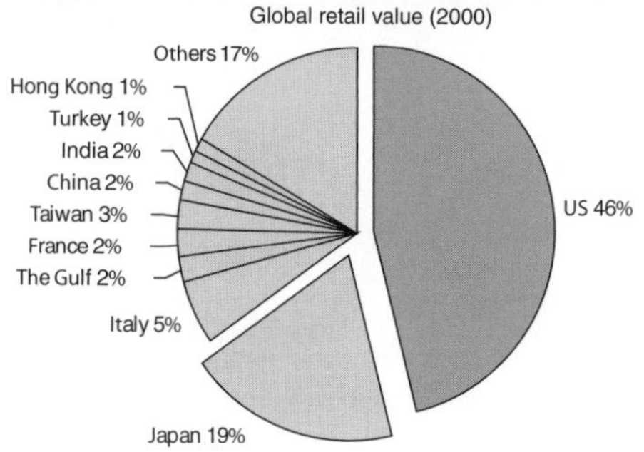
Global retail value (2000)
Others 17%
Hong Kong 1%
Turkey 1%
India 2%
China 2%
Taiwan 3%
France 2%
The Gulf 2%
Italy 5%
Japan 19%
US 46%

Source: Commissioned research: Total Market Study

Having decided on the US as the engine for global growth, what growth would it need to deliver? The US market needed to grow by at least the same level as GDP – at the time 3.8% per year, or 25% over six years.[1]

If this could be achieved it would compensate for the decline in markets elsewhere.

The retail problem

De Beers' decision to focus on the US market brought its own challenges (see Figure 5).

- it is one of the most saturated markets, with penetration at 86%
- engagement ring sales have been flat for many years
- purchase had been brought forward with gifting in the millennium[2]
- the US industry is notoriously fragmented, both vertically and horizontally, consisting of more than 30,000 US retailers.

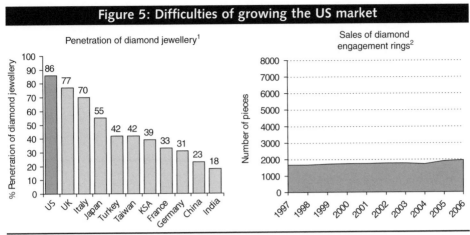

Figure 5: Difficulties of growing the US market

Sources: 1 Commissioned research: Research International Global Tracking Survey, 2005
2 Commissioned research: Total Market Survey

Beyond the specific US issues, there is an overarching challenge for De Beers. It sits at one end of a lengthy pipeline; any retail effect needs to be far greater for the same return than for most businesses.[3]

Strategy

Facing these challenges we developed a strategy to increase the value of the US diamond jewellery market (see Figure 6); we will describe each in turn.

Figure 6: The strategy

Increase the number of (younger) Heavy Owners

First, we decided to prioritise and focus on Heavy Owners – women with eight or more pieces of diamond jewellery. We knew Heavy Owners were a small group who drove the market, contributing 62% of category value (see Figure 7).

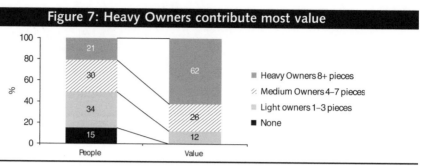

Figure 7: Heavy Owners contribute most value

Base: All US women 18–74
Source: Commissioned research: Total Market Survey, 2006

However, we wanted not only to create more Heavy Owners but for them to become Heavy Owners *as early as possible* in their life, to increase their lifelong value to the category.

As consumers buy more pieces, the time between each purchase shortens. Each acquisition creates greater passion for diamonds, shortening the purchase cycle (see Figure 8).

Figure 8: Time between purchase shortens with each subsequent purchase

Years between each purchase

| 3.9 | 3.0 | 2.6 | 2.2 | 2.0 | 2.0 | 1.8 | 1.5 | 1.4 |

| 1st Piece | 2nd Piece | 3rd Piece | 4th Piece | 5th Piece | 6th Piece | 7th Piece | 8th Piece | 9th Piece | 10th Piece |

Heavy Owners

Source: Commissioned research: Ownership Survey, 2005

If you are a woman in your twenties who already owns eight pieces of diamond jewellery, you are likely to spend the equivalent of almost US$45,000 in your life on diamond jewellery. If you are in your fifties, you'll spend a third as much (see Figure 9).

If we could get consumers to acquire eight pieces early in life, there would still be time for them to acquire piece nine, ten and eleven.

Encourage more sales at higher prices

We knew Heavy Owners were enthusiasts and therefore saw the opportunity to also increase the value of the category by encouraging more higher-priced sales.

Figure 9: Younger Heavy Owners spend more on diamond jewellery during their life

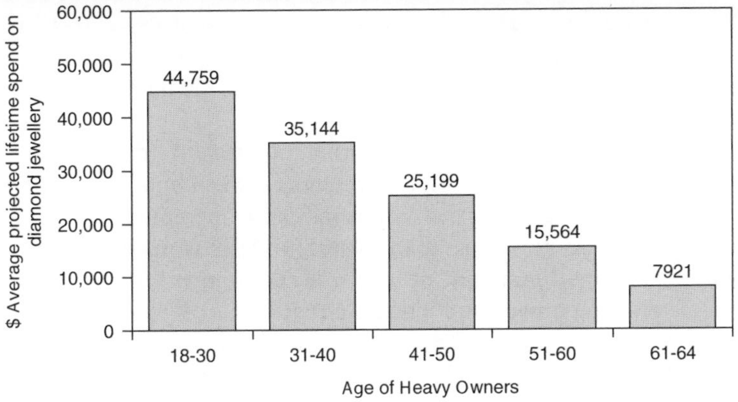

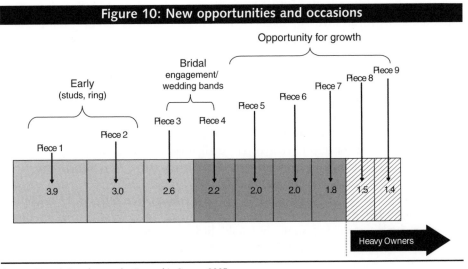

Source: Commissioned research: Ownership Survey, 2005

Furthermore, purchases driven by love provide additional emotional benefits and are therefore less price sensitive.

Provide new opportunities and occasions to buy diamond jewellery

But how were we going to increase the number of younger Heavy Owners and generate greater sales at higher prices? Given they already had diamond stud earrings, an engagement ring and the like, we needed to find new occasions and opportunities for them to buy additional pieces and to increase their connection with diamond jewellery (see Figure 10).

Figure 10: New opportunities and occasions

Source: Commissioned research: Ownership Survey, 2005

To provide this we needed greater insight into why people buy diamond jewellery – an insight that led us to develop the 'Justifying Narrative'.

In the world of love, people need stories, dreams, fantasies. The magic of diamonds is their ability to carry these stories, to represent these dreams.

A woman may want to reaffirm her independence. A man may not be able (or not feel comfortable) to express complex emotions to his partner. A woman may crave affirmation of his commitment.

Diamonds are a way to express these stories and dreams – the man does not buy jewellery for its sparkle but for what it represents between him and his partner. The Justifying Narrative captures the emotions and meanings a diamond can symbolise. For instance, for more than 50 years we have nurtured the narrative that diamonds are the ultimate gift of love – 'a diamond is forever'.

Finally, it is also the power of a narrative that enhances the emotional value of diamonds – key to encouraging more sales at higher prices.

So we needed to create new Justifying Narratives to encourage new opportunities and occasions.

Create awareness and desire for new ideas

Communications needed to create awareness for these stories and Justifying Narratives to increase the desire for them among women and men. We had to explain, romance and excite people around new possibilities of the use of diamonds to express and symbolise their feelings.

Beacons

We developed and launched three ideas, called *Beacons*: identifying the opportunity, developing the narrative and story, bringing this to life in a product concept and design, rallying the trade and creating consumer-facing communications.

Beacon 1: Past, present and future

There are many forms love can take, but up to now diamonds had only represented one: 'engagement love' – pure, innocent, perfect love.

To increase opportunities to acquire, we needed to broaden the meaning of love to make it relevant to potential Heavy Owners.

Qualitative research involving paired and then separate interviews demonstrated how difficult it is for couples to tell each other what they feel – only when alone could they open up. We discovered that, as love changes through the years, it also stays the same. Women look for reaffirmation from their man that, while aspects of their relationship have evolved, their love remains absolute.

There was a clear opportunity to launch a new narrative to represent the three stages of love – its past, present and future.

To launch the idea, we needed a product that could communicate the narrative – the solution being to use a product already in existence. Three-stone jewellery and rings had existed for years but sold little volume, being considered old-fashioned and, most importantly, carrying no meaning.

Figure 11: Past, Present, Future product

The new idea was that jewellery with three stones could tell a unique story: one stone symbolising your past, one your present and the final one your future. Hence, a new tradition began – Past, Present, Future (see Figure 11).

An entire integrated launch campaign was developed as shown in Figure 12, preceded by an intense lobbying of trade to maximise industry support.

Meaning was brought to the existing design through an emotionally charged TV launch, alongside impactful call-to-action press. This positioned the idea around gifting, with a focus around anniversaries (see Figures 13–17).

Figure 12: Past, Present, Future integrated launch

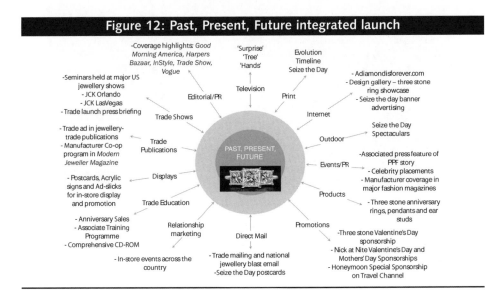

Figure 13: Past, Present, Future trade launch

Figure 14: Past, Present, Future digital design gallery

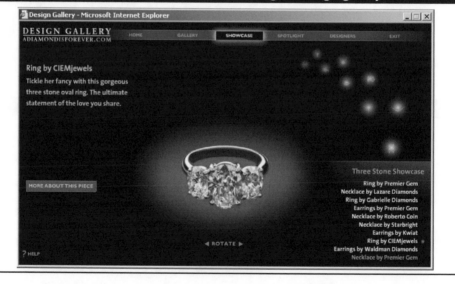

Figure 15: Past, Present, Future TVC

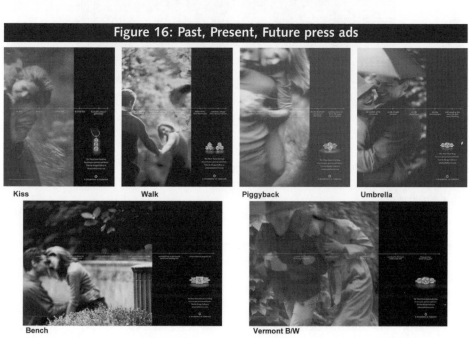

Kiss　　Walk　　Piggyback　　Umbrella

Bench　　Vermont B/W

Figure 17: Past, Present, Future press ads

Beacon 2: Right-Hand Ring

A woman values her relationship and connection with her partner, while also cherishing her independence. For a generation of women, diamonds represented only the former.

To grow opportunities for diamond jewellery we looked to broaden the meaning with a new narrative. Could we bring a new emotional imperative to diamonds without competing with the romantic dream?

If the left-hand ring – the wedding and engagement ring – celebrated her *relationship*, then the right-hand ring is a celebration of *her*: 'the left hand says "we", your right hand says "me"'.

This idea of Right-Hand Ring captured the zeitgeist of the *Sex and the City* generation, allowing women to use diamond jewellery to express their unique spirit/style. The narrative was as relevant to married women as it was for single women, with whom we had never before spoken.

To communicate the idea through the product, we developed a specific design brief, creating sophisticated yet flamboyant designs (see Figure 18). This reflected the independent spirit and that this was most likely to be a self-purchase.

Figure 18: Right-Hand Ring product

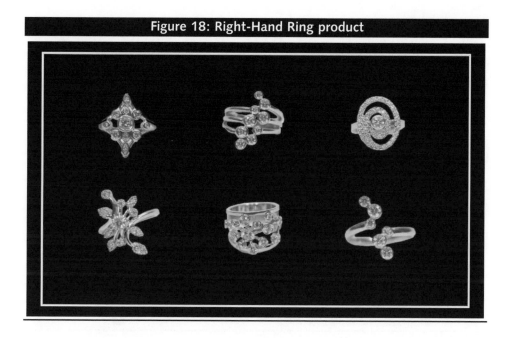

The communications again followed a multi-channel strategy, the heart of the launch being PR – as the idea needed to be elevated to that of a social movement – followed by advertising and trade support (see Figures 19–23).

Figure 19: Right-Hand Ring integrated launch

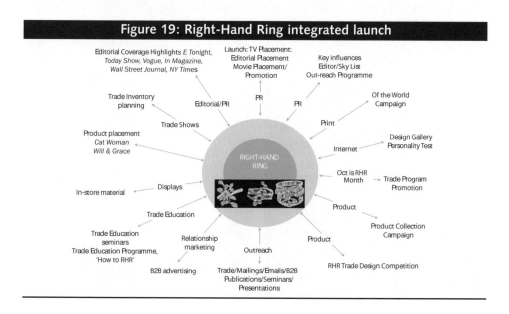

Figure 20: Right-Hand Ring PR

Figure 21: Right-Hand Ring press ads

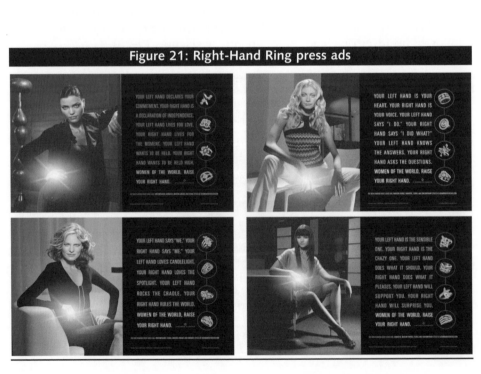

Figure 22: Right-Hand Ring trade support

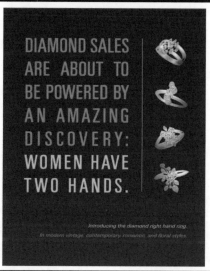

Figure 23: Right-Hand Ring trade alignment

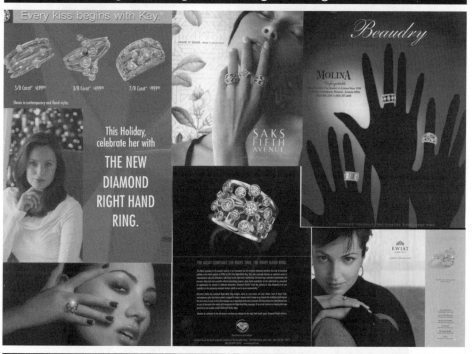

Beacon 3: Journey

As any couple knows, love is a continuous experience with highs and lows, growing stronger as a result.

For many years love has been viewed through an idealised 'perfect' filter and it blinded us to the real and true: every relationship has good and bad; prevailing relationships are stronger as a result.

Our idea was that *love is a journey*, not a destination; during a relationship, there are twists and turns and, as a couple weather these along the way, their love deepens.

We spoke with consumers to develop designs that best evoked the Journey idea; this provided a less obvious design route than previous Beacons. We then worked with a designer to create archetypal designs to provide inspiration for the industry and trade (see Figures 24 and 25).

Figure 24: Journey design development

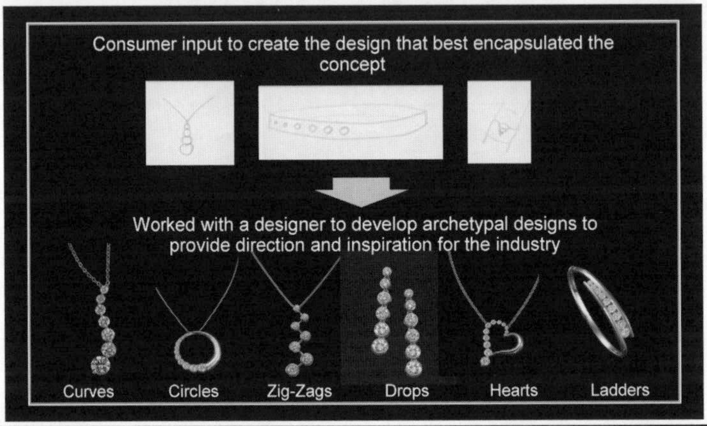

Consumer input to create the design that best encapsulated the concept

Worked with a designer to develop archetypal designs to provide direction and inspiration for the industry

Curves   Circles   Zig-Zags   Drops   Hearts   Ladders

Source: Journey qualitative research, February 2005

Figure 25: Final Journey product

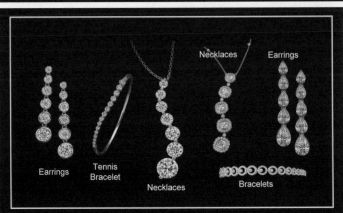

Necklaces   Earrings

Earrings

Tennis
Bracelet

Necklaces   Bracelets

This design was heroed in an engaging print campaign, as well as communicated through more emotionally charged press and TV (see Figures 26–30).

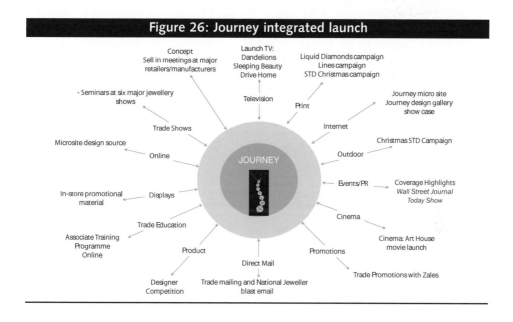

Figure 26: Journey integrated launch

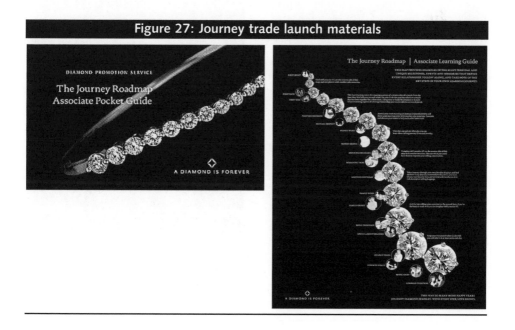

Figure 27: Journey trade launch materials

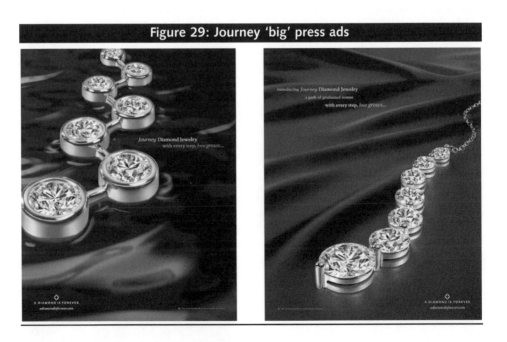

Figure 28: Journey trade alignment

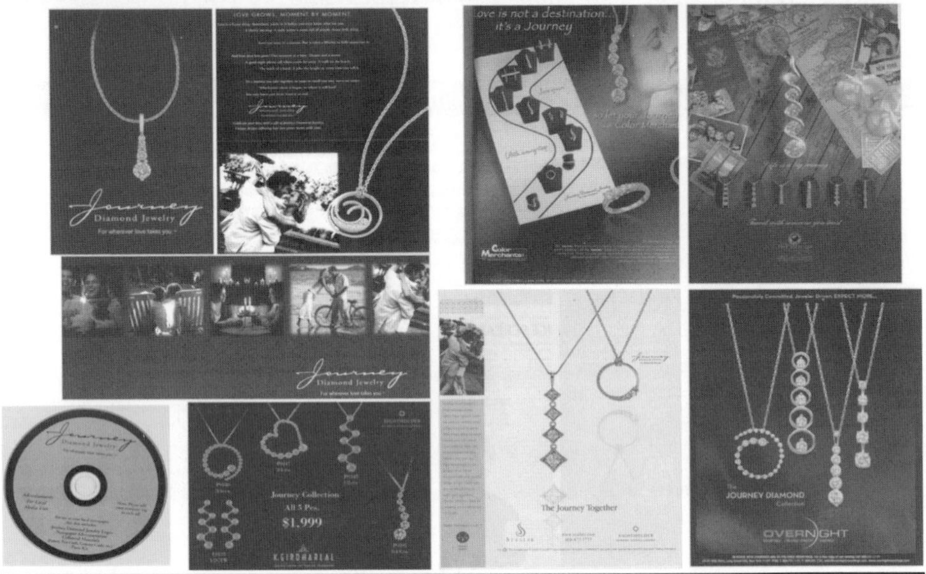

Figure 29: Journey 'big' press ads

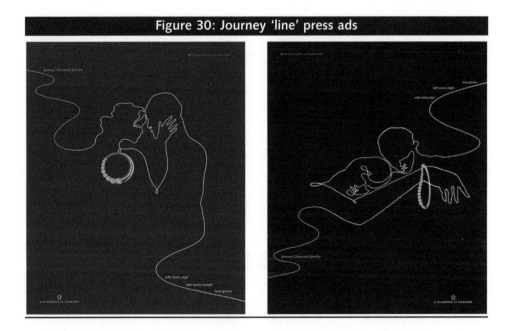

Figure 30: Journey 'line' press ads

Beacons overall

The Beacon ideas and campaigns were launched over a period of six years and continue to this day, as shown in Figure 31.

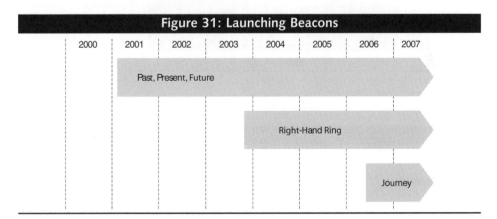

Figure 31: Launching Beacons

Each idea provided consumers with a Justifying Narrative and allowed them to create their own personal narratives and reasons to buy (see Figure 32).

The investment in the Beacon campaigns has remained constant with the launch of each new idea (see Figure 33).

One of the success criteria has been to multiply the communication impact of the ideas by harnessing the trade. Accordingly, the measure of quality trade spend has increased by 50% from 2003 to 2006 (see Figure 34).

Figure 32: Beacon justifying narratives

Macro narrative	Diamonds are the ultimate gift of love		
Conceptual narratives	Past, Present, Future	Right-Hand Ring	Journey
	The three-stone ring represents enduring love; our past, present and future together	Right-Hand Ring is an enduring expression of my unique spirit and style	Love is a journey with its ups or downs, but along the way our love deepens and strengthens
Personal narratives	Kate: 'James has been away so much over the past year ... this was our way of reaffirming our vows'	Debbie: 'I was really pleased to be promoted as I'd worked so hard. I thought I deserved a little celebration.'	Tom: 'Nicole and I have had some rough times but I wanted to find a way to tell her how strongly I love her'
New opportunity/ occasion	Increase purchase for anniversaries	Increase self-purchase for fashion rings	Increase propensity of diamonds for gift-giving

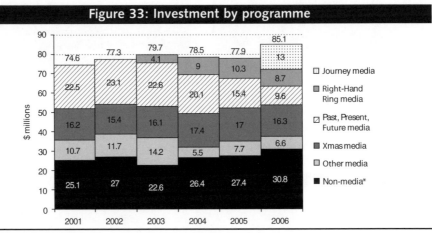

Figure 33: Investment by programme

Source: DTC Trade Spend Data
* = Trade, PR, Direct, Trade, Production

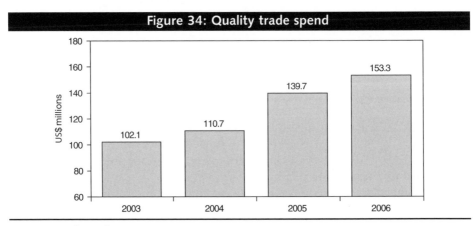

Figure 34: Quality trade spend

Source: DTC Trade Spend Data

Performance

In the six years from 2001 to 2006, Beacons sold 21.6 million pieces of diamond jewellery, *adding US$18.9bn retail sales value* to non-bridal diamond jewellery. By 2006 alone, Beacons grew to US$6.4bn annual sales value (see Figure 35).

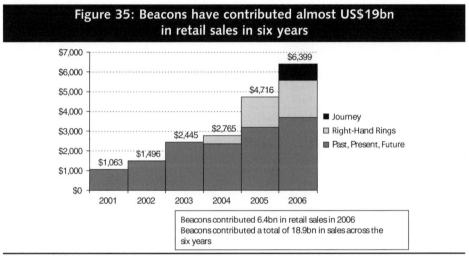

Figure 35: Beacons have contributed almost US$19bn in retail sales in six years

Beacons contributed 6.4bn in retail sales in 2006
Beacons contributed a total of 18.9bn in sales across the six years

Source: Commissioned research: Total Market Survey

To assess the effectiveness of the ideas in delivering retail sales we will evaluate each stage of the strategy (see Figure 36 for a diagrammatic representation).

Figure 36: The strategy

Increase the value of US diamond jewellery market

Increase the number of (younger) Heavy Owners

Increase the value of purchases

Provide new opportunities and occasions to buy diamond jewellery

Create awareness and desire for new Ideas

Increase the value of diamond jewellery market

During the Beacon period (2001–2006), the total US diamond jewellery category grew by US$9.2bn – an increase of 35% from 2001. This exceeded the business objectives of 25% by a net US$6.7bn over the six years.[4]

Figure 37: Growth since 2001 driven mostly by Beacons

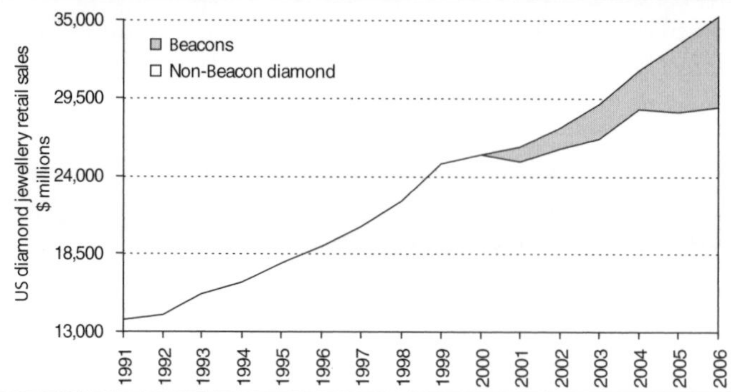

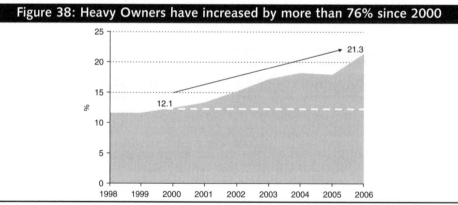

Source: Commissioned research: Total Market Survey

Of all the growth in the market over those six years, Beacon sales represent 70% (see Figure 37).

Increase the number of Heavy Owners

The number of Heavy Owners (8+ pieces) increased by 76% from 2000 to 2006, representing an additional 9.34 million (see Figure 38) women.

The number of Heavy Owners increased across all age groupings, including young women, with an increase of 51% among women aged 18–30 or an additional 1.1 million women (see Figure 40).

Figure 38: Heavy Owners have increased by more than 76% since 2000

Source: Commissioned research: Total Market Survey

There has also been a significant increase in the number of Medium Owners (four to seven pieces), resulting in a total Medium or Heavy Owners increase from 37.6% to 51.8% in six years – an additional 14.42 million women (see Figure 39).

Increase the value of purchases

The average price for Beacon pieces is US$1,118 compared with the price of an average piece of non-bridal diamond jewellery of US$725 – an increase of 54% (see Figure 41).

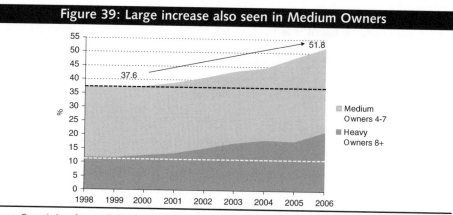

Figure 39: Large increase also seen in Medium Owners

Source: Commissioned research: Total Market Survey

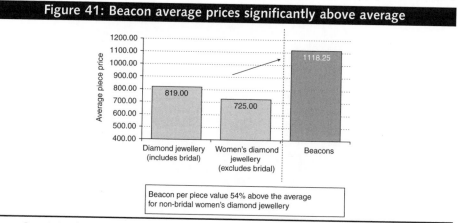

Figure 40: Additional 2.4 million Heavy Owners aged under 40

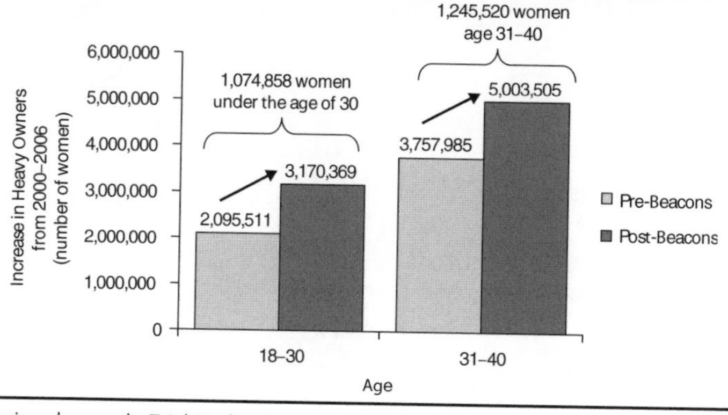

Source: Commissioned research: Total Market Survey 2000, 2006

Figure 41: Beacon average prices significantly above average

Source: Commissioned research: Total Market Survey, 2001–2006

Furthermore, the average diamond content for Beacon pieces is significantly higher than the average of non-bridal jewellery – 29.4% compared with 24.7%.

Provide new opportunities and occasions

The basis of the strategy was that we could provide women with new occasions and opportunities to acquire diamond jewellery.

1. Past, Present, Future

The key opportunity leveraged by Past, Present, Future was to provide new reasons and occasions for gift-giving, with a specific emphasis on anniversary occasions. Both these measures have shown significant increases, as illustrated in Figures 42 and 43.

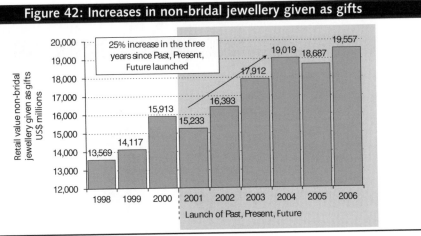

Figure 42: Increases in non-bridal jewellery given as gifts

Source: Commissioned research: Total Market Survey

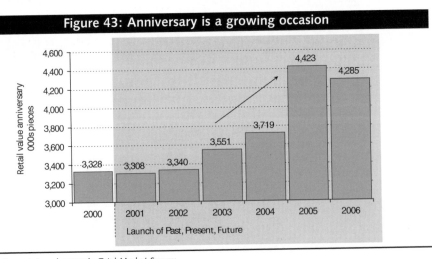

Figure 43: Anniversary is a growing occasion

Source: Commissioned research: Total Market Survey

2. Right-Hand Ring

Right-Hand Ring aimed to provide women with the opportunity to express their own identity and independence. As a result we've seen substantial increases in the amount of money women are spending themselves on diamond jewellery (see Figure 44).

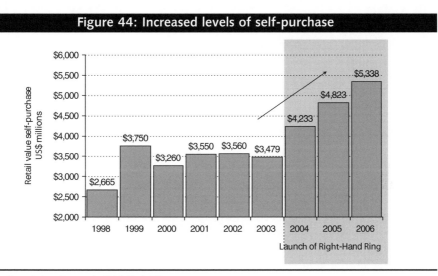

Figure 44: Increased levels of self-purchase

Source: Commissioned research: Total Market Survey

Although the idea was appealing to single women and married women alike, it was the single women with whom we had rarely spoken and given reasons to acquire. The Right-Hand Ring campaign changed this (see Figure 45).

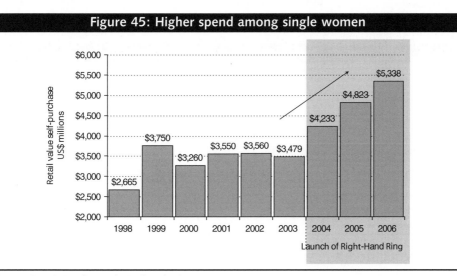

Figure 45: Higher spend among single women

Source: Commissioned research: Total Market Survey

3. Journey

It is too soon to see substantial changes as a result of Journey; however, 2006 was the highest year of retail value of gift-giving, with US$19.6bn. Indications from trade are that Journey played a substantial role in delivering this.

Together Journey and three-stone jewellery are just on fire.

Tom Hart, VP Merchandising, Bailey Banks and Biddle

We project that the Journey pieces will be a big success this Christmas based on the fact that we had good feedback from our clients.

Chris Moeller, CEO

I think we will sell every piece of Journey diamond jewellery that we have in the store.

Pamela Roamo, President, Friedmens Jewellers

Create awareness and desire for Beacon ideas

We had two communication objectives: first, to create awareness of the narrative and opportunity for acquisition; and, second, to create desire.

All three Beacons had high awareness. Past, Present, Future scored the highest, having been in the market longest. Journey, despite only being in the market for less than three months, achieved awareness of 24% among all women.

Right-Hand Ring generated awareness not only for the narrative but also for the very idea of women buying themselves diamond jewellery – a success of PR.

Looking at the desire created by communications, all three Beacons have achieved levels above norm for 'making diamond jewellery more appealing' and 'reminding me why diamonds are so special'.

Most importantly, this desire has translated into intent, with above-norm scores for more likely to buy/acquire. Some 14.2 million women in the US would most like to acquire a Past, Present, Future piece as their next diamond acquisition. Even more significantly, the figures indicate that 17.2 million US women would like to acquire a Right-Hand Ring as their next piece (see Table 1).

Table 1: Role of communication

1. Create awareness			
	Awareness of type of jewellery		
Past, Present, Future	75% two years after launch [A]		
Right-Hand Ring	39% six months after launch [B]	27% awareness of buying diamonds for self [B]	
Journey	24% three months after launch [A]		
2. Generate desire			
Relative to norms	Ad made diamond jewellery more appealing [A]	Ad reminds me why diamonds are so special [A]	Ad made me more likely to buy [A]
Past, Present, Future (TV)	+5	+8	+16
Right-Hand Ring (press)	+16	+6	+8
Journey (TV)	+4	+5	+10

Base: Women
A Millward Brown Advertising Tracking Study (ATS)
B Right-Hand Ring Momentum Study
C Total Market Survey

What other factors need to be considered?

Obviously, in this story every element of the marketing mix has been communication – from the product designs, to the distribution gained, to the press advertising. All these things have been driven by the idea. Nevertheless, it is worth a discussion of some of these points, but more important are the macro-factors, which we will come on to.

Price reduction

A reduction in price was not a factor in driving growth as increasing price levels of Beacon products was one of the stated aims.

Increase in investment

There has been no substantial change in investment – incremental sales were not from incremental investment (see Figure 46). Therefore, it is clear that it was the content of the investment that must have created the effect, as opposed to its weight – in other words the Justifying Narrative.

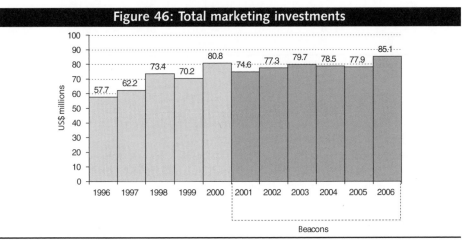

Figure 46: Total marketing investments

Source: DTC Investment Data

Distribution

There were no new kinds of distribution that were associated with Beacon ideas distinct from all other diamond jewellery.

New product

The product was a key part of the communication and as such was beautifully designed. While any new product will attract sales, the Beacon products have created huge uplifts across the United States.

It is also worth remembering that three-quarters of Beacon growth was Past, Present, Future – not even a new product – just a new narrative laid on to an existing product.

Changing demographics

Did Heavy Owners come from people just getting older and moving into older age brackets and acquiring more? The short answer is no; the increase in Heavy Owners was not just among the older – each age bracket has seen increases in the number of Heavy Owners since 2000, especially younger women aged 18–30 (see Figure 47).

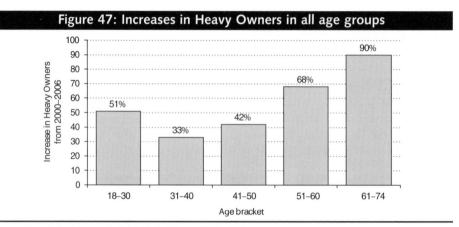

Figure 47: Increases in Heavy Owners in all age groups

Source: Commissioned research: Total Market Survey 2000–2006

Women's growing income parity

Women have experienced increased income levels relative to men. However, this could not have driven the sales effects witnessed.

Diamond jewellery is unique in that, typically, sales are tied into the complex role between man and woman. She hints and, more than 75% of the time, he buys. Therefore household income levels are a closer representation.

Measuring payback

> *History shows that there is a close relationship between GDP and consumer confidence, and between consumer confidence and sales of diamond jewellery.*
>
> M. Baskin, De Beers, IPA Effectiveness Awards, 1996

The Beacons directly drove retail sales of US$18.9bn; however, to establish payback to De Beers we need to determine the incremental growth. What would have happened to the market in the absence of Beacons?

Economic conditions

The economic conditions from 2001 to 2006 were far weaker than expected in 2000. A sharp slowdown in 2001 led many economists to claim the US had entered a recession. Growth during the six years of Beacons was less than two-thirds that of the previous six years. Consumer confidence was also hit – an average index of 26 points from before the Beacons (see Figure 48).

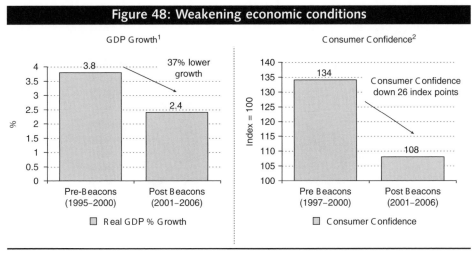

Figure 48: Weakening economic conditions

Sources: 1 – US Census Data
        2 – The Conference Board

Finally, income remained flat for the entire period – the longest time without real income growth in US data since 1967. The last time there was a similar fall (1991) diamond jewellery retail sales fell by 15%: flat or declining real income affects money available for discretionary expenditure (see Figure 49).

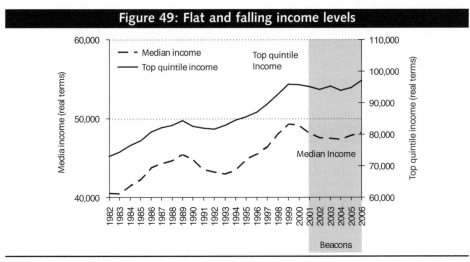

Figure 49: Flat and falling income levels

Source: US Census Data

Comparing top quintile income levels historically with non-bridal diamond jewellery sales shows a close relationship over time, except since 2001, when Beacon sales appear to have continued category growth (see Figure 50).

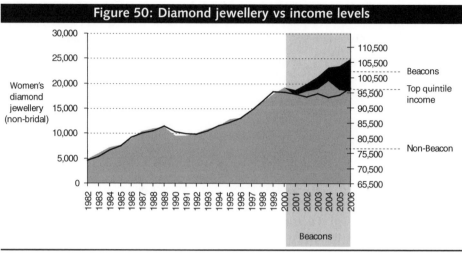

Figure 50: Diamond jewellery vs income levels

Source: US Census Data, commissioned research: Total Market Survey

Macroeconomic regression model

To quantify and establish the impact of these economic factors we established a regression model of the macroeconomic environment that incorporated the Beacon activity, allowing us to estimate what would have happened in the absence of Beacons.

We developed the model using annual sales data from 1982 to 2006. These are the earliest data available and, while limiting the model to 25 data points, we believed it more insightful to model with this limitation than not to model at all.

After testing many different input variables, the optimal model was composed of four: total disposable income in the economy, which implicitly includes population growth; median income levels; Beacon investment; and a time trend (see Figure 51).

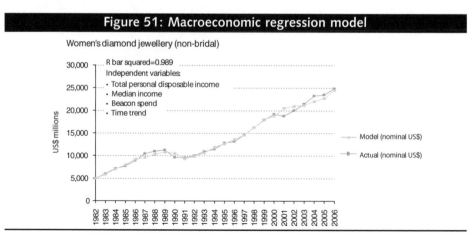

Figure 51: Macroeconomic regression model

Source: US Census Data, commissioned research: Total Market Survey

The model demonstrated there was incremental growth due to Beacon sales as well as halo effects, in addition to some cannibalisation. As seen already, the total retail sales effect of the Beacons over the six years was US$18.9bn. This model demonstrably proves an *incremental sales effect of US$14.7bn.*

Comparison with other diamond jewellery markets

For validation of incremental impact, we compared growth in the US with that in Europe.[5] All three European markets are mature and have developed diamond jewellery markets with similar historical growth.

A comparison with Europe shows very similar growth in diamond jewellery retail value during the 1990s, with a sharp slowdown in Europe following the millennium with five years without growth. This is despite increased European marketing investment (see Figures 52 and 53).

Figure 52: US grew faster than Europe's largest markets

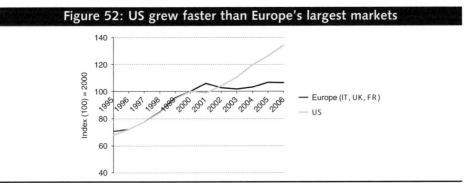

Source: Commissioned research: Total Market Survey

Figure 53: Economic growth lower in both US and Europe

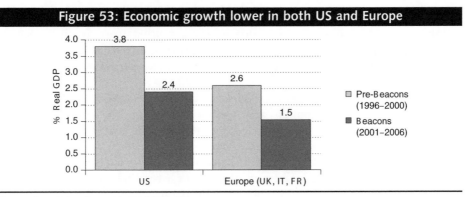

Source: Commissioned research: Total Market Survey

Comparison with non-diamond jewellery

Diamond jewellery's success is not matched by non-diamond jewellery, which has been weak and mostly in decline over the same period (see Figure 54).

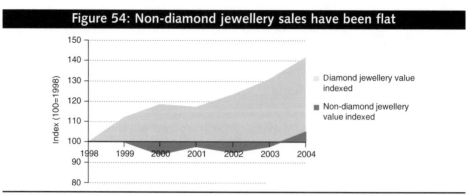

Figure 54: Non-diamond jewellery sales have been flat

Source: Commissioned research, Total Market Survey

Return to De Beers

Having established both the sales effect of the Beacons and the incremental market effect, we need to demonstrate the return to the De Beers business, deducting investment costs.

Of all business models, De Beers' is arguably the most difficult in terms of determining accurate payback. The only previous IPA paper dealing with De Beers (Baskin, 1996) avoided payback altogether because of the various challenges:

- confidentiality of pricing and rough sales to Sightholders (large buyers of rough diamonds)
- length of pipeline between retailer and De Beers
- time lag in diamond pipeline between rough sales and retail sales
- inability to track a gem sold at retail through to a particular rough producer
- variation in per-carat prices and content based on size/quality of rough diamonds.

Although it is not possible to calculate the *actual* payback, we believe it is possible to prove there was *a net payback* by using industry estimates. We have estimated one payback calculation over the entire six-year period in nominal terms (see Figures 55 and 56).[6]

The most difficult measure to establish is the incremental cost of goods sold; this is both difficult to obtain and confidential. To prove conclusively the programmes delivered a payback, we can use the absolute cost of goods sold for the entire business of 82.1%.[7]

Even with this most conservative of calculations, the net return is US$130m, with a return on marketing investment of 1.73: for every US$1.00 spent, De Beers received a net return of US$1.73. Therefore, for the formal purposes of this paper we can demonstrate that the investment did in fact pay back.

However, it is common sense, given the high fixed costs involved in any mining operation, and De Beers' reputation among industry analysts as one of the most efficient operators,[8] that the *incremental* cost of additional goods is likely to be far lower. In the scenario of 33% efficiencies the ROMI equals 4.37, whereas at 66% efficiencies it equals 7.03 (see Table 2).

Figure 55: Measuring payback

Determine incremental sales	100%
Determine content of polished diamonds in retail value (Polished Wholesale Price – PWP)	29.3% [1]
Estimate rough value as a proportion of PWP	21.4% [2]
Estimated incremental COGS	
Calculate net value to De Beers	5.1%–8.1% [3]
Deduct marketing costs	
Net return after costs return on marketing investment	4.37–7.03 [3]

Sources: (1) Beacon diamond content, Total Market Survey, 2006; (2) Estimate, IDEX Diamond Pipeline 2006; (3) Estimated share of rough and incremental COGS

Figure 56: Diamond pipeline value ratios

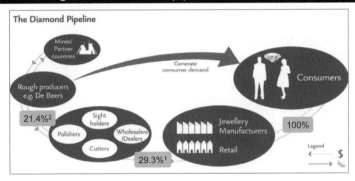

Flow of value of Beacon Diamond Jewellery

Sources: (1) Beacon diamond content, Total Market Survey, 2006; (2) Estimate, IDEX Diamond Pipeline 2006
Note: Rough to PWP value ratio of 73.2%

Table 2: Calculating return on marketing investment

	Zero efficiencies	33% efficiencies	66% efficiencies
Modelled incremental sales	14.70bn	14.70bn	14.70bn
Polished wholesale price (PWP) for Beacon products	4.31bn	4.31bn	4.31bn
Estimated rough value	3.15bn	3.15bn	3.15bn
Estimated incremental COGS	82.1% [1]	54.7%	27.3%
Net value to De Beers	307.5m	1,012m	1,192m
Less marketing costs	177.5m	177.5m	177.5m
Net return after costs	130m	600m	1,070m
ROMI	1.73	4.37	7.03

Source: US Census Data; Commissioned research: Total Market Survey

Impact on business

During the six years, sales of rough diamonds by De Beers increased by 38%, despite increased competition and global economic weakening (see Figure 57).

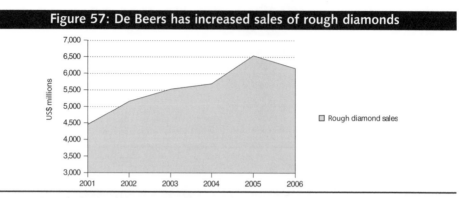

Figure 57: De Beers has increased sales of rough diamonds

Source: De Beers Group Annual Reports 2001–2006

Since 2000, De Beers has globally increased production of rough diamonds in carats by 42%. To put this in context, the Beacons in 2006 represent 3.7 million carats of diamond content, approximately 8% of De Beers' global output (see Figure 58).

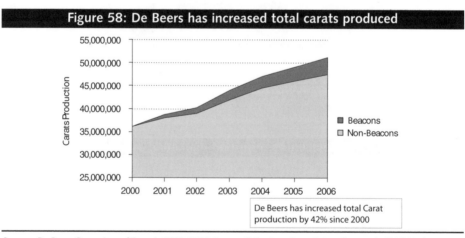

Figure 58: De Beers has increased total carats produced

De Beers has increased total Carat production by 42% since 2000

Sources: De Beers Group Annual Reports 2001–2006; Beacon Estimate – Commissioned research: Total Market Survey

The importance of the US to global retail value over the period increased from 46% in 2000 to 50% in 2006, demonstrating its critical importance in maintaining global consumer demand.

Global roll-out

Ideas so compelling tend to travel well, and Beacons have been rolled out globally. For instance, in Japan, Past, Present, Future has been adapted and has achieved significant success (see Figure 59).

Figure 59: Japanese Past, Present, Future print

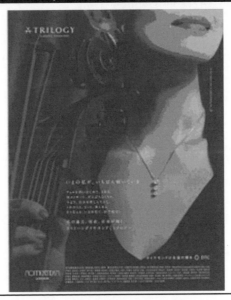

The trilogy campaign has continued its phenomenal success in the US and grows at an outstanding 35% year on year in Japan.

Operating and financial review 2006 – Lorett Penny, De Beers

In conclusion

Reflecting on the state of the US diamond jewellery market in 2001 and how it has developed, it is clear that only the most powerful ideas could have spurred such growth.

Powerful ideas – not just advertising or communication ideas, but business ideas that successfully drove all elements of the mix.

This paper has demonstrably proven the following:

- JWT and De Beers developed and communicated truly big ideas that consumers felt were meaningful and relevant to their lives.
- The focused strategy of prioritising Heavy Owners in the US market provided huge wins for the business globally.
- Ideas drove more than US$14.7bn of retail sales and provided payback on investment.

■ A strong partnership built on trust, collaboration and a desire for effectiveness was a key factor of our success.

Today, a diamond is *still* forever, and still a perfect way to mark and celebrate marriage. But now, thanks to the Beacons, diamonds can allow people to express and celebrate other emotions. Besides the financial contribution of these one billion dollar ideas, this is a contribution to the world about which we feel very proud.

For it is love, in the end, that conquers all.

Notes

1. The average US GDP from 1996 to 2000 was 3.8 so, projecting forward, this measure was used as a benchmark.
2. One in three women in the year 2000 received a diamond as a gift. Source: Total Market Survey, 2000.
3. It is estimated that for every US$10 of retail sales generated, only US$1 represents rough diamond value that is likely to return to De Beers. This is before cost of goods sold and market costs. To put this into context many companies, such as fmcg companies, may look to receive many times higher.
4. In nominal terms.
5. Europe represented by a weighted average of Italy, France and United Kingdom, which represents two-thirds of all European sales.
6. The variable lag between a rough diamond being sold at a producer level and being bought at a consumer level makes it much more complex to estimate payback for any given year. However, calculating one payback over the six years reduces the potential impact of a lag in the pipeline in the calculation.
7. Reported in De Beers Group Annual Reports 2001–2006, averaged in nominal terms.
8. 'De Beers operates the most efficient and safe diamond mines. It's there where the bulk of the company's 25,000 workers are employed, and, basically, an occasional strike notwithstanding, the risk for negative reputational fallout is negligible. De Beers is simply a darn good mining company.' Chaim Even-Zohar, Diamond Intelligence Briefs, 4 December 2007.

Chapter 16

Direct Payment

Giving it to you straight

By Andy Nairn and Jamie Kenny, Miles Calcraft Briginshaw Duffy

Editor's summary

For years, millions of Britons had been used to receiving social security benefits and pensions through paper-based methods. However, the Government announced that from 2003, electronic payments would become the norm, a move that was met with widespread hostility. This paper demonstrates how an integrated communications campaign neutralised the emotionally charged atmosphere, by providing a stream of straightforward, non-threatening information about the new scheme. After two years, 95 per cent of claimants had switched to electronic payments, compared to 43 per cent previously. Over seven years, the campaign is estimated to have delivered payback of £29 per £1 spent.

Introduction

This is a story of integration on a grand scale.[1]

It will tell how one of the biggest, and most controversial, Government initiatives in history was introduced smoothly, thanks to a joined-up approach to communications.

But, more importantly, it will tell how this integrated approach more than paid for itself, generating savings worth hundreds of millions of pounds, with an ROI of approximately £29 per £1 spent.

Background

Every year, the Department of Work and Pensions (DWP) pays out over £115bn in social security benefits and state pensions, via 5 billion separate transactions. However, until recently, the majority of these transactions were conducted via a paper-based system (giros and order books), rather than electronically.

While generations of Britons had become accustomed to their regular trip to the Post Office to collect their cash, the traditional process was clearly inefficient for a modern organisation.

In addition, it was very expensive: the cost of processing each giro was £1.47, as opposed to just 1p for an electronic transfer.[2]

Moreover, paper-based systems carried additional costs, related to their greater vulnerability to fraud (estimated at £50m per annum).[3]

Taking all this into account, the Government announced that from 2003 it would be moving towards electronic transfer as the normal method of payment. More specifically, it set a Public Service Agreement (PSA) target, for 85% of all claimants to be paid electronically by the end of 2005 – compared to 43% in 2003. The Government estimated that achieving this target would generate savings of around £450m every year.[4]

The scale of the task

Several factors combined to make this an extremely difficult task.

- the change would affect 13 million people, from vastly different backgrounds[5]
- these people were 'overwhelmingly negative'[6] about the proposed changes, with 88% believing that electronic transfer would have disadvantages[7] and 73% making 'wholly negative comments'[8]
- fears ranged from practical concerns ('I would never be able to manage a bank account') to social ones ('I will miss going to the Post Office for a chat'); and a general resistance to change ('It's fine the way it is – why muck it up?')[9]
- there were other stakeholders to consider, and again many of these had strong reservations about the scheme. Sub-postmasters (who run 97% of Post Offices) were actively lobbying against the plans, fearing they would result in branch closures.[10] Charities such as Age Concern and Scope were also vocal with their concerns, although not actively obstructive
- opposition politicians were also campaigning against the system[11]

- early media coverage was very critical[12]
- claimants would not be offered any financial incentive for switching
- on the other hand, neither would they be penalised if they didn't switch (e.g. by having their benefits withdrawn): crucially, the whole scheme was to be non-compulsory, with claimants allowed to use paper-based methods if they insisted. This point cannot be emphasised often enough: we could not run the risk of people taking action on account of perceived failed legal obligation – and so we ensured there was none[13]
- the changes were due to take place in what was considered to be an 'exceedingly short time span' of two years[14]
- there was no precedent to learn from: nothing on this scale had previously been attempted in the UK or indeed elsewhere[15]
- finally, there was an IT issue to consider: the DWP's system could not deal with 13 million new customer records at once. So the client brief required us to make people want to switch but not to respond immediately, until they had been personally invited to do so, via a formal letter.

No wonder the National Audit Office called it 'a major challenge',[16] and the *Guardian* described it as 'a mammoth task'.[17]

Our integrated strategy

In summer 2002, MCBD and ZenithOptimedia won the pitch to launch the Payment Modernisation Programme (as it was then called). We soon set about addressing every aspect of the marketing mix.

Overarching strategy

Faced with the challenges described earlier, it was tempting to move into traditional marketing mode: trumpeting the scheme's benefits until people were persuaded that it was a good idea. A charm offensive, if you like.

However, our research suggested that this was actually the last thing we should do. Public opinion was already inflamed, so that any suspicion of 'spin' would only make things worse. Instead of *evoking* an emotional response, as communications usually seek to do, we needed to *avoid* one. Hence we simply set out to inform people, in a very straightforward way, about what the changes entailed and how they should act.

Brand identity

Next we needed to create a consumer-facing brand that fitted with the straightforward strategy described above. Our solution was the device shown in Figure 1.

The name 'Direct Payment' was more straightforward than 'The Payment Modernisation Programme'. The arrow device suggested progress and invited action. And the endline not only told people how they would receive their money, but reinforced our spin-free tone. In research, the device was found to be 'very successful … memorable … simple … concise … credible … a unifying device'.[18]

Figure 1: A straightforward brand

Channel planning

Although we are primarily an advertising agency, we realised that above-the-line activity alone could not pick off all the different audiences or provide the detail required. Thus we gave DM a significant role in the campaign, with a virtually continuous stream of mailings, tailored to different groups, over a period of two years.

Fulfilment

As noted earlier, one of the challenges of this brief was that we couldn't encourage everybody to switch at once. So as well as sending DM to people we *did* want to switch, we needed to allow for other people seeing the campaign and wanting information. With COI, we therefore recommended that a separate phone line be set up, to send out leaflets to anyone who called. This phone number would be highlighted in all campaign materials, equipping communications with a contact mechanism while still fulfilling the client requirement not to directly drive switching until later.

Messaging and phasing

Finally, we assessed when we needed to convey the many different pieces of information we had to communicate. This resulted in a highly sophisticated messaging matrix, which we adjusted continually over time, but which we have greatly simplified to a three-stage model. We will now outline the three stages in the sections below.

Stage 1: Launch

Objective

Our first task was to launch the idea of 'Direct Payment' and begin addressing some basic concerns.

As the initial wave of activity, this phase involved some delicate balancing acts, which we had to get right first time.

Targeting strategy

On the one hand, we needed to take a broad approach to targeting so that all 13 million of our audience understood that change was on its way. On the other hand, we also needed to reflect the many differences within our audience (e.g. the fact that pensioners wouldn't respond well to communications that grouped them together with benefits recipients).

Messaging

Clearly, the main priority was to communicate that 'the way benefits and pensions are paid is changing'. However, we also needed to reassure people that they would still receive the same amount of money, just as regularly as before.

Media strategy

We needed to drive high coverage and frequency in a short period – something we accomplished using TV, national press and radio. However, we also needed to build trust and familiarity – hence we used more intimate channels such as local press and community outdoor (bus headliners, bingo halls and GPs' surgeries). And, as stated above, we needed to carry fairly detailed information, which meant that DM played a huge part.

Creative approach

Finally, we needed a straightforward, yet high-standout vehicle to launch the initiative. Hence we developed a TV campaign featuring familiar faces (the actors Annette Crosbie and Chris Walker) talking matter-of-factly about the changes, and reassuring people that they'd be receiving 'a letter and leaflet with information about what to do next' (see Figure 2).

Figure 2: Stage 1 TV

All other channels (from print and radio to DM) then used ordinary people to explain the implications of the change for specific customer groups (e.g. Income Support, Incapacity Benefit, Disability Living Allowance recipients). Naturally, the Direct Payment brand device ran across all activity, ensuring an extremely coherent campaign feel (see Figure 3).

Figure 3: Stage 1 press, letter, leaflet, bingo hall poster, bus headliner

Stage 2: Information

Objective

Having launched the basic idea of 'Direct Payment', next we needed to build deeper understanding of what it entailed.

Messaging

In particular, we needed to communicate more detailed information about the account options available and where people could access their money.

Target audience

Hence we started targeting people in terms of their experience (e.g. whether they'd ever had a bank account before, or whether they'd ever used an ATM) rather than their benefit type.

Media strategy

Likewise, we now supplemented the channels from Stage 1 with channels that could convey a more detailed message – including radio marketing, press advertorials and roadshows (in 74 venues, nationwide).

Creative approach

Finally, we evolved our creative approach, in line with our shifting needs.

In TV, we started using ordinary people (as per the rest of the campaign), the logic being that we now had such high levels of awareness that we no longer needed additional fame from celebrities. We also moved to a video diary format, so that these people could talk directly about how easy it was to access their money via Direct Payment (see Figure 4).

Figure 4: Stage 2 TV

The other media then provided more detailed information, such as what to do if you had never had a bank account before.

Again, we evolved our creative approach – in this case using illustrated silhouettes, rather than photography, to enable people to identify with the characterisations (see Figure 5).

Figure 5: Stage 2 press and roadshow

Stage 3: Last call

Objective

Finally, by January 2005, all customers had received at least one mailing about Direct Payment, almost all customers were aware of the impending changes and the majority had already switched. So our objective was simple: call generation to drive the last remaining conversions.

Target audience

Targeting was equally simple: we needed to focus on the few people (regardless of their background) who hadn't switched yet.

Message

Likewise, our messaging needed to take on a more urgent, assertive tone: creating the idea of a final deadline and encouraging people to 'call today' or 'act now'.

Media strategy

For this stage, TV and press were chosen as the main channels, since analysis had shown that radio was not as effective in driving telephone response. We also focused our roadshows in key underperforming areas, and used ethnic media to encourage switching among underperforming communities. DM was now similarly targeted, and the other media also referenced the mailings and encouraged people to respond to their letters.

Creative approach

Finally, while we maintained the basic creative approach, we evolved the use of the arrow, so that it now functioned more like a call-to-action device, pointing to the telephone response number (see Figures 6 and 7).

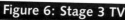

Figure 6: Stage 3 TV

The overall look of the campaign is shown in Figure 8.

Key business results

The key PSA target (for 85% of claimants to opt for Direct Payment by the end of 2005) was met one year early – against all predictions. It has since continued to grow, to virtually universal levels (see Figure 9).

Perhaps more tellingly, the shift has been far smoother than anticipated, with 95% of users declaring themselves happy with the new system[19] and 86% describing it as an improvement.[20]

Ofcom now cites Direct Payment as an example of best practice when delivering large switchover campaigns to vulnerable audiences.[21]

Likewise, the National Audit Office, in a review of 24 successful change programmes from around the world,[22] cites Direct Payment as a rare example of a project that has 'delivered real and lasting benefits to citizens'.

As noted earlier, these benefits amount to around £450m in savings per year. We will now go on to:

- describe how the campaign contributed to these savings
- eliminate other possible explanations
- quantify the campaign's return on investment.

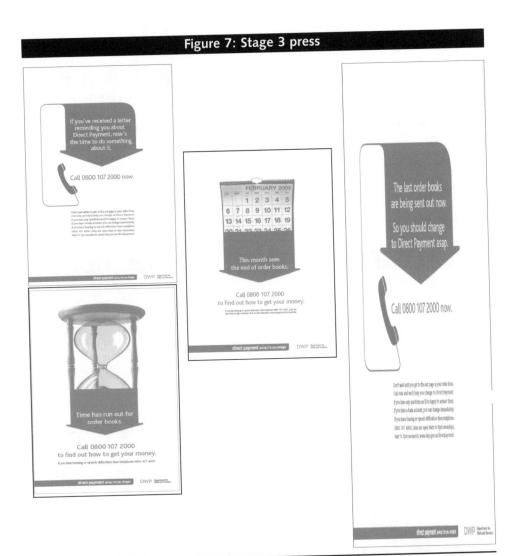

Figure 7: Stage 3 press

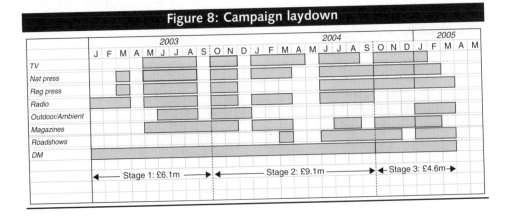

Figure 8: Campaign laydown

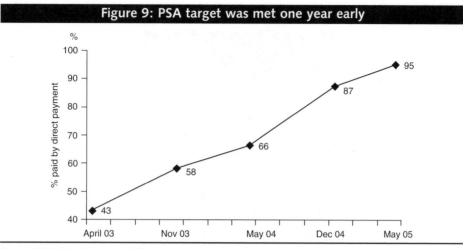

Figure 9: PSA target was met one year early

Source: DWP (N.B. data are available only at roughly six-monthly intervals)

How the campaign contributed to these savings

The campaign cut through and enjoyed very high levels of ad awareness, from start to finish (see Figure 10).

More importantly, the campaign greatly raised awareness of the changes themselves (see Figure 11).

Indeed, the campaign quickly became consumers' main source of information on this issue, with TV advertising overtaking the Post Office almost immediately, and the DM campaign surpassing it by Stage 2 (see Figure 12).

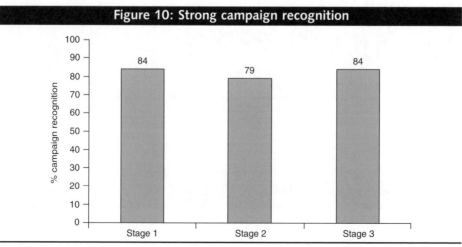

Figure 10: Strong campaign recognition

Base: Non-electronic customers. Source: RSGB Tracking

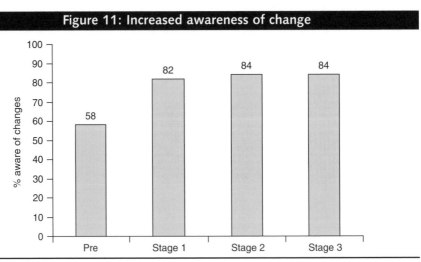

Figure 11: Increased awareness of change

Base: Non-electronic customers. Source: RSGB Tracking

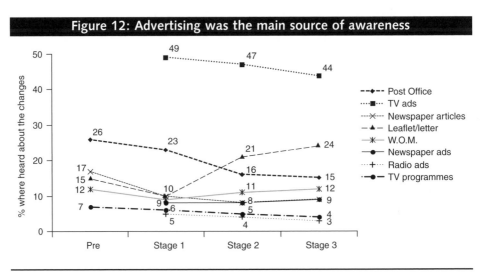

Figure 12: Advertising was the main source of awareness

Base: Non-electronic customers, aware of change. Source: RSGB Tracking

With the campaign now firmly installed as the main provider of information, deeper understanding of the changes developed, just as we had planned (see Figure 13). People became more familiar with the specifics of Direct Payment (see Figure 14). Likewise, they became more familiar with the brand name and logo (see Figure 15). Most importantly, people were presented with all this new information in a clear, reassuring way (see Figure 16).

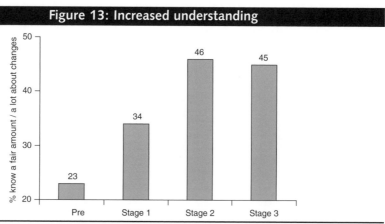

Figure 13: Increased understanding

Base: Non-electronic customers. Source: RSGB Tracking

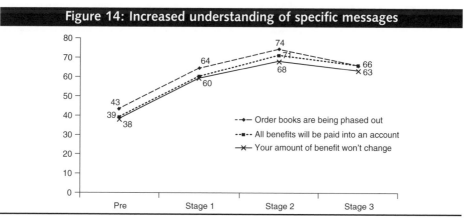

Figure 14: Increased understanding of specific messages

Base: Non-electronic customers. Source: RSGB Tracking

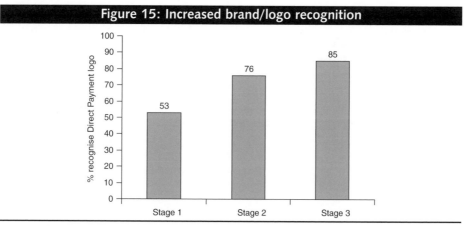

Figure 15: Increased brand/logo recognition

Base: Non-electronic customers. Source: RSGB Tracking

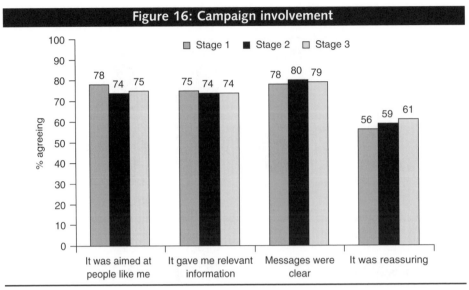

Figure 16: Campaign involvement

Base: Non-electronic customers. Source: RSGB Tracking

Hence researchers were soon able to report that:

To a large extent, the new advertising addresses the misconceptions and reservations about Direct Payment. As consumers become better informed about Direct Payment, it is increasingly difficult to justify not taking it up.[23]

Similarly, frontline workers, such as Jobcentre Plus staff, were soon reporting that our strategy of 'giving it to them straight' helped them clarify how they spoke about the changes to claimants.[24]

Likewise, call centre staff were eager to tell us that our collateral left no stone unturned, as it provided the answers to all the callers' questions, in clear unequivocal language.[25]

Even groups who had initially been resistant – such as Age Concern – began to order bulk supplies of materials, so that they too could explain in straightforward language about the transition.

Gradually, people began to engage with change, rather than reject it. For instance, by November 2004, 137,000 people had *chosen* to attend one of our roadshows for more in-depth advice (see Figure 17).

Likewise, call volumes were strong from the start, despite the fact that TV was not intended to be the primary response generator during the first two stages. Calls really took off at Stage 3, true to our campaign strategy. In total, 824,833 calls were generated and, again, the causal effect of the campaign is clear (see Figure 18).

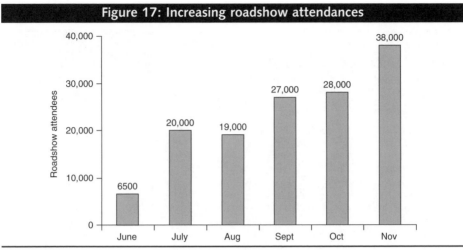

Figure 17: Increasing roadshow attendances

Source: DWP

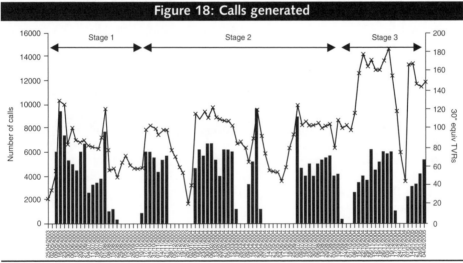

Figure 18: Calls generated

Source: DWP

Eliminating other factors

The natural drift to electronic payments

It's true that, even before the campaign began, take-up of electronic payment of benefits and pensions was growing at three percentage points per year. However, it's also clear that this 'natural drift' cannot explain the step-change witnessed. If this trend had continued in linear fashion, it would have taken 14 years to meet the 85% target, let alone surpass it. Even if natural drift had grown exponentially (which we accept is more likely, as with most 'technological' trends), it would have

329

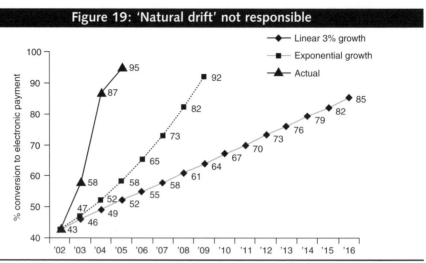

Figure 19: 'Natural drift' not responsible

Source: DWP

taken a long time to reach the desired levels. For instance, if the growth rate accelerated by one percentage point each year, it would still take seven years to reach 85% (see Figure 19).

The influence of Post Office workers

It's also true that some people heard about the changes via Post Office staff, rather than the campaign. However, we know from Figure 12 that there were relatively few of these (15% vs 44% for TV advertising alone). In addition, we know that Post Office staff were often hostile to the new system; indeed Postwatch acknowledged that 'some submasters produced unofficial literature on the migration programme, some of which has been unclear and misleading'.[26] So relying on this channel rather than paid-for communications would have been a very risky move.

The influence of editorial coverage

Similarly, while it's true that some people heard about the changes via the media, we know from Figure 12 that editorial coverage was far less influential in people's decision making than our paid-for campaign. And, as with Post Office workers, we know that the media's reporting of Direct Payment was not always accurate or positive. Again, it would have been very dangerous for the Government to have relied solely on this channel to get its message across.

The influence of other partners

Next, we should acknowledge that many other organisations, from charities to local authorities and banks, gave informal advice on the impending changes. However, research found that these sources 'appeared to play virtually no role [in converting customers]'.[27] Indeed, these organisations themselves were at pains to stress that they were not equipped to provide information on the scale required.[28]

Weren't people compelled to take action anyway?

Finally, it might be thought that people simply switched because they were forced to do so. But just to reiterate: there was no legal requirement upon claimants to move to Direct Payment; there was no prospect of benefits being withheld for people who didn't switch; there were no penalties wielded; and the Government confirmed all of this right up until the last minute.[29]

So in many ways, the campaign's greatest triumph was precisely that it persuaded people to act, *without* using legal threats, even though early research had concluded that 'the majority of customers would do nothing unless they had to'.[30]

Quantifying the campaign's ROI

As noted above, it has been estimated that increasing electronic take-up of benefit payments from 43% to 85% has saved the Government around £450m per year. However, to isolate the specific contribution of the campaign, we have to take into account the natural drift to electronic payment, and then calculate the *incremental* savings generated each year.

For example, let's say that natural drift would indeed have accelerated at the exponential rate suggested in Figure 19. This would suggest seven-year savings of £1,510m (see Table 1).

Table 1: Seven-year savings			
Year	Actual conversion[31]	Projected ('natural') conversion, assuming exponential growth[32]	Incremental savings[33] (£m)
2003	58	47	110
2004	87	52	350
2005	95	58	370
2006	95	65	300
2007	95	73	220
2008	95	82	130
2009	95	92	30
Total			1,510

Now let's err on the safe side (after all, the exponential rate we have used above is merely a hypothesis of what might have happened – perhaps natural drift might have accelerated even more sharply in reality: we'll never know). So instead of using average annual savings of £216m, as suggested above, let's round this figure down to a steady annual saving of £200m per annum, or £1,400m over seven years.

Next, let's acknowledge that not everybody found out about Direct Payment from the campaign (although this was by far and away the most important source of information).

Again, let's be conservative here and assume that only 44% of customers were motivated to switch by the campaign.[34] Applying this percentage to the savings outlined above would give us a figure of £616m savings generated by the campaign.

Based on a total campaign spend of £21,226,638,[35] this would give us an ROI of approximately £29 per £1 spent.

Conclusions and new learnings

Everything about Direct Payment was unusual: from the scale of the project, to the complexity of the audience, to the strength of people's opposition.

Hence it required a novel communications approach to make it run so smoothly – *without the need for any compulsion whatsoever*.

From the beginning, the agency played an unusually upstream role, developing the brand identity and helping to create an information helpline. Likewise, we gave an unusually central role to DM (and executed the campaign to boot). Most unusually of all, we sought only to inform people and actively avoided persuading them emotionally.

This makes Direct Payment very atypical in the context of the IPA Effectiveness Awards.[36] However, as commercial challenges become ever more complex, the joined-up approach described in this paper will be increasingly demanded by clients. And at a time when marketing is often confused with spin, we hope we've proved that unashamedly straightforward communications can pay dividends, too.

Notes

1. This paper was originally entered in the 2007 IPA Effectiveness Awards (for agencies with incomes of £20m or less), where it won a Silver prize and a special prize for 'Best Read'. For the purposes of these Awards, we have updated it by adding additional qualitative feedback, effects on call centre staff and other stakeholders.
2. Source: Select Committee on Work and Pensions Third Report, 23 February 2005.
3. Source: Select Committee on Work and Pensions Third Report, 23 February 2005.
4. Source: Select Committee on Work and Pensions Third Report, 23 February 2005.
5. Some 13 million individuals were receiving their benefits via giros or order books. They ranged from disabled octogenarians to 18-year-old job seekers, income support recipients to high-earning child benefit claimants.
6. Source: Kempson & Whyley, December 2000.
7. Source: Kempson & Whyley, December 2000.
8. Source: Kempson & Whyley, December 2000.
9. Source: Creative Research Limited, October 2002.
10. In a 2003 submission to the Trade and Industry Select Committee, Postwatch acknowledged that 'some submasters produced unofficial literature on the migration programme, some of which has been unclear and misleading'. This was also noted in the *Guardian* (29 March 2003). Charities such as Age Concern and Scope were also vocal with their concerns, though not actively obstructive.
11. For instance, John Barrett, the MP for Edinburgh West, was running a 'Save the pension book' campaign in his constituency, using his personal website and a petition.
12. Headlines included: 'Benefit changeover could bring chaos' (*Independent*, 4 December 2002); 'Fight on to save pension books' (*Daily Record*, 18 February 2003); 'Total letdown for Post Offices' (*Times*, 4 December 2002); 'Postmaster blames changes for closure' (*BBC News*, 28 January 2003).
13. While the existing order books and giros were being phased out in favour of electronic payments, the Government also introduced a new paper-based system – called the 'Cheque payment scheme' – for those who could not or would not make the shift.
14. Source: Kempson and Whyley, 2000.
15. Source: Kempson and Whyley, 2000. Likewise the public-sector website Kablenet.com described the change as a 'step into unknown territory'.
16. Source: NAO, 13 December 2004.
17. Source: *Guardian*, 29 March 2003.
18. Source: Creative Research Ltd, October 2002.
19. Source: EDS, 2005.
20. Source: *BBC News*, 24 September 2004.
21. Ofcom, 2006 ('Vulnerable consumers in switchover: lessons from parallel experiences').
22. Source: National Audit Office, 2006 ('Improving procurement').
23. Source: Cragg Ross Dawson, March 2004.

24. Source: MCBD informal interviews, 2005.
25. Source: MCBD informal interviews, 2005
26. See note 10, above.
27. Source: Wardle McLean, July 2003.
28. For example, Age Concern Scotland insisted that neither the charities nor the banks, nor the Citizens Advice Bureau could handle a communications campaign of this size, while Southwark Council (Review of Direct Payment in Southwark 2004–5) made a similar plea on behalf of local authorities.
29. Source: *Hansard*, 7 July 2005.
30. Source: Creative Research Ltd, May 2002.
31. To be conservative, we have assumed that actual conversions will never increase beyond the 95% achieved in May 2005.
32. Again, to be conservative, we have used the exponential rate of 'natural drift' set out in Figure 19, rather than a linear, three percentage points per annum growth rate based on historical data.
33. Once more, to be conservative, we have assumed that one percentage point represents £10m savings. Actually, £450m divided by 42 (85-43) = £10.7m. But this is a relatively inexact science, where not all percentage points are necessarily equal in value. For instance, converting 1% of weekly benefits recipients would generate twice the savings of converting 1% of fortnightly claimants. Rather than pretend we are using a very precise formula, we have erred on the side of caution and rounded this figure down.
34. We know from Figure 12 that between 44% and 49% of benefits claimants became aware of Direct Payment through the TV campaign alone. So we have ignored all other campaign media and applied the lower percentage figure.
35. Including all media, production and agency fees.
36. The only comparable campaign (in terms of scale, complexity, negative media context, role played by brand identity and active avoidance of emotional communications) is the 2004 Gold-winning paper on the Central London Congestion Charge.

Other company involved in campaign: Media company: Zenith Optimedia

Chapter 17

Dove

Dove's Big Ideal: from real curves to growth curves

By Nicolette Robinson and Haruna McWilliams, Ogilvy Advertising, and Felix Bullinger and Clay Schouest, Mindshare
Contributing author: Simeon Duckworth, Mindshare

Editor's summary

This paper shows how Dove rejected the conventions of the beauty product category, as well as popular cultural beliefs, to forge a strong and rewarding connection with its customers, across the world.

The communication campaign was based upon a simple, but big belief (or 'ideal') that the world would be a better place if we could make more women feel more beautiful everyday. And so was born the 'campaign for real beauty'.

Featuring and celebrating real women and their true, unadulterated, beauty Dove was able to get a wide audience to identify with their message and their brands. However, it wasn't just the message that was fresh and different, the channel strategy made great use of conventional and more word-of-mouth generating media.

The result was a more engaged audience across key markets including the USA, the UK and Germany. This led to sales increases equating to US$3 for every US$1 spent and a huge leap in market share across these territories and despite strong competitors such as Nivea and Olay. As the authors rightly say, this is a case about real curves and growth curves.

Introduction

Can a mainstream brand reject the conventions of its category yet still forge a strong enough connection with consumers to make a significant impact and be more profitable? This was the pivotal question asked of Dove in 2003.

The answer to the question is yes – if at the heart of the brand there is a powerful ideal. One that is compelling enough to engage and connect with consumers in such a way that they embrace it, talk about it, run with it and make it their own.

The story of Dove since 2003 is one of truth and participation. Most competitors were promising an unattainable image to consumers – lying even by implication about the potential of their products to help achieve the impossible.

Dove decided to defy the category 'rules' – to turn this convention around and confront the truth, and in so doing help make more women feel more attractive. A *Big Ideal*[1] was created, which was then to form the heart of all communication for Dove:

> *Dove believes that the world would be a better place if we could make more women **feel** more beautiful every day.*

Dove, as a head-to-toe beauty brand, would embody this and attract support from a large group of real women as well as provoking a debate within society as a whole.

Participation of these women, and word of mouth inspired by communication that provoked a debate, amplified the effect of paid-for communications and allowed the reach of the brand to go beyond the pure impact of traditional media.

In this paper we will prove that this Big Ideal is not an indulgent altruistic idea but a sound and profitable business strategy. Setting brand principles need not be mutually exclusive from commercial objectives. We'll show that a *Big Ideal* can:

- engage and motivate consumers
- snowball through society, creating enough buzz via word of mouth and PR to generate significant incremental profit
- be infinite – sparking creativity and taking on a life of its own
- have a dramatic effect on business results; it drives 32% of Dove's globally estimated brand value.[2]

As Simon Clift stated in a recent article in the *Wall Street Journal*:

> *In Dove's 'Campaign for Real Beauty'[3] ... ideas are brought to life in every single piece of communication, with the intention of emotionally engaging consumers wherever they see the brand – be it walking past a poster or on the supermarket shelf. Provoking debate that generates dialogue is becoming an important way to stand out. Fundamental to success is having built-in 'talkability' from the outset, that is, linking the brand with an idea that is sufficiently interesting to inspire word-of-mouth communication ... it's about creating infectious campaigns that deliver a better return on media investment.[4]*

The story so far – Dove's transition from dull to colourful

This story starts in 2003 when Dove, a familiar but frumpy brand, was commercially stagnating, with hero products such as Dove bar in the US declining at 1.9%. The brand was falling out of favour with the trade and facing threats of de-listing in key retailers such as Wal-Mart. All in all, a 'life-threatening' loss of momentum was in play (see Table 1).

Table 1: Nielsen SOM growth rates 1998–2003 vs 2004–2007				
		1998–2003 Pre	2004–2007 Post	Post vs pre rate of change	Comments
US	Bar Share	22.6%	30.7%	36.0%	
	Body Wash	12.6%	13.2%	4.6%	
	HBL	na	2.3%		launch in 2004
	Face	1.5%	2.7%	78.7%	pre 2000–2003
DE	Bar Share	9.1%	12.4%	36.5%	
	Body Wash	3.4%	5.4%	58.8%	
	HBL	5.0%	8.3%	67.2%	Pre 2000–2003
Note: Data shift – break in tracking mid-2002					
UK	Bar Share	21.6%	30.0%	39.0%	
	Body Wash	5.4%	7.8%	44.0%	
	HBL	3.7%	10.0%	170.9%	Pre 2000–2003

Source: Nielsen/IRI

In truth, the problems stemmed from a lack of emotional connection with the brand, which had started to lose relevance for consumers. For years, communication had largely relied on 1950s-style testimonials and functional stories of one-quarter moisturising cream, resulting in relatively low engagement and low persuasion (see Figures 1 and 2).

By contrast, many competitors offered far sexier, glamorous images: slim bodies, swirling hair and models of perfection surrounded women every day. Would the temptation be for Dove to follow suit and offer equally unattainable images? (See Figures 3 and 4.)

Challenging the beauty myth

The beauty industry has long wrestled with a contradiction at the heart of its imagery and communication. Put simply, and demonstrated clearly in research, women simultaneously criticise and yet cling to images of female perfection.

In our search for new impetus we thought about the issue differently: '*How do these images impact on a woman's self esteem?*' Asking this question helped us examine the conventions from a very different perspective and provided the liberation to think, and eventually act, differently.

Working with psychologists, the first Dove White Paper[5] was commissioned, revealing that after reading a women's magazine, 72% of women felt worse about themselves.[6]

Figure 1: Dove communication pre beauty theory

Figure 2: Dove preview scores pre beauty theory

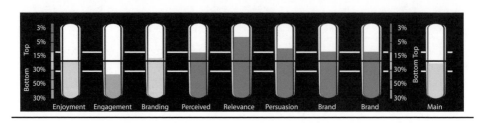

Figure 3: Competitor communication: hair products

Figure 4: Competitor communication: skin products

The images of perfection they craved were reducing their self-esteem – the industry was peddling a cruel drug.

So Dove decided to break not just the rules of its category but also of the wider culture in which we live. Dove realised that a woman's self-esteem is adversely affected by stereotypical images of uniform beauty in the media. Women in fact need to feel accepted by society, to belong, to feel a sense of community and sisterhood rather than striving for an out-of-reach ideal.

Dove's principled solution

Thus Dove's *Big Ideal* was formed to *help make more women feel more beautiful every day*. The theory was: if we could make more women feel better about themselves and encourage them to take greater care of themselves every day, we would have a far more positive impact on their self-esteem and in turn help rebuild that missing emotional connection with the brand.

So Dove took the brave step to go against category norms in order to connect with women in a more profound way – embracing women of all shapes, sizes, ages and races, and projecting a far more accessible, diverse, democratic and principled view of beauty. This more realistic portrayal of beauty would inspire not just our creative work but our whole marketing programme for Dove.

Winning hearts and minds

Before we could realise this new radical direction we had to convince the Unilever board. No easy matter given the importance of Dove to the company. It is their third biggest brand and accounts for 10% of their turnover.[7] Radically changing the brand's point of view had to 'pull on the board's heart strings and appeal to the purse strings'.

To win over the hearts and minds of the key board members we made a huge effort to help key stakeholders embrace and fully support the change. Most of the stakeholders were men, not likely to intuitively recognise the power of this strategy. So in the first place we aimed to appeal to their rational side by highlighting the significantly higher rate of return at 6:1 expected from 'visionary companies' compared to 'comparison companies' (see Figure 5).

However, the case was really made when we brought our strategy to life and closer to home by 'appealing to their hearts', recording their own daughters revealing how they felt about their appearance and beauty (see Figure 6). Following this highly personalised 'micro' version of the communications strategy – making it human, personal, relevant and engaging – the board were convinced.

Bringing the thinking to life

So, with this agreed, how did this new strategy manifest itself in the real world? Two pioneering pieces of communication set the wheels in motion. First, a campaign for firming lotion *challenging* the premise that a size 10 supermodel needs firmer thighs. Second, a campaign called 'Tick Box', asking for *participation* in the beauty debate. Together, these launched the 'Campaign for Real Beauty'.

Figure 5: Ratio of cumulative stock returns to general market, 1926–1990

Visionary companies   US$6,000

Comparison companies   US$1,000

General market   US$400

Figure 6: Dove director's video

Highlights from the two pivotal creative briefs are given in Figure 7.

Figure 7: Highlights from the two creative briefs

Firming: With Dove Firming women can show off their curves
Dove celebrates women's bodies as they are because being curvy is essentially female. Dove makes women feel different and gorgeous instead of feeling they must hide if they are not model perfect.

Tick Box: Genuine beauty comes in lots of shapes, sizes and forms
Dove shows that beauty doesn't have to be perfect. It can be: fatter rather than thin, older rather than younger, a bit lopsided not just symmetrical, with flaws not flawless, grey haired not just blonde, short rather than tall.

The work that developed from these two briefs aimed to drive a strong emotional connection with women. Using *real women* and an honest portrayal of beauty would drive both brand affinity and category differentiation.

Our principled view of beauty was designed to have a significant and positive impact on Dove sales and have global resonance, as it's a fundamental truth about all women, regardless of nationality.

Initial qualitative research into the creative work told us we were onto something good.[8]

> They're caring for me, I can identify with it, and I feel addressed. Dove also knows the other side. They get rid of dissatisfaction, make women more satisfied.

> I'm so grateful for your self esteem campaign for real beauty. Bravo!! Good corporate citizenry works. I went out and just bought Dove products.

> Thank you so much for your campaign for real beauty. Being 17 and growing up in a world where everyone is so obsessed with size 0 ... everyone deserves to feel beautiful about themselves, as everyone is beautiful.

> I think normal women can have firm curves too. If you do something, you can have everything. You only have to do something!

As the new direction was in development, Unilever commissioned a comprehensive global report entitled *The Real Truth about Beauty*,[9] which provided further justification for the strategy. It revealed that only 2% of women worldwide chose to describe themselves as beautiful.

So with the communication validated, Dove introduced Firming: 'Celebrating the curves of real women'. This ran across Europe in early 2004, followed by the US in the latter half of 2004.

The second wave of the campaign introduced the provocative 'Tick Box' executions. 'Tick Box' was a series of non-product, brand opinion ads and, as such, a first for Dove. It launched in the US and Canada in September 2004 and subsequently in Europe and Latin America in January 2005. In the ads Dove encouraged women to participate in the campaign by posing questions such as 'wrinkled or wonderful?', 'fat or fit?' and 'half-empty or half-full?' The Campaign for Real Beauty was born (see Figures 8–10).

Figure 8: Ads for Tick Box

Figure 9: Print ads for Firming

curvy thighs, bigger bums,
rounder stomachs.
What better way to
test our firming range?

new Dove
Firming Range

let's face it, firming the thighs
of a size 8 supermodel
wouldn't have been much of
a challenge.

new Dove
Firming Range

Figure 10: TV ads for Firming

new Dove Firming

Beyond conventional media – the start of the debate

The power of the strategy with a *Big Ideal* at its heart became apparent very quickly. We kick-started it, for example, by buying every billboard in Grand Central Station. Thanks to high-profile placement like this, the Firming and Tick Box campaigns went on to achieve unprecedented PR attention[10] (see Figures 11 and 12).

Figure 11: Firming PR

Figure 12: Tick Box PR

Women noticed Dove, seemingly for the first time, and everyone was talking. Katie Couric, for example, spent 16 minutes on the *Today* show with Dove's Firming girls – exposure that you just can't buy (see Figure 13).

Figure 13: *Today* **show, 14 July 2005**

The *Big Ideal* began to live outside the world of 'pure advertising' and to inform all the marketing mix from advertising to promotions in Wal-Mart, to PR, online and internally within Unilever.

The two pioneering campaigns were followed by engaging category communication in 2006 for Dove Hair, Dove Skin and Dove Deodorant (see Figures 14–16). All embraced the new *Big Ideal*.

Figure 14: Deodorant ads

Figure 15: Hair ads

In February 2006, Dove took the Campaign for Real Beauty a step further, creating the Dove Self Esteem Fund. This offered solutions to enhance the body image of young girls, by running workshops in schools and raising funds for self-esteem-related issues. The Dove Self Esteem Fund (DSEF) was further publicised with a 'Little Girls' film showing during the Super Bowl in North America (see Figure 17). This highlighted the results of the second global study

Figure 16: Skin ads

all skin is beautiful when it's beautifully nourished.
New Dove Body Care with Nutri-Serum.

Figure 17: Little Girls video

Beyond Stereotypes: Rebuilding the Foundation of Beauty Beliefs,[11] which dug deeper into the beauty concerns and motivations of women and girls.

Even the trade re-engaged with the brand, with Wal-Mart creating its own 'real women' TV ads with its own staff, and Asda using real customers in its posters, with excellent results in terms of impact (see Figures 18 and 19).[12]

Figure 18: Wal-Mart involvement

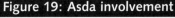

Figure 19: Asda involvement

- Huge PR
- 260 stores
- 272 women
- 5000 pictures

The infinite nature of Dove's new Big Ideal

Evidence of the power of our ideal comes from the range of communications that it has inspired. *Big Ideals* are infinite. In February 2007, Dove tackled the key stereotype of ageing, introducing the Pro-Age product range. This collection of body care, personal wash, face care, deodorant and haircare products was specifically formulated for women aged 50+.

The Pro-Age initiative was also supported by Dove's third global study, *Beauty Comes of Age*.[13] This recommended that we should celebrate women 50+ as they really are – with self-confidence, age spots, wrinkles and grey hair, but still beautiful.

The campaign's launch in the US, Canada and Europe generated a huge buzz. Oprah launched the campaign for Dove in the US by dedicating an entire show to Pro-Age on 5 February 2007. The campaign also received coverage in nearly every major media channel in the UK (January 2007) and Germany (February 2007) (see Figure 20).

Finally, Evolution, a viral ad showing a woman's transformation from 'plain to billboard glamour', was released on YouTube in 2007. This revealed the 'trickery of the beauty industry' in terms of how an ordinary model is transformed into a stunning beauty, winning acclaim at Cannes and sparking much debate on the internet and on major TV channels (see Figure 21).

Figure 20: Oprah and Pro-Age PR

BT has generated free global PR/Buzz of >250 Mio €
> 21 Mio views for Evolution alone.
More than 200 TV stations covered Dove story

No 1 downloaded film on YouTube   A real beauty: Dove's viral makes big splash for n

Beyond the creative component of the *Big Ideal*, channel planning played a pivotal role in cascading the strategy.

Channel communication strategy was devised to help Dove engage women fully

The core creative concept – '*to help more women feel beautiful every day by inspiring them to take greater care of themselves*' – was leveraged through a symbiotic channel communication strategy that focused on engagement beyond non-traditional channels.

Figure 21: Evolution and Evolution PR

The key channel insight was that only a truly 360° strategy would encourage 'real' women to get involved with the campaign. While traditional channels such as TV, press and poster raised awareness for campaigns such as Firming, non-traditional channels would deliver significant buzz for the brand and infiltrate popular culture faster, building audience 'ownership' of the *Big Ideal*.

Previous ROI findings from ATG-Mindshare[14] for Unilever brands suggested that multi-channel communication for brand campaigns was more likely to be effective than any single channel in isolation (i.e. PR, events, sponsorships, print, TV etc.). Prior to Beauty Theory (pre-2004) Dove media channels focused primarily on traditional vehicles and were largely dominated by TV, with some press, radio and out of home (see Table 2).

Table 2: Percentage investment allocated to 360° channels*			
Country	Pre 2004 Dove	Post 2004–2007 (Dove Beauty Masterbrand	% rate of change post vs pre
US	23%	45%	96%
UK	45%	66%	47%
DE	28%	50%	79%
Rest of world	20%	37%	85%

* % of allocation to 360° channels defined as non-traditional excluding TV, radio, press, OOH, cinema

For example in the US only 23% of the pre-2004 total Dove budget was allocated to 'non-traditional' media, while post 2004 the allocation of non-traditional channels was 45% and included PR, sponsorships, digital, CRM, event sponsorships and programming.

The PR effect of Dove's unique take on beauty was huge – pushing against stereotypes in casting and in product communication, challenging the premise of self-esteem in viral activity and involving key celebrities such as Oprah. All raised the beauty debate beyond the actual value of the media spend in isolation.

In addition to the big-ticket 360° items such as the PR partnership with Oprah, or the Super Bowl event with 'Little Girls', the campaign became a turning point for the brand in terms of digital investment. In Germany in 2007, for example, 100% of 'Masterbrand'[15] activity was allocated to digital – a media first for Unilever.

Overall, the combination of 360° channels and usage of consistent creative messages helped encourage women to actively participate in Dove's *Big Ideal*.

Why the campaign worked

There are four reasons why the campaign was so effective.

1. Dove's new *Big Ideal* landed at the heart of the Dove brand positioning. It is embedded with a powerful insight that *engaged* with consumers emotionally, and hence it performed disproportionately well. The most effective and engaging ideas are often rooted in a genuine human truth. This more principled beauty philosophy had a significant impact on differentiation and brand appeal.
2. Women agreed with the brand's principles and felt a strong sense of connection to the core ideal, namely that *all women should feel beautiful*. This elicited high

involvement, generating a positive reaction for Dove; in particular, it drove engagement and persuasion (see Figure 22).

3. There were significant benefits from the PR ability of Dove's Beauty Theory. This huge 'societal effect' was achieved on the premise that great ideas travel fast: they infiltrate popular culture, create buzz and debate, and take on a life of their own. Oprah took the brand deep into popular culture, and women embraced the ideal and made it larger than life.

4. This in turn drove consumer conviction and preference vs competitor offerings. Women bought Dove because they agreed with the brand's point of view. This led to a significant increase in conviction for the brand, which then in turn produced an increase in sales and profitability.

Figure 22: Preview post – Beauty Theory measures

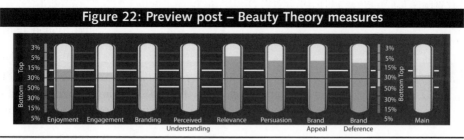

TV ad profile – post Beauty Theory average (all categories)

Evidence in key markets: the US, UK and Germany

Now we'll prove that what made emotional sense made commercial sense, too, by looking in detail at three of Dove's top markets (namely the US, UK and Germany), which account for 60% of global revenue.

Dove's share of market increased by 33% post Dove's new Big Ideal

Using data from 1998 to 2006, both share of market and annual growth rates in our three key markets were higher post Beauty Theory. The weighted share of market for Dove across categories and countries shifted from 17.8% to 23.8%, which equates to a 33.2% increase (see Table 3).

Table 3: Matrix of market growth

Weighted growth by country

		1998–2003 pre	2004–2007 post	Post vs pre rate of change
Total Dove active categories	US	20.3%	26.7%	31.6%
	UK	7.5%	10.5%	40.1%
	DE	16.6%	23.4%	41.0%
Total Dove weighted by value		17.80%	23.80%	33.20%

Source: Nielsen/IRI

353

The Dove media investment model helped Dove outperform competitors in 75% of cases

We know that media spend alone was not responsible for the growth. The strategy itself was commercially successful.

Dove has successfully translated communication spend into share of market growth across its portfolio and key markets during the Beauty Theory campaign periods. In the majority of cases Dove significantly outperformed its key competitors.

The media performance snapshots illustrate this. Using the US skin cleansing category as an example, during the campaign period Dove had a share of spend to share of market ratio of 130 and as a result delivered 92 BPS growth.[16] Moreover, in terms of media performance, Dove outperformed all its competitors in translating investment (SOS:SOM > 100) to growth (see Figure 23).

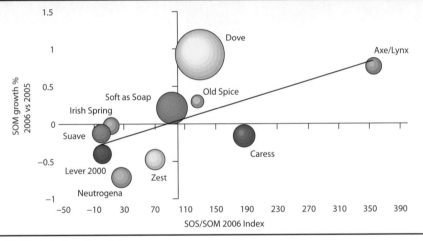

Figure 23: Dove share of spend vs growth chart (US) – Dove US Skin Cleansing category SOS/SOM vs SOM growth 2005 vs 2006

Size of bubble indicative of brand size

In 75% (9 out of 12) of the cases analysed using the above method, across the UK, Germany and the US, Dove outperforms the average category growth linked to SOS/SOM levels (see Figure 24).

Dove's Big Ideal gave us greater differentiation, and engagement increased by 12%

Dove's *Big Ideal* differentiated our positioning in key markets. In fact, all key measures increased post Beauty Theory from enjoyment, relevance and brand appeal to increases in differentiation and persuasion. Engagement in particular increased a staggering 12% (see Table 4).

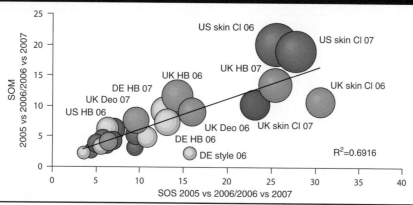

Figure 24: Global share of spend/share of market – Dove in category SOS–SOM relationship for Germany, US, UK

Notes: US skin cleansing (Bar and Personal Wash) is the largest in sales revenue for any Dove category
Size of bubble indicative of brand size

Table 4: Preview Beauty Theory measures

Metric	Pre-Beauty Theory (Normalised Index)	Post-Beauty Theory (Normalised Index)	Change
Enjoyment	100	107	+3
Engagement	92	104	+12
Branding	102	100	–2
Understanding	105	100	–5
Persuasion	107	110	+3
Brand appeal	106	111	+5
Makes brand really different	105	109	+4
Relevance	112	111	–1
Key benefit communication	99	102	+3 Dove value equation

Dove's Big Ideal significantly increased brand loyalty and conviction to the tune of US$12.9m sales in the US

As might be expected, Beauty Theory operates at the top end of the Millward Brown affinity pyramid, and had a significant impact on brand loyalty and conviction (see Figure 25 – the top of the Pyramid is where we would expect the mission to have an impact).

Conviction has a significant correlation to sales (see Table 5). As evidenced, using the US as an example, the impact of Beauty Theory is equivalent to the impact of trade and consumer promotions combined at a total sales value of US$12.9m (see Figure 26).

Figure 25: Millward Brown affinity pyramid

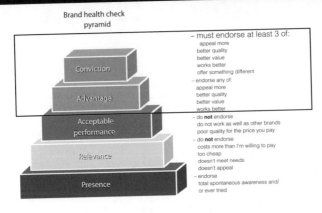

Brand health check pyramid

Conviction
Advantage
Acceptable performance
Relevance
Presence

– must endorse at least 3 of:
  appeal more
  better quality
  better value
  works better
  offer something different
– endorse any of:
  appeal more
  better quality
  better value
  works better
– do **not** endorse
  do not work as well as other brands
  poor quality for the price you pay
– do **not** endorse
  costs more than I'm willing to pay
  too cheap
  doesn't meet needs
  doesn't appeal
– endorse
  total spontaneous awareness and/
  or ever tried

Area most likely to be impacted by the Mission work

Table 5: Conviction to Dove tied to base sales

	UK PW	US Deo*	UK HBL	DE HBL
Contribution of conviction to base sales volume	18% 327,635 units	10% 3,922,130 eq units	17% 260,313 units	8% 381,072 units
R^2	.78	.80	.98	.91

Across categories, conviction contributes 8% to 18% of base sales volume
  * Stronger effects are seen when Dove is more differentiated on beauty statement

Figure 26: US Beauty Theory impact

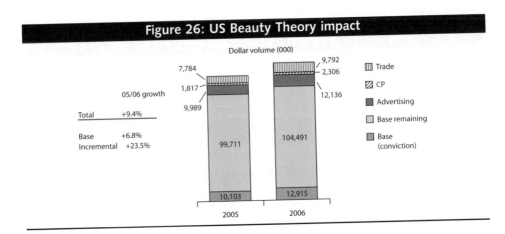

Dollar volume (000)

05/06 growth

Total	+9.4%
Base	+6.8%
Incremental	+23.5%

2005: 7,784 / 1,817 / 9,989 / 99,711 / 10,103
2006: 9,792 / 2,306 / 12,136 / 104,491 / 12,915

Trade
CP
Advertising
Base remaining
Base (conviction)

2005   2006

The broader societal halo effect impacted on conviction; the 'Oprah effect' returns US$6 for every dollar spent

The communication 'halo effect' as a result of combining traditional media (TV, print, PR) with new media (online, virals/downloads, word of mouth) meant that our communications impact became bigger than just the TVRs. Dove became one of the most talked-about brands.

In particular, thanks to 'the Oprah effect' the impact of the campaign escalated and Oprah had the most significant payback on revenue at 6:1 (see Figure 27).

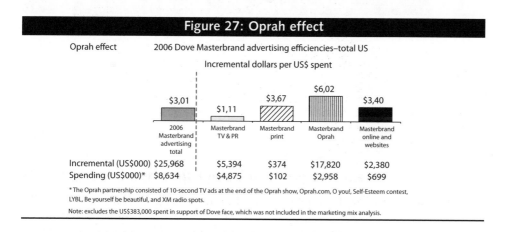

Figure 27: Oprah effect

From Buzzmetrics, we can see that Dove leads the way. Consumers say Dove is taking a leading role in changing advertising's standards towards women. Dove dominates discussion in the personal wash, haircare and deodorant categories, with three times the buzz of competitors such as Olay (see Figure 28).

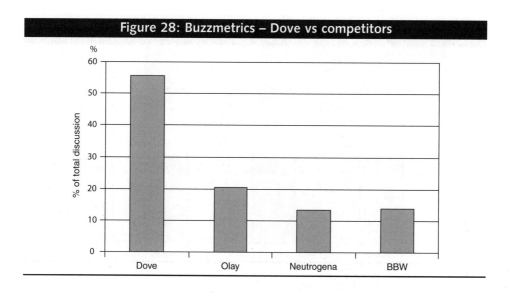

Figure 28: Buzzmetrics – Dove vs competitors

'Evolution' is the top discussion driver for Dove and was on the 'most viewed' list on YouTube. The video's viral nature prompted a major spike in discussion after its release, and it continues to drive moderate and steady buzz levels. Evolution made up 42% of campaign discussion for Dove, with an 8,000% increase in weekly traffic on CFRB.com after its launch. In total the estimated free global buzz amounted to more than €250m. In the US over 21 million people viewed Evolution alone (see Figure 29).

Figure 29: Buzzmetrics – Evolution

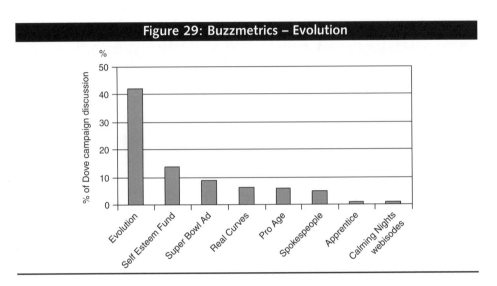

Further evidence of consumer engagement comes as women have adapted the idea and made it their own (see Figures 30 and 31).

Figure 30: Campaign for Real Beauty – Slob Evolution

Figure 31: Campaign for Real Beauty for Dogs

Path modelling: connection of key Beauty Theory activities to conviction and link to sales volume (Figure 32)

Figure 32: Path modelling

- Structural equation models: shows impact of media activity on consumer perceptions and conviction, Allows us to understand how various measures are related

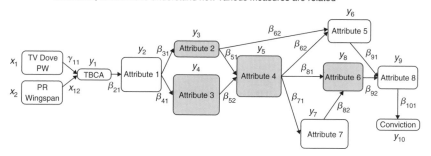

- Dynamic structural models: estimates the relationship between conviction and base sales

$$Y_t = \alpha_{0t} + \alpha_{1t} \times t + \sum_{j=1}^{T} \gamma_{jt} \times \delta_{jt} + \sum_{i=1}^{n} \beta_{it} \times X_{it}$$

☐ Beauty Theory-related attributes

Here we show the impact of media activity on consumer perceptions and conviction, which allows us to understand how various measures are related. Path modelling clearly shows that the key Beauty Theory statements had an impact on conviction across categories and that conviction increased from 8 to 18% dependent on category (as shown earlier, in Table 5). In general, when Dove is more differentiated on Beauty Theory statements, there is a significantly bigger impact on base sales (see Table 6).

Table 6: Summary of key relationships – differentiation and impact

	UK PW	US Deo	UK HBL	DE HBL	US Masterbrand
Impact of beauty statement on conviction (rank among key drivers)	7th of 8	NA – distinct approach	5th of 9	3rd of 6	2nd of 7 (represented by multiple statements)
Relative differentiation of Dove on beauty statement	+2	+26	+13	+13	NA – multiple statements (beauty comes in lots of different shapes and sizes, promotes an honest and attainable portrait of beauty)

In general, when Dove is more differentiated on beauty statement, the beauty concept has a bigger impact on base sales

Again, since the relationship between the beauty statement and conviction is not present in analyses of competitive brands, this re-enforces that differentiation for Dove on this dimension is a competitive advantage

We can prove that Dove's specific mix of emotional and functional attributes has an impact on conviction (see Table 7). Key Beauty Theory statements are as follows:

Are brands that believe you don't have to be model perfect to look great.

Make you feel good about yourself.

Make you feel feminine.

Make you look and feel beautiful.

Table 7: Key attributes measured relating to Beauty Theory			
Increasing Dove conviction by 10% (2.6 pts) in the UK HBL category would lead to a 2.4% increase in base sales for Dove			
	2006 modelled	2006 simulated	% change
Total brand communication awareness	60.5%	71.6%	18.4%
Attribute 1	35.7%	42.2%	18.1%
Attribute 2	47.4%	51.9%	9.3%
Attribute 3	49.2%	52.9%	7.7%
Attribute 4	36.5%	41.0%	12.4%
Attribute 5	28.9%	33.3%	15.1%
Attribute 6	33.7%	38.3%	13.7%
Attribute 7	60.8%	64.9%	6.6%
Attribute 8	41.8%	46.8%	11.8%
Attribute 9	46.1%	50.4%	9.3%
Conviction	26.4%	29.0%	10%
Base sales	930,802 units	953,235 units	2.4%

In the UK, Dove conviction in the Hand and Body Lotion category has continued to rise over the years as Beauty Theory gets stronger (see Figure 33).

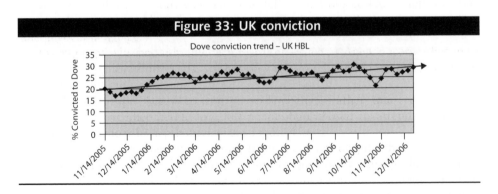

Figure 33: UK conviction

For example, increasing Dove conviction by 10% (2.6 percentage points) in the UK Hand and Body Lotion category would lead to a 2.4% increase in base sales for Dove. Further strengthening our position on these measures would generate increased sales. Figure 34 shows the UK path model for the HBL road to conviction.

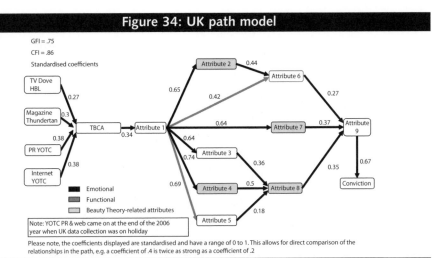

Figure 34: UK path model

GFI = .75
CFI = .86
Standardised coefficients

Note: YOTC PR & web came on at the end of the 2006 year when UK data collection was on holiday

Please note, the coefficients displayed are standardised and have a range of 0 to 1. This allows for direct comparison of the relationships in the path, e.g. a coefficient of .4 is twice as strong as a coefficient of .2

In Germany, increasing conviction to Dove by 20% (6.8 percentage points) in HBL led to a 1.7% increase in base sales (see Figure 35 and Table 8).

Figure 35: Germany conviction

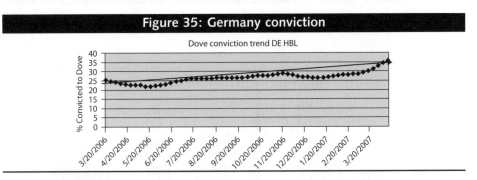

Table 8: Attributes measured for Hand and Body Lotion – Germany

Increasing conviction to Dove by 20% (6.8 pts) in DE HBL will lead to a 1.7% increase in base sales; DE HBL had the lowest contribution of conviction to base sales of any country we modelled, which explains why a big jump in conviction is needed to see a sales increase

	2006 modelled	2006 simulated	% change
TV ad awareness	48.8%	60.2%	18.8%
Totaol brand communication awareness	71.3%	83.2%	14.2%
Attribute 1	36.3%	44.4%	18.3%
Attribute 2*	47.5%	56.8%	16.4%
Attribute 3	37.9%	42.6%	11.0%
Attribute 4*	50.1%	58.1%	13.8%
Attribute 5	37.0%	43.2%	14.4%
Attribute 6*	42.9%	50.9%	15.6%
Conviction	27.2%	34.0%	20.0%
Base sales	3,124,601 units	3,176,179 units	1.7%

* Beauty Theory-related attributes

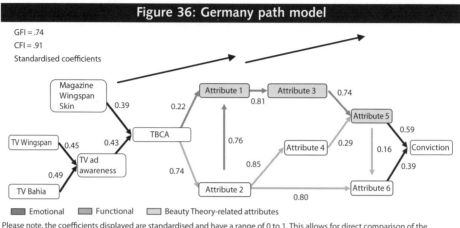

Figure 36: Germany path model

GFI = .74
CFI = .91
Standardised coefficients

Emotional   Functional   Beauty Theory-related attributes

Please note, the coefficients displayed are standardised and have a range of 0 to 1. This allows for direct comparison of the relationships in the path, e.g. a coefficient of .4 is twice as strong as a coefficient of .2

The path model for growth of Hand and Body Lotion conviction in Germany is given in Figure 36.

We further validated these findings by category and then double-checked that the model could not work for other key category competitors, such as Nivea, in the UK, Germany and the US (see Figure 37).

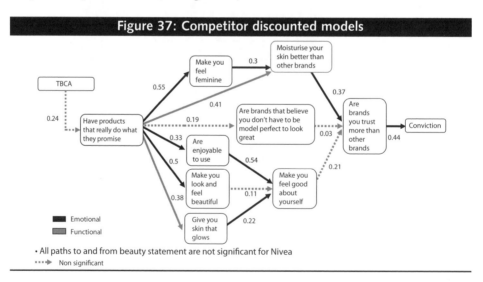

Figure 37: Competitor discounted models

Emotional
Functional

• All paths to and from beauty statement are not significant for Nivea
•••• Non significant

These findings were further endorsed by an independent study in Canada looking at correlations between Dove's associations with self-esteem and purchase intent (see Table 9).

The distinction between product and Masterbrand-driven (i.e. not specifically linked to any product or category) conviction enabled us to measure the financial effectiveness of Dove's Beauty Theory activities in 2005 and 2006: in the US alone

Table 9: Canada purchase intent data

	Correlation with purchase intent
■ Supports a positive self-image	0.39
■ Different from traditional beauty	0.34
■ More realistic beauty	0.38
■ Moisturises skin	0.40
■ Leave skin feeling clean	0.42

a 10% increase in conviction in 2006 would result in US$2.97m, or a 2.3% increase in short- and long-term sales (see Figure 38).

Figure 38: US path model

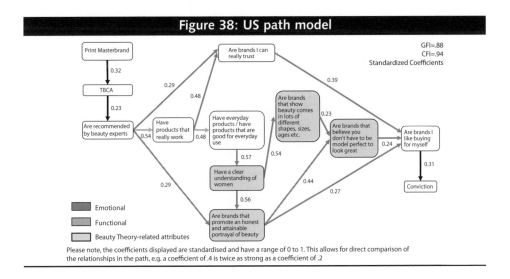

Please note, the coefficients displayed are standardised and have a range of 0 to 1. This allows for direct comparison of the relationships in the path, e.g. a coefficient of .4 is twice as strong as a coefficient of .2

Beauty Theory drives 32%[17] of Dove's globally estimated brand value
Figures 39 and 40 and Table 10 show ROMI calculations.

Figure 39: ROMI calculation – measuring average decay

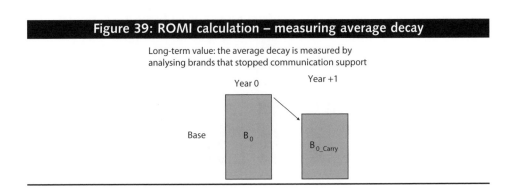

Long-term value: the average decay is measured by analysing brands that stopped communication support

Figure 40: ROMI calculation – identifying the 'new' base

Long-term value: with the average base decay figure
the 'new' base can be identified for each brand
that is supported in the following year

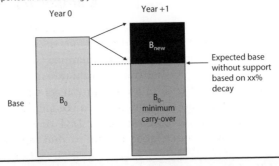

Year 0

Year +1

B_{new}

Expected base
without support
based on xx%
decay

Base B_0

B_{0-}
minimum
carry-over

Table 10: ROMI calculation – incremental sales driven by advertising

Long-term value: incremental sales driven by
advertising explain 'new' base best

	Correlation with New Base %	Sigma	Cases
Incremental sales share due to advertising	0.65	99%	27
Share of spend	0.61	99%	27
Conviction	0.56	99%	25
Voltage	0.49	99%	25
Incremental promotional sales share	0.40	96%	27

Figure 41: Incremental volume breakdown – Dove Bar Soap

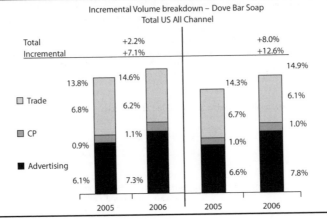

Incremental Volume breakdown – Dove Bar Soap
Total US All Channel

| Total Incremental | +2.2% +7.1% | | +8.0% +12.6% |

14.9%

Trade   13.8%   14.6%   14.3%   6.1%

6.8%   6.2%   6.7%   1.0%

CP

0.9%   1.1%   1.0%

Advertising

6.1%   7.3%   6.6%   7.8%

2005   2006   2005   2006

We have discounted other factors such as pricing, promotion and distribution increases by using market mix modelling (see Figure 41).

Modelling studies on Beauty Theory effects by Nielsen across Hair, Deodorant, Hand and Body Lotion as well as Skin Cleansing for Dove helped to isolate significant Beauty Theory communication effects from the other marketing influences (see Figures 42–47).

Figure 42: Best-fit model: US Nielsen market mix modelling 2005–2006, Dove Bar Soap

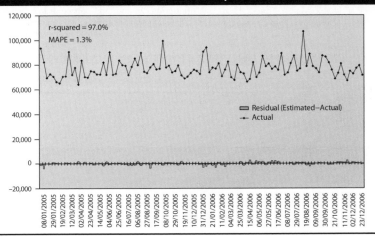

Figure 43: Best-fit model: US Nielsen market mix modelling 2005–2006, Dove Body Wash

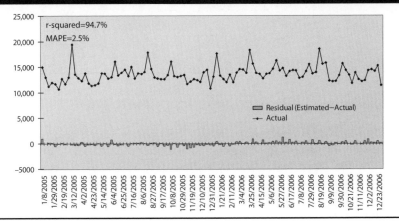

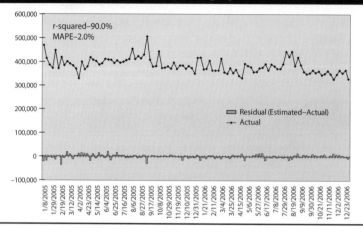

Figure 44: Best-fit model: US Nielsen market mix modelling 2005–2006, Bar Soap category

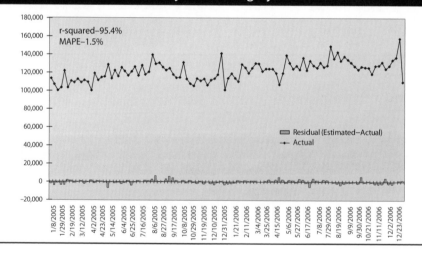

Figure 45: Best-fit model: US Nielsen market mix modelling 2005–2006, Body Wash category

For instance, sales modelling in the US demonstrates that a US$12.4m communication investment in Masterbrand activities in 2005–2006 drove US$38m worth of revenue, delivering a healthy ROI of over 300%, or 3:1 (see Figure 48).

Relating this to global Masterbrand investments of US$91.6m leads us to the conclusion that Dove's global Masterbrand activities drove US$280m of short-term revenue.

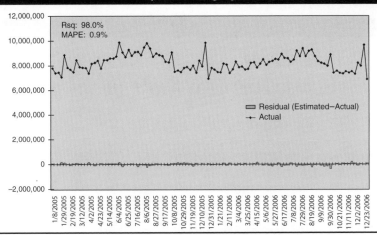

Figure 46: Best-fit models: US Nielsen market mix modelling 2005–2006, ApDeo category

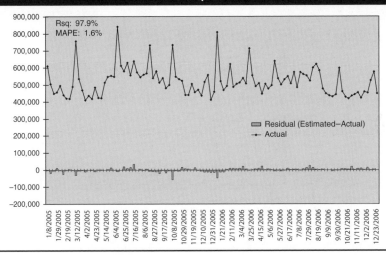

Figure 47: Best-fit model: US Nielsen market mix modelling 2005–2006, Dove ApDeo

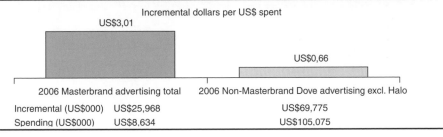

Figure 48: ACNielsen market mix modelling 2006 advertising efficacy (ROI)

367

Value analysis of ROI – summary

Figure 49 gives a diagrammatic summation of the value analysis of ROI.

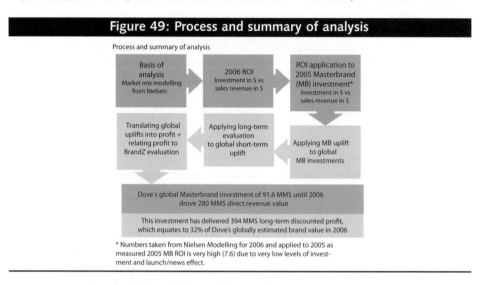

Figure 49: Process and summary of analysis

The discounted long-term value of the Masterbrand investment, which is estimated by Mindshare's Long-term Value Measurement,[18] sums to US$394m profit contribution, which equates to 32% of Dove's globally estimated Brand Value by BrandZ. In conclusion, Dove's *Big Ideal* accounts for almost one-third of the Brand's total value – this was a risk well worth taking!

Dove global brand value from BrandZ

Table 11 gives a breakdown of the Dove global brand value from BrandZ.

Table 11: Dove global brand value from BrandZ = US$1.2bn

PERSONAL CARE – Top 20 by brand value

#	Brand	BV '06 (US$m)	BC '06	BM '06	BV change	# change	
1	Gillette	17,954	4	7.5	1%	=	
2	L'Oréal	12,303	4	6.5	15%	=	
3	Colgate	7,711	4	5	32%	1	
4	Avon	6,558	3	5.5	−1%	−1	Premium position in market drives growth
5	Garnier	4,159	3	5	18%	=	
6	Nivea	3,148	3	4.5	33%	=	
7	Lancôme	3,090	3	6.5	21%	−1	
8	Oral B	2,545	3	5.5	57%		
9	Crest	2,294	3	5.5	51%		
10	Olay	2,284	4	6	83%		Benefiting from P&G strong business value increase as well as more of a premium position
11	Estée Lauder	2,008	3	6	−1%	−3	
12	Shiseido	1,863	3	5	88%	2	
13	Dove	1,214	3	5	6%	=	
14	Clarins	1,127	4	6.5	28%	1	
15	Neutrogena	1,102	3	4	−6%	−3	
16	Pantene	726	4	6	3%	1	
17	Aquafresh	714	3	3	1%	−1	
18	Pond's	605	2	3.5	−2%	1	
19	Signal	544	3	3.5	−17%	−1	
20	Sensodyne	472	3	3.5	−5%	=	

A final word – Big Ideals infiltrate culture

So, beyond the financial implications of the campaign, what are the other 'softer success factors'? The impact of the Dove campaign has infiltrated Unilever both internally and externally. Dove is one of the most applauded Unilever examples of excellent marketing, featured in *Fortune* and other leading magazines and the successful Harvard Business Case Study.[19] Dove has featured in all of Unilever's quarterly results to investors since 2005. It's the most quoted brand of graduate recruitment for Unilever – Dove has touched the lives of 1.8 million young girls through its self-esteem workshops and it is a key example of bringing to life the Unilever Company Vitality mission (see Figures 50 and 51).

Figure 50: Internal motivation

More than 100 Dove Days spend on a global level.
Numerous Local Dove Marketeers in National Print or TV.

Figure 51: Beauty Theory has brought Vitality to life for Dove and Unilever

But truly *Big Ideals* go beyond their immediate environment: they infiltrate popular culture and society. As recently summed up by Oprah (see Figure 52): 'What you guys are doing is amazing for women; it can change the way we look at ourselves ... I applaud Dove, I'm gonna go and get me a bar of Dove soap.'

Figure 52: Oprah TV show on 15 November 2005

Notes

1. Ogilvy bespoke tool.
2. ROMI measure.
3. CFRB became the communications expression of the Big Ideal. 'Beauty Theory' is Dove's internal expression of the Big Ideal.
4. Simon Clift, 'Brand new world', *Wall Street Journal*, 13 March 2008.
5. *The Real Truth About Beauty: A Global Report*, Strategy One.
6. Dove White Paper fact: 72% of women feel worse after reading a woman's magazine thanks to the beauty pressure they experience.
7. Unilever company data.
8. *Qualitative to Review Influences on Self-esteem and Beauty Ideals of Women*, Rheingold Message Tuner™.
9. *The Real Truth About Beauty: A Global Report*, Strategy One.
10. PR on Firming and Tick Box.
11. *Beyond Stereotypes: Rebuilding the Foundation of Beauty Beliefs*, Strategy One.
12. Wal-Mart/Asda involvement.
13. *Beauty Comes of Age*, Strategy One.
14. Advance Techniques Group: Global experts in market mix modelling.
15. Masterbrand = non-product-related activity.
16. BPS: bases points; 100 bases points = 1% share of market.
17. ROMI calculation.
18. Long-term Value Measurement from Mindshare is based upon empirically measured short-term ROI (ideally from market mix modelling) and incorporates a proprietary method to estimate the long-term advertising effect. It furthermore then applies financial factors such as discounted cash flow and profit margins to arrive at an objective total profit contribution of current marketing investments.
19. 'Dove: Evolution of a Brand', *Harvard Business Review*, 25 March 2008.

Other companies involved in campaign: Digital company: OgilvyOne; PR company: Edelman.

Chapter 18

Lucozade Sport

How we doubled sales by focusing on less

By Chris Binns, MediaCom, James Joice, M&C Saatchi, and Clare Newman, MediaCom

Editor's summary

This paper shows how Lucozade Sport sales doubled over three years by having more engaged conversations with a smaller group of people. The 'Before, Fuel, Edge' communications strategy was developed to connect Lucozade Sport with the needs of athletes; using it 'before' sport as preparation, providing 'fuel' through functionality and scientific credentials, and ensuring its availability at events for participants and spectators ('edge'). The campaign created a wide variety of partnerships, experiences and content to deliver this multi-faceted strategy and directly connect with the right people. It has generated a short-term payback of £1.04 per every £1 spent.

The management summary: less is more

This is the story of a specific period in Lucozade Sport's life cycle, namely 2004–2007. During this period we reduced our marketing investment but have grown the brand at an unprecedented speed. Specifically we have achieved the following:

1. Doubled the size of the brand while investing less in marketing (see Figure 1).

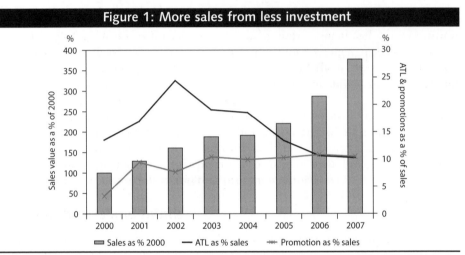

Figure 1: More sales from less investment

Source: Millward Brown

2. Focused on attracting and keeping a high usage audience of competitive Sports Warriors (see Figure 2).

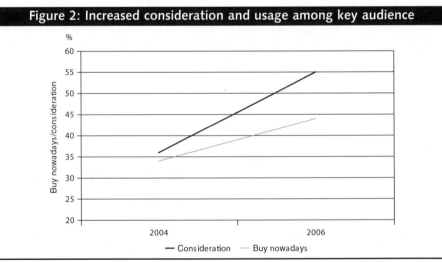

Figure 2: Increased consideration and usage among key audience

Source: Millward Brown

Why are these numbers important? Because in 2003, 69% of sales came from the 25% of our users who were Sports Participants.[1]

3. Delivered an unrivalled ROI[2] for fmcg and a ROMI that is profitable in the short to medium term (see Table 1).

Table 1: ROI and ROMI, 2005–2007[3]			
	2005	2006	2007
ROI (£)	1.51	2.36	3.63
ROMI (£)	0.43	0.80	1.04

We have done this by focusing our efforts on a smaller group of people and having better conversations with them, by putting metrics and effective communications diagnostics at the heart of what we do, and we have done this by aligning all agencies[4] behind one communications strategy – namely Before, Fuel and Edge – to achieve one goal – namely selling more for less.

The challenge

Launched in 1990, by 2004 Lucozade Sport had grown to a £50m brand. While our focus is not on explaining the idiosyncratic delivery of the 4Ps in the first 14 years, we need to explain the brand's situation in 2004 to underline the importance of what we achieved to the business: the year-on-year growth provided by a massive distribution drive had faded away (see Figure 3).[5]

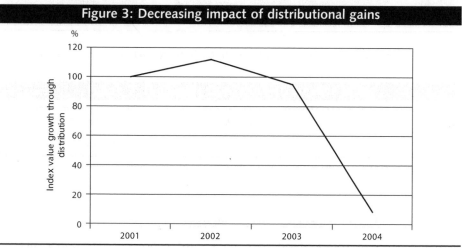

Figure 3: Decreasing impact of distributional gains

%

Index value growth through distribution

Source: GSK/ACNielsen

The magic-wand claims we had made for years[6] were starting to fall on deaf ears. This impacted in three ways:

1. year-on-year sales growth stalled (see Figure 4)

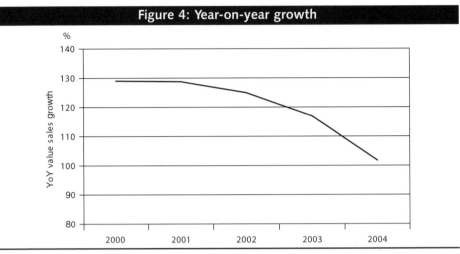

Figure 4: Year-on-year growth

Source: GSK

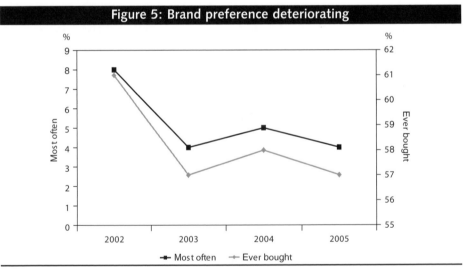

Figure 5: Brand preference deteriorating

Source: Millward Brown

2. claimed usage and consideration was falling (see Figure 5)
3. penetration had fallen by over 4%.[7]

It was into this environment that the mighty Coca-Cola corporation launched Powerade. On the back of Coca-Cola's successful distribution muscle and investing in share of voice well ahead of its share of market,[8] Powerade quickly gained some real traction (see Figures 6 and 7).

If we did not act swiftly and decisively the future growth and profitability of Lucozade Sport was going to be under severe pressure.

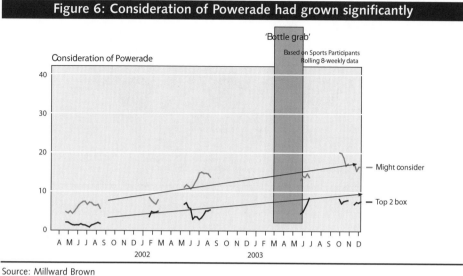

Figure 6: Consideration of Powerade had grown significantly

Source: Millward Brown

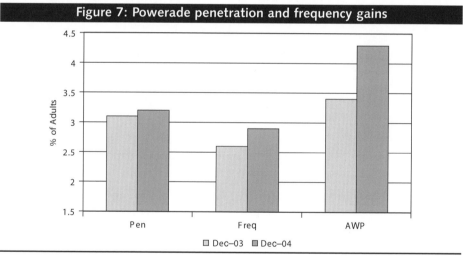

Figure 7: Powerade penetration and frequency gains

Source: TNS

The audience – fewer people, more of the right sports people

Lucozade Sport's early approach to communications[9] followed a similar approach to most fmcg products – speaking to a wide range of people with a massive reliance on TV. Probably right for the time, the net long-term impact of this approach is highlighted in Figure 8.

Only 18% of Sports Participants were drinking Lucozade Sport. Why were these numbers important? Because we knew that Sports Participants have a higher average weight of purchase (see Table 2).

Figure 8: Only 18% of Sports Participants drink Lucozade Sport

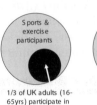

1/3 of UK adults (16-65yrs) participate in sport and/or exercise = 16.9m

Of these, 22% use a sports drink = 3.7m

Of these, 85% are drinking Lucozade = 3.14m

Of these, 74% are drinking Lucozade Sport = 2.32m

Source: MediaCom/TGI: GB Index

Table 2: Lucozade Sport consumption

	Sports Participants	Non-participants
Average value sales (%)	69	31
Average of user base (%)	25	75

Source: GSK 2003 Usage Omnibus

An increase in penetration among Sports Participants would be more beneficial than a similar increase in penetration of a wider audience. However, we couldn't target all the 16.9 million people who claim to participate in sport;[10] they would have a wide and varied set of attitudes towards sport, frequency of participation and requirement for Lucozade Sport. In order to focus our resources we conducted two pieces of audience research:

1. a U&A-driven segmentation of the Sports Participant marketplace
2. a TGI recontact to quantify and make actionable the opportunities.

What we found drove us to focus on a smaller group within Sports Participants.

■ There is a massive range in the frequency of sports participation (and therefore a massive range in frequency of needstate) (see Figure 9).
■ There is also a range of engagement with sports participation (from sport as a means to an end, through sport being about participation, to sport being about winning) (see Figure 10).
■ Within those who play sport frequently and are engaged with sports participation there is a final important scale between Sports Mad and Sports Social (see Figure 11).
■ The opportunity within Competitive Warriors, the most frequent, most engaged and most serious of the six segments above, was 24% greater than the next closest segment.[11] In fact those Competitive Warriors we did already have, had a frequency of 7.5 vs 3.67 for adults who were not Competitive Warriors. We also found that we had only 29% of them: there were still just under a million Competitive Warriors for us to convert to Lucozade Sport.[12]

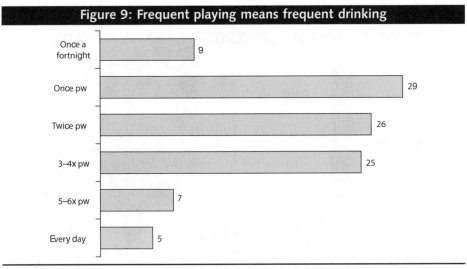

Figure 9: Frequent playing means frequent drinking

Source: Engage Research

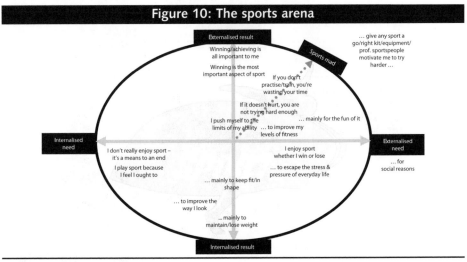

Figure 10: The sports arena

Source: Engage Research

What we also quantified was the long-tail effect within Competitive Warriors' sports participation: 76% of them regularly took part in either football or running.[13] This gave us a focal point for the majority of our efforts. Beyond this there was a wide distribution of sports participation,[14] that highlighted additional opportunities to maximise the business potential (see Figure 12).

We had found a smaller group of people[15] with greater potential business benefit. Next we needed to understand how to open up the opportunity.

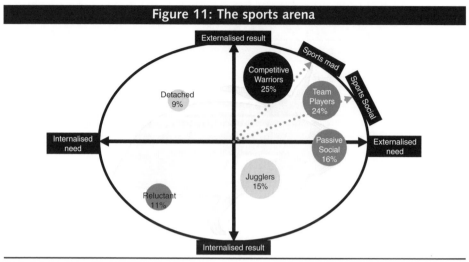

Figure 11: The sports arena

Source: Engage Research

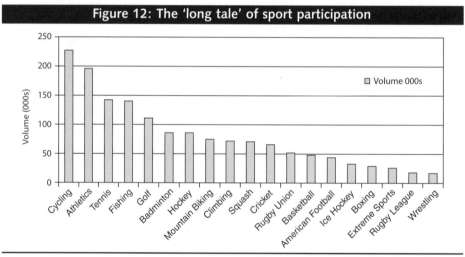

Figure 12: The 'long tale' of sport participation

Source: TGI

The insight: less magic wand, more essential sporting kit

We talked to Competitive Warriors at both a qualitative and quantitative level[16] to understand two key areas: their relationship with sport;[17] and their relationship with Lucozade Sport.[18]

The overall sporting context of a Competitive Warrior

The life of a Competitive Warrior is one of passion and commitment – a constant cycle of training and improvement to reach the intended goals. They love watching, reading, gaining new knowledge about sport and improving their performance.[19] As one Competitive Warrior put it:

> *I put a lot of effort into my sport because if you don't practise you're wasting your time. I'm always last off the pitch! If I under-perform this time I'll try harder next time. I always say that if it doesn't hurt, you are not trying hard enough.*

Source: Engage Research U&A

Time and again what we heard was that preparation and personal effort were key to achieving personal sporting goals at every serious level:

> *There is no recovery; everything I do is preparation.*

Competitive Warrior and team captain in qual group

> *We didn't win the World Cup by a mile, we won it by an inch, we won it in the 20th minute of extra time and we did it by preparing properly.*

Sir Clive Woodward, Rugby World Cup-winning coach

We saw an unwavering point of view emerge that you get out what you put in, and that this was a personal achievement gained through personal investment in time, in preparation and in passion.

The Competitive Warrior's relationship with Lucozade Sport

What we discovered was threefold:

1. We had no perceived role in preparation: we were seen as slaking thirst during sports participation.
2. Lucozade Sport was perceived as too sugary or no better than water, creating a barrier of credibility.
3. The claim we had spent years hammering into the national psyche (33% longer) lacked believability: there was too much of the magic wand about it.

We needed a strategy that tapped into the passion involved in preparation (Before), which challenged head-on the perception of Lucozade Sport being no better than water. We needed to achieve this with a scientific and statistical conversation about how your body reacts to pressure situations (Fuel) and we needed to stop claiming to be a magic wand and recognise the tiny margin (Edge) that separates glory/achievement from disappointment.

The communications strategy – Before, Fuel, Edge

We translated the insights above into three pillars of activity and a set of simple communications behaviours across all disciplines.[20]

- **Before: getting involved with the fabric of preparation so that the product would be consumed before sport.** Rewarding Competitive Warriors by creating bespoke content and advertising that made us true training and preparation partners.
- **Fuel: giving the product functionality and scientific credentials to raise credibility.** Placing Lucozade Sport at the heart of credible and compelling sports science.

■ **Edge: reducing our claim and aligning our channels to the small but meaningful margins in sport.** Ensuring Lucozade Sport was present at the events that mattered to Competitive Warriors, whether participating or spectating on the edge of their seats.

This was the blueprint for whether we should be conducting activity or not; whether we were going to overcome the issues we had. Where this really came to life was in the multi-faceted execution.

The channels: a little more conversation a little less shouting

We focused channel investment into creating pointy, targeted partnerships and experiences. What follows is granular detail as to what we have done, why, whom we managed to reach in doing this and what the effect has been.[21] These activities are arranged under each of the three pillars of Before, Fuel and Edge because that is how they were developed. They cover a wide range of executions and specialisms because we needed to get involved rather than comment from the sidelines but, as the soft and hard measures show, this was the right thing to do.

Before: getting involved with the fabric of preparation

Three key pieces of activity integrated Lucozade Sport into the fabric and rituals of preparation.

1. A partnership with *Runner's World*

Serious runners use *Runner's World* as both a friend and a coach. We invested in specialist press titles for pure display in 2004 and witnessed a strong return from our investment in terms of claimed purchase (see Figure 13).

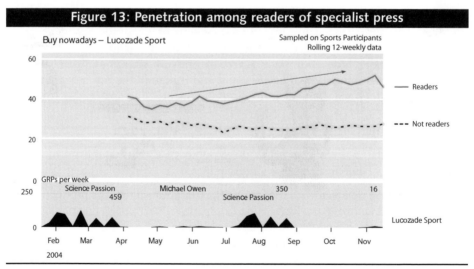

Figure 13: Penetration among readers of specialist press

Source: Millward Brown

To build on this, we developed a four-pillar partnership with *Runner's World*.[22]

- A monthly running calendar. This enabled readers to record training times, gave helpful advice and also detailed running events that Lucozade was attending[23] (see Figure 14).

Figure 14: Monthly running calendar

- A series of training guides focusing on the build-up to specific running events[24] (see Figure 15).
- Monthly readers' running route competition. Competitive Warriors sent us their favourite training routes and each month we showcased the best one (see Figure 16).
- A series of display advertisements showcasing running-specific product (see Figure 17).

2. Football focus on Saturdays
For Competitive Warriors who play football, Saturday is different, Saturday has its own rituals: which sock goes on first, who is driving to the game, who takes the warm-up. The devouring of the sports pages of national press titles is a key part of these preparation rituals.[25] We developed an ongoing presence in national press titles targeted at football coverage[26] (see Figure 18).

Figure 15: Training guides

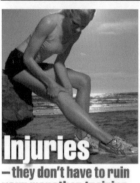

LUCOZADE SPORTS SCIENCE ACADEMY ADVICE

Injuries
– they don't have to ruin your marathon training

Runners expect a few aches and pains, but this invaluable advice from *Runner's World* and Lucozade Sport will keep you on track

LUCOZADE SPORT SCIENCE ACADEMY ADVICE

NICK MORGAN, SPORT SCIENTIST

Boosting performance

Exploding the myths about caffeine's use in running

Figure 16: Running route competition

reader's run route

Well done to Peter Hewitt for winning August's Reader's Run Route of the Month with Lucozade Sport. As well as having his route published in the magazine and online at www.runnersworld.co.uk, Peter will receive a fantastic Lucozade Sport Runners' Training Pack

Gunpowder Park: Enfield, North London - six miles

Win fame and fuel!

Runner's World Tip: For many runners, the secret to successful hydration for a 10K run will depend on starting the race properly hydrated. Drink 200–500ml of a scientifically-formulated sports drink shortly before you exercise. For example, Lucozade Sport's Hydro Active hypotonic drink contains essential electrolytes, vitamins and calcium to help replace the salts and fluid you lose during exercise.

Figure 17: Running product ad

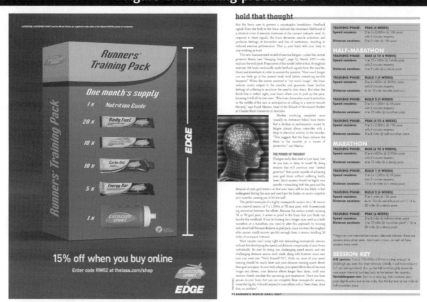

Figure 18: Ads in national football press

3. A Marathon content partnership with *Talksport*

Talksport is the bastion of sports obsessives: when they are not playing, they like to discuss and analyse sport. So what better place to advertise than a sports talk radio programme?[27]

We funded a London Marathon update segment on *Talksport* every Saturday morning. *Talksport* recruited people to train for and run the London Marathon, and every Saturday the *Talksport* presenter would interview one of the training team live on air about the problems they were facing and how they were progressing. The section would then be rounded off with training tips and advice from Jon Brewer, who is Lucozade Sport's training guru. This piece of activity cemented a believable role for Lucozade Sport's in preparation.

This partnership has fuelled believability and challenged listeners' points of view about the brand (see Figure 19).

Figure 19: Impact of *Talksport* activity on Sports Participants

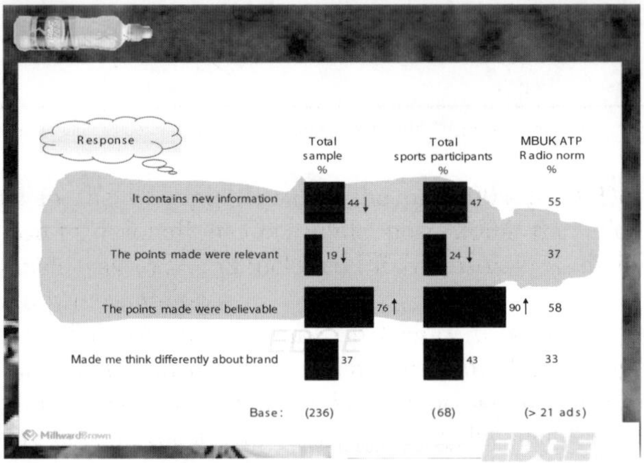

Response	Total sample %	Total sports participants %	MBUK ATP Radio norm %
It contains new information	44 ↓	47	55
The points made were relevant	19 ↓	24 ↓	37
The points made were believable	76 ↑	90 ↑	58
Made me think differently about brand	37	43	33
Base:	(236)	(68)	(> 21 ads)

Source: Millward Brown

Fuel: giving the product functionality and scientific credentials

Three strands of activity challenged the point of view that Lucozade Sport is 'no better than water' or 'just sugar'.

1. Fuelling elite and club sportsmen and women

In 2003, we developed the Lucozade Sports Science Academy (LSSA), predominantly to provide credible science-based research into sports nutrition and performance.[28] We hadn't truly leveraged the LSSA in communications to date, so we developed activity centred on LSSA to drive better understanding of the science behind Lucozade Sport. Therefore we:

- created partnerships with national governing bodies (NGBs) (see Figure 20)[29]
- provided product, education and R&D services to international teams and elite athletes
- offered discounts for members (see Figure 21)

Figure 20: Reciprocal links between Lucozade Sport and NGB websites

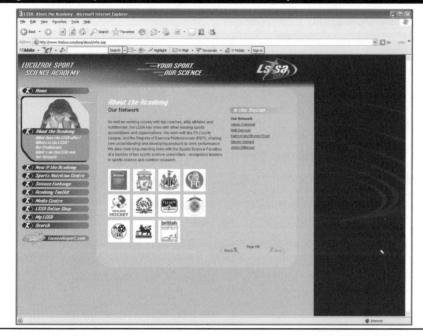

Figure 21: NGB members gaining discount on product through partnership

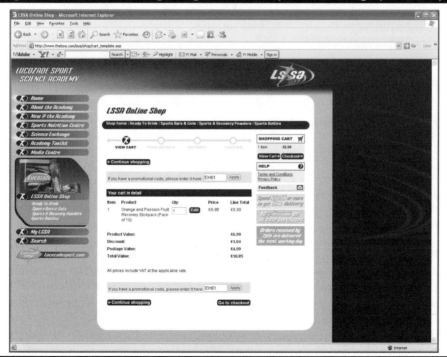

Figure 22: England Hockey electronic newsletter and Nutritional Support

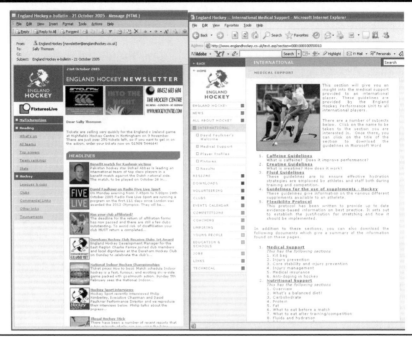

- gained direct access to NGB members via club posters, electronic membership newsletters and positive PR in core specialist publications (see Figure 22)
- backed this up with display activity in bibles of those sports with which we had created partnerships.[30]

The nature of this approach also drove perceived endorsement from the heads of the NGBs of these sports:

> *The ... partnership we have entered into with Lucozade Sport is an extremely positive step for the sport and will be of huge benefit to all our members. Having access to reliable and effective sports nutrition products will help alleviate any possible contamination concerns that our members may previously have had.*

> Philip Kimberley, Executive Chairman, England Hockey

By 2006, we had created collaborations with 12 key NGBs, covering a membership base of 2,036,250 Sports Participants. This was a significant step away from being seen as 'no better than water' or 'just sugar'.

2. Getting to where fuel was needed – product placement in live football

Some 73% of Competitive Warriors claim to admire top sportsmen and women, and 72% of Competitive Warriors who play football also watch it on TV.[31] We identified an opportunity to push our credibility by getting our product in the hands of sporting icons as they appeared in TV sports coverage.

We focused our attention on the most visible and widely supported clubs and players in the sporting media (see Figure 23).

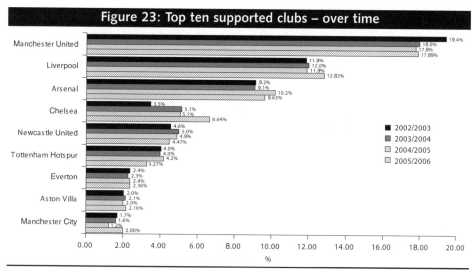

Figure 23: Top ten supported clubs – over time

Source: TNS

We developed deeper, more engaged relationships with Chelsea, Liverpool, Manchester United and Arsenal, and key players from each of these clubs created an immediate step-change in the visibility of our brand in the hand (see Figure 24).

Figure 24: Key players seen with brand in hand

During the 2005/6 season the total number of viewers exposed to Lucozade Sport products through this route was 1,040,520,000. By 2007 our tracking score for 'Trusted by Elite Athletes' was massively different for those who watch Premiership Football vs those who do not (see Figure 25).

Figure 25: Clear effect on credibility and consideration driven by brand in hand

	Total 2007	Watch Premiership football	Don't watch Premiership football
Play football		67	14
Aware of sponsorship		26	8
Heard of		92	84
Ever tried		66	43
Buy now		37	17
Buy most		5	2
Top 2 box consideration		46	26
Trusted by elite athletes		72	17
Ideal preparation for sport		72	64
Base:		(1115)	(1414)

Source: Millward Brown

3. We created a sports science and statistics-based partnership with *The Times*
This strand was designed to position Lucozade Sport clearly at the heart of under-standing the nature of sports performance, pushing our credibility but also driving increased engagement with Competitive Warriors. Tapping in to the Saturday-morning preparation pitstop and the rise of football stats,[32] we partnered with Daniel Finkelstein to sponsor 'The Fink Tank'.

This relationship embedded Lucozade Sport within the arena of science and statistics about sport, an area of obsession for our Competitive Warriors. The Fink Tank produced weekly predicted results for Premiership football matches, based upon previous statistics. Every week readers were engaged and incentivised to try to beat 'The Fink Tank Predictor' (see Figure 26).[33]

Edge: The small but meaningful margins in sport
We have executed three strands of Edge activity:

1. Experiential – when the Edge is moments away
In 2006, we built the Lucozade Sport Performance Zone. Staffed by sports scientists, the rig is designed to engage Competitive Warriors at both an emotional and a rational level, offering an opportunity to explain the benefits of Lucozade Sport, sample our product and, hopefully, the opportunity for our audience to learn something new.

Figure 26: The Fink Tank

Fink Tank research is fuelled by Lucozade Sport

In 2006, we took this to 19 different major running events including the Great North Run, the Great South Run, the London and Edinburgh Marathons as well as 36 Football Powerleague centres. In 2007, we broadened the running element to 26 different events, adding sites including the Bath Half Marathon, the Great Wales Run and the Great Yorkshire Run, and continued our relationship with the Powerleague centres. In 2007, our sports scientists engaged just over 200,000 Competitive Warriors[34] (see Figure 27).

This strand of activity has created a longer dialogue with Competitive Warriors than other channels could achieve (7 minutes vs 30 seconds for the average TV ad), and increased claimed usage by 27%.[35]

Figure 27: Lucozade Sport Performance Zone –
rigs visited major running events

2. Sports marketing

We have developed a handful of key relationships in football (Arsenal, Manchester United, Liverpool, Chelsea, the Premier League and the FA); and the same in running (London Marathon and Great North Run).

These relationships are executed and leveraged at many levels. For runners, we provide training and preparation advice and nutritional support; drinks stations on race days. Within football, our relationships with clubs have allowed access to players and medical staff to test both the players and the products, and assess the potential benefits of using certain products. This has been invaluable in helping drive both the LSSA and the overall credibility message: for the 2007 launch of Lucozade Sport Caffeine Boost we were able to claim that it was 'developed alongside Premiership footballers'. The overall models for football, running, hockey and rowing are outlined in Figures 28–31 respectively.

With the smaller-volume sports, we focus on engaging Competitive Warriors on a personal basis, from involvement in research and development via High Performance Panels to simply getting our message into rowing clubs.

The impact of this activity on Fuel, Edge and Consideration has been marked (see Figure 32).

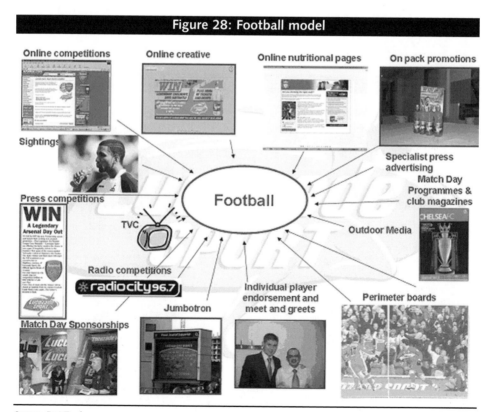

Figure 28: Football model

Source: Fast Track

Figure 29: Running model

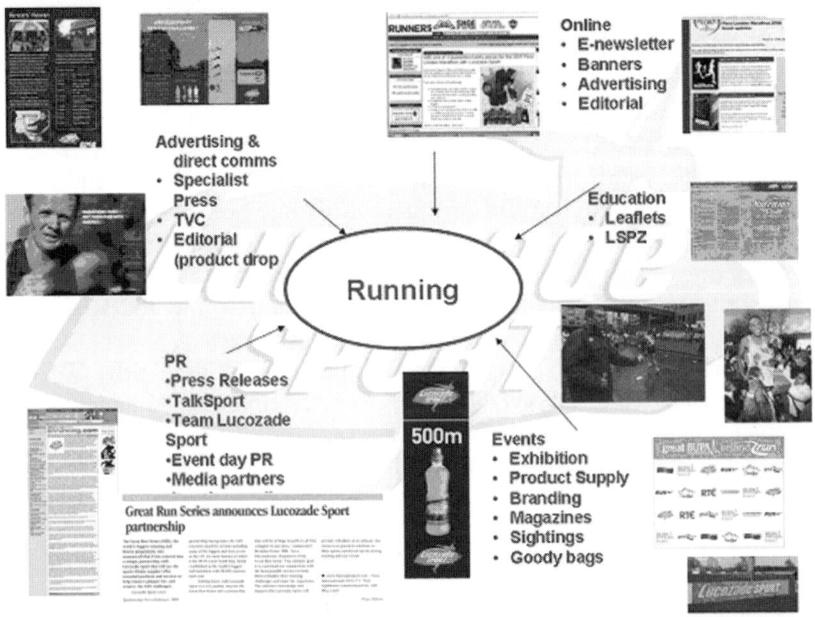

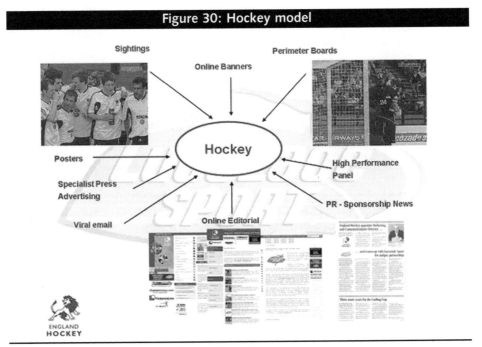

Online
- E-newsletter
- Banners
- Advertising
- Editorial

Advertising &
direct comms
- Specialist Press
- TVC
- Editorial (product drop

Education
- Leaflets
- LSPZ

Running

PR
- Press Releases
- TalkSport
- Team Lucozade Sport
- Event day PR
- Media partners

500m

Events
- Exhibition
- Product Supply
- Branding
- Magazines
- Sightings
- Goody bags

Great Run Series announces Lucozade Sport partnership

Source: Fast Track

Figure 30: Hockey model

Sightings   Perimeter Boards

Online Banners

Hockey

Posters

Specialist Press
Advertising

High Performance
Panel

PR - Sponsorship News

Viral email   Online Editorial

ENGLAND
HOCKEY

Source: Fast Track

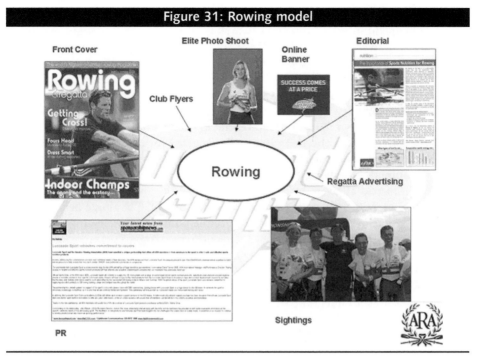

Figure 31: Rowing model

Source: Fast Track

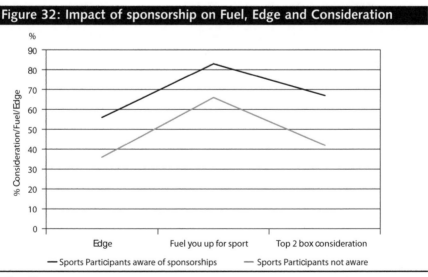

Figure 32: Impact of sponsorship on Fuel, Edge and Consideration

Source: Millward Brown

3. TV – quality not quantity

TV is a key medium for Competitive Warriors to watch, analyse and learn from their heroes. Between 2004 and 2007 we have focused on quality of exposure on TV, not pure quantity of adults. Some 83% of Competitive Warriors who play football specifically choose to watch one of the key football-focused programmes every week; 80% alone watch the Champions League.

In 2005 and 2006 we focused our use of TV into two strands: first, live and competitive sport, moving from broad reach via *Coronation Street* to the Edge via the Champions League, the Boat Race, the Rugby World Cup; second, broader spot selection targeted at delivering purity of an audience who play sport rather than a traditional TV-buying audience of 16–34 adults.[36] Having looked in detail at the econometric analysis of the period 2005–2006 and at delivery of Sports Participants, in 2007 we pulled out of broader use of TV altogether, focusing purely on live and competitive sport, closer to the point of Edge, as this strand had delivered incrementally higher ROI.[37]

The TV messaging evolved in a similar manner, initially focusing on weaving Lucozade Sport into the fabric of athletes' preparation. We reflected the different rituals that Competitive Warriors had told us they performed, and positioned Lucozade Sport as an integral part of that process.

Figure 33: 'Before' TV stills

In 2006 this was followed by a commercial that defined the product as a Fuel. Using brand ambassador Steven Gerrard, we were able to play off the football world's description of Gerrard as the 'midfield engine' for both Liverpool and England and position Lucozade Sport as the fuel that powers him.

Figure 34: 'Fuel' TV stills

Having established our roles in preparation and as more than just water, in 2007 we shifted emphasis to the Edge, to the slender margins that can prove so critical in sport – literally equating the winning margin to a bottle of Lucozade Sport.

Figure 35: 'Edge' TV skills

Summary

This strategy represented a wholesale shift away from punting messages at people to engaging Competitive Warriors in a longer conversation. We have engaged, created content, developed partnerships, used key opinion leaders as communications conduits, developed a thorough and deep experiential strand, pushed sports marketing on and sharpened the blunt tool of TV to a very specific edge. The question is – did it work?

What did we achieve?

During the period 2004–2007 we doubled the size of the brand while investing less in marketing (see Figure 36).

Figure 36: Year-on-year sales and A&P investment growth

%

140

130

120

110

100

90

80

% growth in sales and A&P

2003   2004   2005   2006   2007

— Year-on-year sales growth   — A&P year-on-year as % of sales

Source: GSK

We achieved this by driving penetration where the potential was greatest (see Figure 37).

This was about fuelling credibility and believability as to our role in sport: that we were part of the preparation ritual (Before) (see Figure 38).

And that we were credible and trusted as more than just sugar (Fuel) (see Figure 39).

The net effect of which was more than 50% of our audience believing we gave them an Edge (see Figure 40).

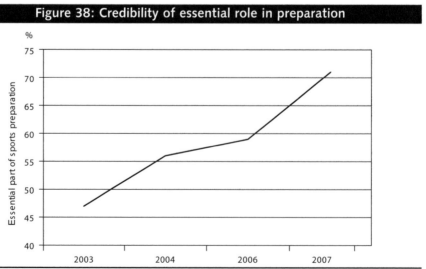

Figure 37: Penetration among Sports participants has grown significantly

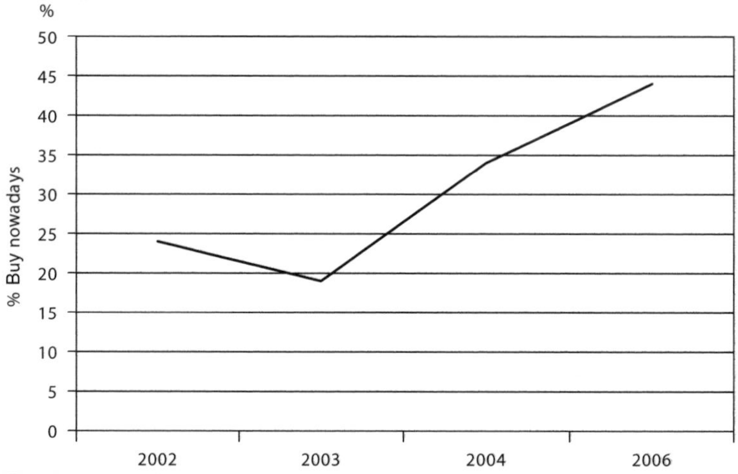

Source: Millward Brown

Figure 38: Credibility of essential role in preparation

Source: Millward Brown

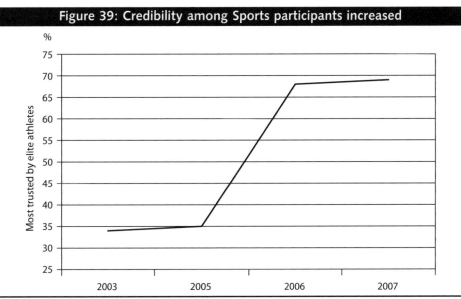

Figure 39: Credibility among Sports participants increased

Source: Millward Brown

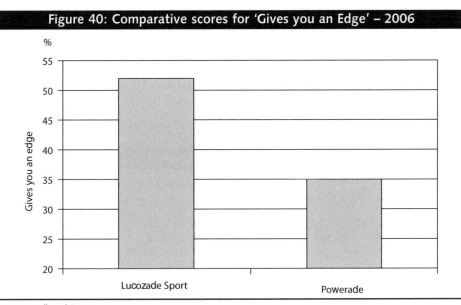

Figure 40: Comparative scores for 'Gives you an Edge' – 2006

Source: Millward Brown

Proving the effectiveness of communications: eliminating other factors

Before we discuss the return generated from our communications, it is worth discussing the other key sales drivers and their contribution, if any, to the growth in Lucozade Sport.

Distribution

From 2004 to 2007 distribution remained fairly constant rather than seeing any significant gains (see Figure 41).

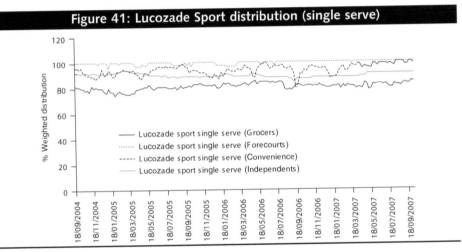

Figure 41: Lucozade Sport distribution (single serve)

Source: ACNielsen

Price and promotions

There was little movement in retail non-promotion price (see Figure 42).

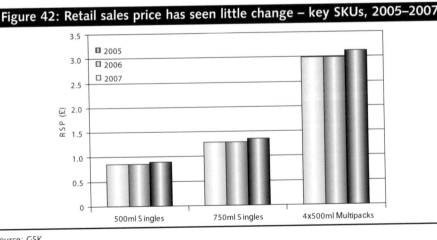

Figure 42: Retail sales price has seen little change – key SKUs, 2005–2007

Source: GSK

There was however a slight decrease in promotional activity in 2007, meaning the percentage of sales sold on promotion decreased slightly. That Lucozade Sport experienced growth despite a fall in the use of promotions was fantastic news (see Figure 43).

Figure 43: Percentage sold on promotion decreased in 2007

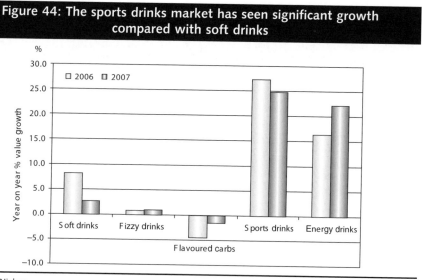

Source: GSK/MediaCom Economiser

The market

While we recognise Lucozade Sport operates within the broad soft drinks market, sports drinks have been significantly outperforming soft drinks for the last few years (see Figure 44).

Figure 44: The sports drinks market has seen significant growth compared with soft drinks

Source: ACNielsen

It is therefore key to look closer to home within the sports drinks market to understand market trends. This market consists of two key brands, of which Lucozade Sport is the dominant player with 77% of the market (2007). Powerade is the closest competitor, with 22% of the market, and the remaining 1% comes from two smaller sports brands.

While Powerade also saw growth over this period, it is important to note that Lucozade Sport is almost 3.5 times larger than Powerade, therefore its 2007 growth in value terms is still twice that of Powerade (see Figures 45 and 46). This growth has been taken into account within our econometric models to ensure communication impacts are not overestimated.

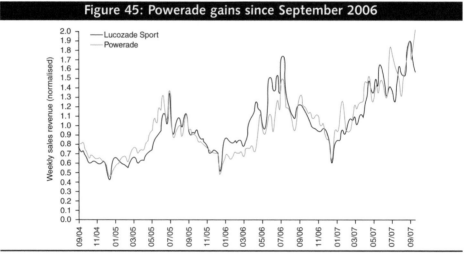

Figure 45: Powerade gains since September 2006

Source: ACNielsen

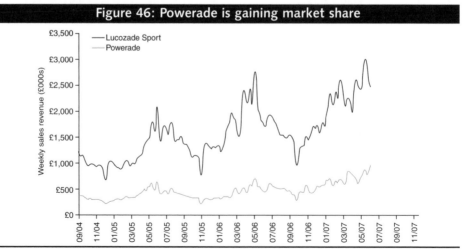

Figure 46: Powerade is gaining market share

Source: ACNielsen

New product development

Lucozade Sport has introduced new flavours to the portfolio.[38] These new flavours have taken the place of previous flavours and not stemmed the growth seen in the core Orange flavour over this period (see Figure 47).

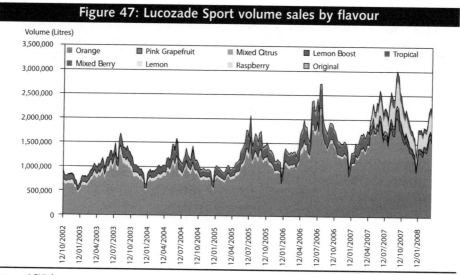

Figure 47: Lucozade Sport volume sales by flavour

Source: ACNielsen

Communications

Econometric models for Lucozade Sport were set up in 2004 specifically to evaluate the effectiveness of the new communications strategy.[39] This ongoing analysis has been crucial in driving accountability, providing the Lucozade Sport team with confidence in the direction of the communication strategy and helping to optimise the channel mix investment for subsequent campaigns without increasing budgets (see Figure 48).

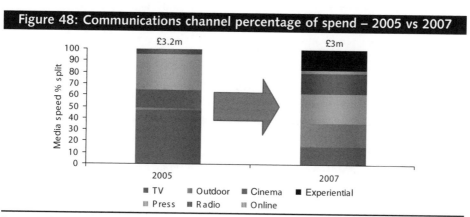

Figure 48: Communications channel percentage of spend – 2005 vs 2007

Source: MediaCom/Nielsen Research Media

We have accounted for key drivers in the market and been able to understand and quantify the effects of all communications. Figure 49 demonstrates the effects of advertising separated from other factors (such as price, distribution, temperature, and so on). Having this understanding helped fine-tune the communications mix over the last three years, delivering increased levels of efficiency.

Figure 49: Contribution to advertising from Lucozade Sport sales (example multiple grocers)

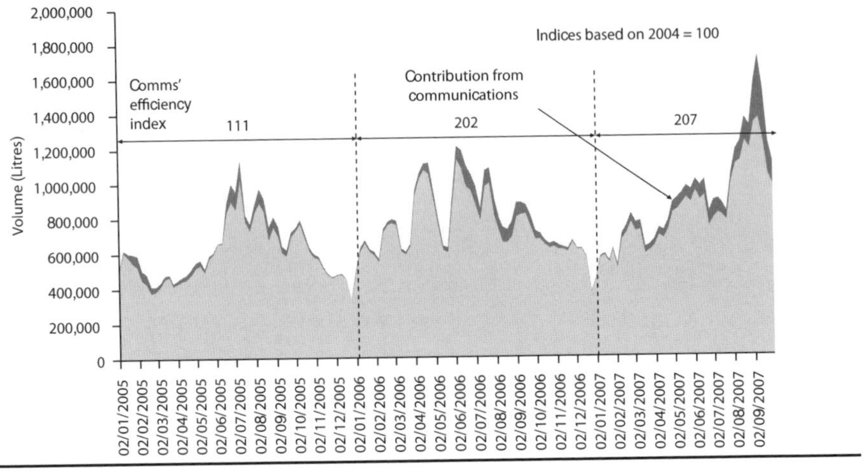

Source: MediaCom Economiser

Payback

It is well known that fmcg brands struggle to make an immediate return on investment. From all our studies we have seen that the average incremental revenue per £1 of communications investment for fmcg brands is 59p.[40] The equivalent figure for Lucozade Sport across the period 2004–2007 was £2.39.

Furthermore, we can see from Figure 50 that our activity managed to grow this rate of return consistently across the period, achieving a revenue return of £3.63 in 2007.

The next stage is to analyse the impact on profit. GSK's profit margins are commercially sensitive. However, we can confirm that our calculations show that the return on marketing investment grew in 2007 to £1.04 per £1 invested.

Having shown that communications provided a healthy return in the short term, we will go on to estimate the value it adds in the long term. This is much harder to quantify, especially as we are talking about future sales, but by applying some simple calculations we are able to estimate what the long-term impact will be.

Lucozade has experienced significant growth in base sales over the period 2004–2007 (see Figure 51).

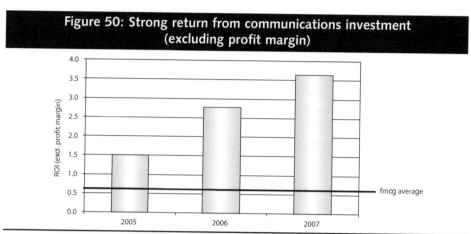

Figure 50: Strong return from communications investment (excluding profit margin)

Source: MediaCom Economiser

Figure 51: Base sales have seen significant growth (example multiple grocers)

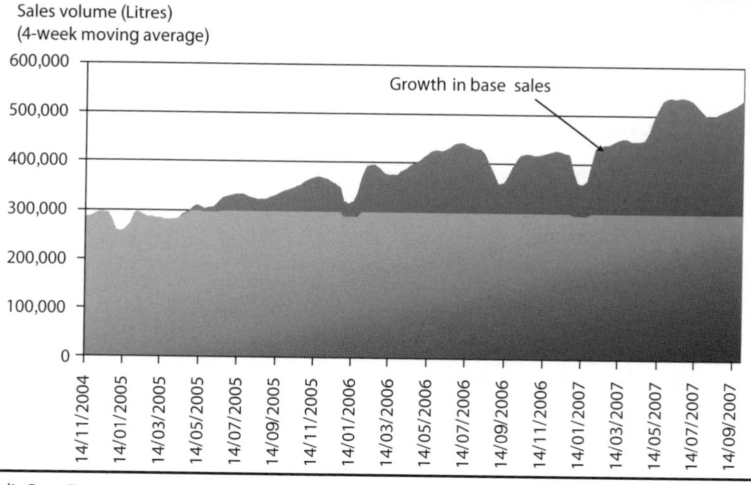

Source: MediaCom Economiser

This growth is represented in our models by a trend variable. All short-term variations of sales have been accounted for through marketing activity and, as there has been little change in these factors year on year, it is reasonable to assume that a considerable proportion of this trend is driven by communications.

We have assumed that communications contributed to base growth in the same proportion that communications contribute to the short/medium-term sales (i.e. 7.6% of sales).[41] This would generate an additional £9m from 2007 communications in the longer term, achieving an extremely healthy ROMI of £1.47. We feel this in itself is a pessimistic view given the longer-term focus of communications.

Summary

We set out to show the benefit of focusing Lucozade Sport's communications. We have shown you a tale for our times: one of engagement, content, experiential; one of integration across a wide base of agencies.

By focusing on a smaller audience and better conversations, concentrating on metrics and insight, we have been able to drive value and decrease proportional A&P over time. We have doubled the size of the brand, increased profits and short-term return from communications investment. We have given Lucozade Sport its Edge: less is more.

Notes

1. Source: 2003 U&A study.
2. MediaCom average fmcg ROI = £0.59. This is pure ROI not ROMI, so excludes cost of goods.
3. See section entitled 'Payback'. ROMI figures include subtractions for COGs and production, ROI figures do not.
4. MediaCom (media), M&C Saatchi (advertising), Fast Track (sports marketing), Extentio (experiential), hereafter referred to as 'we'.
5. GSK analysis on drivers of growth and the impact of distribution on brand.
6. Effectively, makes you go 33% longer.
7. From 7.2% to 6.9%. Source: ACNielsen Data.
8. Powerade's 2003 SOV was 29%; SOM was 19%.
9. During the 1990s and early 2000s.
10. Source: TGI GB Index.
11. Source: Engage research U&A.
12. Source: TGI GB Index GSK recontact.
13. Source: Engage research U&A.
14. Source: TGI GB Index GSK recontact.
15. Competitive Warriors.
16. Source: Qual groups, Engage U&A and the TGI recontact.
17. To explore the context of the role Lucozade Sport could play.
18. Specifically why those who did were buying and why those who didn't weren't buying.
19. They index at 1,188 for taking their sport seriously, at 455 for pushing themselves to the best of their abilities and at 736 for winning/achieving as all important: TGI recontact.
20. Advertising, media, sport marketing, experiential, digital, content, PR.
21. Soft measures, e.g. claimed usage, key image statements such as trusted by elite athletes, are dealt with in this section; harder ROI and ROMI measures are dealt with in the section entitled 'Payback'.
22. *Runner's World* delivers 88,567 runners through the magazine and has 97,000 unique users online.
23. Where more advice and samples would be offered.
24. The Flora London Marathon and the Great North Run.
25. Some 63% of Competitive Warriors who play football read a national press title on a Saturday. Source: TGI GB Index GSK recontact.
26. In 2006 this campaign delivered 57% of Competitive Warriors at a frequency of 8.5 OTS; in 2007 we delivered 54% at a slightly higher frequency of 12 OTS.
27. According to Millward Brown tracking, 22% of Sports Participants are regular listeners to *Talksport*. Competitive Warriors who are regular runners index at 285 for having listened to *Talksport* in the last week. Source: TGI GB Index GSK recontact.
28. Also to develop relevant products in response to the needs of elite and serious sports participants.
29. Known as NGBs, these included the Amateur Rowing Association, England Hockey, British Triathlon and the Professional Footballers Association.
30. Titles range from *Runner's World* through *Regatte* to *220 Triathlon*.
31. Source: TGI GB Index GSK recontact.
32. Witness the rise in the prevalence of opta index stats in football coverage, e.g. how far a player has run in Champions League games.
33. In 2007, the partnership delivered 24% of Competitive Warriors at 24.1 OTS. Source: NRS.
34. Extentio estimate.
35. Source: Hall & Partners Experiential Tracking.
36. Achieved using bespoke MediaCom tool Advantedge. As an example, in April 2006, *Bad Lad's Army* delivered 6.4 16–34 adult ratings and *Prison Break* delivered 5.4. However, *Bad Lad's Army* delivered 5.6 ratings against

Sports Participants and *Prison Break* delivered 6.6 ratings, therefore flipping which would be the better programme to be in.

37. ROI from TV in 2006 was £1.60, in 2007 £2.70 – see final section for more detail on how these numbers are worked out. Although we spoke to fewer people (200 ratings in live sport delivers 42% of all people who play sport; 200 ratings in all programming would deliver 58%), because we got them in the right mind-set, the payback was greater.
38. In particular Lemon Boost, Raspberry and Tropical in 2007.
39. Econometric models were created at SKU level for both Multiple Grocer and Impulse sales.
40. MediaCom Business Science Benchmarks.
41. MediaCom Economiser.

Other companies involved in campaign: Sports marketing company: Fast Track; Experimental agency: Extention; Digital agency: Fuse

Chapter 19

Public awareness campaign for helmet wearing

Winning Vietnam's helmet war

 By Alexander Clegg, Ogilvy & Mather Vietnam

Editor's summary

In 2007, 97 per cent of the 21 million Vietnamese motorcycle riders and passengers were not wearing helmets. Asia Injury Prevention Foundation's public awareness campaign aimed to reverse that situation. The creative strategy involved turning the poor excuses people give for not wearing helmets into life threats. Using previously unavailable outdoor advertising on buses alongside TV, print and digital, the campaign raised over US$1m, tripled the number of helmet wearers and influenced the government to advance nationwide helmet wearing legislation by six months. This has saved approximately 38 lives per day and has ensured a 99 per cent compliance rate of the new law.

Context and background

Vietnam has been at peace for well over two decades now and the desire to concentrate on a bright future has replaced the years of agony that defined what was once a deeply divided nation. Over the last 15 years, however, another war has emerged as the country has transformed into one of the world's economic stars. Rapid motorisation unaccompanied by necessary safety legislation led to a situation where 97% of motorcycle riders and passengers were driving without wearing a helmet in early 2007. The streets of Vietnam carry over 21 million motorbikes, making it the most rapidly motorised nation in the world. Even in 1997 the number of casualties increased 300% year on year. More recently, traffic accidents account for, on average, 38 deaths per day, approximately 14,000 deaths per year, and 30,000 cases of severe brain damage and head injury per year. The National Traffic Safety Committee states that approximately 4,200 children were killed in 2007 and 7,000 suffered traumatic head injury. The Viet-Duc Hospital in Hanoi, one of the country's leading traffic injury hospitals, alone treated 1,637 children under the age of 15. That number is equivalent to four children each day. And for those aged between 18 and 45, traffic crashes have become the country's leading killer.

The Asian Development Bank[1] reports that this carnage costs approximately US$900m per year in property damage, administrative costs, lost output, and medical and human costs, equating to 2.7% of Vietnam's GDP.

The World Health Organization[2] estimates that wearing a properly fitting helmet decreases the severity of injury by 72% and decreases the likelihood of death by 39%. In early 2007, only 3% of the population wore a helmet when on a motorbike.

This is a new kind of war, one that the Vietnamese have never had to fight before.

From cyclo to motorbike

In Vietnam the motorbike is a symbol of progress. It has replaced the 'cyclo' as the iconic, ubiquitous mode of transport. Families can ride together. Market traders can transport goods quickly and easily. Streets buzzing with motorised transport show the world how the lives of Vietnamese people are developing. International brands such as Honda, BP, Castrol, Yamaha and Suzuki have become household names. People can travel further, quicker. They can visit relatives in home towns now only two or three hours' drive away. The government no longer restricts movement around the country and the motorbike perfectly symbolises the society's new-found energy, mobility and freedom.

Tourists come to Vietnam and discover a country that is 'like Thailand 20 years ago'. Undiscovered beaches, villages, forests and, most significantly, friendly people. All these are accessed mostly by motorbike. And driving without the constricting influence of a helmet makes the 'experience' all the more 'authentic' and exciting.

Motorbike 'taxi drivers' are everywhere, taking people to work, to lunch, shopping or back home after a night on the town. They have become known as Xe Om, 'drivers you hug', or even Honda Om, 'Honda [drivers] you hug'. How unlike the image of taxi drivers anywhere else in the world!

Men and women flirt and chat with each other as they drive along city streets, or at traffic lights. Couples go 'motoring' on balmy evenings, hugging each other as they pass through their constantly changing cities and towns, looking out for new shops, eateries, sales or other as yet undiscovered 'finds'.

When the Vietnam football team beats Laos, Singapore or even Malaysia in the South East Asian games, supporters immediately jump on their motorbikes and drive through their towns and cities waving flags, hooting horns and cheering to express their joy and pride.

Given the lack of private space in homes, young couples sit and date, or 'make out', on their motorbikes while parked under the shade of trees, on pavements or in deserted alleyways (see Figure 1).

Figure 1: Young couples 'making out'

In a matter of only a few years the Vietnamese have grown to love their motorbikes in the same way that Americans learnt to love their cars in the 1950s. Just like the car, the motorbike has become a powerful symbol of freedom and progress, now available, for the first time ever, to the majority of Vietnamese people.

The idea of wearing a helmet or even that a motorbike itself could be a cause of danger just doesn't fit with the spirit of the times.

The government made an attempt in 2001 to introduce a law for helmet wearing nationwide but the general public simply refused to comply and the necessary resources required for enforcement were not available. According to the Asia Injury Prevention Foundation there was insufficient education, preparation, helmets and enforcement officers to implement such a policy.

In 2004, a law was introduced to enforce helmet wearing only on the most critical highways. Helmet sellers quickly set up stands at the entries and exits to the highways, where drivers and passengers could hire helmets for the journey. While this legislation was largely enforced and did create the habit of wearing a helmet when travelling on certain highways, it also spawned the excuse that wearing a helmet was necessary only on a highway and not a requirement for all other journeys. As a consequence people felt there was little difference between riding a motorbike at 40 or 50 kilometres an hour through busy urban traffic and riding a bicycle at 10 kilometres an hour (any faster is not really an option given the heat and the physical exertion required). If you don't need to wear a helmet when riding a bicycle around town why would you need to wear one when on a motorbike?

In addition to this experience, learnings from neighbouring Thailand, where helmet wearing is a frequently ignored law, also reveal that enforcement alone is not successful in bringing about behaviour change. Only when combined with education can enforcement really deliver against the objectives of changing drivers' and passengers' habits when it comes to wearing a helmet.

Another key factor that needs to be explained in order to set out a clear picture of the context and background to this campaign is the heritage and culture of public service communications that exist in Vietnam. Only a few years ago, involving an independent, non-government organisation in the development of communications designed to educate the general public was unthinkable. In particular, communications that highlight any kind of issue or problem in society would be interpreted as critical of the government itself and would therefore be unacceptable.

This campaign, and its success, is therefore a highly significant indication of the change in political and economic climate in Vietnam. In terms of the tone, the content and the process by which the campaign was developed, all represent firsts in Vietnam. This was the first public service campaign that did not adopt the Sino/Soviet/Vietnamese style of propaganda that traditionally relies heavily on 'painted posters', radio broadcasts and editorial. These reasons, in addition to the quality of the creative work, explain why the campaign received such a great deal of publicity and also won the grand prize at the Golden Bell award show (Vietnam's annual creative award show for advertising) for the best TVC in 2007.

Gathering momentum for the war

The Asia Injury Prevention Foundation first began fighting the war against non-helmet wearing in 1999. Since then this battle has been fought on many fronts, including:

■ government lobbying and collaboration with Vietnam's Ministry of Transport and the National Traffic Safety Committee (NTSC)
■ conferences and workshops including the landmark Global Road Safety Initiative Helmet Conference held in Hanoi in December 2006; the recom-

mendations of this conference formed the foundation of Government Resolution 32/CP, Vietnam's latest, nationwide helmet law

■ a public awareness campaign
■ Protec Helmets – non-profit 'tropical' helmet company, producing high-quality and affordable helmets designed specifically for tropical conditions
■ Helmets For Kids – a helmet donation and road safety programme where corporations and other organisations sponsor free Protec Helmets and traffic safety education for school children.

In 2005, the Asia Injury Prevention Foundation approached Ogilvy & Mather Vietnam to help develop its public awareness campaign. It is the effectiveness of this campaign that is the focus of this paper.

Objectives

Given the very apparent nature of the problem, the objective in one sense was pretty simple, namely to get everyone to wear helmets when they ride or are driven on a motorbike. However, making that a reality was a little more complex.

One of the first challenges was finding funding for the campaign. Although many potential sponsors expressed an interest in supporting a public awareness campaign, few were prepared to give money until they had seen what the campaign might look like and had some sense that it was endorsed by the government. Being involved in a public awareness campaign of this nature without such endorsement was risky.

The first objective therefore was to develop a campaign idea and materials that could be used as fundraising tools, and also serve as a means of securing government endorsement. These funds would be used to pay for the media investment and production costs. In short, the campaign needed to persuade backers and the government in order to run.

The second issue was more specifically focused on the communication itself. What was the best way to get motorbike drivers and passengers to reassess their deeply entrenched habit and buy and wear a helmet whenever they got on a motorbike? In an environment where even the doctors and medical staff in the hospitals treating victims of motorbike accidents didn't wear helmets, initially this felt like an insurmountable challenge.

In addition, other than the casualty information, there were absolutely no data available and no money for research. However, in a sense, none was required as anyone looking out on the streets of any town, city or village anywhere in Vietnam would see that, with the exception of those travelling along the 'critical' highways, nobody wore helmets.

The second objective therefore was to fundamentally challenge current habits and change behaviour among those most open to change.

The third objective of the campaign was harder still. The Asia Injury Prevention Foundation believed that as part of its multi-faceted approach, a powerful public awareness campaign could also possibly impact the government's own legislative process, giving them the confidence that this time around enforcement could work given that the necessary task of education had already been tackled.

The third objective therefore was to generate significant talkability around the issue and thereby influence the legislative process, which would lead to the implementation and enforcement of a comprehensive helmet law.

The solution

Ogilvy & Mather Vietnam focused first on the second objective, namely 'fundamentally challenge current habits among those most open to change'.

Given Vietnam's extraordinarily young demographic – approximately 60% of the population is under 30 – initially a decision was made to focus on young adults who were possibly first-time drivers/owners of a motorbike and theoretically less entrenched in terms of habits.

Research revealed two shocking insights among this target group:

1. Everyone to whom the agency spoke knew someone who had been killed or seriously injured in a motorbike accident. More shocking still was the number of stories the agency heard about 'bread-winners' who were turned into financial and emotional burdens for their families as a result of severe brain damage caused by a motorbike accident. The accident clearly did not just affect the individual concerned but in these instances its tragic impact on a family was almost more dramatic than if a younger member of the family was killed outright. Furthermore, all the respondents in the research had themselves been involved in some minor motorbike accident in the past 18 months to two years.
2. Despite their awareness of the severe consequences of being involved in a motorbike accident and the prevalence of accidents, none of the respondents felt that it was necessary to wear a helmet when driving anywhere other than on the major highways. Moreover, and more interestingly, the same excuses for why it was not necessary emerged again and again:

   - it ruins my hair
   - wearing a helmet is so uncomfortable and hot
   - you look stupid wearing a helmet when no one else is
   - it won't happen to me
   - I drive very slowly in the city so it's not necessary
   - I can't hear when I'm wearing a helmet; it's like wearing a rice-cooker on your head.

The contrast between the awareness of the severity and prevalence of crashes and the superficiality of the excuses people gave was striking to say the least. And it led directly to the core creative thought:

Turn stupid excuses into life threats

With this core thought in mind the agency then developed materials that could be used to deliver against the first objective: develop a campaign idea and materials that could be used as fundraising tools. In addition to a storyboard for television, print, outdoor and digital ideas, postcards were developed, printed and used as tools for presenting the idea to potential backers and the government.

The look and feel of the campaign is unlike any public service announcement that has ever been produced in Vietnam before. Excuses are juxtaposed with black and white images of crash victims. Some of the images appear horizontally to emphasise the contrast between the triteness of the excuse and the severity of the consequence. The image also references the specific nature of the excuse, so for example when the excuse talks about 'it messes up my hair' the image is that of the top of a person's head, which has been shaved and is covered with stitches and scars (see Figure 2).

In the television commercial, emphasis is also placed on the burden that falls on a family when caring for someone who has become physically and mentally disabled as a result of not wearing a helmet in an accident.

There was much discussion about the shocking tone and manner of the creative work. Was it too much in a country that had only recently suffered so much tragedy? Would the public feel that the campaign punched 'below the belt' and therefore inspire them to screen out the message, or would it inspire them and the media to pick up on the issue and think again?

Figure 2: Haircut

"I DON'T LIKE WEARING A **HELMET**
(HUONG LY - NEURO SURGERY PATIENT)
IT RUINS MY HAIR"

EVERY YEAR OVER 12,000 PEOPLE DIE ON OUR ROADS AND 30,000 ARE SERIOUSLY INJURED. THAT MEANS THOUSANDS OF FAMILIES LEFT PICKING UP THE PIECES. FAMILIES TORTURED BY THE LOSS OF A LOVED ONE, CRIPPLED BY REDUCED INCOME OR THE SUDDEN NEED TO CARE FOR A RELATIVE WITH PERMANENT BRAIN DAMAGE. THE SAD TRUTH IS THAT MOST OF THESE CASES COULD HAVE BEEN PREVENTED BY SIMPLY WEARING A HELMET. WHEN YOU THINK ABOUT IT, THERE ARE NO EXCUSES.

SPONSORED BY AIP

WEAR A **HELMET**. THERE ARE NO EXCUSES.

Figure 3: Head

"I NEVER WEAR A **HELMET**,
(NGUYỄN LAN - CRANIAL SURGERY PATIENT)
THEY **DON'T LOOK COOL**"

EVERY YEAR **OVER 12,000 PEOPLE DIE** ON OUR **ROADS** AND **30,000** ARE SERIOUSLY INJURED. THAT MEANS **THOUSANDS OF FAMILIES** LEFT **PICKING UP THE PIECES**. FAMILIES TORTURED BY THE **LOSS OF A LOVED ONE**, CRIPPLED BY **REDUCED INCOME** OR THE SUDDEN NEED TO CARE FOR A RELATIVE WITH **PERMANENT BRAIN DAMAGE**. THE SAD TRUTH IS THAT **MOST** OF THESE CASES COULD HAVE BEEN **PREVENTED** BY SIMPLY WEARING A **HELMET**. WHEN YOU THINK ABOUT IT, THERE ARE **NO EXCUSES**.

SPONSORED BY AIP

WEAR A **HELMET**. THERE ARE NO EXCUSES.

Figure 4: Feeding

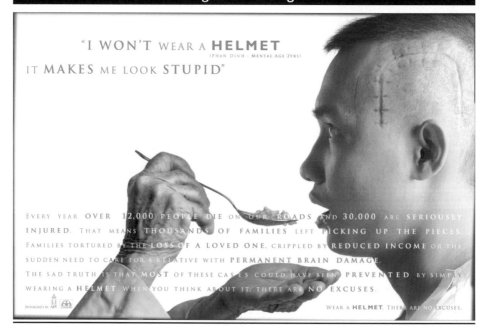

"I WON'T WEAR A **HELMET**
(PHAN ĐINH - MENTAL AGE 2YRS)
IT **MAKES** ME LOOK **STUPID**"

EVERY YEAR **OVER 12,000 PEOPLE DIE** ON OUR **ROADS** AND **30,000** ARE SERIOUSLY INJURED. THAT MEANS **THOUSANDS OF FAMILIES** LEFT **PICKING UP THE PIECES**. FAMILIES TORTURED BY THE **LOSS OF A LOVED ONE**, CRIPPLED BY **REDUCED INCOME** OR THE SUDDEN NEED TO CARE FOR A RELATIVE WITH **PERMANENT BRAIN DAMAGE**. THE SAD TRUTH IS THAT **MOST** OF THESE CASES COULD HAVE BEEN **PREVENTED** BY SIMPLY WEARING A **HELMET**. WHEN YOU THINK ABOUT IT, THERE ARE **NO EXCUSES**.

SPONSORED BY AIP

WEAR A **HELMET**. THERE ARE NO EXCUSES.

The activity

When sufficient funds were raised and the necessary backing of the National Traffic Safety Committee secured, the campaign broke across a range of touchpoints in June 2007. Obviously getting the message onto the streets was a key priority; however, the outdoor environment is extremely heavily regulated in Vietnam. The support of the government through the NTSC enabled previously unavailable outdoor, eye-level sites to be created.

Advertising on buses – not usually allowed in many Vietnamese cities – was also used for the first time as part of the campaign.

The TVC aired on national television stations HTV and VTV. Print ads appeared in Vietnamese and English press, and the TVC itself was one of the first Vietnamese ads to be posted on YouTube.

Postcards were distributed in coffee shops and bars. A website, www.wear-a-helmet.com, was also developed.

To launch the campaign, a news conference was held and was attended by both international and local journalists.

The results

Ogilvy & Mather conducted street-level, vox pop research when the campaign broke, which yielded interesting findings in terms of how the creative was working. The outdoor images in particular seemed to convey a very direct, persuasive message:

If I don't wear a helmet, that's what is going to happen to me.

That's the same reason I give for not wearing a helmet ... and clearly it's not a very good reason!

These verbatims typified the response. The campaign seemed to be working as designed. The shocking images caught the attention, and the familiar nature of the excuse built relevance and also drove persuasion.

We now look in turn at how each of the three objectives was achieved.

First objective

The first objective was to develop a campaign idea and materials that could be used as fund-raising tools and as a means of securing government endorsement.

In six months the campaign was able to secure US$500,000 from the following donors: VTV, HTV, the Asian Development Bank, the National Traffic Safety Commission, the Australian Embassy (AusAid), the Royal Danish Embassy, the US Embassy, the World Bank, the World Health Organization, Intel Vietnam and Michelin South East Asia.

Subsequently, since the launch of the campaign and its proven success, funding has increased to US$1,073,000.

The initial creative work also obtained the backing of the government through the NTSC, which was instrumental in securing new outdoor sites that served as a key touchpoint in the campaign.

Nguyen Vu Khue, a permanent member of Ho Chi Minh City's traffic safety committee, said when interviewed by Ogilvy & Mather Vietnam:

I really appreciate the communications [campaign] and I do think it really works. It's a breakthrough in propaganda.

Second objective

The second objective was to fundamentally challenge current habits and change behaviour among those most open to change.

In order to assess the results of the campaign the Asia Injury Prevention Foundation commissioned associate professor Dr Nguyen Thi Thieng and associate staff from the Institute of Population and Social Affairs in Hanoi to conduct a survey assessing the effectiveness of the initial phase of the public awareness campaign. This survey produced the following results.

- Within four months of the launch of the campaign, and prior to any change in legislation, the percentage of helmet wearers increased from 3% to over 10% – more than triple. In Hanoi and Ho Chi Minh City the percentage almost doubled, from 10.8% to 19.1%. The percentage of motorcyclists wearing helmets when driving out of the cities increased by 15.7%, from 61.3% to 77%.
- The effect was particularly pronounced among 18–24 year olds. Prior to the campaign, only 5.3% claimed they always wore a helmet when riding a motorbike; four months later that figure had more than doubled, to 11.3%.
- Quite unexpectedly the campaign had an equally pronounced effect among 45+ riders. Prior to the campaign 14.2% claimed to wear a helmet every time they got on a bike; four months later that number had risen to 28.8%.
- For those driving out of the cities the effect was again very noticeable. Among 18–24 year olds the percentage of those always wearing a helmet shifted from 52.4% to 69.2%, among 25–44 year olds from 56.7% to 77.2%, and among those 45+ from 55.1% to 84.3%.
- Despite the shocking nature of what was in essence a public service campaign – hitherto unthinkable – the survey revealed that the overwhelming majority felt that the images and messages conveyed were appropriate. For the three key images used in print, outdoor and online, close to 70% of the respondents felt they were 'appropriate'.

Third objective

The third objective was to generate significant talkability around the issue and thereby influence the legislative process, which would lead to the implementation and enforcement of a comprehensive helmet law.

In June and July 2007, the campaign itself was heavily reported in Vietnam's top online and offline media. These included articles in:

Tin Chieu (Evening News)
Tien Phong (Pioneer)

Tin Tuc (News)
Saigon Times
Vietnam News
Sinh Vien (Student)
Vietnam Economic Times
Nguoi Lao Dong Online (People's Labour)
Vietnam Net Online
Vietnam News Agency (online)
Vietnam Express (online)
Thanh Nien Online (youth)
Vietnam News Online
24h.com.vn

On 15 September 2007 it became mandatory on all national highways – not just the critical ones – to wear a helmet.

Most significant of all, however, is that the impact the campaign had is credited with influencing the government's decision to bring forward the new nationwide helmet legislation (Resolution 32), originally planned for summer 2008, to 15 December 2007. This was the legislation that the Asia Injury Prevention Foundation had been lobbying so hard for for nine years. From now on, no matter where, no matter who, all drivers and passengers on motorbikes must wear a helmet.

According to Tran Quang Phuong from the NTSC:

Asia Injury Prevention Foundation's recent campaign on helmet wearing has influenced the government to bring forward the law requiring all motorbike riders to wear helmets on all roads to December 15th 2007 instead of next year.

In terms of the months that legislation was brought forward, every day has saved approximately 38 lives and countless injured.

The most significant result of all, however, is that on 15 December 2007, in contrast to the earlier attempt to introduce nationwide legislation in 2001, up to 99% of Vietnamese bike riders and passengers wore helmets. It is an astonishing compliance rate, bearing in mind that it not only requires a change in habit but also an investment of approximately US$5 per person to buy a helmet. That's US$20 for an average family with two children in a country where the average monthly per capita income is under US$70.

Or compare this to seatbelt wearing compliance rates, for example. In 1999 a report was published by the Scottish Government. It showed that even though seatbelt wearing was made law in Great Britain in 1983, in 1999, 16 years later, compliance was still only at 86%.

Accident victim statistics covering the time period after the enactment of Resolution 32 are now becoming available. The Asia Injury Prevention Foundation has been communicating with various hospitals, the Ministry of Health and the NTSC to gauge the differences in pre- and post-helmet law casualties. A summary of these statistics is as follows:

- Adult head trauma and fatalities from motorbike crashes have declined significantly. Most hospitals report substantial drops in casualties, by as much as 25–50%.
- Cho-Ray Hospital reported a 20% decrease in head injuries and a 9% decrease in fatalities from road accidents for December 2007 vs December 2006.
- Thu Duc Hospital reported a 50% decrease in brain trauma cases compared to the pre-helmet period.
- HCMC Police reported traffic accident fatalities had decreased by 26.7% and injuries had decreased by 39.5% for December to January year on year.

Payback

It is too early for any financial figures to emerge. However, given the almost universal compliance rate, of the US$900 million per year cost, one can make a conservative estimate of 25% savings (the bottom end of the scale regarding drop in casualties that most hospitals report), which equates to US$225 million per year.

Summary

Ogilvy & Mather Vietnam together with the Asia Injury Prevention Foundation developed Vietnam's first ever independent public awareness campaign that was not only instrumental in raising funds for the campaign but also more than tripled the number of motorbike riders and passengers wearing a helmet. In addition, it generated such significant levels of awareness that it influenced the government to bring forward legislation by approximately six months, and played a role in ensuring an astonishing 99% compliance rate when the law was introduced.

Legislation had been introduced a few years earlier but compliance did not follow. A key difference was the preparation and education delivered in large part by this public awareness campaign.

Notes

1. ADB Regional Road Safety Program Accident Costing Report Vietnam, 2003.
2. WHO: *Road Safety Manual for Decision Makers and Practitioners*, Geneva, 2006.

Other companies involved in campaign: PR company: Ocean Communications; Sponsors: WHO, The World Bank, ADB, US Embassy, Australian Embassy, Danish Embassy, Intel, Michelin and FIA Foundation.

Chapter 20

Radley

From bags to riches

By Julian Calderara, DDB London, Les Binet, DDB Matrix and Sarah Carter, DDB London
Contributing author: Monika Jakubczak, DDB London

Editor's summary

This is a case about an unlikely partnership – a fashion designer and the private equity community. This is also a case that illustrates the potential of a small marketing budget to make a big difference.

At the end of 2007, Radley + Co, makers of distinctive handbags branded with a small Scottie dog, exchanged hands for £130m, only two years after it had been valued at £42m in its first private equity deal. This phenomenal increase was in no small part down to the 'Truly, Radley, Deeply' communications campaign.

The campaign was tasked with several simple objectives – increase awareness of Radley bags and get them talked about; improve their image and desirability; underpin more expensive bags; strengthen penetration in London/SE. But all this had to be achieved while staying true to the brand's quirky identity.

The stand out and integrated campaign succeeded in meeting all these challenges, driving up the brand's image and desirability across the UK including London/SE. Sales volume increased correspondingly, but value sales rose even more markedly as the brand traded buyers up its range.

Within a year of the advertising Radley became the nation's favourite handbag designer, making the brand a very attractive proposition for further private equity involvement to help take Radley to the next level.

Introduction

This is a story about Scottie dogs, dogged ambition and phenomenal commercial success.

It is a story of unlikely bedfellows: an intellectual architect and the ephemeral world of fashion; handbags and the private equity community; and a tiny media budget set against the big-bucks glossy spend of international fashion houses.

At the end of 2007, Radley + Co – makers of distinctive handbags branded with a small Scottie dog – exchanged hands for £130m – only two years after it had been valued at £42m in its first private equity deal.

Truly bags to riches ...

The advertising campaign was cited as a key contributor to this success.

the profile of the Radley brand has been raised considerably through a
highly acclaimed national advertising campaign.

Exponent website, 20 December 2007

Fashion brands have, until now, been conspicuous by their absence from the IPA Effectiveness Awards.

Fragmented markets, small media budgets and limited industry research data have tended to result in advertising being an 'act of faith' rather than rigorously evaluated. However, when private equity is invested in a brand to the tune of £42m, an act of faith is not good enough.

This case shows that fashion advertising can have a huge financial payback, and that it *can* be measured rigorously. Along the way, we will discover a new kind of advertising effect, and a new method of evaluation.

How it all began

In 1984, Lowell Harder, an Australian-born architect (see Figure 1), opened a stall at Camden Market selling men's work-bags under the name Hidesign.

Figure 1: Lowell Harder with one of her later women's designs

Whether it was her architectural training, or something deeper in her nature, the bags were unusual – eccentric even.

Her business grew, and by 1991 merged with Tula Group (an established high-street handbag company), giving Lowell two brands to play with – Hidesign and Tula.

But, ever restless, Lowell felt that there was room for something new, colourful and surprising for women. In 1998 she launched a third brand, called Radley, and added a brightly coloured Scottie dog. The result was an immediate hit. Soon there were Scotties on every Radley bag (see Figure 2).

Figure 2: The Radley Scottie dog

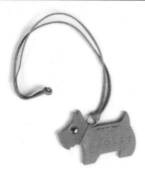

A new owner for Radley

In February 2006, Tula Group was acquired by Phoenix Equity Partners for £42m. Phoenix considered the potential of its three handbag brands – Hidesign, Tula and Radley (see Figure 3).

Figure 3: UK handbag market

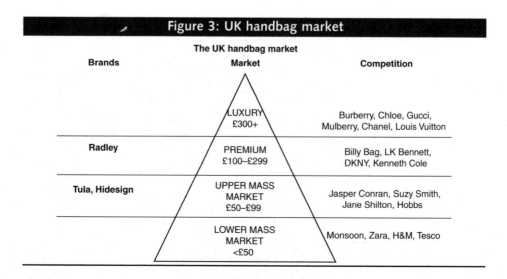

The UK handbag market

Brands	Market	Competition
	LUXURY £300+	Burberry, Chloe, Gucci, Mulberry, Chanel, Louis Vuitton
Radley	PREMIUM £100–£299	Billy Bag, LK Bennett, DKNY, Kenneth Cole
Tula, Hidesign	UPPER MASS MARKET £50–£99	Jasper Conran, Suzy Smith, Jane Shilton, Hobbs
	LOWER MASS MARKET <£50	Monsoon, Zara, H&M, Tesco

It was clear the Radley brand had the greatest potential. It was:

- the biggest, with sales of £23m
- the most profitable, competing in the more expensive premium segment
- by far the most distinctive in design terms
- already gaining a small, almost cultish, following.

The new company was renamed Radley + Co, and a bold business plan was agreed.

Business objectives for Radley bags

The new private equity ownership was looking for rapid and significant growth over the next three years:

- £57m of sales – up from £35m
- £11m profit – up from £6m.

And, with this, development:

- into retail by opening Radley shops across the UK
- into profitable markets such as sunglasses and footwear
- overseas.

Marketing objectives for Radley bags

The marketing plan was as follows:

- encourage *more women* to buy Radley bags
- build Radley's *premium values*, encouraging women to trade up to more expensive bags and increasing average pricing
- establish the brand's *credentials* in the industry, supporting extension into new merchandise areas *and* internationally.

Phoenix agreed an annual budget of £800k for its first Radley advertising campaign and the management appointed Burkitt DDB[1] to the task.

A full brand communications launch was needed for 1 March 2007. The agency was short of time ...

Developing the role for communications

Lowell Harder's unique philosophy

Lowell is a maverick in the fashion industry.

While she's *in* the industry, she doesn't necessarily *like* it.

- she believes in functionality, good design, quality and value
- she dislikes selling to women by exploiting their *insecurity*. Why, she argues, can't a fashion company be *on the side of* women?
- she likes colour and whimsy – not serious, monochrome 'fashion'.

Figure 4: Radley product characteristics

Multicoloured leather charm

Woven leather strap

Intricate embroidered design

Stitching detail in contrasting colour

Option of long or short shoulder strap

Practical across-chest shoulder strap

Comfortable leather shoulder strap

Walkies range with flying Scottie dog pattern

The bags themselves

Her bags were truly unusual – from materials, to stitching, construction, colour and texture. The designs might seem classic – but open them up and the pink, polka dot lining would say 'this is no ordinary bag'.

Radley fanatics

Radley had built a loyal fan base of handbag devotees. Typically they were middle-aged, upmarket and from the north. They liked the quirky, colourful designs and sense of fun. For some, interest bordered on the obsessive.

I have been collecting Radley bags for five years. There's nothing else like them. They're beautifully made and always different. I am an addict.

Radley fan, 2005

But other women didn't 'get' Radley

It was also clear that this distinctiveness was both an opportunity and a problem. Radley was an unusually polarising brand. While owners adored their bags, non-owners often didn't 'get it'.

The non-Radley buyer is a different species, a different stylist, a different 'brand hunter'.

Source: The Difference Engine, 2005

Qualitative and quantitative research at this time confirmed that encouraging more women to buy our bags was not going to be easy. Non-Radley buyers saw the brand as functional, good quality but sadly lacking in excitement and style appeal.

It makes me think of a woman at work – she's the kind that has soft toys on her car parcel shelf.

The designs are cutesie and childish – a bit whacky for me.

I've seen them in John Lewis but they look a bit childish to me ... not something I'd want to be seen with.

Source: Qualitative research, December 2005

And they thought that women who bought Radley were in turn lacking in fashion savvy.

This polarisation – between lovers and non-lovers – can be seen from Figure 5, taken from a qualitative debrief in 2005.

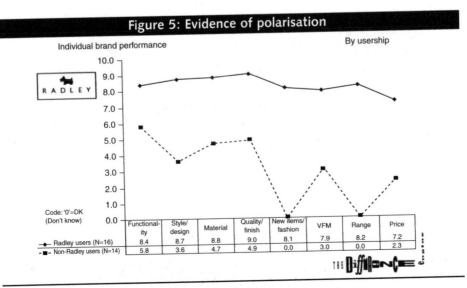

Figure 5: Evidence of polarisation

Individual brand performance — By usership

Code: '0'=DK (Don't know)

	Functional-ity	Style/design	Material	Quality/finish	New items/fashion	VFM	Range	Price
Radley users (N=16)	8.4	8.7	8.8	9.0	8.1	7.9	8.2	7.2
Non-Radley users (N=14)	5.8	3.6	4.7	4.9	0.0	3.0	0.0	2.3

So not only did awareness of Radley bags need to be increased but there were issues of desirability. It was functional, but not fashionable.

And quantitative research confirmed this: Radley achieved a low score of 6% 'for people like me' among women (see Figure 6). Not something we could ignore.

Weaknesses in London and the south-east

As Figure 6 shows, Radley had a particular weakness in the south-east – probably because the brand here was more swamped by international and luxury competition. So, impressing fashion industry opinion formers – who were also in London and vital for the development of the brand – was a particular challenge.

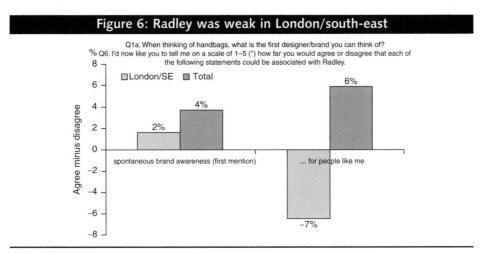

Figure 6: Radley was weak in London/south-east

Q1a. When thinking of handbags, what is the first designer/brand you can think of?
% Q6. I'd now like you to tell me on a scale of 1–5 (*) how far you would agree or disagree that each of the following statements could be associated with Radley.

Source: Dipsticks
Base: Women, magazine readers, London/SE: pre (62); rest of UK: pre (73).
Date: Pre (20/03/07–02/04/07).
* Where 1 means strongly disagree and 5 strongly agree. In our calculations we subtracted % responding 1 and 2 from % responding 4 and 5.

Communication objectives, December 2005

Nick Vance, Radley's new marketing director,[2] summed up the need as follows:

- increase awareness of Radley bags and get them talked about
- improve their image and desirability
- improve the value proposition to underpin more expensive bags
- do this with particular emphasis on London and the south-east
- but stay true to the brand's identity, keeping Radley fanatics on side.

We agreed a creative brief, as shown in Figure 7.

Figure 7: The agency's creative brief

Creative brief

Target audience

    –   Women who may have heard of Radley but don't see it as a brand for them. Broad age range from 25+ But also make loyal Radley lovers feel good about their brand.

Proposition

    –   Fall in love with Radley's bags

Reason why

    –   Beautifully made bags from a company with a different attitude.

Values
    –   Creative, colourful, surprising and real.

A challenging task

It was clear to us that the scale of the task was significant.

> *It doesn't appear that the non-Radley buyer is 'convertible'.*
>
> Source: The Difference Engine, 2005

We would be moving into the cut-throat and glossy world of high fashion; the world of 'it bags'; celeb magazines chronicling Posh's latest Hermès; and daunting ad budgets.

To put this into perspective:

- Radley's total annual media budget of £800k was dwarfed by fashion market spend, which can top £8m in one month
- in any given month of Radley spend, we could expect a share of voice of no more than 3%.

How was the Scottie dog going to be able to make any impression in this tough new world?

The creative idea

At the end of November 2006 DDB presented the idea. It was:

'Truly Radley Deeply'.

We started with a manifesto. Lowell loved it and it has remained a touchstone in Radley ever since. Figure 8 shows how it read, in its original form.

This idea was unanimously endorsed by Radley's management.

It went on to be used for briefing the new city owners, staff, the PR agency, and the design company.

This was the brand's point of view: but what about the ads? With our tiny budget we knew we had to be bold and different.

The cliché of handbag industry ads is moody-looking model + product + big logo (see Figure 9). But we decided to:

- avoid showing people, and focus on the bags
- be colourful, surprising and real vs the serious world of 'heroin chic'.

Figure 8: The Truly Radley Deeply manifesto

RADLEY

Because women love handbags, Radley do everything possible to make their bags as attractive, as desirable as well made, as good value and as unique as possible. Radley love handbags too. But we think of everything we make differently. Rather than think of ours as a fashion company which promotes the 'next must-have item' we see Radley as a creative company where choice and individuality are paramount. So we think of the things we make as an artist thinks of her prints. Short-run artworks, not high-stakes fashion statements. For example while many women own Radley bags, very few own the same bag. And just as the artist strives for originality; for unusual colour or texture or materials, so do we. There's no run of the mill; nothing is standard, except the desire to make something that someone can fall in love with. And all of this is underpinned by the way we work. We work with companies all over the world. But always in a way that puts something back. Be it embroidery clubs in Bangladesh or beachcombers in Malaysia who provide many of the startling details that add colour, texture and fun to our products. This approach is not cheap. But the end result is not extravagant. We offer an honest luxury. Before you can fall in love with an item from Radley we have to fall in love with an idea, enough to want to make it. We love bags. You love bags. It's the depth of that shared feeling that means we can say

TRULY **RADLEY** DEEPLY

Figure 9: Montage of typical competitor fashion advertising

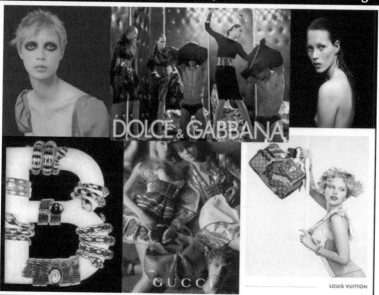

Radley's new advertising campaign: March 2007

The campaign idea unified the *inspiration* for the bag with the *bag itself*. Figure 10 shows the Moccasin bag, capturing the fun and the summery feel of the design; Figure 11 shows the Souk bag, using a real artist's palate to bring colour to life.

Figure 10: Moccasin bag

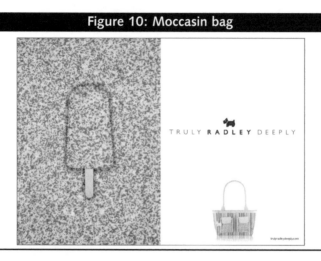

Figure 11: Souk bag

Figures 12 and 13 show other Radley bags whose designs were inspired by the campaign idea.

The Radley journal

The Truly Radley Deeply idea was further brought to life by creating a journal celebrating the brand and its meaning (see Figure 14). Numbered copies were given to all staff.

Figure 12: Leather Loom bag

Figure 13: Origami bag

Figure 14: The Truly Radley Deeply journal

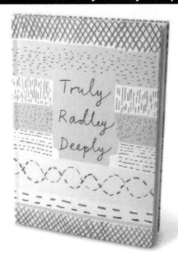

Two of the journal's pages are shown below. The first, the introduction, deals with the brand's mission (see Figure 15).

Figure 15: Introduction to the journal

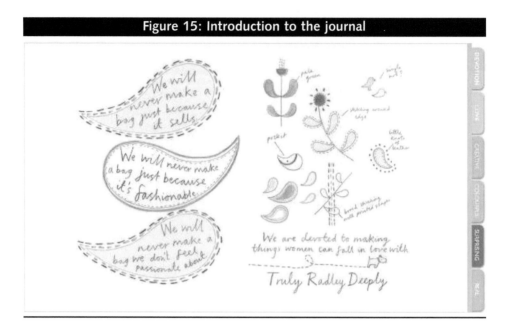

The page shown in Figure 16 talks about Radley's use of colour.

Figure 16: Radley's use of colour

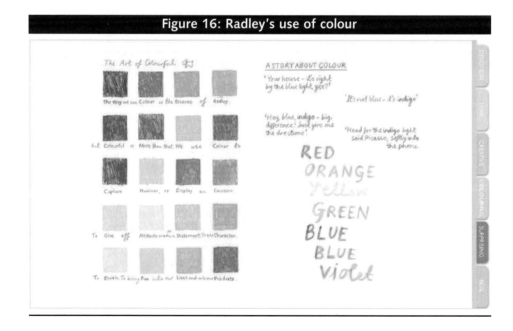

Point of sale and digital

And of course the campaign was taken to the point of sale. The display board shown in Figure 17 was used in retail across the UK (in particular, John Lewis windows).

Figure 17: Point-of-sale board

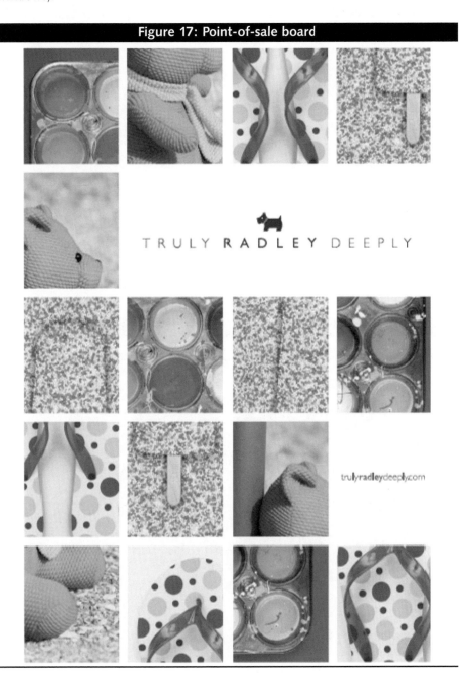

Figure 18 shows examples of counter displays and postcards, and Figure 19 is a shot of a John Lewis window display – the first time the Partnership had sanctioned such a campaign.

Figure 18: Counter displays and postcards

Figure 19: John Lewis windows

Figure 20: Website landing page

The campaign was also exposed digitally; Figure 20 shows the trulymadlydeeply.com landing page.

The second campaign wave, autumn 2007

This integrated approach was continued for the second wave of advertising, for autumn/winter 2007, which again used four new executions for the new season's bags.

Figure 21 shows the softest leather in the Soho bag, the debut of Radley's £300 range.

Figure 21: Soho bag

Pencils focused on colour for the Tannin bag (see Figure 22).

Figure 22: Tannin bag

Figures 23 and 24 respectively show the London Fields bag and the Daisy Daisy bag, and their accompanying advertising designs.

Figure 23: London Fields bag

Figure 24: Daisy Daisy bag

Media solution

Not surprisingly we decided to use women's glossies as the focus of the campaign; they offered us the right environment to talk to women and reached the opinion-forming fashion world.

But for Radley to have any chance of cutting through on such a small budget we needed to be smart and take some risks:

- to secure front half positions in the all-important women's international glossies (hard for an unknown advertiser)
- to create the impression we had a much bigger budget than the reality
- to get the campaign noticed and talked about by the fashion press opinion formers who we needed to impress for Radley's future ambitions.

How could we get Radley bags into glossies like *Vogue*?

Using the creative work in the buying process

We believed that our best help in negotiating with media buyers for these glossies would be for them to *see the ads for themselves*. So our media department took the unusual step of physically taking our ads round to show to magazine owners. This turned out to be an inspired move … They loved the ads.

The creative is fabulous.

Vanity Fair

The creative looks great for Radley and we would love to carry the business.

Vogue

Obviously we would love to carry it in You *magazine.*

M.O.S.

Love it.

Fashion Editor, *The Times*

Titles originally unsure of taking Radley were converted. Together, we selected executions that would leap out in each publication. Lolly in *Vogue* (Food in a fashion bible?; see Figure 25), Paint in *Vanity Fair*, Teddy in *Tatler*, for example.

Figure 25: Lolly in *Vogue*

We were also bold:

- paying more for prestigious positions in the front of magazines – usually reserved for long-term fashion-house advertisers – and among major editorial sites
- running two double-page spreads in the same magazine at launch.

Easy enough for the agency to recommend. Harder for a client short on funds to justify.

But Radley's management team were determined that the campaign should be launched with real impact.

The campaign targeted a national cross-section of women interested in fashion, but in addition it:

- naturally upweighted London/south-east – our weakest area
- hit the fashion opinion formers vital to Radley's longer-term ambitions.

Figure 26 outlines Radley's 2007 media plan.

Figure 26: The 2007 media plan

Radley 2007

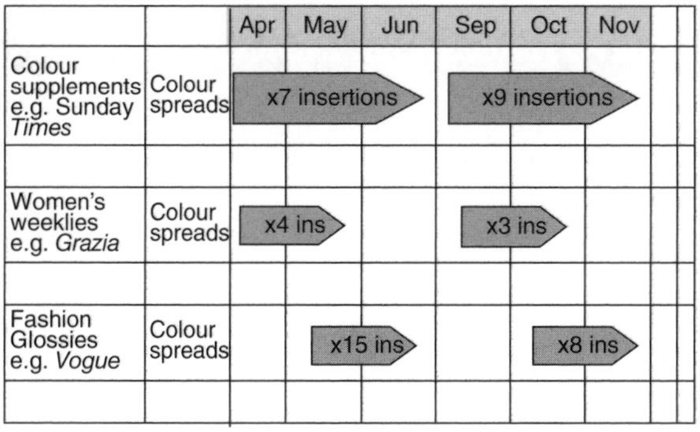

First insertions used two double page spreads for added impact

Our new website – www.trulyradleydeeply.com – was featured on all the ads, too.

The results of the campaign

Results were remarkable. Across 2007, Radley spent only £800k, including production on the new advertising – tiny in the fashion market. Yet impact on the brand and business was startling. In some cases, so much so that we had to double-check results.

Women certainly noticed our new advertising

After only eight months, awareness of our advertising put us in the fashion handbag top five, level with Chanel, fashion's single biggest spender (see Table 1).

Table 1: Spontaneous ad awareness post advertising

	Spontaneous ad awareness	Rank
Gucci	12%	1
Prada	9%	2
Louis Vuitton	8%	3
Chloe	6%	4
Radley	5%	5
Chanel	5%	5
Burberry	4%	6
Mulberry	4%	7
Dior	3%	8
Fendi	3%	9
D & G	1%	10

Source: Dipsticks
Base: Women, magazine readers, post (257); date: post (15/10/07–26/10/07)

Press advertising was responsible for this increase in awareness: 53% of women claimed to have seen the ads in magazines. But the point of sale based on our advertising was also having an effect: 17% of women claimed to have seen the brand advertised in-store (see Figure 27).

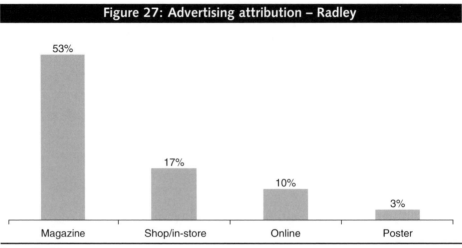

Figure 27: Advertising attribution – Radley

Source: Dipsticks
Base: Women, magazine readers, post (287); post (15/10/07–26/10/07)

So women certainly noticed our advertising – more so than that of some of our huge competitors.

The advertising got people talking about Radley

To increase Radley's profile, we needed to create a 'buzz' around Radley.

This seemed to be happening. Visits to Radley's two websites (www.radley.co.uk and www.trulyradleydeeply.com) increased significantly from the very day that our advertising appeared (see Figure 28).

And opinion formers and the press soon got interested, too. Press coverage had been fairly static, but when our ads broke, articles mentioning Radley increased, and by year end had doubled (see Figure 29).

> *Radley's campaign captures the attention of the discerning customer with wit and visual clarity that reflect the brand itself.*
>
> *Vogue*

> *Please tell Lowell how brilliant the print campaign is.*
>
> *New Woman*

> *I love the Radley campaign because it's truly original and different.*
>
> *You magazine*

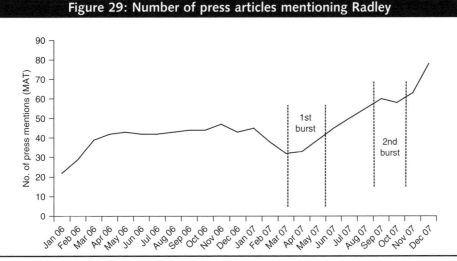

Figure 28: As soon as the ads broke, web traffic surged

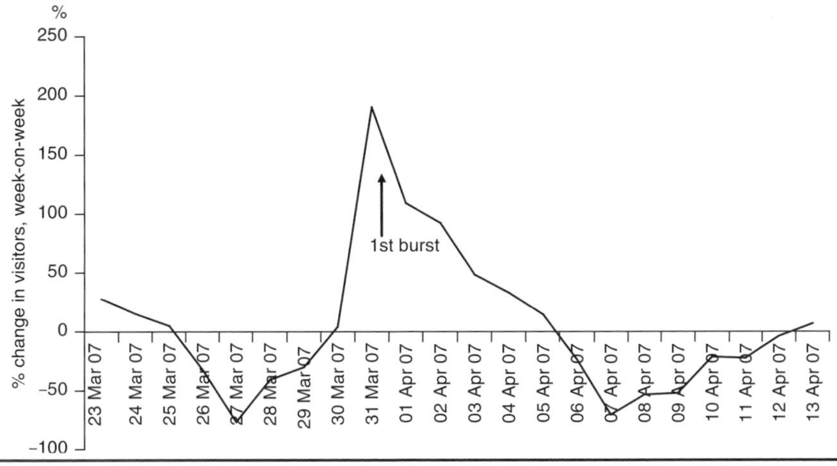

1st burst

Source: Radley + Co.

Figure 29: Number of press articles mentioning Radley

1st burst

2nd burst

Source: Radley + Co.

Radley became famous and desirable

Women became far more aware of Radley and found it far more appealing.

1. Brand awareness increased substantially

When we asked women what handbag brand came to mind, the results were astonishing. Prompted awareness increased by 18%, and spontaneous mentions of Radley tripled (see Table 2).

439

Table 2: Awareness of the Radley brand

	Pre	Post	% change
Prompted brand awareness	45%	53%	+18%
Spontaneous brand awareness (total)	8%	23%	+188%
Spontaneous brand awareness (first mention)	4%	12%	+200%

Source: Dipsticks
Base: Women, magazine readers, pre (135), post (257); pre (20/03/07–02/04/07), post (15/10/07–26/10/07)

Only Gucci was mentioned more often. After only eight months, we were the second most top-of-mind handbag brand (see Figure 30).

Figure 30: Spontaneous brand awareness – first mention

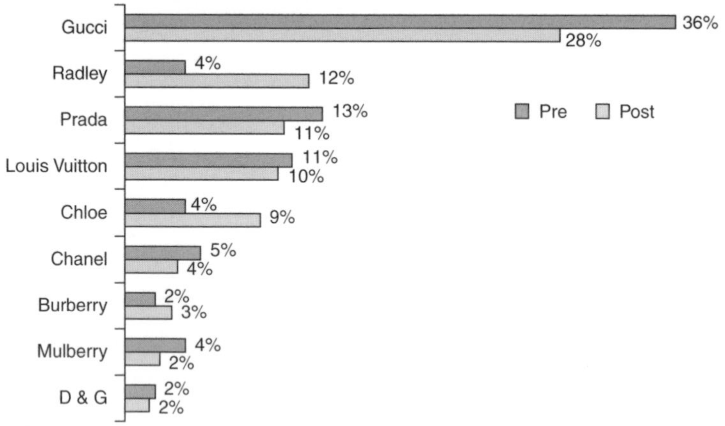

Gucci: 36%, 28%
Radley: 4%, 12%
Prada: 13%, 11%
Louis Vuitton: 11%, 10%
Chloe: 4%, 9%
Chanel: 5%, 4%
Burberry: 2%, 3%
Mulberry: 4%, 2%
D & G: 2%, 2%

Pre   Post

Source: Dipsticks
Base: Women, magazine readers, pre (135), post (257); pre (20/03/07–02/04/07), post (15/10/07–26/10/07)

2. We became the nation's favourite handbag designer

When we asked women who would be their first-choice handbag designer, we saw a fourfold improvement. This was so remarkable that we had to recheck the data. Radley was now the nation's favourite handbag designer, trouncing Gucci and even Chloe – makers of the 2007 'It' bag, according to the press (see Figure 31).

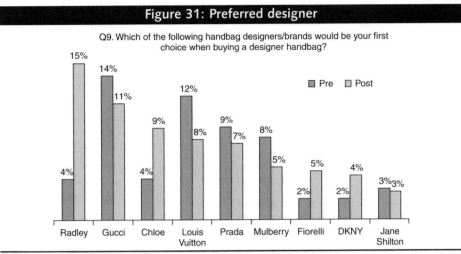

Figure 31: Preferred designer

Q9. Which of the following handbag designers/brands would be your first choice when buying a designer handbag?

■ Pre □ Post

Source: Dipsticks
Base: Women, magazine readers, pre (135), post (257); pre (20/03/07–02/04/07), post (15/10/07–26/10/07)

This was an amazing achievement, especially considering the huge budgets and press coverage that these two competitor brands enjoy (see Figure 32).

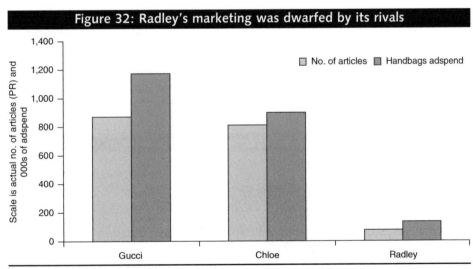

Figure 32: Radley's marketing was dwarfed by its rivals

□ No. of articles ■ Handbags adspend

Source: Nielsen, DDB Research

Radley became less polarising

Radley was a polarising brand. But now, something very good was happening. The number of women who felt that the brand was 'for people like me' increased, while the number disagreeing decreased (see Figure 33).

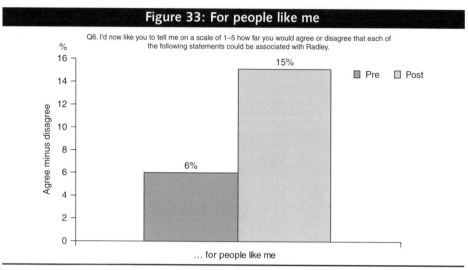

Figure 33: For people like me

Q6. I'd now like you to tell me on a scale of 1–5 how far you would agree or disagree that each of the following statements could be associated with Radley.

Source: Dipsticks
Base: Women, magazine readers, pre (135), post (257); pre (20/03/07–02/04/07), post (15/10/07–26/10/07)

I just couldn't believe it when I saw the Radley advert in Vogue. *Brilliant.*

Loyal Radley customer

I love the simplicity and the colours. The bags almost look yummy.

New Radley customer

Radley bags became more popular

Not surprisingly, this led to strong growth in numbers of women saying they would like to buy a Radley handbag (see Figure 34).

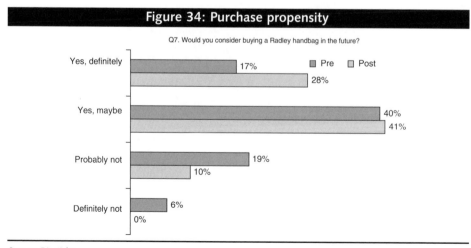

Figure 34: Purchase propensity

Q7. Would you consider buying a Radley handbag in the future?

Source: Dipsticks
Base: Women, magazine readers, pre (135), post (257); pre (20/03/07–02/04/07), post (15/10/07–26/10/07)

We exceeded all our business targets

With such extraordinary shifts in brand perceptions, you'd expect some pretty impressive business results. And you'd be right.

Radley's plan presumed that as value increased there would be some slowdown in volume. But volume sales of Radley handbags *increased* by 9% in 2007 (see Figure 35).[3]

Figure 35: The number of Radley bags sold increased by 9% in 2007

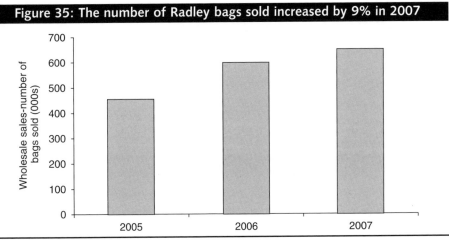

Source: PWC

Market share also increased to 12.5% by volume, *making Radley now the brand leader*; one in every eight handbags sold in Britain was now a Radley (see Table 3).

Table 3: Market share increased

	Before advertising (2006)	After advertising (2007)	Change
Radley share of handbag market	11.6%	12.5%	+7.5%

Source: PWC

And this share of growth was not explained by discounting or lowering pricing. Indeed the opposite took place: Radley was able to move its pricing up (see Figure 36), and more women traded up to more expensive Radley bags.

Value sales therefore increased faster than volume, growing by 21% over the previous year (see Figure 37).

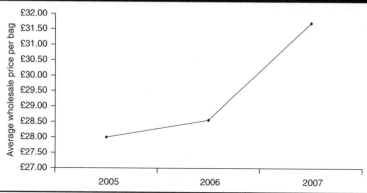

Figure 36: Radley managed to increase prices by 10% in 2007 – the first time in two years

Source: PWC

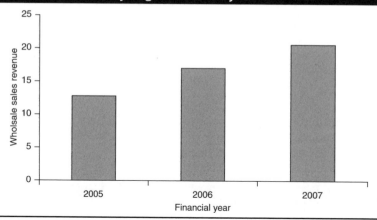

Figure 37: Sales of Radley bags increased by 21% in value terms in 2007

Source: PWC

The result: Radley's contribution to company profit increased by 51% (see Figure 38).

In combination, this meant that Radley + Co would meet its three-year business objective *a year earlier than planned*.

Proof that the advertising was responsible

Radley + Co underwent a remarkable transformation during 2007. In January it was a small company operating out of a converted dairy in Dollis Hill. By Christmas it was on the top floor of Greater London House and the number one player in the handbag market.

Figure 38: As a result, the contribution the Radley brand made to the company's profits increased by 51% in 2007

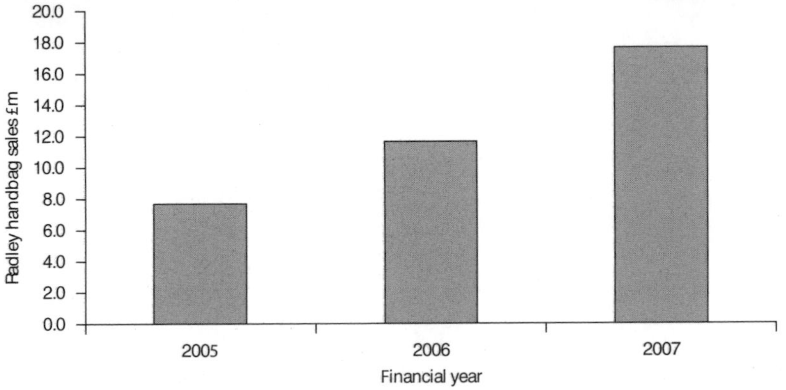

Source: PWC

Clearly this success was driven by the Radley brand. The other two brands, Tula and Hidesign, actually lost sales (see Table 4).

Table 4: Change in Radley, Tula and Hidesign sales

	%Change 2006–2007		
	Radley	Tula	Hidesign
Volume sales	+13%	–32%	–42%
Retail price	+13%	+16%	–1%
Value sales	+28%	–21%	–42%

But how much of Radley's success was due to advertising? The fact that Radley was advertised and grew, while the other two brands shrank, is suggestive; however, it is not conclusive. Fortunately, we have three more pieces of evidence:

1. timing of sales uplifts match timing of advertising
2. brand perceptions shift exactly as planned
3. regional results match advertising exposure.

Timing of sales uplifts matches timing of ads

Radley sales were already growing modestly; however, as soon as advertising broke, rate of growth increased significantly (see Figure 39).

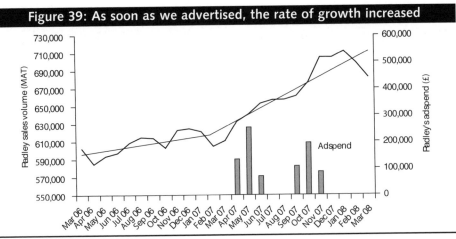

Figure 39: As soon as we advertised, the rate of growth increased

Source: NMR, Radley + Co.

And year-on-year changes in Radley sales match advertising spend closely. As soon as the ads broke, sales jumped 60% on the preceding year. Similarly, the second burst saw sales almost 50% up. Regression analysis shows the correlation between growth and advertising is highly statistically significant (see Figure 40).

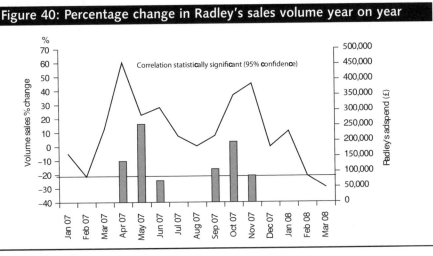

Figure 40: Percentage change in Radley's sales volume year on year

Source: NMR, Radley + Co.

Brand perceptions shifted exactly as planned

What was changing women's minds about Radley? A clue comes from the shifts in brand image. The biggest shifts came in two areas.

1. image dimensions related to colour, beauty and creativity – the qualities on which we'd focused advertising (see Figure 41)

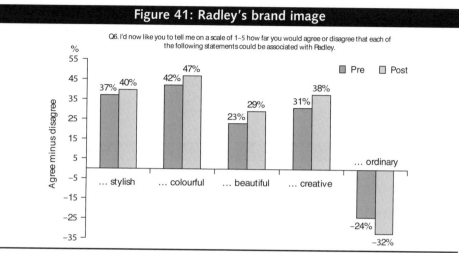

Figure 41: Radley's brand image

Q6. I'd now like you to tell me on a scale of 1–5 how far you would agree or disagree that each of the following statements could be associated with Radley.

Source: Dipsticks
Base: Women, magazine readers, pre (135), post (257); pre (20/03/07–02/04/07), post (15/10/07–26/10/07)

2. image dimensions relating to price positioning. Our high-profile advertising was conveying a suitably premium brand image (see Figure 42).

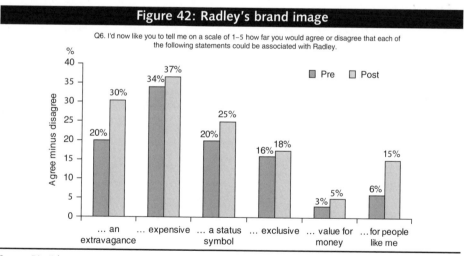

Figure 42: Radley's brand image

Q6. I'd now like you to tell me on a scale of 1–5 how far you would agree or disagree that each of the following statements could be associated with Radley.

Source: Dipsticks
Base: Women, magazine readers, pre (135), post (257); pre (20/03/07–02/04/07), post (15/10/07–26/10/07)

Remarkably, we managed to improve Radley's image for 'upmarket' and 'expensive' *and* 'good value' and 'for me'. This explains how we were able to increase both volume *and* price.

Regional results matched advertising exposure

Our ads were planned to give us extra exposure in the weaker London/south-east region. As we will see, this region improved most.

1. Advertising awareness was higher in London/south-east

As one would expect, given the media bias, the biggest shifts in advertising awareness occurred in London/south-east (see Table 5).

Table 5: Awareness of Radley's advertising

	Pre	Post	Change
Spontaneous			
London/SE	0%	6.6%	+6.6%
Rest of country	4.1%	3.6%	–0.5%
Prompted			
London/SE	4.8%	12.1%	7.3%
Rest of country	6.8%	12%	5.2%

Source: Dipsticks
Base: Women, magazine readers, pre (135), post (257); pre (20/03/07–02/04/07), post (15/10/07–26/10/07)

2. Improvements in brand image were also bigger in London/south-east

Importantly, the biggest shifts in brand image also occurred in London/south-east, in a way that reflected the ads; for example, here Radley became seen as significantly more 'beautiful' (see Figure 43).

Figure 43: Radley's brand image – Beautiful

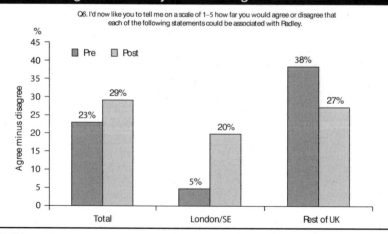

Q6. I'd now like you to tell me on a scale of 1–5 how far you would agree or disagree that each of the following statements could be associated with Radley.

Source: Dipsticks
Base: Women, magazine readers; total: pre (135), post (257); London/SE: pre (62), post (91); Rest of UK: pre (73), post (186); pre (20/03/07–02/04/07), post (15/10/07–26/10/07)

Similarly, in this region Radley was now rated as more 'stylish' (see Figure 44) and more of a 'status symbol' (see Figure 45).

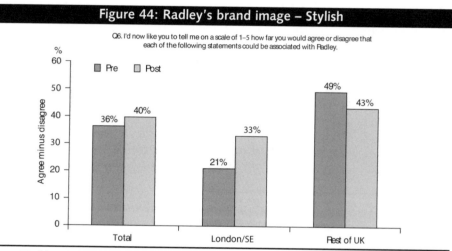

Figure 44: Radley's brand image – Stylish

Q6. I'd now like you to tell me on a scale of 1–5 how far you would agree or disagree that each of the following statements could be associated with Radley.

Source: Dipsticks
Base: Women, magazine readers; total: pre (135), post (257); London/SE: pre (62), post (91); Rest of UK: pre (73), post (186); pre (20/03/07–02/04/07), post (15/10/07–26/10/07)

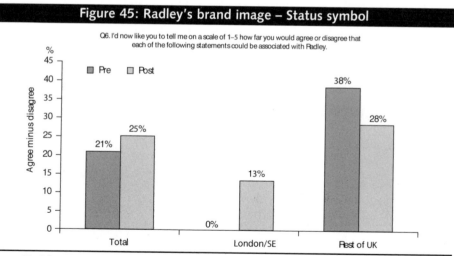

Figure 45: Radley's brand image – Status symbol

Q6. I'd now like you to tell me on a scale of 1–5 how far you would agree or disagree that each of the following statements could be associated with Radley.

Source: Dipsticks
Base: Women, magazine readers; total: pre (135), post (257); London/SE: pre (62), post (91); Rest of UK: pre (73), post (186); pre (20/03/07–02/04/07), post (15/10/07–26/10/07)

3. Desirability increased most in London/south-east too

In London/south-east, Radley became increasingly seen as 'for people like me', moving from a net negative position to a positive one (see Figure 46).

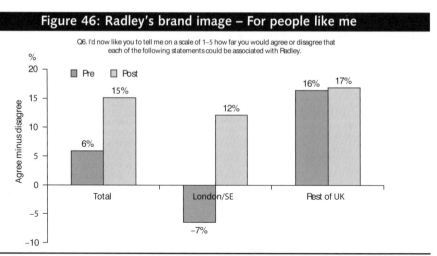

Figure 46: Radley's brand image – For people like me

Q6. I'd now like you to tell me on a scale of 1–5 how far you would agree or disagree that each of the following statements could be associated with Radley.

Source: Dipsticks
Base: Women, magazine readers; total: pre (135), post (257); London/SE: pre (62), post (91); Rest of UK: pre (73), post (186); pre (20/03/07–02/04/07), post (15/10/07–26/10/07)

4. And, finally, sales grew fastest in London/south-east

John Lewis, Radley's largest wholesale client, gives us a picture of sales to the public on a regional level; we have been able to obtain sales by outlet for 2006 and 2007.

Rate of growth in John Lewis' London/south-east stores was three times higher than the rest of the country – where historically Radley had been strongest (see Figure 47).

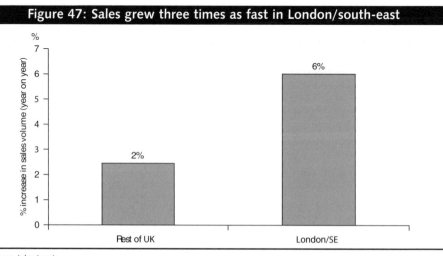

Figure 47: Sales grew three times as fast in London/south-east

Source: John Lewis
Pre = April 2006 to March 2007, post = April 2007 to March 2008

Could anything else explain Radley's success?

So women noticed our ads and changed their perceptions of Radley in line with our strategy. The bags became more desirable, which meant we sold more bags at higher prices. And we've seen how all these things correlate with advertising, by brand, by region and over time.

But could some other factor explain all this?

It wasn't price

Radley's sales did not rise as a result of discounting its product. Radley's prices increased across the board, shifting the brand further up into the premium segment (see Figure 48).

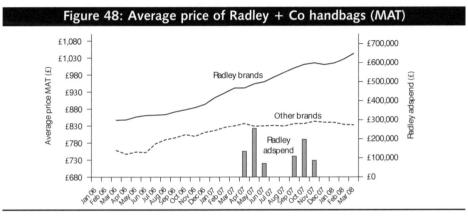

Figure 48: Average price of Radley + Co handbags (MAT)

Source: NMR, Radley + Co.

It wasn't distribution

The total number of stores stocking Radley actually *fell* (see Figure 49).

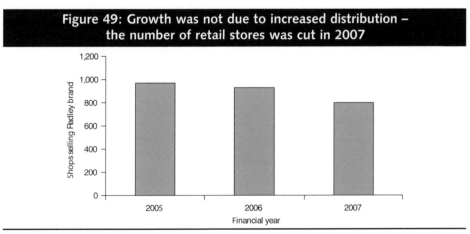

Figure 49: Growth was not due to increased distribution – the number of retail stores was cut in 2007

Source: PWC

For Radley to build share on the back of declining distribution meant it was more dependent on a smaller base where rate of sale needed to increase. And this is exactly what happened – a classic sign that demand for Radley had increased (see Figure 50).

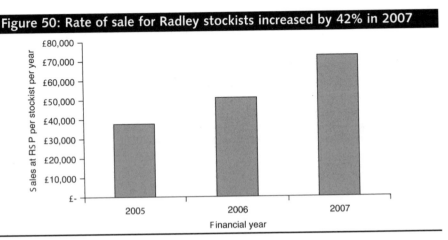

Figure 50: Rate of sale for Radley stockists increased by 42% in 2007

Source: PWC

It wasn't the market

Radley's performance can't be explained by market growth: we've seen how market share increased. Radley's rate-of-sale data are even more compelling – increasing three times faster than the market (see Figure 51).

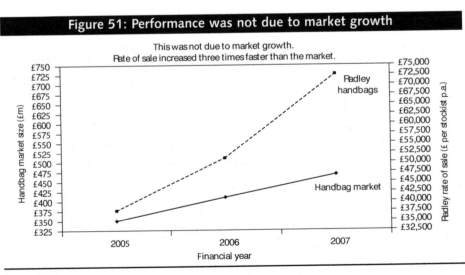

Figure 51: Performance was not due to market growth

Source: PWC

It wasn't new products

The ongoing business – 'continuity' products – showed the same improvement in success that newer, more seasonal products were enjoying (see Figure 52).

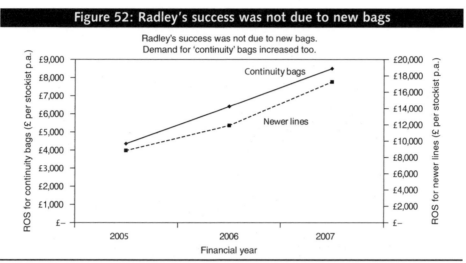

Figure 52: Radley's success was not due to new bags

And, of course, changes to the range can't explain the regional patterns we observed – the same bags were sold across the country.

It wasn't a lack of competition

Competitors' spend continued to dwarf ours (see Figure 53).

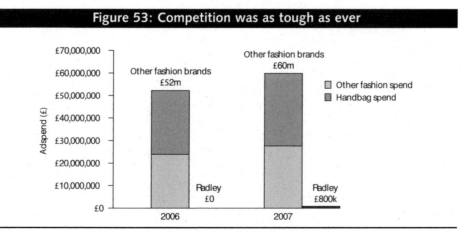

Figure 53: Competition was as tough as ever

It wasn't just in-store activity

We've seen how campaign point-of-sale material contributed to awareness, but the John Lewis data provides a natural control here as the same material was used in all stores (see Figures 54 and 55).

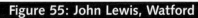

Figure 54: John Lewis, Liverpool

Figure 55: John Lewis, Watford

Yet, as we've seen, regional sales patterns in John Lewis match regional ad support, with sales growing three times faster in the heavily advertised London/south-east region.

It wasn't retail expansion

Radley started 2007 with one specialist store in the King's Road (trading since 2005). Two new stores opened in 2007.[4] However, they were a tiny part of the business and they have been excluded from all the analysis so far (which is based on wholesale data to give an unbiased picture).

It wasn't online sales

From October 2007, it became possible to buy direct from the Radley website. However, this business is still small, came late in the year, and in any event has been removed from all previous sales analyses.

Short-term payback

We have estimated advertising payback in two ways:

1. Sales grew 2.4 times faster when we advertised.
Sales were already growing before we advertised, but as soon as the campaign started, rate of growth increased by a factor of 2.42. Given the evidence we have presented, it seems clear the main reason for this was advertising (see Figure 56).

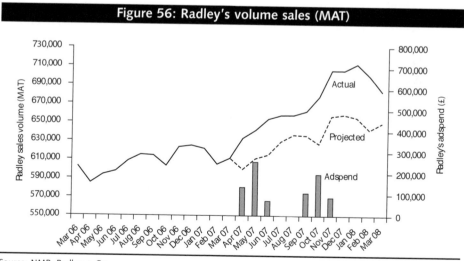

Figure 56: Radley's volume sales (MAT)

Source: NMR, Radley + Co.

2. Sales grew 2.4 times faster where our ads were concentrated.
Sales in London/south-east grew 2.45 times faster than in the rest of the country. The only thing that can explain this is advertising – all other factors affected the different stores equally.

Our two methods lead to exactly the same conclusion: advertising increased the rate of growth by a factor of 2.4. From this, we can calculate immediate payback. We estimate that the advertising paid for itself 1.47 times over, giving a return on marketing investment (ROMI) of 47%.

This is an impressive payback, especially over such a short time span. But it is only part of the picture.

Longer and broader effects

There are several other ways in which advertising created value:

1. Women came to value the brand more.
The campaign lifted perceptions of what a Radley bag was worth and how much one should pay, allowing Radley to charge higher prices.

2. Retail expansion became more feasible
Now that Radley is a stronger brand, selling direct to the public is easier. Whether it's online or on the high street, women are now more likely to want to visit a Radley shop. That's important, because retail margins are higher than wholesale. Radley has aggressive plans to expand its retail network.

3. The brand became more extendible
Radley has already launched purses and luggage. Now the brand is stronger, it can be extended into other categories.

4. Radley secured distribution abroad
This was a key campaign outcome: as intended, international fashion buyers noticed and were impressed with Radley. As a result, distribution has already been secured in North America (via Lord and Taylor and Bloomingdales department store chains). We expect more to follow.

Calculating the value of all these effects would be difficult. Fortunately, we don't have to, because the market did it for us.

The big payback – a new kind of ad effect

If the market is efficient, the effects of advertising should all be reflected in the value of the company.

When Phoenix bought the company in 2006, it had a three-year plan to transform the business. Our advertising helped it to achieve its targets in half that time. As a result, it was able to sell at the end of 2007.

And that's where the big payback came from. Phoenix acquired Radley + Co for £42m in February 2006. By November 2007, Exponent (another private equity group) paid £130m for it – regarded as one of the private equity deals of the year (see Figure 57).

The value of the company had tripled, creating £88m worth of value in just 19 months. An extraordinary achievement, especially since, by late 2007, the credit crisis was causing lesser deals to fail.

Figure 57: Two *Sunday Times* **awards: 'Top 100 private equity-backed companies with the fastest growing profits' and 'Ones to Watch'**

It's instructive to examine where that value came from (see Table 6). Exponent's rationale for the increased valuation was based on two factors:

1. having a stronger brand doubled the potential for profit
2. having a stronger brand made those profits more secure, allowing use of a higher profit multiple when calculating the company's value.

To our knowledge, the latter is an advertising effect that has never been properly identified or measured before.

Table 6: Extraordinary value creation: how Exponent valued Radley

	2006	2007
Profit	£6m	£13.0m
Profit multiple	X7	X10
Market value of company	£42m	£130m

Source: Exponent

We can use Exponent's calculations to estimate the total effect of the advertising, including the longer and broader effects.

We know:

- ads increased earnings by £375k in 2007
- Exponent applied a multiple of 10 to those earnings when valuing the company.

Therefore the ads increased the value of the company by at least £3.75m.

True payback will be even greater, since advertising also helped increase the multiple from 7 to 10.

Since we only spent £800k, this means the campaign paid for itself 5.7 times over, giving a ROMI of 470%. As Table 7 shows, this is one of the highest returns ever measured in the entire history of the IPA Effectiveness Awards.

Table 7: The ten most profitable IPA cases		
Case	Year	ROMI
1 O_2	2006	8000%
2 O_2	2004	6100%
3 Eurostar	2006	1510%
4 Virgin Mobile	2004	758%
5 Homebase	2006	690%
6 Ackermans	2004	590%
7 Ryvita	2006	516%
8 Radley	2008	470%
9 Sainsbury's	2002	445%
10 Marks & Spencer	2004	412%

Source: IPA dataBANK, all cases with valid ROMI (39).

Conclusions and learnings

A number of conclusions arise from this story of the unlikely alliance between the worlds of high fashion and high finance.

- 'Small budgets' can produce remarkably big commercial effects – even when dwarfed by much larger competitor budgets.
- 'Small budgets' can and should be as rigorously evaluated as large ones – even in sectors such as the fashion industry, not known for rigorous communication evaluation.
- In the hands of visionary management, great advertising both builds brands *and* directly increases the value of companies.
- And we outline *new evaluation learning*, showing how ads have a double effect on company value – increasing profits *and* making those profits more secure.

A parting thought: perhaps we can all humbly learn something here from the recently much-maligned world of private equity.

Free from the short-term demands of listed companies, private equity companies can surprisingly offer far more fertile ground in which brands can flourish securely over the long term.

Far from being dismissive of brands and slashing support in the interests of short-term profit gains, Phoenix was smart enough to do the opposite, providing bold commitment and financial backing for its new brand Radley. And, in turn, demanding a rigorous approach to analysing return on its investment.

The result: a textbook case of how advertising creates hard financial value. Truly from bags to riches ...

We are building an iconic brand for women throughout the world and advertising is a key component in that. The benefits of last year's campaign go way beyond the strong sales and awareness gains we experienced last year.

The Radley brand continues to take market share in the UK and with DDB this spring we have embarked on our heaviest ever media campaign. Just like Phoenix, our new private equity partners – Exponent – are totally supportive in our goal to keep growing through investment behind our Radley brand.

The collaboration with DDB and our design and PR agencies – Liquid and Halpern – is producing some outstanding results for the company and work that we are very proud of. Something we all appreciate. Like Radley, it's fun.

The last word from Radley's CEO, Roger Best

Notes

1. Now merged into DDB London.
2. Who'd joined following the Phoenix acquisition, from Levi's Dockers.
3. These are wholesale figures. But, as we will see later, total sales increased slightly faster, due to expansion into retail. However, throughout this section we will use wholesale figures, in order to provide a fair like-for-like comparison.
4. In Floral Street, Covent Garden, in April and Manchester in October.

Other companies involved in campaign: Design company: Liquid; PR company: Halpern; Market Research company: Dipsticks.

Chapter 21

Virgin Atlantic

How 15 years of communications helped break the British Airways stranglehold

By Emily James, RKCR/Y&R, and Sergen Ozbek, Brand Science
Contributing authors: Joanna Bamford and Elizabeth Boulter, RKCR/Y&R, and Matt Bement, Manning Gottlieb OMD

Editor's summary

This paper demonstrates how communications over a 15-year period helped enhance 'Virginness' and strengthen performance for the Virgin Atlantic brand. The creative approach incorporated the elements of Richard Branson's innovative, maverick image and persona into the communications campaigns, reinforcing them with iconic personalities and imagery. Working on a small budget, the media strategy ensured advertising was seen alongside that of the big established brands. Despite being a relatively small operation, Virgin Atlantic is now perceived as an airline industry heavyweight and is one of the most valuable asset in the Virgin Group. Econometric modelling estimates that communications have produced a return of £10.76 for every £1 invested.

Introduction

It is easy to forget that, 15 years ago, British Airways probably was the world's favourite airline, while Virgin Atlantic was still operating in a minor league of the airline industry. A lot has changed in 15 years.

In 1993, British Airways, one of the great success stories of the Thatcher years, had a virtual stranglehold on the UK airline market. With 241 aircraft servicing 165 routes across the globe, and annual profits in excess of £300m, the company seemed unassailable. By comparison, Virgin Atlantic was a minuscule operation. With just 13 aircraft servicing seven routes, it was having a hard time. The 1980s had been profitable but the UK recession of the early 1990s brought more turbulent times. That year the company made a loss of £9.3m.

Today, in spite of remaining a lean operation, Virgin Atlantic is perceived as an airline industry heavyweight, standing head to head with British Airways in UK customer perceptions and surpassing it in virtually every measure of brand preference.

This paper tells the story of how communications, over a 15-year period, helped Virgin Atlantic become one of Virgin Group's most valuable assets. By strengthening 'Virginness' and increasing brand preference, communications helped Virgin Atlantic become a genuine challenger on the routes it operated, and was instrumental in generating incremental passengers and revenue.

It demonstrates how, with a budget less than a third the size of British Airways, Virgin Atlantic has risen to its current status as the UK's favourite airline and flagbearer of the country's most admired brand.[1]

Birth and growing pains

I was fed up with identical seats, identical food, identical service and extortionate fares. I decided to create an airline that I wanted to fly myself.

Richard Branson

Richard Branson launched Virgin Atlantic with a single leased aircraft making its inaugural flight from London Gatwick to Newark Liberty on 22 June 1984. At the time, the idea that a brand best known for launching Culture Club and the Sex Pistols could be extended to encompass an international airline seemed hardly credible.

Against all the odds, and to the surprise of many commentators, Branson turned a profit in his first year of operation and continued to expand Virgin Atlantic over the next decade.

However, ten years later, despite heavy investment in service innovation, Virgin Atlantic had not managed to break British Airways' stranglehold on the UK long-haul market. At the start of the 1990s the UK scheduled airline market was still very much a one-horse race. British Airways carried almost two-thirds of all passengers departing the country. The next largest player, British Midland, had less than a 10% market share.[2]

As the UK economy took a downturn and the airline industry as a whole began to look vulnerable, people were starting to question whether Virgin Atlantic would even be around to challenge the market in the years to come.[3] In 1993, with the company posting its first operating loss since launch, measures had to be put in place to ensure the heavy investment in innovation would deliver a rapid return.

BA seemed invincible and for one of the first times in my life I felt vulnerable.

Richard Branson, 1994

Communications challenge

RKCR/Y&R were invited to work with Virgin Atlantic in 1993. Until this time communications had been intermittent, frequently using Branson as a spokesperson, with a heavy reliance on price and promotions.

The strongest drivers of brand choice in the air travel market are structural. If an airline doesn't fly to your chosen destination or at a convenient time, no amount of brand loyalty will sway your choice.

However, with margins as tight as they are, every passenger counts. And when given a comparable offer the power of the brand can be the difference between an extra booking or not.

Airline profits are made at the margin: the income from most of the seats that fill an aircraft goes towards covering the immense costs of running a network, but it is the last few seats sold that produce all the profit.

K.W. Glaister, *Cases in Strategic Management*, 1995

The role for communications

With a route network less than a twentieth the size of British Airways', Virgin Atlantic could never compete on structural factors. But it could challenge them in the quality of the offer. To secure its position into a second decade of growth the company needed to ensure that, wherever the offer was comparable, Virgin Atlantic was the preferred brand.

This defined the role for communications:[4]

> **Maximise brand preference to a point where, all structural factors being equal, consumers choose Virgin Atlantic.**

Media budget dwarfed by those of competitors

In 1993, Virgin Atlantic's media budget was £1.6m. Although a considerable commitment for such a small operation, it equated to just 3% share of voice in the UK air travel market. By contrast British Airways spent more than £10m in the same year,[5] outspending Virgin Atlantic by a factor of six. This inequality of UK media investment would continue over the next 15 years with British Airways spending almost four times as much as Virgin Atlantic.

To compensate for the imbalance, cut-through was crucial. If Virgin Atlantic was to be perceived as a credible challenger to British Airways, its communications had to work four times harder (see Figure 1).

Figure 1: Virgin Atlantic and British Airways media spend 1993–2007

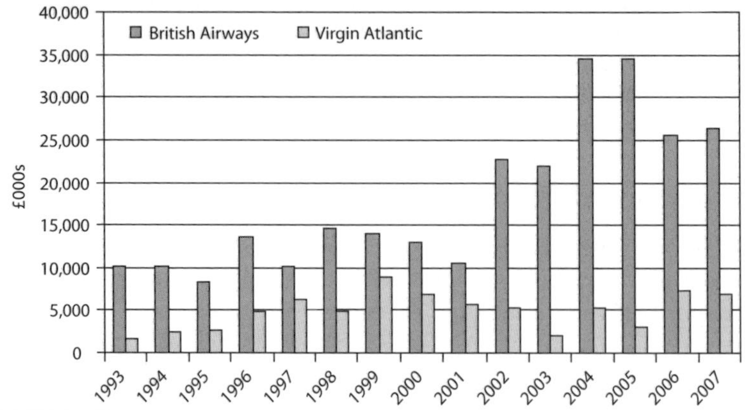

Source: MMS, 2008

The communications strategy

Creative approach

With such a variety of messages to be communicated across each cabin class, target audience, route and channel – it was a tone of voice, rather than any single creative idea, that acted as the golden thread linking everything together.

The most powerful asset at the disposal of the Virgin brand was the mercurial personality of its founder Richard Branson. And it was Branson's style and personality that provided the template upon which the creative approach was fashioned. If the Virgin brand can be said to have attitude, that attitude was Branson's – maverick, challenging, irreverent, witty and innovative.

Our creative approach was to incorporate all the elements of the Branson image and persona into the communications campaigns, reinforcing them with iconic personalities and imagery representing the Virgin Atlantic promise – from Helen Mirren to Terence Stamp; Iggy Pop to Miss Piggy; Alice Cooper to the Wright Brothers. The idea of British Airways using such a cast was unimaginable.

This approach optimised the cut-through of the activity by ensuring that every message a consumer saw or heard, even if not directly relevant to them, added to their understanding of the Virgin Atlantic positioning. This was particularly so when communicating the benefits available in Upper Class, transmitting as it did, a halo effect to other cabins.

Media approach

The Virgin Atlantic attitude was reflected as much in media strategy as creative execution.

Making sure the brand was seen in the company of big established players was critical in creating a sense of scale. Occupying environments best known for premium brands added a sense of sophistication and style to the Virgin Atlantic brand. Media firsts, such as front-page colour strips in the early 1990s and being the first commercial brand to run podcasts, helped reinforce the innovative nature of Virgin Atlantic.

Capitalising on tactical opportunities also added to the brand's sense of dynamism and challenger status. For example:

- placing the Upper Class Suite (newly designed flatbeds) outside the BA lounge
- flying a BA 'Can't Get it Up' blimp above the London Eye
- proactively recruiting BA business flyers during BA strikes.

Fifteen years of award-winning creative communications

Figures 2–7 show some of the creative communications that have been used during the past 15 years.

Figure 2: TV ads

Advertiser: Virgin Atlantic

Title: Chauffer Driven   Agency: Rainey Kelly Campbell Roalfe Y&R

Date: August 1993

HELEN MIRREN: On flights from Heathrow there is one business class which drives you to the airport.

HELEN MIRREN: Checks your bags on for you, bypasses the terminal, then drops you off at passport control.

HELEN MIRREN: Smile and wave, smile and wave....
Super: Upper Class. Virgin Atlantic

Figure 2: TV ads (continued)

Advertiser: Virgin Atlantic

Title: Grim Reaper   Agency: Rainey Kelly Campbell Roalfe Y&R

Date: April 1997

Scene opens with stone angel falling off a building. Church bells ring in the distance as the Grim Reaper appears. Fast paced music starts.

Various scenes of the man's life pass before his eyes, exciting, wild adventures and encounters.

As more and more scenes keep flashing past the Grim Reaper begins to get bored, when eventually he falls asleep.

VO: When your life flashes before your eyes, make sure you have plenty to watch

Figure 2: TV ads (continued)

Advertiser: Virgin Atlantic

Title: Big Seat – Miss Piggy   Agency: Rainey Kelly Campbell Roalfe Y&R

Date:2001

MISS PIGGY: Bonjour- ha ha ha!
Super: Miss Piggy in the Back Seat

MISS PIGGY: Do all Business Class drive you to the Airport?
Do they whisk you past all those dreadful queues?
Do they check your bags in without you even leaving a memo?

MISS PIGGY: No they don't?
Well you picked the wrong airline buster!
Super Virgin Atlantic
MISS PIGGY: Kissy Kissy

Figure 2: TV ads (continued)

Advertiser: Virgin Atlantic

Title: Kitty Hawk   **Agency: Rainey Kelly Campbell Roalfe Y&R**

Date: 2006

Scene opens with the pioneer walking through the sand dunes of Kitty Hawk and meets the Wright brothers by their plane.
Pioneer: So the plane's here. And how do you get to it? Chauffeur, takes you from your door to the airport.

Pioneer: You check in without leaving the vehicle. What's the flight between here and London? 7 hours right? People want to sleep with proper beds on board.

Pioneer: You're looked after by the best people. You have drinks on board, but why not sit at a bar. You eat when you want. You get to the other side another chauffeur takes you right where you're headed. You're gonna need a bigger plane.

We now pan through the new Virgin Upper Class cabin.

Figure 3: Outdoor

1993

1993

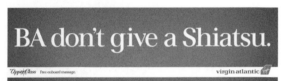

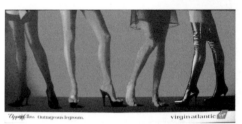

1993

2000

2005

2006

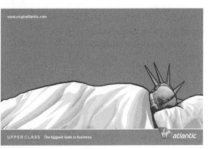

2007

Figure 4: Outdoor – route launches

 1997

1999

 2000

2004

 2004

 2005

2005

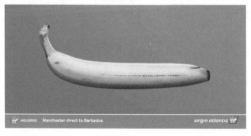 2006

Figure 5: Press

2001

2003

2005

2008

2007

Figure 6: Tactical press

1998

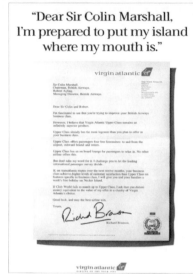

2003

2004

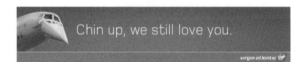

2004

2005

Figure 7: Stunts

2002

2002

2000

2004

What the communications strategy achieved

Approach to measurement

To accommodate inconsistencies in tracking sources over the 15-year period, Y&R's Brand Asset Valuator (BAV) has been used as the principal tracking tool. It is a single source that covers the full communications period and can be used to demonstrate changes in consumer perceptions since 1993.[6] When using BAV to analyse trends over time it is necessary that any brand's position is judged relative to competitors because the BAV methodology ranks individual brands against a total UK brandscape.

Pre and post tracking measures from a range of TV campaigns over the advertising history have been used to illustrate how communications have effected the longer-term change.[7] With five different research agencies over a 15-year period, the measures required for this analysis were not always included in each questionnaire. Consequently the evidence presented is taken from a range of campaigns and time periods using all the sources available.

Business performance since advertising began is shown through a range of measures including passenger numbers, turnover and change in share across key Virgin Atlantic routes.

Given the relatively small impact of communications when compared with structural factors, it is only through econometric modelling that we can isolate the contribution of advertising to the results. The effect of communications on passenger numbers and revenue is illustrated over the 41-month period that modelling has been conducted. A method of back-casting has been used to estimate the total contribution over the full 15 years of communications.

Communications model

The impact of communications on consumer attitudes and behaviour is summarised in Figure 8. This model will be used to summarise the results.

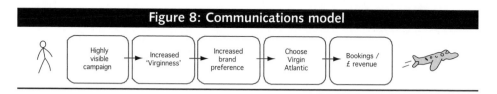

Figure 8: Communications model

Highly visible campaign → Increased 'Virginness' → Increased brand preference → Choose Virgin Atlantic → Bookings / £ revenue

Fifteen years of highly visible communications

Communications have achieved high cut-through with both business and leisure travellers, regardless of the cabin class featured.

For example, the first Helen Mirren execution, 'Legs', launched in December 1995,[8] communicated the extra leg room on Virgin Atlantic aircraft. Almost a year after airing, 73% of consumers still spontaneously recalled it.[9] Another year later a quarter of consumers still spontaneously recalled the execution.[10] Tracking from other activity shows how communications awareness increased post advertising for both audiences (see Figures 9 and 10).

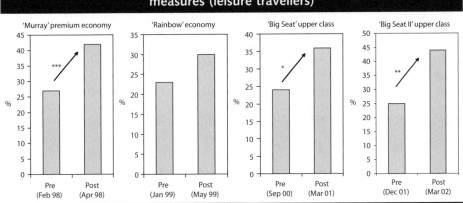

Figure 9: Increase in communications awareness between pre and post measures (business travellers)

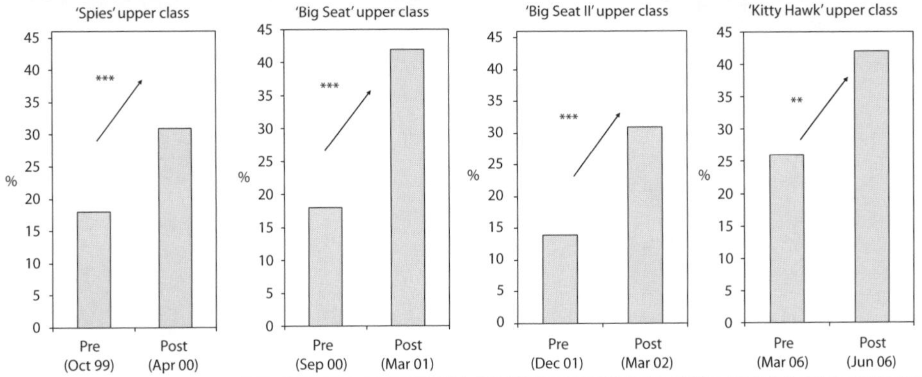

Sources: 'Spies': Consumer Insight Tracking. Pre176, post305; 'Big Seat': Consumer Insight Tracking. Pre284, post300; 'Big Seat II': HPI Tracking. Pre300, post300; 'Kitty Hawk': Hall & Partners Tracking. Pre184, post190

Figure 10: Increase in communications awareness between pre and post measures (leisure travellers)

Sources: 'Murray': Consumer Insight Tracking. Pre192, post203; 'Rainbow': Consumer Insight Tracking. Pre200, post188; 'Big Seat': Consumer Insight Tracking. Pre207, post202; 'Big Seat II': HPI Tracking. Pre200, post200
* p =90%; **p = 95%; ***p = 99%

From all the tracking evidence, there was just one occasion when both British Airways and Virgin Atlantic were targeting the same audience with a similar message about flatbeds. Figure 11 shows how branded recognition for Virgin Atlantic per 100 TVRs was more than double that of British Airways.

These high levels of cut-through were important not just for helping maintain brand salience[11] but for maximising the ability of communication to build perceptions of the brand. We go on to explore this change in the next section.

Figure 11: Branded recognition per 100 TVRs for Virgin Atlantic and British Airways

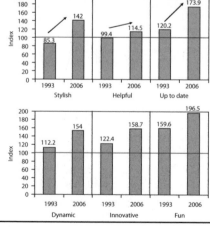

Business travellers

Leisure travellers

Virgin Atlantic – Beauty Sleep

British Airways - Piccadilly

Source: HPI 2004/MMS, including TVRs from Sept–Nov (BA 693 TVRs, VAA 235 TVRs) business sample (223), leisure sample (145)

Atlantic's sense of 'Virginness' strengthened

There are six image attributes on BAV, which reflect the core values of 'Virginness': stylish, helpful, up-to-date, dynamic, innovative and fun.

Figure 12 shows that Virgin Atlantic's position relative to British Airways has increased significantly across all measures, even those where BA originally enjoyed considerable advantage.

Figure 12: Strengthening of 'Virginness' for Virgin Atlantic relative to British Airways between 1993 and 2006

Source: Brand Asset Valuator, 1993 (725) to 2006 (3507)

Even a casual glance at the tracking will show that advertising has helped develop these brand assets over the last 15 years. Figures 13–17 show how Virgin Atlantic brand image shifted pre and post advertising among both business and leisure travellers.

Figure 13: Change in image associations pre and post communications – innovative

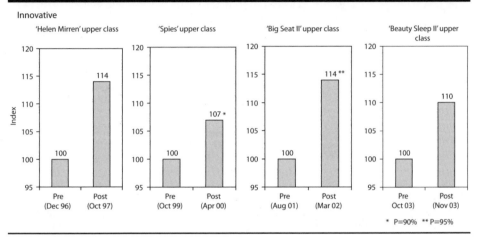

Innovative

Sources: 'Helen Mirren': Critical Research Tracking. Pre60 post112; 'Spies': Consumer Insight Tracking. Pre299, post305; 'Big Seat II': HPI Tracking. Pre300, post300; 'Beauty Sleep II': HPI Tracking. Pre75, post75

Figure 14: Change in image associations pre and post communications – dynamic

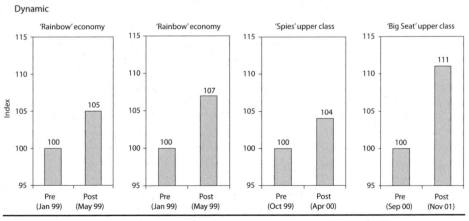

Dynamic

Sources: 'Helen Mirren': Critical Research Tracking. Pre60 post112; 'Spies': Consumer Insight Tracking. Pre299, post305; 'Big Seat II': HPI Tracking. Pre300, post300; 'Beauty Sleep II': HPI Tracking. Pre75, post75

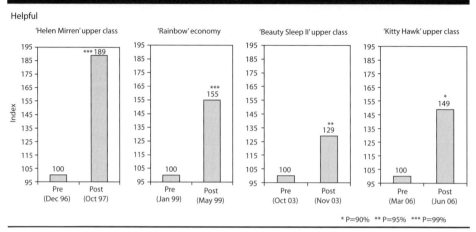

Figure 15: Change in image associations pre and post communications – helpful

Helpful

Sources: 'Helen Mirren': Critical Research Tracking. Pre60 post112; 'Rainbow': Consumer Insight Tracking. Pre200, post188; 'Beauty Sleep II': HPI Tracking. Pre300, post300; 'Kitty Hawk': Hall & Partners Tracking. Pre41, post78

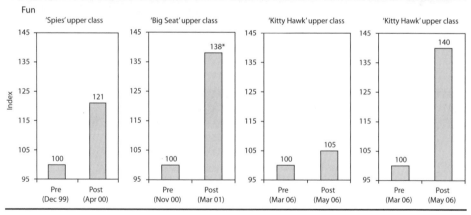

Figure 16: Change in image associations pre and post communications – fun

Fun

Sources: 'Spies': Consumer Insight Tracking. Pre64 post119; 'Big Seat': Consumer Insight Tracking. Pre87, post170; 'Kitty Hawk': Hall & Partners Tracking. Pre74, post76; 'Kitty Hawk': Hall & Partners Tracking. Pre41, post47

'Virginness' is a driver of brand preference

Using BAV it is possible to identify which image attributes most closely correlate with preference for Virgin Atlantic.[12] Based on this analysis it can be seen that the six image attributes that have increased since 1993 are positive drivers of preference (see Figure 18).

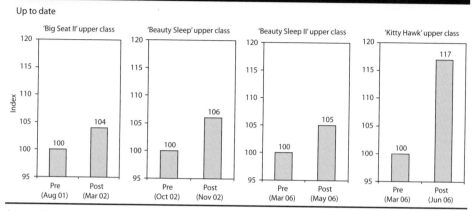

Figure 17: Change in image associations pre and post communications – up-to-date

Sources: 'Big Seat II': HPI Tracking. Pre300 post300; 'Beauty Sleep': HPI Tracking. Pre75, post75; 'Beauty Sleep II': HPI Tracking. Pre50, post50; 'Kitty Hawk': Hall & Partners Tracking. Pre41, post78

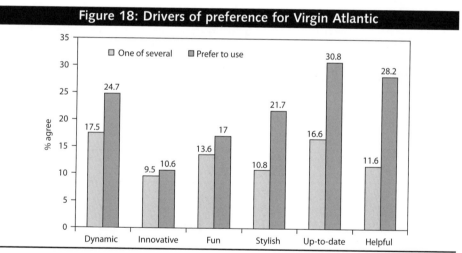

Figure 18: Drivers of preference for Virgin Atlantic

Source: Brand Asset Valuator 2006 (3507)

So far, evidence has shown that communications were highly visible, helping strengthen 'Virginness' for the Virgin Atlantic brand. These six attributes would appear to correlate with preference. In the next section we will explore how brand preference, the objective of communications, has changed over the 15-year period.

Preference for Virgin Atlantic increased

Virgin Atlantic has improved its position on 'prefer to use' relative to British Airways since 2000.[13] The way the question is worded has an implicit element of usage, so the relative sizes of the two brands are reflected in the data (see Figure 19).

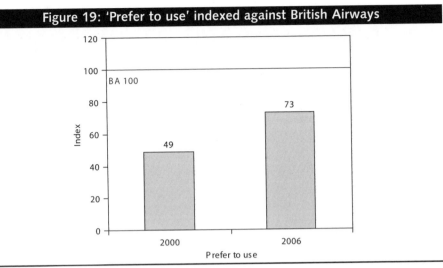

Figure 19: 'Prefer to use' indexed against British Airways

Source: BAV: All adults 2000 (990) 2006 (3507)

Recent research shows that preference for Virgin Atlantic exceeds that of the airline average and British Airways on five different measures (see Figure 20).

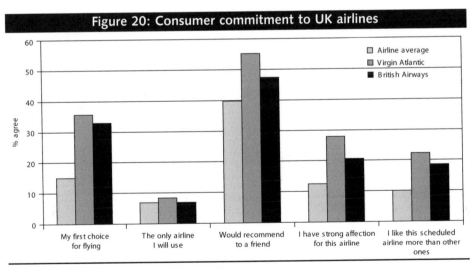

Figure 20: Consumer commitment to UK airlines

Source: CIAO, May 2007. Total sample 2000 adults 16+

Despite less than 30% of those interviewed having actually flown with Virgin Atlantic, more than 50% would consider it in the future. British Airways has considerably higher levels of usage but consideration is half that of Virgin Atlantic.

This would suggest that the high levels of preference for Virgin Atlantic have not solely been driven by the on-board service experience (see Figure 21).

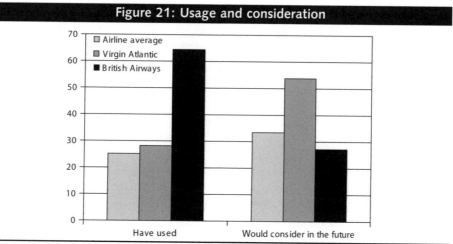

Figure 21: Usage and consideration

Source: CIAO, May 2007. Total sample 2000 adults 16+

Figure 22 illustrates the value consumers place on this brand preference, Virgin Atlantic exceeding the airline average on 'worth paying a bit extra'.

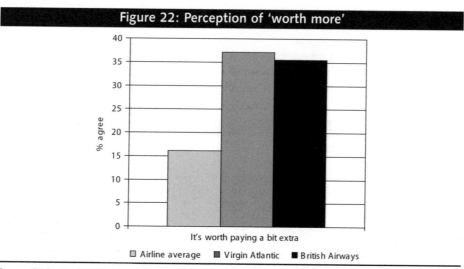

Figure 22: Perception of 'worth more'

Source: CIAO, May 2007. Total sample 2000 adults 16+

Based on BAV and CIAO research, it can be seen that brand preference has increased over the period and Virgin Atlantic now proudly wears the mantle of being Britain's favourite airline. Tracking helps demonstrate what role communications have played in this change.

Analysing preference scores[14] going back to the early days of the Helen Mirren campaign in 1996 right up to 'Kitty Hawk' in 2006 there have been considerable shifts pre and post advertising (see Table 1).

Table 1: Increase in brand preference post advertising

Campaign	Increase (%pt increase)	Pre and post dip dates (sample size)	Tracker statement & tracking company
Helen Mirren (1996–1997)	+ 12 ***	Pre Nov/Dec 96 (250) Post Sep/Oct (502)	One airline I would personally prefer to fly with (source Critical Research)
Spies (1999–2000)	+ 6	Pre Oct 1999 (299) Post April 2000 (305)	Increase in Virgin Atlantic brand preference (source Consumer insight)
Big Seat I (2000)	+ 9 *	Pre Sep 2000 (200) Post Nov 2000 (200)	Increase in Virgin Atlantic brand preference (source Consumer Insight)
Beauty Sleep (2004)	+ 4	Pre May 2004 (300) Post June 2004 (300)	Increase in Virgin Atlantic brand preference (source HPI)
Kitty Hawk (2006)	+ 15 ***	Pre Mar 2006 (74) Post June 2006 (253)	Increase in favourite airline and one I would consider (source Hall & Partners)

* p=90%　*** p=99%

Virgin Atlantic communications have been more efficient at driving preference than British Airways'

Analysing the relationship between communications and preference over the past 22 months of continuous tracking, it can be seen that Virgin Atlantic communications have worked three times harder than British Airways' at driving preference per £1m spent (see Figure 23).

Based on all the evidence presented so far we can see that highly visible communications have impacted image associations, strengthening 'Virginness' over time. Evidence would suggest that this had led to an increase in brand preference,

Figure 23: Efficiency at driving preference per £1m spent

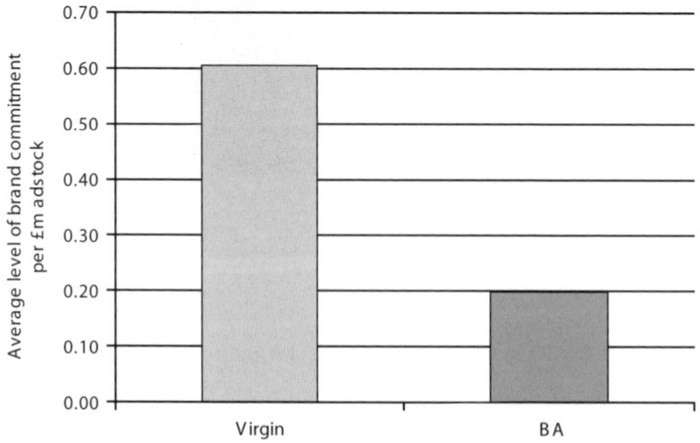

Source: Addynamix/Hall and Partners

today making Virgin Atlantic Britain's favourite airline. This is summarised in our communications model below (see Figure 24).

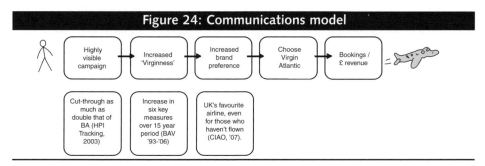

Figure 24: Communications model

Over the next few sections we will analyse the effect this has had at a business level.

Brand preference correlates with market share

Load factor (percentage filled seats on an aircraft) is one way of measuring share in the industry. Based on analysis of routes that Virgin Atlantic flies,[15] it is possible to see a correlation between indexed load factor and brand preference (see Figure 25). Assuming that fares are quickly matched by competitors (which does appear to be the case), this suggests that increasing the 'attractiveness' of the brand has some impact on market share.

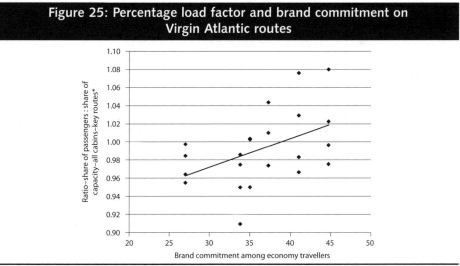

Figure 25: Percentage load factor and brand commitment on Virgin Atlantic routes

Source: IATA/CAA/Hall & Partners

This is supported by analysis showing the key drivers of choice in the airline market. Figure 26 shows that, although structural and functional factors are dominant, almost a third of consumers state 'airline brand name/reputation' as a key influencer.

Figure 26: Drivers of choice in air travel for leisure and business passengers

Leisure

Price	
Direct flight	
Convenience of UK airport	
Convenient flight times/schedule	
On-board experience (ex. staff)	
Service standards of airline staff	
Punctuality	
Airline brand name/reputation	

0 10 20 30 40 50 60 70 80 90
% agree

Business

Direct flight	
Price	
Convenience of UK airport	
Convenient flight times/schedule	
On-board experience (ex. staff)	
Punctuality	
Service standards of airline staff	
Frequent flyer programme	
Airline brand name/reputation	

0 10 20 30 40 50 60
% agree

Source: Harris, 2007

Virgin Atlantic business has grown

Over the past 15 years, Virgin Atlantic has secured its position as a premier-league airline competing successfully alongside national carriers from all over the world.

Both passenger numbers and turnover have increased since 1993, demonstrating the growth of the business in volume and value terms (see Figures 27 and 28).

Market share can be looked at only by route since at an overall level airlines with more routes will automatically have higher share. Moreover it is only on these routes that consumers have a 'like-for-like' choice that Virgin Atlantic hoped to influence.

Figure 29 shows share on four Virgin Atlantic routes selected for their geographical diversity. It can be seen that, on the whole, Virgin Atlantic has made gains while British Airways has remained flat or declined since 1997.

While structural factors can take much of the responsibility for these gains, in the next section we will demonstrate that communications, while secondary, have nevertheless played an impressive role.

Figure 27: Virgin Atlantic annual passengers flown, 1984–2006

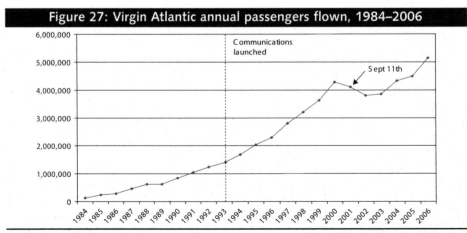

Source: Virgin Atlantic

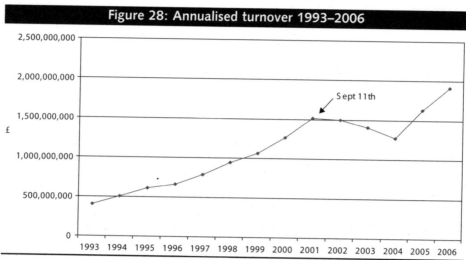

Figure 28: Annualised turnover 1993–2006

Source: Virgin Atlantic

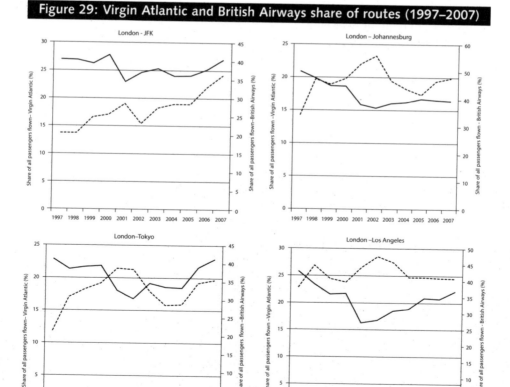

Figure 29: Virgin Atlantic and British Airways share of routes (1997–2007)

Source: Virgin Atlantic

Isolating the contribution of communications

Approach to econometric modelling

Modelling was conducted over a 41-month period and based on bookings as the closest indication of consumer preference.[16] It was constructed in a way that accounted for all influencing factors such as capacity, product and service innovation, seasonality, price, promotions, events, news stories and communications.

In recognition of differences in response between the three cabin classes[17] and of the various channels through which a flight can be booked, we chose to build a suite of models. This allowed us to accurately identify not only how Virgin Atlantic's advertising works but also where it works. For each cabin we modelled bookings through three separate channels: those that come through Virgin's own call centre; its website; and, finally, 'indirect' bookings, i.e. bookings through third parties.[18] This led to a total of nine models.

Contribution of communications to bookings

Amalgamating the nine models, it can be seen that advertising delivered a total of 522,297 bookings over the 41-month period modelled. This equated to:

- 407,894 in Economy
- 46,094 in Premium Economy
- 68,309 in Upper Class.

As would be expected, the majority of incremental bookings were driven in Economy Class, which accounts for the highest capacity. However, as a percentage of total bookings by cabin, communications had the greatest impact in the premium cabins (see Figure 30).

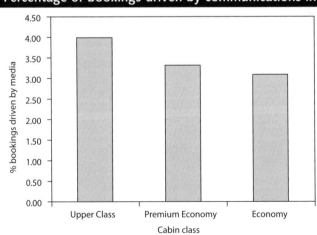

Figure 30: Percentage of bookings driven by communications in each cabin

Source: Brand Science

Evidence of halo effect across cabins

Econometric evidence illustrates the benefit of the strategy at a cross-cabin level with activity having a halo effect between audiences.

In almost every case, advertising for each of Virgin's cabins generates positive halo effects within one or more of the other cabins. A good example is the effect of Upper Class advertising on Premium Economy bookings. Effectively, Upper Class advertising leads potential Premium Economy passengers to upgrade to the comforts of Upper Class. Since Upper Class bookings tend to yield several times more revenue than Premium Economy, this is a rare case of 'positive' cannibalisation. Looking in the other direction we find no evidence of Premium Economy advertising leading to a fall in Upper Class bookings (see Table 2).

Table 2: Incremental bookings driven by advertising across different cabins

| Bookings driven, 2004–2007 (2007 ytd) | | Cabin bookings | | |
Advertising focus		Economy	Premium Economy	Upper Class
	Economy	197,011	52,875	22,337
	Premium Economy	4,255	18,997	0
	Upper Class	46,698	−30,006*	44,152

Source: Brand Science Network, 2007

Reduced impact of British Airways on Virgin Atlantic revenue

The modelling also demonstrates the reduced impact of British Airways communication on Virgin Atlantic revenue over time.

While BA's spend has varied significantly from year to year,[19] the revenue per £1 of BA spend that Virgin Atlantic has lost as a direct result has consistently reduced (see Figure 31).

Figure 31: Revenue lost as a result of British Airways advertising

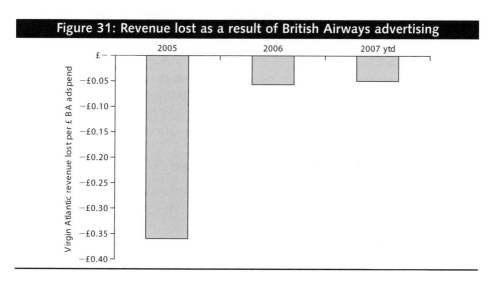

In summary, econometric modelling estimates that 522,297 bookings have been generated as a result of communications over a 41-month period. Although Premium cabins have shown the greatest percentage increases, the highest volume has come from Economy. Activity has been shown to halo across cabins, and British Airways' reduced dominance in the market is evidenced.

Other factors

While all the major influencers are accounted for in the modelling, there are two additional factors that warrant further exploration.

The Branson effect

Richard Branson is a powerful brand in his own right. One could fairly question whether it is his personality, rather than advertising, that has given Virgin Atlantic the dominant presence and status it has acquired over the past 15 years.

There is no question that Richard Branson's influence has been, and remains, a positive influence on the Virgin Atlantic brand. Indeed the distinctive advertising tone of voice that has consistently helped build the brand over the last 15 years was deliberately based on the Branson image and persona.

However, Branson has been a consistent presence throughout the Virgin Atlantic brand's 24-year history, which does not explain the gains the brand has made in the last 15 years. And, although he remains one of the leading entrepreneurs of his time, even Branson is not an absolute guarantee of success. For all the successes of the Virgin empire there remain some exceptions.

What about the Virgin Group?

At the time of writing there are 25 Virgin brands registered in the UK.[20] In building a case for the effectiveness of Virgin Atlantic communications it is important to explore the role sister companies might be playing in the brand's success. To help understand this, Virgin Group has been running tracking research since November 2000.

Looking across the different Virgin Group companies, for both users and non-users, the research shows that, at the time, Virgin Atlantic was the greatest net contributor to the parent brand by some margin (see Figure 32).

Virgin Atlantic is also a major contributor to the Virgin attitude, over-indexing versus the average on key attributes that define the parent brand (see Figure 33).

Based on this evidence it would seem more appropriate to quantify the value Virgin Atlantic communications have had on the rest of the Virgin Group, rather than the other way round.

The value of building 'Virginness' for Virgin Atlantic

To estimate the return on investment in communications we have considered the payback over three timescales:

1. econometric modelling period
2. over 15 years of communications
3. wider campaign value.

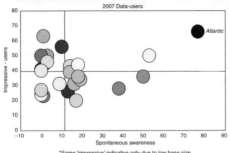
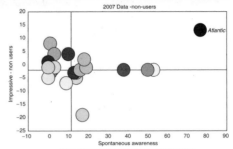

Figure 32: Contribution of group companies to the Virgin brand (spontaneous awareness and impressiveness)

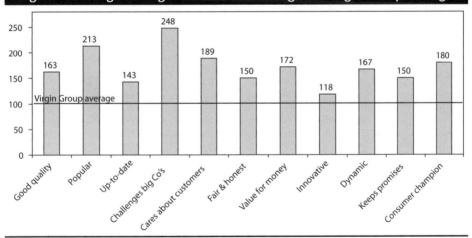

Figure 33: Image of Virgin Atlantic indexed against Virgin Group average

Source: Virgin Management Tracking, HPI, 2007 (Total sample = 2000)

Econometric modelling period

Taking an average revenue generated per booking by cabin, the total revenue return over the 41-month period is £320.8m. The total investment in marketing communications, including production, over the same time frame was £28.9m.[21] Based on these figures the revenue ROI over the modelling period is £10.76 for every £1 invested (see Table 3).

This revenue ROI figure is more than six times the size of the figure estimated for British Airways in the 2004 IPA Effectiveness Awards (see Figure 34).[22]

Revenue contribution is a more appropriate measure of effectiveness for the airline industry because of the high level of fixed costs in the market (estimated at more than 90% by Virgin Atlantic). As such, a measure of profitability would be more a reflection of the airline's operational efficiency than the advertising's

Table 3: Revenue ROI between 2005 and 2007			
Period	Total media spend (£m)	Bookings driven by advertising	Revenue driven by advertising	Revenue ROI (£)
2005	4,960	52,797	54,417,376	10.97
2006	10,786	201,845	103,426,321	9.59
2007 ytd*	5,488	264,017	154,702,819	28.19

*ytd, yet to be determined.

Figure 34: Revenue ROI for Virgin Atlantic compared with British Airways

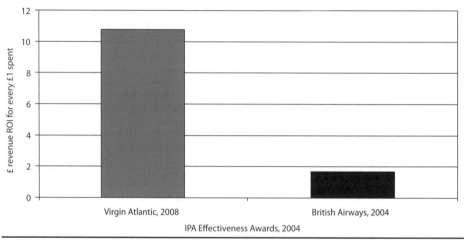

Source: IPA Effectiveness Awards, 2004

effectiveness. This precedent had been set in the British Airways 2004 IPA Effectiveness paper.

Fifteen-year campaign period

The approach to communications has remained relatively consistent over the last 15 years. Therefore, it is reasonable to assume that advertising will have worked in a similar way over this time.

Based on this assumption we are able to estimate the potential revenue return over the full campaign period using a back-casting methodology.

Taking the annual breakdown of media spend against each cabin class between 1993 and 2003 we have estimated, using learning from the model, the total number of bookings generated over the period, accounting for seasonality, world events, competitive activity, and so on.

While not an exact science, this does produce a reasonably robust estimate over the 15-year campaign. Total bookings are estimated at 1.79m, generating a total revenue of £728.3m. With a total of £77.1m media investment and a 15% allowance for production, this then leads to a revenue ROI of £8.22 (see Table 4).

Table 4: Estimated incremental revenue driven by communications since 1993

Year	Annualised Virgin Atlantic turnover (£m)	Economy	Adspend (£m) Premium Economy	Upper Class	Economy	Estimated revenue driven (£m) Premium Economy	Upper Class	Total
1993	400.9	0.000	0.000	1.674	0.000	0.000	16.431	16.431
1994	503.4	0.000	0.000	2.441	0.000	0.000	20.632	20.632
1995	608.4	0.000	0.086	2.549	0.000	0.068	24.120	24.189
1996	660.0	0.004	0.002	4.909	0.018	0.001	27.015	27.034
1997	785.1	0.956	0.001	5.427	4.027	0.001	27.353	31.381
1998	942.3	1.637	0.006	3.330	10.628	0.004	25.861	36.493
1999	1,066.6	0.958	0.004	7.959	3.925	0.001	39.001	42.927
2000	1,267.6	0.000	0.777	6.151	0.000	0.489	46.125	46.614
2001	1,517.5	0.000	0.400	5.231	0.000	0.371	57.773	58.145
2002	1,499.8	0.029	1.429	3.883	0.280	1.381	44.686	46.346
2003	1,401.2	0.030	0.006	2.046	0.690	0.015	56.424	57.128

Wider value of communications

Communications has been shown to have delivered a revenue ROI over the 41 months of econometric modelling and full payback over 15 years has been estimated by back-casting. But, arguably, the true worth of communications in this case goes beyond the scope of this paper.

When Branson sold a 49% stake in Virgin Atlantic to Singapore Airlines in 1999 the £600m price tag was in part a reflection of the strength of the brand. Given the vital role communications have played in building 'Virginness', at least some part of this should be attributed to the campaign.

As one of the flagships of the Virgin Group, leading the rest of the Virgin brands on awareness and impressiveness, the contribution of Virgin Atlantic communications to the Virgin brand is indisputable. What value this has driven for sister companies over the last 15 years is impossible to measure.

Now as Virgin Atlantic enters a new era of increased competition with the launch of the Open Skies agreement, the brand will be one of the key assets to help it compete in this new arena, ensuring that it remains a key player in long-haul air travel.

Summary

This story of Virgin Atlantic exemplifies the value of building a brand in a market of fierce competition and limitations.

Through a consistent and impactful tone of voice, communications have achieved greater cut-through than British Airways, helping compensate for the disparity in media spend.

Fifteen years of creativity have helped build a clear sense of 'Virginness' into the Atlantic brand. This in turn has helped drive brand preference, at a rate three times more efficient than British Airways, making Virgin Atlantic Britain's favourite airline today.

This strength of brand preference has helped ensure Virgin Atlantic is the brand of choice when consumers are faced with a comparable offer, and brand share has grown accordingly.

Figure 35: The Virgin Atlantic story

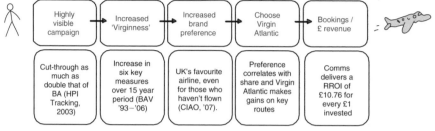

Today, Virgin Atlantic is Britain's favourite airline. And this brand preference has been one of the key assets that have helped Virgin Atlantic break the stranglehold of its once apparently unassailable rival British Airways.

Notes

1. Virgin is the most admired brand in the UK when asked spontaneously. HPI Tracking, 2007 (2000 adults).
2. Source: Mintel, 1991.
3. Air Europe collapsed in March 1991 and Dan-Air was widely reported to be on the verge of liquidation.
4. Virgin Atlantic pitch document, 1993.
5. Enjoying a 20% share of voice.
6. BAV was launched in 1993 and is the world's largest brand database. In the UK it covers roughly 1,500 brands with a sample of over 3,500. The most recent wave of data is from 2006. Given the comparative nature of the data it is not possible to show statistical significance on shifts over time.
7. Tracking was only conducted for TV activity on a regular basis.
8. It ran for six weeks.
9. Critical Research Ltd, November/December 1996 (250).
10. Critical Research Ltd, September/October 1997 (162).
11. Virgin Atlantic has never been far from the limelight and as such had 54% unaided awareness (top two mentions) versus BA's 87% back in 1993. Its position relative to British Airways has since improved (BAV).
12. This is done by comparing the image associations of those people with weak preference, 'one of several I would consider', with those people who have strong preference, 'prefer to use'. The relative agreement with each image attribute can be used to determine to what degree it relates with preference.
13. 'Prefer to use' was added to the questionnaire only in 2000.
14. Preference is asked in a slightly different way across different tracking studies. These are stated in Table 1.
15. To include non-Virgin Atlantic routes would grossly distort the figures given its relatively small share of the market.
16. January 2004 to May 2007.
17. Economy, Premium Economy and Upper Class.
18. For example travel agents and aggregators.
19. See Figure 1.
20. See www.virgin.com.
21. We have allocated a budget that equates to 15% of total media spend for production although actual figures are considerably lower than this.
22. Winning Silver.

Other companies involved in campaign: Media company: Manning Gottlieb OMD; Other company: Brand Science

Chapter 22

Waitrose

David vs Goliath: the rematch

  By Andy Nairn and Mary Tucker, Miles Calcraft Briginshaw Duffy

Editor's summary

In 2002, Waitrose won an IPA Effectiveness Award for its 'Quality food, honestly priced' campaign. However, soon afterwards all the main supermarkets started to move in on Waitrose's territory, with greater activity behind their premium own-label ranges. Going directly up against the might of Tesco, Sainsbury and a renewed M&S, demanded Waitrose build upon their strategy. And that's exactly what they did, marrying quality with ethics, a stance that other supermarkets would be slow to follow.

Using an evolved and integrated campaign across TV, radio, press and in-store media the campaign set out to position Waitrose as an ethical company as well as a retailer of fine foods.

The campaign highlighted Waitrose's partnerships with, and support for, farmers and fisherman in the UK and around the world, helping ensure you have the best food available.

Against a backdrop of increased competitor activity, Waitrose was able to enhance key perceptions around its quality and integrity, increasing customer penetration and transactions as it did so.

Delivering £111 million in incremental profits across the life of the campaign has meant significant return on marketing investment, proving that an ethical approach can be financially rewarding too.

Introduction

In 2002, Waitrose won an IPA Award with a paper entitled 'David versus four Goliaths'.[1]

But unlike the biblical tale, it turned out there was a sequel to this story. And in this latest instalment, the giants would come back stronger than ever.

Our paper[2] tells what happened next:

- how Waitrose evolved its winning strategy, rather than discarding it altogether
- how this shift saw off the grocery giants once more, against all the odds
- and how communications played their part, to the tune of £111m incremental profits over six years and an ROI of £5.05 per £1 spent.

Background – a recap of the 2002 paper

The 2002 IPA paper dealt with the period 1997–2001, and told how advertising had helped Waitrose defend a profitable niche in the face of tough competition from much larger rivals.

The strategy was based on an acknowledgement that many shoppers viewed Waitrose as unduly expensive. In reality, this was an unfair perception, since Waitrose merely offered superior products at an appropriately premium price. However, since consumers tended to define value in relatively simplistic terms ('low cost') and because competitive communications reinforced this, the impression stuck.

Faced with this challenge, Waitrose set out to redefine the value equation, by emphasising that it actually offered 'Quality food, honestly priced'.

At first, it dramatised this idea via a press campaign, which celebrated the quality of individual products and the great value they offered, using classy photography. Unusually, the advertising never actually showed the product itself (see Figure 1).

Figure 1: Launch

Then, after three years, the retailer extended this approach to TV, with a series of equally persuasive commercials (see Figure 2).

Figure 2: Launch

The results were impressive: over five years, quality perceptions rose, price concerns receded, and footfall and basket size increased. Using a mixture of econometrics and other analyses, the campaign's contribution to topline sales was estimated to be £43.75m.

2002–2003 – continued success

Over the next two years, Waitrose stuck with its winning formula.

The press campaign became a well-established favourite of customers and awards juries alike,[3] chalking up 50 executions by the end of 2003. Meanwhile, the retailer increased its use of TV, again to popular and critical acclaim[4] (see Figure 3).

Figure 3: 2003

More importantly, as the campaign wore in, sales and market share increased and brand image steadily improved.[5]

To cap it all, two major competitors – Sainsbury's and M&S – seemed permanently in the doldrums,[6] while two other Goliaths – Tesco and Asda – were concentrating on non-food sales.[7]

With an increased budget (see Figure 4), all seemed well in the world of Waitrose and its advertising.

Figure 4: 2002–2003 media laydown

	2002												2003											
	J	F	M	A	M	J	J	A	S	O	N	D	J	F	M	A	M	J	J	A	S	O	N	D
TV																								
Press																								
Radio																								

Gross media cost: £7.9m   Gross media cost: £8.6m

2004 onwards – the giants awake

By 2004, however, some new challenges began to emerge.

The year started with Morrisons' takeover of Safeway, creating a new grocery giant to be reckoned with – one that immediately positioned itself as standing for 'a passion and flair for food retailing'.[8] Subsequent advertising was very reminiscent of the Waitrose campaign.

Then, in March, Sainsbury's appointed a new Chief Executive, Justin King. He soon pledged to 'Make Sainsbury's great again' by delivering 'Great food at fair prices'.[9] A proposition not a million miles away from Waitrose's long-established endline.

Next, M&S unveiled Stuart Rose as its new boss. He, too, stated that a core part of his revival strategy would be to 'emphasise the quality and uniqueness of our food'.[10] As we all know, he subsequently delivered on this promise.

On top of all this, Tesco was now revisiting its approach to food, prompted by the runaway success of its top-end Finest range.[11]

As the analysts at Verdict noted:

Tesco, Asda and even Morrisons have been stretching their offers upmarket and bolstering premium and fresh ranges in 2004. Waitrose will by no means have everything its own way – should fortunes at M&S, and/or Sainsbury's improve, it will find itself needing to fight harder for profitable sales growth.[12]

In short, the giants of grocery were regrouping and heading straight for Waitrose's territory. Not only that, they were spending ever greater sums on communications,[13] so that Waitrose's share of voice was smaller than ever.[14]

In mid-2004, Waitrose appointed MCBD to address these new challenges.[15]

We realised that we could not hope to meet this attack head on. Instead, we needed to find a new way of reasserting what made Waitrose special.

Our strategic solution – emphasising ethics

We needed to tread carefully as all indicators suggested the existing approach remained broadly effective. In particular, research showed that the overarching campaign idea – 'quality food, honestly priced' – remained valid. We just needed to hone the definition of quality, so that it remained distinctive in the new environment described above.

To this end, we noted that Waitrose's commitment to quality was not just a passing fad or an advertising invention: it stemmed from its unique ownership structure and business model. You see, unlike other supermarkets, Waitrose is a partnership, co-owned by its employees. What's more, this partnership is governed by a constitution (first formalised in 1928), which explicitly states that Waitrose must 'conduct all of its business relationships with integrity … and contribute to the wellbeing of the communities where it operates'. This in turn creates a structural commitment to long-term supplier relationships, small producers and local specialities.

In short, we discerned that Waitrose was not just a retailer of fine foods but a company of fine principles. If we could forge a link between the two elements – quality and ethics – we could guide the brand positioning into a highly motivating territory where the bigger players could not touch us. We defined this added value territory as '*food you can feel good about*'.

Marketing Week devoted its front cover and lead story to the new strategy, hailing it as a 'wise move',[16] while *Marketing* magazine also commented that 'Waitrose's positioning is spot on'.[17]

Our creative approach

We now needed to evolve our creative approach, in line with the strategy above. In TV, this meant setting our product quality stories within a bigger, ethical picture.

For instance, we sold citrus fruit by highlighting Waitrose's support for the South African farmers who grow them (see Figure 5). Likewise, we promoted pork and sausages by emphasising that Waitrose sources them from British pig farmers who conform to the highest standards of animal husbandry (see Figure 6). Similarly, we talked about our British fresh vegetables by explaining that they are bought only from farmers who leave extra wide margins in their fields, to encourage wildlife (see Figure 7). And we supported the fish range by emphasising that Waitrose refuses to sell any fresh fish from unsustainable waters (see Figure 8). Most recently, we publicly expressed our backing for the British farming industry during the 2007 foot-and-mouth outbreak (see Figure 9).

As you'd expect from Waitrose, all the work was beautifully crafted. Or, as one reviewer put it in *Campaign*:

> *Why can't all commercials be like this? It makes you want to record the ads, not avoid them.*[18]

The evolution was perhaps even more marked in print, where we replaced the familiar visual-led campaign (ideal for telling simple product USP stories) with a long-copy approach (better for explaining the bigger picture about Waitrose's way

Figure 5: Citrus fruit TV ad

Female VO: One supermarket has a unique recipe for turning South African citrus fruit into training colleges and crèches.

They simply return a slice of their profits to the workers who grew the fruit.

Here's one they prepared earlier.

South African Satsumas, £1.99/kg

Waitrose. Quality food, honestly priced.

Figure 6: Sausages TV ad

Female VO: The pork and sausages from one supermarket always come from British farmers …

and their pigs always sleep on soft straw.

No wonder they were voted Compassionate Supermarket of the Year.

Waitrose. Quality food, honestly priced.

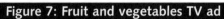

Figure 7: Fruit and vegetables TV ad

Female VO: One supermarket only buys its ...

conventional British fresh fruit and veg
from farmers ...

who leave extra wide field margins
to encourage wildlife.

English Onions 59p/kg

Waitrose. Quality food, honestly priced.

Figure 8: Fish TV ad

Captions: No Bluefin Tuna. No Atlantic Halibut. No Wild Atlantic Salmon. No North Sea Cod.

Female VO: One supermarket refuses to sell any fresh fish from unsustainable waters.

Not only that, they're also protecting another endangered species – their Billingsgate-trained specialists.

Helping you choose from a wider range of sustainable fish …

than any other supermarket.

Waitrose. Quality food, honestly priced.

Figure 9: British farming TV ad

Female VO: Through good times ...   and not so good times,

We have always supported the toughest breed of all: the British farmer.

Figure 10: Press

Paulina's Avocados,
£1.19 each

Mark's Organic Crimini Mushrooms,
£2.59/250g

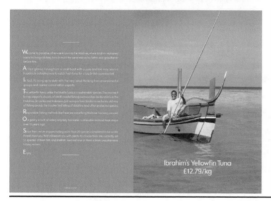

Ibrahim's Yellowfin Tuna
£12.79/kg

Duncan's Bulford Milk Ice Cream,
from £3.95/500ml

of doing business). In particular, we used press to highlight our support for small, local suppliers and producers (see Figure 10).

Research suggested that this blend of product and principle was highly motivating:

> Good treatment of farmers and livestock is seen as right in itself and advantageous because the food will taste better (e.g. unstressed pigs); fair trade and fair pricing means suppliers don't cut corners and instead make a little extra effort, resulting in nice food: everyone wins.[19]

Our channel strategy[20]

TV remains a fantastic channel for long-term, brand-building communications. We have therefore continued to use it as our main medium, maintaining our strategy of buying long-second-length spots in premium airtime across our core regions.[21]

However, since the 2002 paper, we have also pioneered the use of i-TV; for instance, we have used it to explain more about our support for the farmers of South Africa. Moreover, in 2007 we launched our first foray into ad-funded programming, with a show on the Uktv Food Channel: *The Market Kitchen*.[22]

While TV is great for broadcasting the big ethical theme, press is perfect for telling the human stories in more detail. Here, the challenge is to rise above the retail clutter, so we hand-select premium positions in a tightly defined set of weekend supplements and quality magazines, again focused on our southern heartland.[23] Unusually, we buy only double-page spreads as we believe that the extra impact gained more than makes up for the loss of frequency. As with TV, we are also experimenting with branded content; for example, we have recently launched a standalone magazine promoting the ethical sourcing of fish.[24]

The year 2007 saw our first concerted foray into direct marketing (previously we used direct communication on an ad hoc basis).[25] Direct mail supported the TV campaigns, providing greater detail and customer incentives. We also explored tactical email marketing to generate customer interaction with the Waitrose brand both in branch and on Waitrose.com.

Naturally, we follow through our advertised themes in-store via poster boards, shelf barkers and panels (see Figure 11), as well as events, such as Meet the Farmer, whereby local farmers are invited into stores to meet customers and talk about their products.

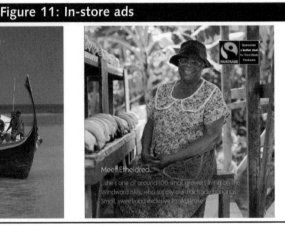

Figure 11: In-store ads

We also use online (where we can explain even more about the ethical subject matter) and our publications, notably *Waitrose Food Illustrated*, which at the time of writing is spearheading a 'Save our Bacon' campaign, in support of British pig farmers (see Figure 12).

Crucially, we ensure that Waitrose staff are well versed in the big issues we're communicating, by sending each store a 'branch pack' of educational DVDs, posters and leaflets, prior to each new piece of activity. The celebrities featured in our advertising are Waitrose staff, so the finished work is highly anticipated.

Likewise, we're always looking for new ways to engage people with the brand. Indeed, in 2006, an idea for using advertorials to support local suppliers won first prize in a national media competition, and £150K worth of free space to boot.[26]

Radio is the only strand that takes a more promotional tack, but even here the tone of voice is very much in keeping with the rest of the brand. Our activity can be summarised as follows (see Figure 13).

Figure 12: Supporting British pig farmers

Figure 13: 2004–2007 media

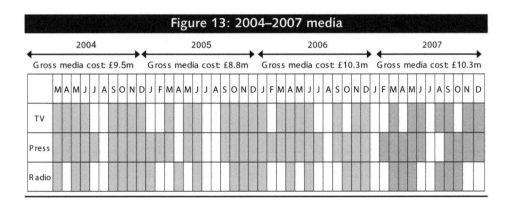

Topline business results

Since the last IPA paper, Waitrose sales have continued to rise impressively, reaching £3.95 billion in 2007 – up 63% on 2002 (see Figure 14). At the time of writing, sales are up a further 8% in 2008.[27]

On a like-for-like basis, the success story is equally clear, recording positive growth figures, year after year (see Figure 15).

Thus, despite all the competitive pressure outlined above, Waitrose has actually outperformed the market, gaining share each year (see Figure 16). Significantly, given the campaign strategy, Waitrose share of Fairtrade and organics is much higher (at 9% and 18% respectively).[28]

Likewise, Waitrose has consistently grown its profits, making £291m in 2007 – almost double the figure achieved in 2002 (see Figure 17).

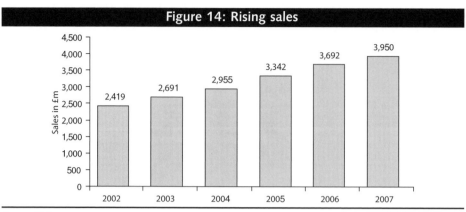

Figure 14: Rising sales

Source: Waitrose

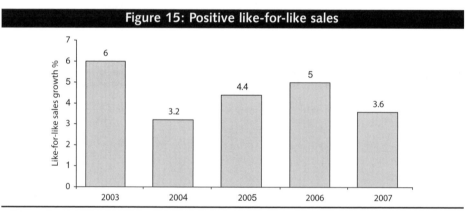

Figure 15: Positive like-for-like sales

Source: Waitrose

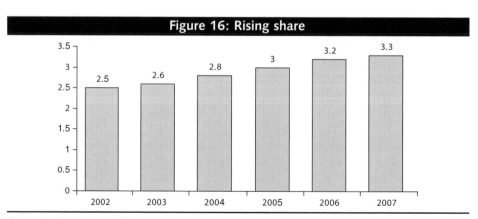

Figure 16: Rising share

Source: Verdict, Grocery Retailers report, 2008

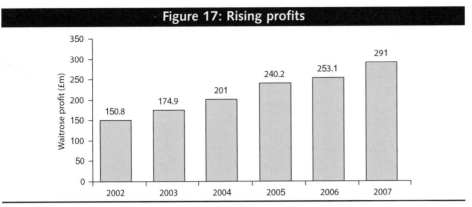

Figure 17: Rising profits

Source: Waitrose

City analysts have already hailed these results as 'proof that Waitrose's advertising and marketing are connecting with the UK consumer'.[29] However, we will now go on to:

■ explain *how* communications have contributed to this success story
■ quantify this contribution
■ calculate a return on investment
■ eliminate other factors.

Explaining the campaign's contribution

First things first. The campaign became more and more impactful over time (Figure 18).

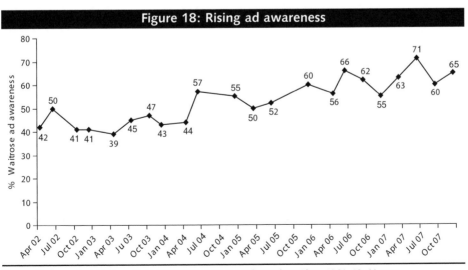

Figure 18: Rising ad awareness

Source: Consumer Insight. Base: Main grocery shoppers in London and Meridian, ABC1, 18–64 years

Likewise, the campaign's branding (which was already excellent, considerably above Consumer Insight's average of 50–55%) improved even further (see Figure 19).

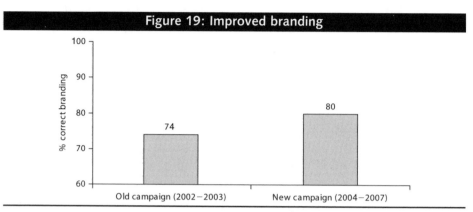

Figure 19: Improved branding

Source: Consumer Insight. Base: All aware of Waitrose advertising

This all happened against the backdrop of an aggressive hike in spend by the competition post-2004, while our spend remained more or less static (see Figure 20).

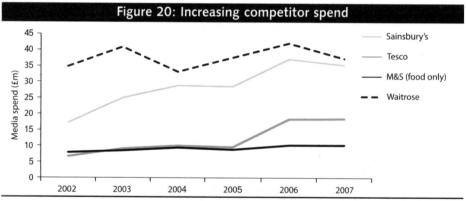

Figure 20: Increasing competitor spend

Source: Waitrose/MMS

As a result of all this, our *effective* share of voice rose, even though our *actual* share of voice declined (see Figure 21).

Crucially, the advertising wasn't just impactful and well branded: it worked powerfully to improve impressions of Waitrose.[30] Indeed its effectiveness at driving positive perceptions rose markedly over the period (see Figure 22).

In particular, the campaign continued to build the brand's core proposition of 'Quality food, honestly priced', despite rivals' attempts to move into the territory (see Figure 23).

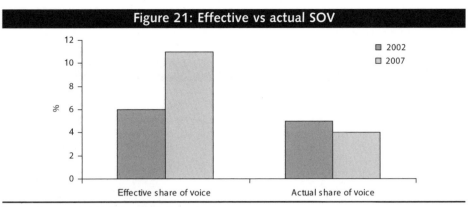

Figure 21: Effective vs actual SOV

Source: Consumer Insight, Nielsen Media Research

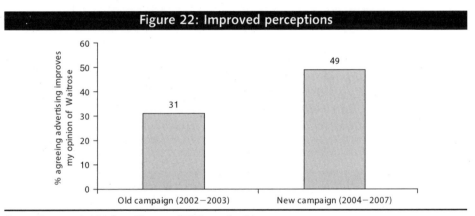

Figure 22: Improved perceptions

Source: Consumer Insight. Base: All aware of Waitrose advertising

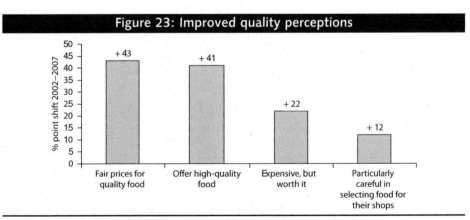

Figure 23: Improved quality perceptions

Source: Consumer Insight. Base: Main grocery shoppers in London and Meridian, ABC1, 18–64 years

On top of this, a broader appreciation of the company's ethical credentials started coming through strongly (see Figure 24).

Figure 24: Improved ethical perceptions

Source: Consumer Insight. Base: Main grocery shoppers in London and Meridian, ABC1, 18–64 years

To put all this into perspective, it's interesting to draw comparisons with the 2005 IPA Awards Grand Prix winner, Marks & Spencer. For while it's true that M&S has experienced a remarkable recovery, it's equally true that Waitrose has maintained its tight grip on customers' quality perceptions (see Figure 25).

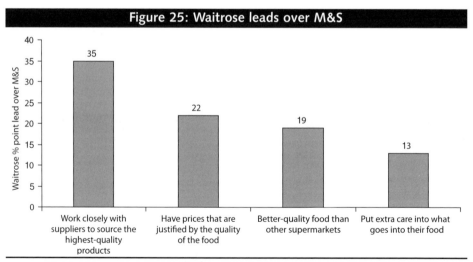

Figure 25: Waitrose leads over M&S

Source: Consumer Insight. Base: Main grocery shoppers in London and Meridian, ABC1, 18–64 years

Indeed, even among M&S shoppers, Waitrose is seen as the leader on most attributes, but especially on ethics (see Figure 26).

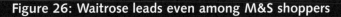

Figure 26: Waitrose leads even among M&S shoppers

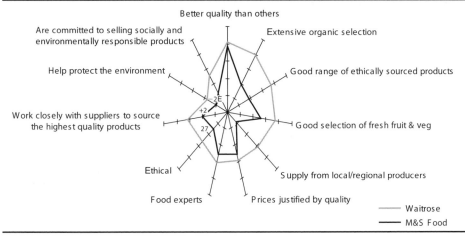

Better quality than others

Are committed to selling socially and environmentally responsible products

Extensive organic selection

Help protect the environment

Good range of ethically sourced products

Work closely with suppliers to source the highest quality products

Good selection of fresh fruit & veg

Ethical

Supply from local/regional producers

Food experts

Prices justified by quality

Waitrose
M&S Food

Source: Consumer Insight. Base: M&S shoppers in London and Meridian, ABC1, 18–64 years

So the campaign boosted brand impressions. But did it have any effect on shopping behaviour?

Well, the campaign certainly boosted intentions to shop at Waitrose, achieving highest ever persuasion scores, significantly above Consumer Insight's 'good average' of 25–30% (see Figure 27).

Figure 27: Improved intentions to shop at Waitrose

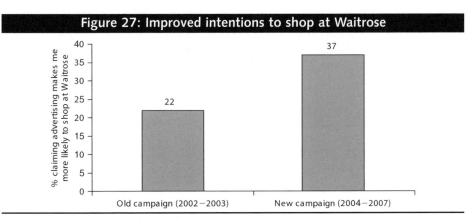

Source: Consumer Insight. Base: All aware of Waitrose advertising

And, sure enough, actual Waitrose penetration rose steadily over the campaign period (see Figure 28).

Likewise, transaction numbers increased (see Figure 29).

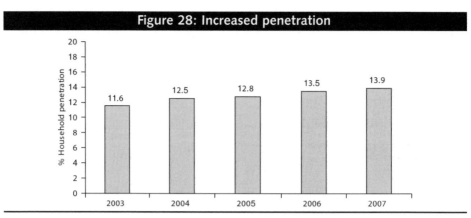

Figure 28: Increased penetration

Source: BMRB TGI. Base: All shopping at Waitrose in last year in advertised regions

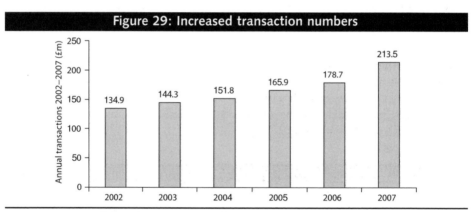

Figure 29: Increased transaction numbers

Source: Waitrose. N.B. All data refer to 52 weeks apart from 2003 (53 weeks)

In the words of Peter Carter, Chairman of Consumer Insight, Waitrose:

The result is a remarkable cumulative response to the campaign that has built over time to create a higher base level of advertising awareness, increasing positive opinion and a clear positioning for Waitrose.

Quantifying the effect of the campaign

We can isolate the campaign's contribution to this business success story by using TNS AdSum[31] – a tool that focuses on the contribution of TV advertising in particular. According to this methodology, the TV campaign alone has generated over £173m in incremental short-term sales since 2002 (see Figure 30).

These incremental sales have largely been gained through increasing the number of shopping visits[32] (see Figure 31).

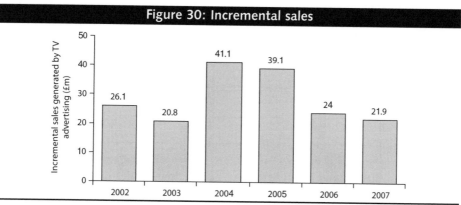

Figure 30: Incremental sales

Source: TNS AdSum

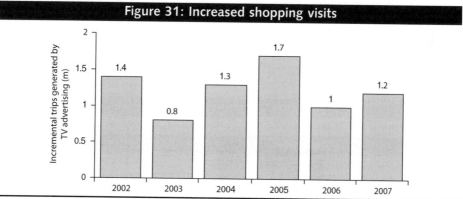

Figure 31: Increased shopping visits

Source: TNS AdSum

Return on investment

Short term

Using the TNS data on incremental sales generated by TV advertising, and applying a proxy margin of 32%,[33] we can calculate the short-term pay back of communications. As can be seen from Table 1, the 2002–2003 campaign comfortably paid for itself in the short term, and from 2004 onwards the evolved strategy has delivered an equally healthy return despite a far tougher competitive environment (see Table 2).

Table 1: Short-term ROI, 2002–2003	
Extra revenue generated 2002–2003	£46.9m
Gross margin @ 32%	£15m
TV campaign spend	£7.2m
Short-term ROI	£2.08 per £1 spent

Table 2: Short-term ROI, 2004–2007	
Extra revenue generated 2004–2007	£126.1m
Gross margin @ 32%	£40.4m
TV campaign spend	£20.2m
Short-term ROI	£2.00 per £1 spent

Medium term

However, this short-term payback is only a small part of the campaign's effectiveness. Indeed, a number of studies in the UK and the US estimate that advertising's effects over 12 months may be 2.5 times larger than the initial sales uplift.[34] Applying this rough ratio, we would see an even greater payback, without even considering the truly long-term picture (see Tables 3 and 4).

Table 3: Medium-term ROI, 2002–2003	
Immediate revenue generated 2002–2003	£46.9m
Medium term revenue × 2.5	£117.3m
Gross margin @ 32%	£37.5m
TV campaign spend	£7.2m
Medium-term ROI	£5.21 per £1 spent

Table 4: Medium-term ROI, 2004–2007	
Immediate revenue generated 2004–2007	£126.1m
Medium term revenue × 2.5	£315.3m
Gross margin @ 32%	£100.9m
TV campaign spend	£20.2m
Medium-term ROI	£5.00 per £1 spent

In other words, we estimate that around £111m incremental profits have been generated by TV advertising alone over the last six years (an ROI of £5.05 per £1 spent). This equates to 8.5% of the £1,311m profits that Waitrose has delivered over the period.

Accounting for other variables

Taking each of the '4Ps' in turn …

Product

We would be the first to acknowledge that Waitrose is a great place to shop.[35] However, perceptions of the shopping experience itself have remained relatively static at the same (very high) levels for the last six years.[36] This is certainly not a case of a poor product dramatically improving.

Price

Waitrose has stayed true to its policy of offering 'Quality food, honestly priced', over this period. It should already be clear from the above that the retailer's growth has come from increased quality perceptions, which in turn have improved perceptions of true value, rather than from slashing prices. But further proof of this is that average item price has not declined over the period.[37]

In fact, *The Grocer*'s Price Survey suggests that the pricing gap between Waitrose and other retailers was constant across 2006 and 2007 at least.[38]

Place

Waitrose has grown its estate significantly, especially by expanding beyond its southern heartland.[39] It is fair to say that this has been a major factor behind the business's overall growth. However, wherever possible we have used data sources that eliminate the effects of this geographical expansion. For instance, we have cited:

- like-for-like sales, which eliminate sales from stores opened in the previous 12 months
- tracking data from mature regions only (London and Meridian)
- TNS AdSum data, which are again based on core, advertised regions, and take store visits and split them out by ad-exposed and non-exposed, to isolate the advertising effect and minimising the effect from new store openings.

Promotion

Finally, we should re-emphasise that Waitrose's advertising share of voice has decreased over the period: this is not a case of a brand spending its way out of trouble.[40] And again, by using TNS AdSum data (which strip out the effects of in-store promotions), we can be confident that an increased presence at point of purchase was not responsible either.

Other effects

While the nature of an IPA paper requires us to focus on the financial return generated for Waitrose, we should emphasise that this campaign has also benefited the world at large. From raising funds for African farmers,[41] through protecting British wildlife,[42] to helping local suppliers,[43] our campaign will have 'longer and broader' effects that will last longer than any ad campaign.

Recruitment

There are many high-calibre people who have worked at Waitrose for some time and in recent years more have been attracted to Waitrose, often citing the advertising as a compelling reason to join. One Partner who has worked at Waitrose for nearly three years said 'Waitrose ads have a really warm feel to them and made me want to be part of it.'[44]

Partner bonus

All Waitrose Partners are awarded an annual bonus proportionate to their salary. The bonus has risen consistently since their award of 8% in 2002 – up to 20% in 2007. Naturally, much of their fortune directly results from their own hard work; however, we believe that through our contribution of circa 8.5% of profits, we helped in a small way to increase the amount they were rewarded.

Partner morale

Partners are informed about and (literally) involved in the development of the advertising. Each year an annual survey is conducted, which shows that Partners' feeling of inclusion has strengthened over time:[45] again, however small, we believe we've played a part. In the words of David Parkin, Branch Manager, who was thrilled his Partners featured in an ad: 'They are hugely proud of their branch and they want to show it off and to be shown off.'[46]

Ethical and environmental impact

Perhaps one of our most wide-reaching effects has been our influence over the competition, as our communication style and message have been widely copied. For instance in 2007, *Marketing* magazine noted that:

> Sainsbury's latest activity ... extolling the supermarket's local sourcing ... will leave viewers with a distinct feeling of déjà vu ... [and] prompt a double-take from many a viewer expecting the ad to be from Waitrose, which has pinned its strategy on local provenance for many years.[47]

Instead of feeling put out by others' adoption of our territory, we are thrilled that the companies involved have started to take seriously those subjects we have believed important for decades. After all, the sustainability of our planet and people's livelihoods within it considerably outweigh any battle over four-week like-for-likes!

New learnings

It is often claimed that 'marketing has never been more ethically driven'.[48] And yet in the entire IPA database of over a thousand papers, only one other advertiser has described a successful, ethically driven campaign.[49] We believe that our case study can therefore serve as a pioneering, textbook example in what seems to be an increasingly important field.

In particular, we would offer three pointers for marketers considering an ethical approach:

1. Ethical marketing must be rooted in organisational fact, rather than advertising sound bite: actions always speak louder than words.
2. Ethical marketing must be viewed as a long-term commitment, not as a passing fad.
3. Ethical marketing still requires a good product to succeed, and can't disguise a poor one.

In conclusion

Waitrose was a latecomer to advertising, only beginning in 1997 at the ripe old age of 93. But since then it has emerged as a champion of long-term, brand-building communications.

'Quality food, honestly priced' is now the longest-running campaign idea in the grocery category.[50]

And, more importantly, Waitrose's run of sales, share and profit gains is now one of the longest in retail. In the words of the Verdict retail analysts:

> The company has built a long-lasting, successful strategy in a market that has grown increasingly competitive. Going forward, Waitrose needs to continue its long-standing strategy communicating the benefits of its brand to justify its premium price positioning.[51]

All of which proves, once again, that a dedicated David can still outsmart Goliath.

Notes

1. The 2002 paper (which won a Silver award) was written by Waitrose's previous agency, Bank Hoggins O'Shea FCB.
2. The current paper was originally entered in the 2007 IPA Effectiveness Awards, for agencies with an income below £20m. Here it won a Gold award. We have significantly updated the paper, to take into account our 2007 campaign, with new sales, share, tracking and modelling data.
3. Banks Hoggins O'Shea FCB's press campaign was named Consumer Magazine Campaign of 2002, by the PPA and also won a Campaign Press Silver in 2002, Best National Press Campaign in 2002 and 2003 at the Grocery Advertising Awards, and D&AD Best Consumer Magazine Ad in 2003.
4. The TV campaign won Best TV in the 2002 Grocery Advertising Awards and took the top Marketing Communications prize in the Marketing Society Awards the same year.
5. See results section for full details, but essentially: LfL sales grew 4% in 2002 and a further 5% in 2003. Likewise, market share grew from 2.4% to 2.5%.
6. In 2003, Sainsbury's was famously overtaken by Asda as the UK's second largest supermarket. Meanwhile, in April 2004, the *Daily Telegraph* noted that M&S was 'one of the worst performing FTSE companies last year'.
7. In 1997, Tesco defined non-food as one of its four strategic imperatives, while in September 2001, Asda massively increased its focus on non-food, introducing 5,000 new, non-food lines, many of which were sourced from Wal-Mart.
8. Sir Ken Morrison, Safeway offer statement, December 2003.
9. The 'Making Sainsbury's Great Again' four-year recovery programme was launched on 19 October 2004.
10. Source: M&S Annual Report 2005, review of 2004 strategy.
11. By late 2003, sales of this range had surpassed those of stalwarts such as Coke and Walkers (*The Grocer*, November 2003).
12. Verdict Grocery Retailers report, 2005.
13. Media spend by the main supermarkets rose by 20% from 2003 to 2004 (Nielsen Media Monitor).
14. Waitrose SOV fell from 5% in 2002–2003 to 4% in 2004 (Nielsen Media Monitor).
15. Technically, Waitrose appointed another agency – HOW – which was part-owned by MCBD. But since HOW was soon rolled into MCBD, along with the Waitrose business, we have referred to the agency as 'MCBD' from this point on.
16. Source: *Marketing Week* (16 March 2006).
17. Source: *Marketing* (9 April 2008).
18. Mark Mendoza, Managing Partner at the Media Planning Group (*Campaign*, 16 June 2006).
19. Qualitative Research, Justin Clouder, 2004.
20. Brand Connection handled Waitrose's media planning until June 2006, since when it has been handled by Manning Gottlieb OMD.
21. Waitrose buys ABC1 housewives in London, Meridian and (from 2006) Central.
22. *The Market Kitchen* is a show about all things culinary, including content about the ethics of food production and supply.
23. Titles include the likes of *Grazia*, *Marie Claire* and *Good Housekeeping*. We were the first to negotiate a southern deal in national publications that allowed us to use national press regionally, hence more efficiently as a predominantly regional supermarket.

24. *A Very Useful Guide to Fish*.
25. DM is handled by Kitcatt Nohr, which was appointed in 2006. Its Fish DM mailer won two DMA Gold awards in 2007.
26. The *Telegraph* 'Create' competition attracted 71 entrants, of which 13 were shortlisted. Sarah Newton, *Telegraph* Create sales director, said: 'Waitrose took the first prize because in addition to providing the *Telegraph* with a true brand partnership, the campaign placed our readers at the heart of the idea – it will be our readers that will bring the campaign to life in a truly engaging way.'
27. First five weeks to 1 March 2008.
28. Source: Waitrose, 2008.
29. Unnamed analysts, quoted in *The Grocer* (November 2005).
30. Consumer Insight's average score is around 30%.
31. In essence, it fuses television data from SkyView with actual shopping data from TNS Worldpanel, thus allowing us to examine immediate sales effects among those exposed to the TV advertising, compared to those who were not exposed to the advertising. This methodology strips out all other variables, such as promotional activity and seasonality, as well as the effects of store expansion and new store openings.
32. Average spend among these incremental shoppers has also risen, but only marginally.
33. This is the margin quoted in M&S's 2006 IPA paper, in relation to its food business, based on Deutsche Bank estimates. Like M&S, Waitrose will not disclose its actual margins but this is a reasonable approximation.
34. Source: T. Broadbent 'How advertising pays back', *Admap*, November 2001. We have used a conservative one-year time frame, although IRI have measured the carry-over effects for years two and three as almost equal to the effects in year one.
35. Every year, the retail analysts at Verdict examine around 70 high-street retailers and ask 6,000 consumers to rank them on a number of key criteria. Waitrose came first overall in 2006 and 2007 as well as runner-up in 2005.
36. Source: Consumer Insight Tracking, 2002–2006. Percentage of those agreeing with the statement 'Waitrose is a supermarket that is a pleasure to shop in' has consistently averaged around 60%.
37. Source: Waitrose internal data (exact data are confidential).
38. Source: *The Grocer* Price Survey.
39. Between 2003 and 2006 Waitrose opened a total of 42 branches, 23 of them outside its core, advertised regions.
40. Waitrose national SOV has declined from 5% in 2002–2003 to a consistent level of 4% in 2007. Its regional SOV (those areas where Waitrose advertises on TV) has declined from around 9.5% in 2003 to 8% in London and the SSE core regions in 2007 (Nielsen Media Research).
41. By promoting the Waitrose Foundation, over £600K has been raised, benefiting more than 7,000 farm workers with the funding of 34 different community initiatives, including much needed training in literacy, IT and life-skills development, as well as classes to enable farm workers to earn an income out of season.
42. By promoting Linking Environment and Farming (LEAF), an independent charitable organisation, we have supported farmers who are committed to conserving the British countryside for future generations. All of Waitrose conventional (non-organic) fruit and vegetables is sourced from LEAF accredited farms.
43. By promoting locally supplied produce, including cake, beer, ice cream and cheese, we have helped the 278 local suppliers who currently supply Waitrose with more than 900 products to branches within a 30-mile radius.
44. Source: Waitrose Partner interviews.
45. The precise data are confidential.
46. Quoted in *The Gazette*, Waitrose's in-house publication, 18 March 2006.
47. *Marketing*, 6 June 2007.
48. Charles Vallance, founding partner VCCP, *Marketing* magazine (21 March 2007).
49. The Cooperative Bank won an IPA Award in 1994 and also submitted an unawarded paper in 2006.
50. Tesco is the only other supermarket to have retained its endline during the same period; however, its campaign idea has changed several times over the years.
51. Verdict Grocery Retailers report, 2007.

Other companies involved in the campaign: DM company: Kitcatt Nohr Alexander Shaw; Media company: Manning Gottlieb OMD

SECTION 5

Bronze winners

Chapter 23

CABWISE™

Creating a brand to help prevent rapes

By Giselle Okin, WCRS; Victoria Sangster, Mediaedge:cia; Robert Thurner, Incentivated, and Fergus Adam, WCRS
Contributing authors: Miranda Leedham, Transport for London; Stuart Bowden, Mediaedge:cia; Jason Cross, Greater London Authority; and Priya Smart, Chemistry Group

Background

Safer Travel at Night is a partnership between the Mayor of London, Transport for London (TFL), and the Metropolitan Police Service. It aims to reduce the use of unlicensed minicabs by increasing public awareness of the dangers of using them. It runs a text service that provides the numbers of local licensed minicab and taxi firms.

Strategy and execution

Between September 2006 and March 2007, with a media spend of only £671,000, we were able to stop the majority of women from using illegal minicabs in London.

This was achieved by creating the CABWISE™ brand, which acted as the glue to hold all activities together. It allowed us to split the marketing task into two stages and employ appropriate media for each.

The first stage was to emotionally dissuade women from using illegal minicabs by taking away their perceived safety net: the false sense of security they felt when getting into a cab with friends or having their mobile phones with them as a lifeline.

The second stage was to provide practical information on how to use the text service in a way that was appropriate to a bar or club environment: useful, memorable and easy to decode.

Results

The campaign significantly decreased incidents of rape and sexual assault committed by illegal minicab drivers. It is our conservative estimate that we helped prevent at least eight rapes and/or sexual assaults between September 2006 and March 2007.

The number of sexual assaults and rapes committed by illegal minicab drivers dropped from an average of 14 during each September–December period over the

Figure 1: Student Union Poster

previous three years, to a total of four during September to December 2006. Although this is still four rapes and sexual assaults too many, it is a significant drop nevertheless and this coincided with the uplift in usage of CABWISE™.

The 12 months following the campaign launch showed an average monthly increase in users of 52% versus the previous 12 months, and the number of individual users doubled. All this was achieved with the same number of illegal cabs on the streets approaching women late at night.

Within the first four months, the entire campaign budget was more than paid for in savings against potential investigation and court costs. In fact, for every £1 spent on this campaign, an estimated £1.13 was saved. This doesn't even begin to take into consideration the emotional costs of the eight crimes that our efforts helped to prevent.

Table 1: Number of sexual assaults and rapes committed by illegal minicab drivers			
	Sept–Dec 2003	Sept–Dec 2004	Sept–Dec 2005	Sept–Dec 2006
Number of serious sexual assaults and/or rapes committed by illegal minicab drivers in London	17	12	13	4

Source: Metropolitan Police/GLA stats

Other company involved in campaign: DM company: Chemistry

Chapter 24

Cadbury Biscuits

Oh Happy Day! How advertising helped biscuit buyers discover a new name in chocolate digestives

By Amanda Fève, Bartle Bogle Hegarty
Contributing authors: Karl Weaver and David Hartley, D2D

Background

This is the story of how advertising heralded the arrival of a new name in chocolate digestives and, in so doing, made Cadbury the fastest-growing chocolate biscuit brand.

Cadbury is a fantastic confectionery brand. It is Britain's most trusted brand of chocolate. But chocolate is an indulgence, and so we try not to eat too much of it. Chocolate digestives, on the other hand, are a permissible treat that we readily enjoy every day. And for 'chocoholics', chocolate digestives are a guilt-free opportunity to sneak an extra bit of chocolate into their day.

Looking to build its biscuit business, Burton's Foods decided to invest in advertising for Cadbury Milk Chocolate Digestives for the first time ever in 2007, having experienced slow but steady growth since launch in 2004.

Strategy

We faced sizeable barriers to growth: a major competitor (McVitie's) and a minor communications budget (less than £1m). Not to mention the fact that Cadbury Digestives were virtually unheard of.

Strategic clarity and executional focus were the consistent themes of the campaign's development. In articulating a clear communications task, a narrowly defined target audience and a single-minded creative strategy, we created a recipe for business success.

Execution

With one high-impact television execution, 'Thank You', we achieved strong awareness levels for Cadbury Milk Chocolate Digestives and, in so doing, unlocked sales growth across the entire Cadbury Biscuits range (which also includes Cadbury Dark Chocolate Digestives, Cadbury Rich Tea, Cadbury Chocolate Chip & Oat, and Cadbury Shortcake).

Figure 1: 'Thank You' ad

A woman in a supermarket stares into space dazed

Two women embrace laughing

A woman in a kitchen laughs hysterically

Cut to pack shot.
VO: **YES!!** Cadbury chocolate is now on a digestive

Results

Every £1 spent on advertising generated £2.59 in revenue, outperforming most fmcg brand advertising and achieving an ROI that would humble many larger, more established brands.

However, the impact of 'Thank You' was more far-reaching than awareness and sales. The campaign also:

- improved perceptions of product quality and taste
- drove more consumers to purchase Cadbury Half Choc biscuits more often
- built loyalty and decreased price sensitivity
- helped Burton's achieve better-quality distribution for the entire Cadbury Half Choc range.

The concert of these effects has given unprecedented momentum to Cadbury Chocolate Biscuits, helping create conditions favourable to long-term growth, and effectively pre-heating the oven for long-term sales.

For Burton's Foods, the story of 'Thank You' is the story of a very happy day indeed.

Figure 2: Milk chocolate digestive value sales pre/post campaign launch

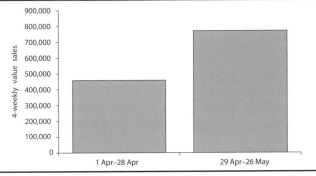

Source: ACNielsen

Other company involved in campaign: Media company: Universal McCann

Chapter 25

Learndirect

Careers Advice from Learndirect: the whole story about being incomplete

By Jon Tipple, RKCR/Y&R
Contributing author: Wanda Gregorek, Brand Science

Background

To be successful in today's global economy, the UK needs to continue to compete at the higher-value end of the market. For this we need a high-quality, dynamic labour pool to draw from – an area in which we currently trail other G8 countries.

Launched in 1999, Learndirect's remit from the government is to improve the employability of adults in the UK, with a specific focus on targeting adults who have low or no qualifications and are seeking work or looking to improve their current situation.

Strategy

In January 2006, Learndirect created a world-class careers advice service. However, creating such a service and making people want to use it are two very separate tasks.

With a brand that few people knew well, and an audience more used to being lectured to and patronised regarding career development, Learndirect successfully engaged people with the idea of fulfilling their potential by showing it understood how they felt: incomplete – a refreshing change in a category of rational service attributes and financial improvement.

Execution

A multimedia campaign was created that took a fresh approach in a category characterised by brands promoting their functional service attributes and/or the possible financial returns on offer. The resulting 'Jigsaw' campaign instead showed that Learndirect empathised with the incompleteness people can feel with their jobs and career. Using simple images of people with jigsaw-piece shapes missing from them, the campaign consciously sought approachability over creative wizardry.

Figure 1: The simple jigsaw icon that promised 'completeness' from Learndirect

Results

At the time of writing, the campaign had already generated a £40m payback.

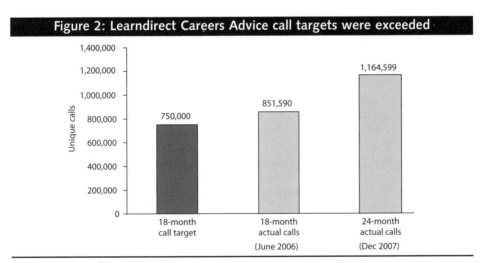

Figure 2: Learndirect Careers Advice call targets were exceeded

Source: Learndirect call data

Other companies involved in the campaign: Media agency: PHD; Digital company: Saint; DM company: Wunderman; PR company: Consolidated; Other company: Brand Science.

Chapter 26

Marmite

Please look after this brand: the launch of Marmite Squeezy

By Kirsty Saddler and Sarah Carter, DDB London; Les Binet, DDB Matrix and Alex Vass, DDB London

Background

Marmite is a national institution, and that means the British public tend to think it belongs to them and not to the brand owners: mess with it at your peril. From 1996 to 2002 Marmite sales had been on an upward curve, but by 2005 the brand seemed to have run out of steam. The future looked troubling too. The biggest usage of Marmite is on toast, but this staple was suffering from changing breakfast trends. Something had to be done to inject new energy into the brand and new occasions alongside it. A radical new growth strategy was needed.

Strategy

The time had come to run the gauntlet and change a cultural icon: enter the new Squeezy jar. The challenge was how to evolve Marmite (this being the first change in over a hundred years) but still keep the brand's devoted followers onside. The communications task was clear: balance the old and much loved with the new and much needed. To achieve this, Marmite fans were involved and engaged in the process. The resulting creative set about dramatising why the Squeezy had been launched, while making the fans feel that the brand was still theirs.

Execution

To achieve these dual tasks it was vital to continue the same provocative 'Love–Hate' strategy that had run successfully for several years. This time the creative featured a man with a broken arm whose love for Marmite can only be continued as a result of the new Squeezy jar. The Marmite community were targeted with the innovative 'MarmArt' campaign, dramatising the convenience of the new jar and encouraging them to get involved with their own creativity. Finally, the Paddington Bear campaign was conceived to highlight how the new jar helps you have Marmite in sandwiches, thereby opening up a new usage occasion.

Figure 1: Print executions with the line 'You either love it or hate it', for the launch of Squeezy Marmite

Results

Marmite saw sales increases that correlate with the advertising, and achieved a sustained annual growth rate of 5% in 2006 and 2007. Communications supported the successful launch of the new Squeezy jar, and then effectively influenced existing eaters to eat more Marmite, and eat more of it in sandwiches. The communications were proven to pay back more than double across long-term projections (a five-year period). Gone are the days when marketing can just impose change on willing customers. Now we've entered a new era of more democratic brand owner–buyer relationships and this communications programme successfully reflected this.

Table 1: Marmite sales performance since Squeezy launch

	Pre Squeezy (2005)	Post Squeezy (2007) (2007 vs 2005)	% change since launch
Volume (thousand kg)	3,679	3,972	+8%
Price per kilo	£8.97	£9.12	+2%
Value (thousand £)	£33,015	£36,207	+10%

Source: ACNielsen

Other companies involved in campaign: Design company: Iris; Digital company: Tribal DDB, AKQA; Media company: Mindshare; PR company: Splendid.

Chapter 27

Morrisons

Fresh growth for Morrisons

By Sandya Piyasena and Alex Kuropatwa, Delaney Lund Knox Warren & Partners
Contributing authors: Michael Bates and Richard Burgess, WM Morrison Supermarkets

Background

Morrisons was founded more than a century ago, with its roots in the markets of West Yorkshire. When Sir Ken Morrison took over the family business, he built it into the north of England's biggest supermarket.

In 2003, Morrisons successfully bid to buy the ailing supermarket chain, Safeway. The deal catapulted Morrisons from regional grocer to national challenger with nearly 15% market share, putting it almost on a par with Asda and Sainsbury's.

The process of integrating Safeway took its toll on Morrisons' performance. Not only did its market share slide to 11.3% but, for the first time in the company's 100-year-plus history, Morrisons issued a string of profit warnings. The company found itself under intense scrutiny. And Sir Ken, in particular, suffered a blow to his reputation.

By the end of 2006 Morrisons emerged, ready to resume growth, but market share had dropped further to 11.1%. The company now had to find a way to stop the seemingly inexorable decline in market share.

Strategy and execution

The single biggest issue holding Morrisons back was the perception of its food quality. Even in its heartland, it ranked bottom of the competitor pack.

Communications needed to improve Morrisons' food credentials. Frustratingly, there was a massive gap between perception and reality.

An amazing story was being hidden at the heart of Morrisons' 'Market Street' offer: Morrisons actually makes and prepares more food fresh in-store than any other supermarket.

The customer benefit of freshly prepared food was motivating, differentiating and had the potential to encourage reappraisal of Morrisons. It also highlighted the opportunity for Morrisons to position itself as the 'food specialist for everyone'.

Figure 1: Example of magazine and newspaper ads

Results

The result was an abrupt reversal of Morrisons' three-year market share decline from 11.1% to 11.6%, and the transformation of Morrisons into Britain's fastest-growing supermarket – a feat recognised by its winning of the prestigious 'Retailer of the Year 2008' award.

The estimated payback of the campaign was £13 extra sales revenue for every £1 invested, and it provided a return on marketing investment of 82%. Significantly, the gain in new customers, and increased spend and frequency among existing customers, gave us confidence that the return would significantly exceed investment in both the immediate and long term.

Figure 2: Spectacular leap in like-for-like sales growth (%)

Source: TNS. Total till roll, 12 w/e January 2007–March 2008

Other company involved in campaign: Media company: Mediaedge:cia

Chapter 28

Motorola

Marketing Motorola in China

By Tim Broadbent, Edward Bell, Anthony Wong, Ogilvy & Mather Advertising Beijing; Weifan Zhang, Mindshare ATG and Zheng Li, Ogilvy & Mather Advertising Beijing

Background

The market for mobile phone handsets in China is huge and growing fast. There are already more than twice as many mobile users in China as there are in America, and the market is growing at over 20% a year. However, in 2005, Motorola had only 13% market share compared to Nokia's 22%. More significantly, Motorola's share in China lagged those it had achieved in other markets. In fact Motorola's global market share was closer to 18%. This paper outlines how marketing worked to bring Motorola in China up to the same levels as the rest of the world.

Strategy

The big issue for Motorola in China in 2005 was its brand image. For Chinese consumers image is the most important consideration in choice of mobile phone. The new strategy for 2005 onwards was based upon making Motorola the 'fashion' phone, building on the growing desire for self-expression among young Chinese people keen to escape drab conformity. This strategy connected well with Motorola's new line of phones, including the RAZR and the PEBL.

Execution

The creative campaign was themed around the 'Moto Tribe', a group of challenging, confident people with a strong personal style. Together they form a 'tribe' of individuals, united only by their choice of phone. Standing apart from the low production values of much Chinese advertising, the campaign was created with the help of leading fashion photographers. It also featured a few celebrities within the mix, including David Beckham and Messrs Dolce & Gabbana. The campaign featured across TV, online and huge iconic outdoor poster sites, celebrating the arresting visuals of the 'tribe'.

Figure 1: Moto RAZR D&G execution

Results

The new Tribe campaign had a significant effect on Motorola's brand image, helping make it more cool and stylish. By the end of 2006 Motorola's market share had risen to 20%. This was a much faster rate of growth than Motorola's global average, demonstrating that growth was due to more than just the new products. A series of econometric models were developed to evaluate effects across various regions of China, and collectively demonstrate that each RMB spent on ATL created around 15 RMB profit.

Table 1: Faster growth in China than global average and competitors		2005 %	2006 %	% increase
Motorola	Global	17.9	21.7	+21%
	China	**12.8**	**20.4**	**+59%**
Nokia	Global	32.5	34.7	+7%
	China	21.7	28.5	+31%
Samsung	Global	12.6	11.3	−10%
	China	10.1	9.9	−2%
Sony Ericsson	Global	6.3	7.5	+19%
	China	4.6	5.0	+9%

Source: Sino-MR, IDC, Strategy Analytics

Other companies involved in campaign: Digital company: OgilvyOne Beijing; Media company: Mindshare Beijing; PR company: H-Line Beijing.

Chapter 29

Road Safety

The longer-term effects of seatbelt advertising

By David Lyle, Julie Anne
Bailie, Dawn McCartney,
Robert Lyle and David
Martin, Lyle Bailie
International

Background

Seatbelt-wearing rates in both Northern Ireland and the Republic of Ireland have historically been lower than their nearest neighbour, Great Britain. The upshot of this has been higher rates of road carnage. In 2000, road deaths per 100,000 of the population were six in Great Britain (GB) compared to 10 in Northern Ireland (NI) and 11 in the Republic of Ireland. Equally, at the turn of the millennium, seatbelt-wearing rates stood at 87% in NI and 55% in the Republic of Ireland, compared with 91% in GB. The challenge was to increase seatbelt compliance and thereby reduce road deaths and injuries, with a consequent reduction in both human tragedy and in the economic cost to the taxpayer.

Strategy

The approach was research, data and psychology led. Findings across all three areas were combined with the learnings from neuroscience to develop a strategic idea based upon 'the memory of a possible future'. The strongest motivations for deciding to wear a seatbelt included the prospect of killing a family member or friend, or of being seriously disabled for life. The desired take-out was simple: 'that could be me'. TV was deployed as the core media for the launch of each seatbelt campaign. It was supported by 'point of danger' radio and activity in car parks and on petrol pumps, to reach motorists and passengers as they travelled by car.

Execution

The brand, 'No Seatbelt – No Excuse', was chosen to summarise the moral consequences of not wearing a seatbelt, and disprove any perception that wearing a seatbelt or not is a personal freedom or choice. From 2001 the TV ad 'Damage' used shocking slow-motion imagery to dramatise the selfishness of not wearing a seatbelt by showing how brain damage and the death of friends are the resulting

Figure 1: The 'Damage' ad

outcomes. From 2006 'Get it on' and 'Selfish' were two further executions to further dramatise the selfishness of parents and younger drivers in not encouraging seatbelt wearing among their passengers.

Results

NI's seatbelt-wearing rates overtook those of GB in 2007, standing at 95% compliance compared to 94% in GB. Improvements were also achieved in the numbers of backseat passengers and young people wearing seatbelts. In the Republic of Ireland a similarly impressive result has been achieved, moving from 55% compliance in 1999 to 88% in 2007. Following the campaign, deaths and serious injuries fell by 30% in NI and 46% in the Republic of Ireland. The economic payback from these reductions is significant: bearing in mind that the cost of a death is estimated at £1.4m and the cost of a serious injury at £160,000, it can be seen that this campaign pays back considerably.

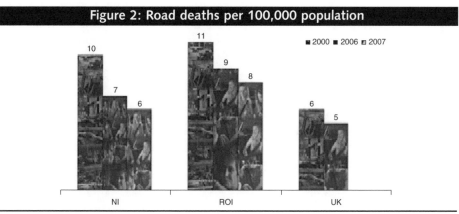

Figure 2: Road deaths per 100,000 population

Source: PSNI/NISRA/Garda/CSO/DFT/National Statistics
NB: UK 2007 road death figures not available

Chapter 30

Trident

Making a small budget go a long way

By Andy Nairn, Miles Calcraft Briginshaw
Duffy, and Matt Buttrick and Duncan
Snowden, MediaCom

Background

In 1998, the Metropolitan Police Service set up a special initiative called 'Trident' to tackle gun crime within London's black community. The reasons were simple: 61% of gun crime offenders in London, and 30% of victims, are black. Communications were tasked with raising gun crime's profile to help create a genuine debate that would help challenge the glamorous image of guns while encouraging the black community to come forward with information. However, the environment within which the campaign was working was a complex one, with myriad social problems and a lack of trust of the police, rendering the tasks particularly challenging.

Strategy

Research showed that black teenagers were particularly susceptible to gun crime's glamorous imagery, so a strategy was developed to demonstrate a different reality. The activity was developed across four phases, starting with rallying the community, which emphasised how a simple phone call could make a big difference. Phase 2 dramatised the fatal consequences of inaction. Stage 3 aimed at winning over the next generation, while stage 4 focused on the consequences for offenders.

Execution

Using the rallying cry 'Stop the guns', the campaign used a huge range of different media to convey its various key messages. Posters and press carried powerful and simple calls to action, while cinema commercials demonstrated how those who remained silent had 'blood on their hands'. To win over the next generation, an anti-gun music track was commissioned from a top 'grime' act and made available across the internet. Finally, ambient media, from petrol pumps to replica cells erected on the streets, highlighted the implications of gun crime for offenders.

Figure 1: Press ad

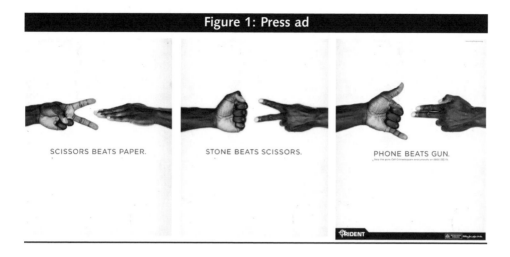

SCISSORS BEATS PAPER.　　　STONE BEATS SCISSORS.　　　PHONE BEATS GUN.

Results

The campaign has succeeded in generating millions of pounds' worth of publicity for an issue that had previously received little media coverage. More significantly, a previously hostile audience of young black men was won over, with 88% supporting the campaign. All this has led to a trebling of telephone calls with actionable intelligence on gun crime. As a result, arrests of offenders have increased, and in 2007 alone Trident officers seized 908 guns, more than in the previous four years combined.

Other company involved in campaign: Digital company: Elvis

How to access the IPA dataBANK

The IPA Effectiveness dataBANK represents the most rigorous and comprehensive examination of marketing communications working in the marketplace, and in the world. Over the 28 years of the IPA Effectiveness Awards competition, the IPA has collected over 1,400 examples of best practice in advertising development and results across a wide spectrum of marketing sectors and expenditures. Each example contains up to 4,000 words of text and is illustrated in full by market, research, sales and profit data.

Access

The dataBANK resides offline in the IPA Information Centre. Simple searches can be run, free of charge for members, across a range of parameters including brand, advertiser, agency, marketing objectives, medium and length of activity and the results supplied by email or other means as required. More sophisticated analyses can be commissioned through the IPA, to their network of specialist dataBANK consultants.

Purchasing IPA case studies

Member agencies are allowed to download a maximum of 12 case studies in any given calendar year, after which they will be able to download case studies from the IPA website (www.ipa.co.uk) at £25 each. Alternatively, members can sign up to WARC Online (see overleaf) at a beneficial IPA rate and can then download case studies as part of that subscription.

Non-IPA members can purchase case studies from the IPA website (www.ipa.co.uk) at £40 per copy.

Further information

For further information, please contact the Information Centre at the IPA, 44 Belgrave Square, London SW1X 8QS
Telephone: +44 (0)20 7235 7020
Fax: +44 (0)20 7245 9904
Website: *www.ipa.co.uk*
Email: *info@ipa.co.uk*

WARC Online

All IPA case studies can be accessed through WARC Online at *www.warc.com*. IPA members can subscribe to WARC Online at a 10% discount.

WARC Online is a unique resource relied upon by major creative and media agency networks, market research companies, media owners, multinational advertisers and business schools to help tackle any marketing challenge. It offers an unrivalled wealth of award-winning case studies, research and best practice guides, consumer insight and marketing intelligence on leading companies and brands.

Content available at WARC Online includes WARC's own publications, such as Admap, and material from 50 WARC Partners worldwide including the Advertising Research Foundation and ESOMAR, as well as the IPA.

For more information visit *www.warc.com*.

www.ipaeffectivenessawards.co.uk

On our dedicated awards website you can find out everything you need to know about the annual IPA Effectiveness Awards competition including how to enter, and who's won what since 1980.

As well as viewing case study summaries and creative work, you'll also find a number of mini brand films. So, if you have a few minutes to spare here's what is on offer:

- The Magners Effect (8:56)
- Original Source: packed with natural stuff (7:42)
- Ryvita Minis: big taste, mini waist. (8:55)
- Trident: stop the guns. (9:54)
- Waitrose: quality food, honestly priced. (8:32)
- Daz: Cleaner Close. (5:57)
- Virgin Trains: the return of the train. (7:17)
- Marks & Spencer: Your M&S (7:55)
- O2: a world that revolves around you (5:45)
- British Heart Foundation: Under My Skin (7:44)
- Smart, inspiring and effective. Richard Storey, Chief Strategy Officer at M&C Saatchi reviews the 2007 Effectiveness Awards cases that caught his eye. (8:20)
- Inside the Effectiveness Awards. Why they matter. (6:36)

Films from the 2008 competition will be added in 2009.

IPA dataBANK case availability

* Denotes winning entries.
** Denotes cases published in *Area Works* volumes 1–5.
(S) Denotes cases published in *Scottish Advertising Works* volumes 1–4.

NEW ENTRIES 2008

2008	Acquisition Crime*
2008	Audi*
2008	BBC iplayer
2008	Bonfire Night
2008	Bradesco
2008	BT
2008	CABWISE (Transport for London)*
2008	Cadbury Dairy Milk
2008	Cadbury Biscuits*
2008	Capital One
2008	Carex
2008	Danone Activia*
2008	Dave*
2008	De Beers*
2008	Dero
2008	Direct Payment*
2008	Dove*
2008	Eurostar
2008	Fairy Liquid
2008	Fairy Non Bio
2008	Heinz Beanz Snap Pots
2008	Hewlett Packard Personal Systems Group (PSG)
2008	Iceland
2008	Johnnie Walker*
2008	KFC*
2008	Learndirect*
2008	Lucozade Sport*
2008	Lurpak
2008	Marmite*
2008	Mastercard
2008	McCain
2008	McDonald's Eurosaver
2008	Morrisons*
2008	Motorola*
2008	O₂ UK
2008	Power of One
2008	Public Awareness Campaign for Helmet Wearing*
2008	Radley*
2008	Road Safety*
2008	Sainsbury's magazine
2008	Sainsbury's*
2008	Scottish Government: Teacher Recruitment
2008	Sky
2008	Thomas Cook
2008	Toyota Yaris
2008	Trident*
2008	Virgin Atlantic*
2008	V-Power
2008	Waitrose*
2008	Yorkshire Tourist Board – Make Yorkshire Yours

Numerical

2000	1001 Mousse*
2003	55 Degrees North**
2006	100.4 smooth fm

A

2004	AA Loans*
1982	Abbey Crunch
1990	Abbey National Building Society
1990	Abbey National Building Society (plc)
1980	Abbey National Building Society Open Bondshares
1990	Aberlour Malt Whisky*
2004	Ackermans (SA)
2008	Acquisition Crime*
2006	Actimel*
1996	Adult Literacy *
2002	Aerogard Mosquito Repellent (Australia)
1999	Agri Plan Finance**
1986	AGS Home Improvements*
1988	AIDS
1994	AIDS*
1986	Air Call
1990	Alex Lawrie Factors
1980	All Clear Shampoo*
1992	Alliance & Leicester Building Society*
1990	Alliance & Leicester Building Society*
1988	Alliance & Leicester Building Society*
1984	Alliance Building Society
1990	Allied Dunbar
1984	Allinson's Bread
1984	Alpen
1990	Alton Towers
2003	Alton Towers 'Air'**
1999	Alton Towers 'Oblivion'**

2007	Knife Crime (Police Service of Northern Ireland)
1990	Knorr Stock Cubes*
1988	Kodak Colour Print Film
1994	Kraft Dairylea
1984	Kraft Dairylea*
1980	Krona Margarine*
1986	Kronenbourg 1664
2006	Kwik-Fit*

L

1990	Lada
2004	Lamb (Meat & Livestock Australia)*
2005	Lancashire Short Breaks*
1990	Lanson Champagne*
2005	Lay Magistrates
1992	Le Creuset
1982	Le Crunch
1990	Le Piat D'or
1986	Le Piat D'or
1996	Le Shuttle
1990	Lea & Perrin's Worcestershire Sauce*
1980	Lea & Perrin's Worcestershire Sauce
2008	Learndirect*
1988	Leeds Permanent Building Society
1988	Lego
2004	Lego Bionicle
1984	Leicester Building Society
1996	Lenor
2002	Levi Strauss Engineered Jeans (Japan)
1992	Levi Strauss UK*
1980	Levi Strauss UK
1988	Levi's 501s*
2005	Lift Off
1996	Lil-lets
1990	Lil-lets*
1996	Lilt
1992	Limelite*
1980	Limmits
1999	Lincoln Financial Group**
2000	Lincoln Insurance
2000	Lincoln USA
1980	Lion Bar
1992	Liquorice Allsorts
1988	Liquorice Allsorts
2004	Listerine
1988	Listerine*
1980	Listerine
1998	Littlewoods Pools
1992	Lloyds Bank
1984	Lloyds Bank*
1999	Local Enterprise Development Unit (NI)**
1990	London Buses Driver Recruitment
1984	London Docklands*
1982	London Docklands

1990	London Philharmonic
1992	London Transport Fare Evasion
1986	London Weekend Television
1980	Lucas Aerospace*
1996	Lucky Lottery
1992	Lucozade
1980	Lucozade*
2008	Lucozade Sport*
2008	Lurpak
2000	Lurpak*
1988	Lurpak
2002	Lynx*
2004	Lynx Pulse*
1994	Lyon's Maid Fab
1988	Lyon's Maid Favourite Centres

M

2004	M&G
1988	Maclaren Prams
2003	Magna Science Adventure Centre**
2007	Magners Irish Cider*
1999	Magnet Kitchens**
2004	Magnum
2006	Make Poverty History (Comic Relief)
1990	Malibu
2006	Manchester City*
2001	Manchester City Centre**
1999	Manchester City Centre**
2003	*Manchester Evening News* Jobs Section**
2002	*Manchester Evening News* (Job Section)*
2003	ManchesterIMAX**
1982	Manger's Sugar Soap*
1988	Manpower Services Commission
2006	Marks & Spencer*
1994	Marks & Spencer
2004	Marks & Spencer Lingerie*
2008	Marmite*
2002	Marmite*
1998	Marmite*
1998	Marmoleum
1988	Marshall Cavendish Discovery
1994	Marston Pedigree*
2001	Maryland Cookies**
2008	Mastercard
2006	Mastercard
1986	Mazda*
1986	Mazola*
2008	McCain
1998	McDonald's
1996	McDonald's
2008	McDonald's Eurosaver
1980	McDougall's Saucy Sponge
1990	Mcpherson's Paints
1988	Mcpherson's Paints

1998	Oxo Lamb Cubes

P

2007	P&O Cruises
2007	P&O Ferries
1986	Paignton Zoo
2000	Pampers South Africa*
1988	Paracodol*
1984	Paul Masson California Carafes
2005	Payment Modernisation Programme
1982	Pedal Cycle Casualties*
1998	Penguin
1994	Peperami*
1994	Pepsi Max
1990	Perrier
1986	Perrier
2000	Persil*
2006	Petits Filous
2000	PG Tips*
1990	PG Tips*
1996	Philadelphia*
1994	Philadelphia
1994	Phileas Fogg
1988	Phileas Fogg
1988	Phileas Fogg
1980	Philips Cooktronic
1980	Philips Video
2003	Phoenix Natural Gas
2003	Phones 4u**
1998	Physical Activity Campaign (HEB Scotland)
2007	Pilkington Activ*
1990	Pilkington Glass
1992	Pilsner
1986	Pink Lady
1998	Pizza Hut*
1996	Pizza Hut
1994	Pizza Hut
1996	Pirelli
1990	Pirelli
1986	Pirelli
1984	Pirelli
1990	Plax
1980	Plessey Communications & Data Systems
1998	Polaroid*
2007	Police Community Support Officers
1994	Police Federation of England and Wales
2004	Police Officer Recruitment (Hertfordshire Constabulary)*
2002	Police Recruitment*
2002	Police Recruitment (Could You?)
2002	Police Recruitment Northern Ireland
2007	Police Service of Northern Ireland (Recruitment)
2001	Police Service of Northern Ireland**
1996	Polo Mints
1984	Polyfoam
2007	Pomegreat
1986	*Portsmouth News*
2004	Postbank (Post Office SA)
2002	Post Office*
1980	Post Office Mis-sorts
1986	Post Office Special Issue Stamps
1996	Potato Marketing Board
1998	Pot Noodle
2008	Power of One
1984	Presto
1980	Pretty Polly*
2006	Privilege Insurance
2005	Progressive Building Society – Financial Services
1992	Prudential
2008	Public Awareness Campaign for Helmet Wearing*

Q

1984	QE2
2003	Qjump.co.uk
1988	Quaker Harvest Chewy Bars*
1982	Qualcast Concorde Lawn Mower*
1986	Quatro
1986	Quickstart
1996	Quorn Burgers

R

1982	Racal Redec Cadet
1990	Radion Automatic*
1994	Radio Rentals
1990	Radio Rentals
2008	Radley*
1996	RAF Recruitment
1980	RAF Recruitment*
2004	Rainbow (evaporated milk)*
1994	Range Rover
2000	Reading and Literacy*
1992	Real McCoys
2000	Rear Seatbelts*
1998	Red Meat Market*
1984	Red Meat Consumption
1988	Red Mountain*
1996	Reebok*
1990	Reliant Metrocabs
1994	Remegel
1998	Renault
1986	Renault 5
1990	Renault 19*
1996	Renault Clio*
1992	Renault Clio*
1984	Renault Trafic & Master
2005	ResponsibleTravel.Com

2004	Sony Ericsson T610*		1986	Touche Remnant Unit Trusts
1996	Springers by K (Shoes)		1992	Tower of London
2006	Sprite		2004	Toyota Corolla
1984	St Ivel Gold*		1996	Toyota RAV4
2004	Standard Bank (SA)		2008	Toyota Yaris
2005	Standard Life (S)		2003	Translink CityBus
2000	Star Alliance		2007	Translink Metro
2002	Stella Artois*		2003	Translink Smartlink
2000	Stella Artois*		1982	Trans World Airlines
1998	Stella Artois		2006	Travelocity.co.uk*
1996	Stella Artois*		2005	Travelocity.co.uk*
1992	Stella Artois*		1984	Tri-ac (Skincare)
2002	Strathclyde Police		2008	Trident*
1994	Strepsils*		2007	Trident (Metropolitan Police)*
1990	Strongbow		2004	Tritace
2007	Subway*		1980	Triumph Dolomite
1982	Summers the Plumbers		2006	Tropicana Pure Premium*
1980	Sunblest Sunbran		1994	TSB
1990	Supasnaps		1988	TSB*
2000	Surf*		1986	TSB*
1980	Swan Vestas*		2004	TUI (Germany)
1984	SWEB Security Systems		1982	Turkish Delight*
1992	Swinton Insurance		1986	TV Licence Evasion*
1998	Switch		2006	TV Licensing*
1996	Switch		2000	Twix Denmark
2003	Syndol (painkillers)**			
			U	
T			1984	UK Canned Salmon
1992	Tandon Computers		1986	Umbongo Tropical Juice Drink
1990	Tango		2003	UniBond
1986	TCP*		1999	UniBond No More Nails**
2006	Teacher Recruitment*		2005	UniBond Sealant Range*
2003	Teacher Training Agency**		2005	University of Dundee* (S)
2001	Teacher Training Agency**		1998	UPS
1986	Teletext		2003	UTV Internet
1986	Territorial Army Recruitment		1990	Uvistat*
2000	Terry's Chocolate Orange*			
2002	Tesco*		**V**	
2000	Tesco*		1988	Varilux lenses
1980	Tesco		1994	Vauxhall Astra
2007	Tesco (Green Clubcard)		1996	Vauxhall Cavalier
1990	Tetley Tea Bags		1990	Vauxhall Cavalier
2004	The Number 118 118*		1999	Vauxhall Network Q**
2008	Thomas Cook		1996	Vegetarian Society
1984	Thomas Cook		2006	Vehicle Crime Prevention (The Home Office)*
1992	Tia Maria			
1990	Tia Maria		2004	Vehicle Crime Reduction (Home Office)
1990	*Times, The*			
1994	Tizer		2001	Vimto**
2005	Tizer*		2008	Virgin Atlantic*
1980	Tjaereborg Rejser*		1986	Virgin Atlantic
2004	Tobacco Control (DH)*		2004	Virgin Mobile*
1980	Tolly's Original		2004	Virgin Mobile Australia*
2002	Tommy's: The Baby Charity*		2004	Virgin Trains*
1984	Torbay Tourist Board*		2006	Virgin Trains*
1986	Toshiba*		1994	Visa

2006	Visit London	2005	Waste Awareness
1986	Vodafone	1984	Websters Yorkshire Bitter
1998	Volkswagen*	2007	Weetabix*
2002	Volkswagen (Brand)*	2004	Weetabix*
2004	Volkswagen Diesel*	1988	Weight Watchers Slimming Clubs
2006	Volkswagen Golf*	2002	West End Quay
2006	Volkswagen Golf GTI Mk5*	2005	West Midlands Hub of Museums*
2002	Volkswagen Passat*	1990	Westwood Tractors
2008	V-Power	1992	Whipsnade Wild Animal Park*
1992	VW Golf*	1980	Whitegate's Estate Agents*
		1990	Wilson's Ultra Golf Balls
W		1988	Winalot Prime*
1980	Waistline	1994	Wonderbra*
2008	Waitrose*	2006	Women's Aid*
2007	Waitrose*		
2002	Waitrose*	**Y**	
2003	Wake Up To Waste (Northern	2000	Yellow Pages Norway
	Ireland)**	1980	Yeoman Pie Fillings
1992	Wales Tourist Board	1980	Yorkie
2002	Walkers Crisps*	1982	Yorkshire Bank
1996	Walkers Crisps*	2002	Yorkshire Forward/Yorkshire Tourist
1998	Wallis		Board
1980	Wall's Cornetto	2008	Yorkshire Tourist Board – Make
2006	Wall's Sausages		Yorkshire Yours
1996	Wall's Viennetta		
1984	Wall's Viennetta*	**Z**	
1984	Walnut Whips	1984	Zanussi*
2003	Warburtons	1994	Zovirax
1990	Warburtons Bread*		

In compiling this list, the IPA has made every effort to ensure an accurate record of all cases currently available in the IPA dataBANK.

Index

Learner Services

Please return on or before the last date stamped below

CITY COLLEGE
NORWICH

2 2 MAR 2011